EXPLAINING INDIAN DEMO
A FIFTY-YEAR PERSPECTIVE, 1

Volume II

The Realm of Institutions

'...an exceptionally important volume...[the] essays tell a veritable story about the character and politics of state formation in India...rich and full of incidental insights...It is a tribute to the power of these essays that they not only have a fresh feel about them, they also speak to contemporary themes.'

—Pratap Bhanu Mehta
Centre for Policy Research, New Delhi

'Publication of...the works of Lloyd and Susanne Rudolph is simultaneously an academic event, a part of India's journey into the postcolonial world, and a splendid form of cultural exchange... [It] is a tribute to the five decades of engagement with India of the Rudolphs and their commitment to a humane political science.'

—Ashis Nandy
Centre for the Study of Developing Societies, Delhi

'These volumes bring together the work of two extraordinary scholars. In their more recent work on political economy, the complications of hybridized identities during the colonial period, and the need for methodological pluralism in the social sciences, the Rudolphs have made us examine India, and our own scholarship more broadly, through new lenses.'

—Steven I. Wilkinson
Yale University

EXPLAINING INDIAN DEMOCRACY
A FIFTY-YEAR PERSPECTIVE, 1956–2006

Volume II

The Realm of Institutions
State Formation and Institutional Change

Lloyd I. Rudolph
&
Susanne Hoeber Rudolph

OXFORD
UNIVERSITY PRESS

OXFORD
UNIVERSITY PRESS

Oxford University Press is a department of the University of Oxford.
It furthers the University's objective of excellence in research, scholarship,
and education by publishing worldwide. Oxford is a registered trademark of
Oxford University Press in the UK and in certain other countries

Published in India by
Oxford University Press
YMCA Library Building, 1 Jai Singh Road, New Delhi 110 001, India

ISBN-13: 978-0-19-945339-9
ISBN-10: 0-19-945339-X

Typeset in Typeset in Giovanni Book 10/12.6
by Eleven Arts, Keshav Puram, Delhi 110 035
Printed in India by Avantika Printers Pvt Ltd, New Delhi 110 065

Contents

Preface

Our academic careers began roughly fifty years ago when we arrived in India in 1956 with two Ford Foundation Foreign Area Training Fellowships. Our teaching careers came to a close at the University of Chicago on April 2003 with a Festschrift conference on 'Area Studies Redux: Situating Knowledge in a Globalizing World'. These two singular moments in our academic lives emphasize that 'area studies' were central to our inquiries in the fifty-one essays found in the three volumes of *Explaining Indian Democracy: A Fifty-Year Perspective*.

Area studies captures a central tendency of the method and substance of our work on Indian politics. Our early take on area studies is indicated by the title of the book we wrote on the basis of the research for the 1956 foreign area training grants, *The Modernity of Tradition*. Unlike the view of the then regnant modernization theory—that tradition would be swept into the dustbin of history and that 'they' were destined to become like 'us'—we found that tradition was often adaptive, change dialectical, not dichotomous, and that 'we' could learn from 'them'.

In *The Modernity of Tradition's* introduction, we warned readers about 'the imperialism of categories and historical possibilities'. Was a prosperous middle class, as Seymour Martin Lipset held, a 'requisite of democracy' in India?[1] Could social change in India be explained by the dichotomous 'pattern variables' posited by Edward Shils and Talcott Parsons,[2] or captured

---

[1] See S.M. Lipset, 'Some Social Requisites of Democracy: Economic Development and Political Legitimacy', *American Political Science Review*, 53, March, 1959, for the hypothesis and supporting evidence that democracy should be an utter failure in India.

[2] For the dichotomous 'pattern variables', see Talcott Parsons, and Edward Shils, 'Categories of the Orientation and Organization of Action', in *Toward a General Theory of Action*, by Talcott

by the structural–functional variables posited by Gabriel Almond?[3] We took an alternative view, a view captured in the topics addressed in the three parts of *The Modernity of Tradition*, 'Traditional Structures and Modern Politics: Caste'; 'The Traditional Roots of Charisma: Gandhi'; and 'Legal Cultures and Social Change: Panchayats, Pandits and Professionals'. Change in India, we found, could be best understood as adaptations of a complex and variegated traditional society and culture.

Almost fifty years later, the 'Area Studies Redux' conference in April 2003 revisited area studies[4] by confronting issues raised by global processes and formal modes of inquiry. 11 September had challenged America's parochialism by reminding it that the country lived in a diverse and complex world, but lacked adequate means to grasp its meanings. 9/11 brought to the fore the realization that knowledge of the other's languages, ways of life, and worldviews mattered for America's security and prosperity. Instead of asking 'why can't they be more like us', Americans should be asking, what can we learn about them, and how can we live with difference?

Long before the events of 9/11 challenged American parochialism, social scientists had begun to bypass area studies in favour of using data sets to statistically test formal models and run 'large-n' country studies. As Princeton professor Stephen Kotkin put it in a *New York Times* article of 7 September 2002, if you tried to find

a full-time political scientist who specializes in the Middle East or South Asia at the nation's universities, you'd almost be out of luck. The absence of regional experts in political science departments of many elite universities goes back to long-running,

---

Parsons and Edward Shils (eds), Cambridge: Harvard University Press, 1951. The variables are: (*i*) Affectivity—Affective Neutrality; (*ii*) Self-orientation—Collectivity-orientation; (*iii*) Universalism—Particularism; (*iv*) Ascription—Achievement; (*v*) Specificity—Diffuseness (p. 77).

[3]In 'A Functional Approach to Comparative Politics', which introduced *The Politics of the Developing Areas*, the first of seven volumes on 'Studies in Political Development' sponsored by the Committee on Comparative Politics of the Social Science Research Council, Gabriel Almond wrote '... the concept of political system [serves] ... to separate out analytically the structures which perform functions in all societies regardless of scale of differentiation, and culture ...' Those functions are divided into 'input functions', that is, (*i*) political socialization and recruitment; (*ii*) interest articulation; (*iii*) interest aggregation; (*iv*) political communication; and 'output functions', that is, (*v*) rule-making; (*vi*) rule application; and (*vii*) rule adjudication. The essay is found in Gabriel Almond, *Political Development: Essays in Heuristic Theory*, Boston: Little Brown and Company, 1970, pp. 79–151. The quote is from pp. 81–2 and the input and output functions are at p. 96.

[4]For a recent critical but positive evaluation of area studies, see David Szanton's essay, 'Introduction: The Origin, Nature and Challenges of Area Studies in the United States', in *The Politics of Knowledge: Area Studies and the Disciplines*, by David Szanton (ed.), Berkeley and Los Angeles: University of California Press, 2004, pp. 1–33.

rancorous debate over the best method for understanding the way the world works: is it using statistics and econometrics to identify universal patterns that underlie all economic and political systems, or zeroing in on a particular area and mastering its languages, cultures and institutions?

By 2003 we had come to understand area studies knowledge as situated knowledge, knowledge that is located and marked by time and place and circumstance. It is unlike the objective knowledge on offer by those who adhere to a universal social science epistemology based on the obsolete methods of Newtonian science, a science which purports to be true everywhere and always. Unlike such theory-driven universal social science knowledge, area studies knowledge tends to be problem-driven and more prone to inductive generalization than to deductive reasoning.

In 1956 we had recently finished our degrees at Harvard. We were among the first generation of American scholars to do research in post-colonial India. We purchased a Land Rover for delivery in London, and set off in mid-July on an overland journey across Europe to Turkey, Iran, and Afghanistan, crossing into the Indian subcontinent over the Khyber Pass to Peshawar, travelling through the Punjab to Lahore and Amritsar, and then on to New Delhi and Jaipur, the capital city of Rajasthan in India's northwest. During six months of research in Jaipur we lived with an Indian family, struck roots and made friends.[5] In February we travelled overland by Land Rover to Madras in southeast India. We were committed to learning about India's south as well as its north, and British as well as princely India. Our route took us first to Bombay on the west coast, and then to Bangalore in the Deccan, in 1957 a bustling post-colonial city, now the heart of India's information technology industry. The first was 1956–7, and 1999–2000 was the last of eleven years spent in India doing academic research. Starting in 1962–3 with the first of our three children, we took them along. They attended Indian schools where they made friends, competed in sports, and learned Hindi.

The articles in the three volumes of *Explaining Indian Democracy: A Fifty-Year Perspective*, span fifty years of scholarship on Indian politics. The first, published in 1958 in *Public Opinion Quarterly*, analyses the results of one of the first random sample surveys done in India. Carried out in the state of Madras, it examined the relationship between media exposure and political attitudes. Our field experience led us to raise questions about the

---

[5]Several of our books are about Rajasthan. We have helped to organize five international conferences on Rajasthan and a Rajasthan Studies Group listserv, and participated in the publication of six composite books on what might be called Rajasthan studies.

methodological individualist assumptions of opinion and electoral research. Among the last published are essays in a volume edited by Kristen Monroe[6] on the pluralist challenge by the Perestroika movement to efforts within the American Political Science Association to establish the hegemony of formal modelling, rational choice, and large-n studies.

We have more to say about modes of inquiry and ways to ask and answer questions, as well as about substance in introductions to the sections in which the three volumes of the selected works have been organized. The articles in Volume I, *The Realm of Ideas: Inquiry and Theory*, have been organized in two sections: 1. Modes of Inquiry, and 2. Theorizing Politics and Society; those in Volume II, *The Realm of Institutions: State Formation and Institutional Change*, in two sections, 1. Processes of State Formation, and 2. Processes of Institutional Change; and those in Volume III, *The Realm of the Public Sphere: Identity and Policy*, in four sections, 1. Identity Politics, 2. Interpreting Lives: Amar Singh and Gandhi, 3. Making US Foreign Policy, and 4. Writing as Public Intellectuals.

Writing about Indian politics, society, and history for fifty years has kept us fully engaged. We are still at it.

REFERENCES[7]

The Modernity of Tradition: Political Development in India, Chicago: University of Chicago Press, 1967, Phoenix Books, 1967; New Delhi: Orient Longman, 1969, Midway Edition, 1984; Bombay: Orient Longman, 1987.

Education and Politics in India: Studies in Organization, Society and Policy, Cambridge, MA: Harvard University Press, 1972; New Delhi: Oxford University Press, 1972. Electronic edition available via info@ideaindia.com.

The Regional Imperative: The Administration of U.S. Foreign Policy Towards South Asia Under Presidents Johnson and Nixon, New Delhi: Concept Publishing Company, 1980; Atlantic Highlands, NJ: Humanities Press, 1980.

Gandhi: The Traditional Roots of Charisma, Chicago: University of Chicago Press, 1983; New Delhi: Orient Longman, 1983. Hindi translation by Chitranjan Dutt, New Delhi: Orient Longman, 1999.

Essays on Rajputana: Reflections on History, Culture and Administration, New Delhi: Concept Publishing Company, 1984.

Rudolph, Lloyd I. (ed.), *Cultural Policy in India*, Delhi: Chanakya Publishing Company, 1984.

Rudolph, Susanne Hoeber *et al.* (eds), *Agrarian Power and Agricultural Productivity in*

[6]Kristen Renwick Monroe (ed.), *Perestroika: The Raucous Revolution in Political Science*, New Haven, CT: Yale University Press, 2005.
[7]All books listed are co-authored or co-edited unless otherwise indicated.

South Asia, Berkeley and Los Angeles: University of California Press; New Delhi: Oxford University Press, 1984.

In Pursuit of Lakshmi: The Political Economy of the Indian State, Chicago: University of Chicago Press, 1987; Bombay: Orient Longman, 1987.

Rudolph, Lloyd I. *et al.* (eds), *The Idea of Rajasthan. Vol. I: Constructions; Vol. II: Institutions*, New Delhi: Manohar Publishers, 1994.

Rudolph, Susanne Hoeber and James Piscatori (eds), *Transnational Religion and Fading States*, Boulder, CO: Westview Press, 1997.

Reversing the Gaze: Amar Singh's Diary, A Colonial Subject's Narrative of Imperial India, New Delhi: Oxford University Press, 2000; Boulder: Westview Press, 2002.

Postmodern Gandhi and Other Essays: Gandhi in the World and at Home, New Delhi: Oxford University Press, 2006; Chicago: University of Chicago Press, 2006.

Rudolph, Lloyd I. and J.K. Jacobsen (eds), *Experiencing the State*, New Delhi and New York: Oxford University Press, 2006.

Making US Foreign Policy Toward South Asia, New Delhi: Concept Publishing Company and Bloomington, IN: Indiana University Press, 2008.

Acknowledgements

First and foremost, we want to recognize the imagination, ingenuity, and diligence of Jeannie Koops-Elson. She tracked down, scanned, and 'cleaned' the fifty-one articles and book chapters included in the three volumes of *Explaining Indian Democracy*. She also sought and obtained permission to publish the articles and book chapters from publishers who were sometimes hard to find or slow to reply. Equally important, she was a cheerful and charming presence in our lives during the several years it has taken to bring these tasks to pass.

We also want to acknowledge the unfailing helpfulness and good humour of our editors at Oxford University Press, New Delhi, who provided steady support. Thanks are also due to the Director of Academic Publishing who has initiated this endeavour, and provided the necessary encouragement to keep it moving.

As mentioned in our Preface, the articles and chapters in these volumes represent work done over fifty years, from 1956 to 2006. Most could not have been written without the help and cooperation of fellow academics, librarians, and archivists, administrators and political leaders from prime ministers and presidents to *sarpanches*. We have been welcomed and dealt with forthrightly.

We now spend part of each year living in Jaipur. India is home for us. We thank our friends in Jaipur, New Delhi, and elsewhere in India for making this so.

Publisher's Acknowledgements

The publisher acknowledges the following for permission to include articles/extracts in this volume.

Oxford and IBH Publishing Company, for 'The Subcontinental Empire and the Regional Kingdom in Indian State Formation', in Paul Wallace (ed.), *Region and Nation in India*, New Delhi, 1985, pp. 40–59.

The Journal of Asian Studies, for 'Presidential Address: State Formation in Asia—Prolegomenon to a Comparative Study', XLVI (4), November 1987, pp. 731–45.

University of Chicago Press, for 'State Formation in India: Building and Wasting Assets', in Lloyd I. Rudolph and Susanne Hoeber Rudolph, *In Pursuit of Lakshmi: The Political Economy of the Indian State*, Chicago, 1987, pp. 60–102, and 425–36.

Westview Press, for 'Introduction: Religion, States, and Transnational Civil Society', in Susanne Hoeber Rudolph and James Piscatori (eds), *Transnational Religion and Fading States*, Boulder, Co., 1997, pp. 1–24.

Pacific Affairs, for 'Generals and Politicians in India', XXXVII (6), Spring 1964, pp. 5–19; and for 'Rethinking Secularism: Genesis and Implications of the Textbook Controversy, 1977–79', 56 (1), Spring 1983, pp. 15–37.

Asian Survey, for 'The Centrist Future of Indian Politics', XX (6), June 1980, pp. 575–94.

Journal of Commonwealth and Comparative Politics, for 'Judicial Review *versus* Parliamentary Sovereignty: The Struggle over Stateness in India', XIX (3),

November 1981, pp. 231–56; and for 'Demand Groups and Pluralist Representation in India', XXIV (3), November 1986, pp. 227–38.

Economic and Political Weekly, for 'Iconisation of Chandrababu: Sharing Sovereignty in India's Federal Market Economy', 5 May 2001, pp. 1541–52.

Cambridge University Press, for 'Redoing the constitutional design: from an interventionist to a regulatory state', in Atul Kohli (ed.), *The Success of India's Democracy*, Cambridge, 2001, pp. 127–62.

Journal of Democracy, for 'New Dimensions of Indian Democracy', 13 (1), January 2002, pp. 52–66.

I
Processes of State Formation

Our engagement with state formation in India began in 1957, twenty-eight years before the first of the five articles in this section, 'The Subcontinental Empire and the Regional Kingdom in Indian State Formation', was published. As we set about creating a reading list and a course outline for our first course on Indian government and politics, we confronted the absence of historical and comparative analysis or theoretical writing about state formation in Asia in general, and India in particular. In our education as postgraduate students interested in comparative politics, scholarship on the state in Europe and America was readily available. There was nothing equivalent for Asia, no conventional wisdom elegantly summed up in definitive textbooks such as Carl J. Friedrich's *Constitutional Government and Democracy*, or Herman Finer's *The Theory and Practice of Modern Government*. Friedrich and Finer referred to Greece and Rome, the Renaissance and the Enlightenment, to Plato and Aristotle, Machiavelli, Hobbes and Bodin, Locke and Rousseau, the Magna Carta and the Treaty of Westphalia. No such iconic references were available for studying the state in India.

In the pre-war period and for a decade afterwards, the study of comparative politics was unreflexively Euro-centric. When, after de-colonization, the study of 'new' and 'developing' nations began, modernization theory, structural functionalism, and Marxism called for the obliteration of the past. Knowledge about the state in Asia, of ancient kingdoms and empires, of political thought and texts, or of colonial states was neither sought nor created. European state formation was naturalized, and the modern state universalized.

What passed for knowledge about the state in Asia in European thought was associated with the concept of 'Oriental Despotism'. Montesquieu, echoing Aristotle, held that 'In Asia ... there reigns a spirit of servitude which has never quitted it; and in the entire history of the continent it is impossible to find a single trait that marks a free soul; only the heroism of slavery is to be seen.' Major state thinkers such as Freidrich Hegel, Adam Smith, James Mill, Karl Marx, even Max Weber, wove variations on Aristotle's and Montesquieu's theme of states based on a pervasive spirit of servitude. From Constantinople to Shanghai, state-subject relations in Asia were depicted as standing in marked contrast to the freedom and consent that were said to characterize the modern state in Europe.

Susanne Hoeber Rudolph's 1987 'State Formation in Asia—Prolegomenon to a Comparative Study', provides a larger comparative historical framework in which the phenomena of Indian state formation can be understood. It includes critiques of Oriental Despotism's doctrines of servitude and the absence in Asia of intermediate powers and land ownership. In India, the space between the imperial ruler and his subjects was not empty; on the contrary, it was thickly populated with regional and lesser kings (*rajas*, *nawabs*), local chiefs (*zamindars*, *jagirdars*), and village, caste, tribe, and sect councils who often resisted (*fitna*) by refusing tribute, attendance at court, and taxes. And in marked contrast to sovereignty and social contract state theory in Europe, in Indian political thought the institutions of society preceded and limited state authority. The good king was enjoined to uphold the self-regulating village, caste, guild, and sect orders of society.

In our 1985 article, 'The Subcontinental Empire and the Regional Kingdom in Indian State Formation', we contrast the loosely structured, segmentary, power-sharing, multinational imperial form characteristic of Indian state formation with the centralized, monopoly sovereignty, nation-state form, whose story European analysts projected as the evolutionary culmination of the state formation story, and that Lloyd I. Rudolph depicts in his 2006 article 'Historicizing the Modern State'.

Had the Holy Roman Empire continued as the dominant European state form after the twelfth century, European state formation might have taken a course akin to that found in Asia. With the benefit of hindsight, Joseph Strayer opined that 'By 1300 it was evident that the dominant state form in Western Europe was going to be the sovereign state'.[1] Yet in the first half of the sixteenth century the Holy Roman Emperor, Charles V, ruled most of Western Europe,[2] and it wasn't until 1806, after Napoleon's victory over Prussia at Jena, that the Holy Roman Empire formally came to an end. Nor was it the case that sovereign states were the only state form after 1300; in the Dutch

---

[1]Joseph Strayer, *On the Medieval Origins of the Modern State*, Princeton, NJ: Princeton University Press, 1970, p. 10.

[2]The Hapsburg Charles V was Holy Roman Emperor from 1519 to 1556. Concurrently, he was ruler of Burgundian Netherlands, King of Aragon, King of Castile, King of Naples and Sicily, and Archduke of Austria.

Republic, the Swiss Confederation and the German iteration of the Holy Roman Empire versions of states that shared sovereignty proved viable.[3]

The collapse of the Ottoman, Hapsburg, and Tsarist empires at the end of World War I seemed to confirm that the imperial state form was an anachronism in Europe. And Selig Harrison's 1960 book, *India, the Most Dangerous Decades*,[4] suggested that India's multinational federal state, a latter-day version of the subcontinental empire, would soon disintegrate into nation-states, thereby confirming that the imperial state form was an anachronism in Asia too. However, at roughly the moment when Harrison was predicting the demise of India's federal state, six European countries signed the Treaty of Rome (1957) joining them in a European Community that, in 1992, became the European Union, which includes states from Eastern as well as Western Europe. Europe had returned to the shared sovereignty of the imperial state form and India's federal state, far from disintegrating, has become a model of democratic multiculturalism.

Contrary to received wisdom, it has been the territorial sovereign nation-state that has become increasingly anachronistic, and the shared sovereignty of federal states and cooperative international institutions that seem more appropriate for a globalizing and localizing world. Failing and failed modern states have become more frequent and troubling. And the interdependence engendered by global processes have spawned not only cooperative international institutions, but also the criminal as well as the benign non-state actors of the sort that Susanne Hoeber Rudolph characterizes in her 1997 article, 'Religion, States, and Transnational Civil Society'.

[3]See Dimitrios Karmis and Wayne Norman (eds), *Theories of Federalism: A Reader*, New York: Palgrave/Macmillan, 2005, and Joon Suk Kim, 'Making States Federatively: Different Routes of State Formation in Late Medieval and Early Modern Europe,' Ph.D., Department of Political Science, 2004.

[4]Selig Harrison, *India, the Most Dangerous Decades*, Princeton, NJ: Princeton University Press, 1960.

1

The Subcontinental Empire and the Regional Kingdom in Indian State Formation*

LLOYD I. RUDOLPH AND SUSANNE HOEBER RUDOLPH

INTRODUCTION

The recent return to the state as an object of inquiry arises from a renewed recognition of its capacity for institutional autonomy. Rather than standing in a reflexive relation to one or several social forces (for example, status orders, classes, nationalisms, interest groups, parties), recent scholarship treats the state as a distinct and potentially independent, and sometimes superordinate domain in relation to the economic, social, and cultural domains.

Scholarship on state formation in Europe and scholarship about the state in Asia have tended to consider each other as, at best, peripheral. Both the evidence used and the concepts employed by each have bypassed the other. Empirically, this has meant marginal or superficial treatment. Conceptually and theoretically, it has meant ignoring the other, or treating it as a residual or irrelevant category. We propose to remedy this defect by attending to both historical experiences in terms of a comparative universe characterized by similarities as well as differences.

Our objectives are (*i*) to appraise critically the new literature on the state with a view to enriching and qualifying it with reference to the evidence and alternative conceptual possibilities provided by South Asian institutions; and (*ii*) to reformulate the understanding and explanation of state formation

*Originally published as 'The Subcontinental Empire and the Regional Kingdom in Indian State Formation', in Paul Wallace (ed.), *Region and Nation in India*, New Delhi: Oxford and IBH Publishing Company, 1985, pp. 40–59.

in India by using in modified form the concepts provided by the new literature. The two objectives are substantively parallel, but interact conceptually.

RECENT STUDY OF STATE FORMATION AND STATENESS

The state, as an object of inquiry, has its own history. State formation is part of that history in a double sense, establishing the 'origins' of the state, and conceptualizing the relation between state and society. While distinct at the level of analysis and explanation, the study of origins and that of the state-society relationship are united in a common problematic, the variable relationship between states on the one hand, and the social, economic, and ideological determinants of political action and the use of power on the other. From this perspective, regardless of whether the object of inquiry is state origins or the state-society relation, state formation remains a *continuous process* within which the relationship of a state to its society can be conceptualized as reflexive, constrained, autonomous, or totalistic. Which of the four modalities prevails can be known, but it can be known only as a result of historical and contextual analysis and explanation. None of these modalities is more permanent, essential, or 'evolved' than the others. Each has found expression at certain historical moments.

The history of the study of the state reveals a variety of approaches. Until recently, liberal pluralist and Marxian interpretations of the origins of the modern state and of the relationship between state and society tended to be based on reflexive theories. Liberal pluralists, particularly American liberal pluralists, tended to explain the nature of the state or its actions in terms of the play of organized interests within parameters set by political culture or ideology. Marxists tended to explain the origins of the state in the West (as contrasted with 'the Orient') and its actions in terms of the struggle among classes formed and motivated by the mode and relations of production. The reflexive state, then, simply mirrored the balance of interests, or the interests of the dominant class.

The publication in 1968 of an article, largely unheralded at the time, by Peter Nettl on 'The State as a Conceptual Variable',[1] can be taken as a convenient turning point in the contemporary study of the modern state by social scientists and historians. Nettl's use of the term 'stateness' to indicate the degree to which particular states were relatively autonomous or constrained rather than reflexive in relation to organized economic and social forces, and his parallel concern with how history and political culture

---

[1] *World Politics*, 20, July 1968, pp. 559–92.

affected the variability of stateness over time signalled a change in the contemporary study of the state, even if it did not necessarily bring it about.

The change became evident among those working in the liberal pluralist tradition when the Social Science Research Council (SSRC) Committee on Comparative Politics, which had since 1954 devoted its resources to the study of political development in the Third World in ways that focused primary attention to nation-building and treated the state as reflexive, began in 1969–70 to study political development in terms of state-building in Europe. The results, published in 1975 in a volume edited by Charles Tilly,[2] made a strong case for the prior development, at least in Europe, of states as against nations and, given the authors' attention to periods (seventeenth and eighteenth centuries) when the primacy of states was still open to question, for the autonomy of those states that 'succeeded'.

At about the same time (1974), Philippe Schmitter published an article[3] that drew attention to what the late Andrew Shonfield and Samuel H. Beer had argued was the case in a variety of national contexts—that states aspired to and often succeeded in organizing and dominating interest groups, particularly producer interest groups.[4] Shonfield and Beer, unlike Schmitter, recognized that state corporatism in the form of mercantilism and 'virtual representation' preceded and to a degree 'caused' post-industrial state corporatism. The 'rediscovery' of the relatively autonomous or constrained state was accompanied by considerable ambivalence about its desirability, with Tilly and his co-authors and Schmitter aware of and concerned about the repressive, extractive, and aggressive features of the modern state, and Shonfield and Beer more inclined to feature its potential capacity to plan and manage the economy in ways that promote equality, growth, or welfare.

At about the same time that liberal pluralists were rediscovering the state, so too were some Marxists. The newly translated writings of Gramsci (Italy), Poulantzas, Althusser and Godelier (France), and Miliband (England), for example, tended in a variety of ways and for somewhat different reasons to find Marx's remarks about the state in *The Eighteenth Brumaire of Louis Bonaparte* (for instance, that '... under the second Bonaparte ... the state ... made itself completely independent' with the result that '... the executive power subordinated society to itself') more germane under a wide variety of

---

[2]*The Formation of National States in Western Europe*, Princeton: Princeton University Press, 1975.

[3]'Still the Century of Corporatism', *Review of Politics*, 36, January 1974, pp. 85–131.

[4]Their books, respectively, were *Modern Capitalism; The Changing Balance of Public and Private Power*, New York: Oxford, 1965; and *British Politics in the Collectivist Age*, New York: Knopf, 1966.

circumstances than his reflexive view of the state as an executive committee of the ruling class.[5] Marx's and Engels' views of the state and the economy in Asia (oriental despotism, the Asiatic mode of production, the village system), and their view that Asian 'history' was immutable (change required the impact of Western imperialism) were less questioned by Western Marxists and scholars of Marx; indeed, they were even elaborated by Karl Wittfogel[6] and others even though the Russian and Chinese revolutions provided massive evidence on the contrary on how and why revolutionary change occurred.[7] In India, Marxist-oriented scholars such as Irfan Habib have challenged Marx's understanding of the mode and relations of production and the role of the state, and have provided alternative explanations grounded in new and detailed historical research.[8]

Although a lot more can be said about the degree of and reasons for the revival of interest in the state by Marxist-oriented scholars, there is sufficiently strong evidence showing that a revisionist view is well-established among them. Among the most relevant for our concern with state formation is the recent important work by Perry Anderson. His *Lineages of the Absolute State* (and his earlier *Passages from Antiquity to Feudalism*) takes state formation as central for the explanation of historical change, even though Anderson remains wedded to the Marxian (and Weberian) notion of Western uniqueness and consequent superiority.[9]

Finally, the recent history of the state as an object of inquiry includes the work of those influenced by Weber. They too have had to rediscover the state, despite the fact that their master placed domination at the centre of his political sociology. S.N. Eisenstadt and Reinhard Bendix, after major

[5]Antonio Gramsci, *Letters from Prison*, translated by Lynne Lawner, New York: Harper and Row, 1973; *The Modern Prince and Other Writings*, New York: International Publishers, 1972. Nicos Poulantzas, *Political Power and Social Classes*, London: New Left Books, and Sheed and Ward, Ltd., 1973. Louis Althusser, *For Marx*, New York: Vintage Books, 1969. Maurice Godelier, 'The Notion of the "Asiatic Mode of Production" in Marx and Engels', *Enquiry*, New Series, 11 (2), 1965. Ralph Miliband, *The State in Capitalist Society*, New York: Basic Books, Inc., 1969.

[6]*Oriental Despotism, A Comparative Study of Total Power*, New Haven: Yale University Press, 1957.

[7]The works, *inter alia*, of Benjamin Schwartz and Stuart Schram amend and critique Western Marxism in the light of China's experience and Mao Tse Tung's interpretation of it. Schram, Stuart and Helen Carrere D'Encausse, *Marxism and Asia*, London: Alan Lane, The Penguin Press, 1969. Benjamin Schwartz, *Chinese Communism and the Rise of Mao*, Cambridge: Harvard University Press, 1961.

[8]Irfan Habib, 'An Examination of Wittfogel's Theory of Oriental Despotism', *Enquiry* VI, 1961, and *Agrarian System of Mughal India*, Bombay: Asian Publishing House, 1963.

[9]Perry Anderson, *Lineages of the Absolutist State*, London: New Left Books, 1977; *Passages from Antiquity to Feudalism*, London: New Left Books, 1974.

works dealing with processes of change that paid limited attention to state formation and treated the state as reflexive of cultural, ideological, or social forces, produced studies that deal centrally with state formation, *The Political Systems of Empires; The Rise and Fall of the Historical Bureaucratic Societies;* and *Kings or People: Power and the Mandate to Rule.*[10]

CRITIQUE OF EXTANT STATE THEORY

STATE FORMATION IN ASIA AND EUROPE: A RECONCEPTUALIZATION

Explanations of state formation, the state-society relationship, and stateness have been based on interpretations of the history of the West. The failure to take account of non-Western historical experiences presents critical obstacles to an understanding of the state in Asia. Social and political changes in Asia have been both like and unlike changes in the West. In fact, different social conditions and doctrines in Europe and India produced contrasting state types, the nation-state in Europe and the subcontinental empire in India. As Nettl put it,

The European experience of stateness was essentially the product of a particularization or narrowing of sovereignty into ethnically homogeneous or at least ethnically defined areas. ... Developing countries, on the other hand, have in common the extension of central authority across ethnic boundaries and particular, hitherto 'sovereign, communities'.[11]

The conceptions of state, society, and the relationship between them have been formulated differently in India from the way they have been in Europe. In Europe, the Greek idea of common citizenship and the Christian ideal of a community of believers contributed to the seventeenth-century concept of a civil society that ultimately shaped the process of state formation, which eventually led to the nation-state. The European concept of civil society and state sovereignty established a superordinate moral and political community of the state, which encompassed and transcended social diversities and inequalities. In contrast, classical Hindu thought of the *dharmasastras* (legal texts) recognized ordered heterogeneity. It rationalized and legitimized a society of distinct cultural and functional communities that shared a sense of brotherhood within themselves, but lived as races apart in their relationship to each other. State power was constrained by society's autonomous claims to self-regulation. Communities were not united to each other by fellow feeling—quite the reverse—and yet they constituted non-antagonistic

---

[10]New York: The Free Press, 1969, and Berkeley: University of California Press, 1978.
[11]Nettl, 'The State', see p. 590.

strata[12] whose cultural differences, social interaction, and functional interdependence were ordered and integrated within a larger social architectonic that the state was meant to uphold and protect.

For Brahmin social theorists, the dharmasastra was a means to assimilate the diverse customs of *mlecchas* (foreigners) within the customs of the Vedic/Aryan peoples as they moved down the Gangetic plain from their 'homeland' in the Punjab. Brahmin theorists used the same conceptions and techniques to assimilate waves of subsequent conquerors, Greeks, Sakas, Kushanas, Huns. The characteristic strategy of the law books was a compartmentalization of diversity, rather than homogenization. It was a strategy designed to establish and legitimize vertical and horizontal social distance within a larger social order. A correlate of the strategy was the conception that society, the laws and customs of particular social groups, was prior to the state. It was the duty of kings to uphold the pre-existing and self-regulating diverse laws and customs of social groups.

Appropriate state ideologies for ordered heterogeneity are prefigured in doctrines about religious diversity that subcontinental empires have articulated. An Asokan pillar of the Mauryan empire enjoins: 'King Priyadarsi, Beloved of the Gods, honours men of all religious communities with gifts and honours ... other sects should be daily honoured in everyway. ...'[13] Islam, too, in its Indian environment, was obliged to recognize this mode of social integration. The twelfth-century conceptions of militant Islam of the early Turkic invaders entailed the conversion of conquered peoples, that is, homogenization rather than compartmentalization. In the event, Indian social reality proved more intractable than that of other peoples. The exemptions generally extended to people of the book, Jews and Christians, were extended first to Brahmins, and eventually to other Hindu subjects. Badaoni, writing in the sixteenth century as a contemporary about Akbar, the greatest of the Mughal emperors, tells us: 'As a result of all the influences which were brought to bear on his Majesty, there grew ... gradually as the outline on a stone, the conviction in his heart that there were sensible men in all religions. ...'[14]

Rulers who violated the norm of upholding the laws and customs of social groups by intervening to change them, as Aurangzeb did in the later part of his reign and the British did just prior to 1857, endangered the

[12]André Béteille, 'The Politics of "Non-Antagonistic" Strata', *Contributions to Indian Sociology*, n.s., III, December 1969.

[13]Asokan Rock Edict, No. XIII, Shahbazgari text, in Sircar, D.C., *Inscriptions of Asoka*, Delhi: Government of India, Publications Division, 1975.

[14]Badaoni, as cited in *The Abul-Fazl-i-'Allami*, The A' in-i Akbari. Translated by H.F. Blochmann and H.S. Jarrett and further annotated by Jadunath Sarkar, second edition, Calcutta: Asiatic Society of Bengal, 1927, vol. II, p. 256.

foundations of the subcontinental empire. The British policy eventually echoed the practice of previous imperial states, subventions to and protection of all sects. These doctrines about religious diversity are relevant for other diversities, such as language, caste, and religion, as well.

In Europe, states sought sovereignty over intermediary orders that articulated and represented civil society. The existence and viability of the state and society were mutually determined and interdependent. In India, diverse social groups did not participate in a civil society based on a common moral and political community. Instead, society conceptualized as diverse social groups possessed of particular laws and customs was taken to be prior to the state, and independent of it. The obligation of rulers as public persons was not, as in Europe's sovereignty-seeking states, to embody and articulate the values and interests of a civil society, but to protect and uphold the respective customs and laws of the self-regulating social orders. These two possibilities, the heterogeneous conception of Indian society integrated by compartmentalization within a larger social order, and the more homogeneous conception of society in Europe that the shared moral and political community of civil society engendered, shaped the divergent processes of state formation, the subcontinental empire and the nation-state.

State formation in India was less affected than it was in Europe by its relation to society. Hence, state formation was more subject to internal or exogenous causes of growth and decay. In Europe, where the state-society relationship was more intimate and mutually dependent, growth and decay, including the possibility of revolution, were more dependent on the viability of the state's relation to society. In the post-absolutist era, Europe's sovereignty-seeking states were often constrained by conceptions of a contractual and consenting civil society and citizens' rights. In India, the prior existence of the multiple-layered self-regulating society, and the injunction that the 'good king' protects and upholds it, helps to explain the instrumental and constrained nature of the state.

ORIENTAL DESPOTISM, ASIATIC MODE OF PRODUCTION, AND THE VILLAGE COMMUNE

Much theory about state formation in Europe depends on misconceived or historically false contrasts with Asia. A considerable amount of literature has begun to dis-establish such concepts as Oriental despotism, the Asiatic mode of production, and the village commune because they distort explanations of state formation not only in Asia, but also in Europe. A proper conception of state formation in Asia requires a consolidation of these criticisms. An account of state formation also requires an account of the extra-continental environment of state formation. That environment includes influential state models (Ottoman, Safavid, Mongol, British), world ideologies (Islam, *laissez faire* liberalism), the world economy, and the impact on the subcontinent of intruding external actors and forces.

The Frenchman Francois Bernier, physician to the Mughal emperor Aurangzeb between 1656 and 1668, was a principal source in Europe of the Indian variant of Oriental despotism. Visiting the Mughal court at a time when the imperial state was already in crisis, he perceived and interpreted it in terms of Renaissance Europe's image of a powerful, threatening, and despotic Ottoman empire. Bodin, in the sixteenth century, had noted Oriental despotism's lack of respect for persons and goods; Bacon, its absence of an hereditary aristocracy; Harrington, its juridicial monopoly over landed property. To this catalogue, Adam Smith in the eighteenth century contributed the conception of hydraulic civilization, of a state that dominates society by controlling the means to improve the land. In the nineteenth century, Marx, who echoed all these conceptions, added the idea of the self-sufficient classless village engaged in collective production, without history, but subject to the extractions of the Oriental despotic state.[15]

By the eighteenth century, 'Oriental despotism' had created contradictory images for European state theory. For Machiavelli, impressed with the Ottoman military organization, a despotic prince could rule more effectively. For Voltaire, a despot could be the instrument of enlightenment. It was the 'liberal' Montesquieu, however, whose depiction of Oriental despotism had the greatest influence on Western state theory, albeit in a manner he did not intend. Montesquieu meant to criticize French absolutism in a safe way, by pretending (in the *Persian Letters*) to condemn Persian usages. Louis XIV, the Sun King, was a despot 'who had violated the French constitution, corrupted French society, and introduced Oriental practices'.[16] By noting this resemblance, his Persian characters provide a vehicle for criticizing and condemning the absolute state in France. It is via Montesquieu's *Persian Letters* that the concept of despotism becomes enormously significant in European political discourse through the designation of a system of total domination. 'Despotism for Montesquieu and for subsequent European theory of the state is the rule of a single person subject to no restraint, constitutional or moral. The ruler's caprice and passions prevail through deputies who act out of fear.'[17] The result, which Montesquieu finds at home in France, is its centralization of absolute authority and its exercise by an

---

[15]See Anderson, *Lineages*, pp. 399 ff, 472 ff.

[16]Charles de Secondat, Baron de Montesquieu, *The Persian Letters*, translated by John Davidson, London: Routledge and Sons, 1923; Melvin Richter, *The Political Theory of Montesquieu*, New York: Cambridge University Press, 1977, p. 31.

[17]Ibid., p. 46.

anonymous patrimonial bureaucracy. In one of the greater ironies in the sociology of knowledge, the *Persian Letters'* image of Oriental despotism is exorcized and projected to the states of the East, which are taken, by Hegel, the Mills, Marx, Weber, and others, to be its home.

This view requires both empirical and theoretical revision. Empirically, the most important revision has to do with what Indian rulers did recognize and protect: the customs, activities, and prerogatives of communities, castes, sects, status orders, and guilds (craft and commercial). While practice often departed from norm, state theory recognized that such social formations, far from being creations or instruments of the state, existed *prior* to the state, and were governed by their own laws and customs. It was the first duty of rulers to preserve and protect them.

The privileges and immunities of castes, communities, sects, and guilds do not parallel feudal liberties and rights.[18] India's social formations were not *Stände*, nor were they recognized institutionally in a *Standes-Staat*.[19] However, social theory in authoritative and widely influential texts vested ascriptive and functional communities with privileges and immunities, and enjoined rulers seeking legitimacy to recognize and protect them. The good king's duty was to uphold the society which preceded him, and was a necessary condition for his rule. The good ruler's obligation to defer to the privileges and immunities of pre-existing social formations did not eventuate, as it did in European doctrine or practice, in a constitutional monarchy or a liberal state derived from feudal liberties or rights.[20] But it did conceptualize and value the state, that is, the ruler and his patrimonial bureaucracy, and society as separate and exclusive domains, and established sacred and secular restraints on the arbitrary exercise of power.

For Marx, whose vision of India reflected the widely shared nineteenth-century conceptions epitomized by James Mill, Oriental despotism consisted of the overwhelming state on the one hand and the atomized village communities on the other, separated, as it were, by empty social and political

---

[18]Basic primary texts are Georg Buhler, *The Laws of Manu*, Delhi: Reprint by Motilal Banarsidass, 1975, and R.P. Kangle, *The Kautiliya Arthasastra*, 3 vols, Bombay: T.V. Chidambaram for the University of Bombay Studies, 1960–5. Consult also A.L. Basham, *The Wonder that was India*, New York: Grove Press, 1959; Romila Thapar, *History of India*, Baltimore: Penguin Books, 1965.

[19]Ernest Barker, *The Development of the Public Services in Europe*, New York: Oxford University Press, 1944.

[20]For the theory of European liberties and rights, see Charles MacIlwain, *The Growth of Political Thought in the West, from the Greeks to the End of the Middle Ages*, New York: Macmillan, 1932; Guido de Ruggiero, *The History of European Liberalism*, translated by R.G. Collingwood, London: Oxford, 1927; T.H. Marshall, *Class, Citizenship and Social Development*, Chicago: University of Chicago Press, 1977.

space. Their circumstances were dictated by the absence of private property. Marx wrote:

The stationary character of this part of Asia [India]—despite all the aimless movement in the political surface—is fully explained by two circumstances which supplement each other: (1) the public works were the business of the central government; (2) besides this the whole empire, not counting the few larger towns, was divided into villages, each of which possessed a completely separate organization and formed a little world in itself. ... As to the question of property, this is a very controversial one among the English writers on India—In the broken hill country south of Krishna [sic], property in land does seem to have existed. ... In any case it seems to have been Mohamedens who first established the principle of 'no property in land' throughout the whole of Asia.[21]

Writing in a different tradition, Henry Mayne shared elements of Marx's view. Isolation and self-sufficiency allegedly insulated village communities, confined their horizons to local concerns,[22] and facilitated a fatalistic acceptance of the all-powerful state. In fact, they were not isolates. Villages were complexly connected by a variety of networks. Marriage ties, especially in northern India, might link as many as 100,000 persons over hundreds of miles. The clan networks and kinship ties of local rulers and dominant landlord communities created links among regional elites. Religious ties of regional sects, popular pilgrimages, and periodic devotional festivals constituted vital channels of cultural communication. Trade networks, in which credit and cash transactions played a role, were, from the most ancient times, critical to linking villages to sub-regions and to the world.[23] Nor was the Indian political landscape exhausted by the duality that both Marx and Henry Mayne posit, of an all-powerful and despotic state confronting a universe of passive isolates—the villages of India. In fact, as we have pointed out, the social and political space between the village and the state was richly populated. The improbable nature of the 'empty space' between village and state posited by the theory of Oriental despotism is suggested in Habib's account of the sects, caste communities, and regional patron-client networks that resisted late Mughal rule.[24]

---

[21]Marx to Engels, 14 June 1953, in *Karl Marx and Friedrich Engels: Selected Correspondence*, Moscow: Foreign Language Publishing House, no date, c. 1953, pp. 102–4.

[22]Henry Sumner Mayne, *Village Communities in the East and West*, London: John Murray, 1895.

[23]See Bernard S. Cohn and McKim Marriott, 'Networks and Centers in Indian Civilization', *Journal of Social Research*, 1 (1), 1958; Romila Thapar, *The Past and Prejudice*, Patel Memorial Lectures, Delhi: Government of India, Ministry of Information and Broadcasting, Publications Division, c. 1974, pp. 42–9, for trade networks; Iravati Karve, *Kinship Organization in India*, Poona: Deccan College, 1951, for kin networks; G. Ghurye, *Indian Sadhus*, Bombay: Popular Book Depot, 1953, for religious networks.

[24]Habib, *Agrarian System*.

Contrary to European understanding, ancient and medieval epigraphic and textual evidence shows that entitlement to land existed. Property rights paralleled the conditional and parcelled form found in feudal Europe before revived conceptions of Roman law removed many limitations on the rights that accompanied 'ownership'.[25] The mistaken idea of an exclusive 'state ownership' of land under Oriental despotism, which was inferred in part from the primary and uncontested right of the state to a share of the land's product as revenue, obscured the existence of a variety of claims to the entitlement to land, and shares in its product. This variation makes it possible to speak of class differences and conflict and, in the Marxian sense, 'history', as against the image prior to and after Marx of a classless, ahistorical village commune subject to extractions by the owner-state. Irrigation, which constituted the 'public works' to which Marx refers, and on which Wittfogel builds his theory of hydraulic states, was controlled by a wide variety of agencies, from village communes through individual landholders, temples, and regional kingdoms.[26] It was by no means the monopoly of the state, and provides a basis for political pluralism, not centralization.

In sum, state formation and the state-society relation in India cannot be understood in the light of a theory whose principal concepts are Oriental despotism, the Asian mode of production, and the village commune. More relevant are the doctrine and practice of the Mauryan and Gupta empires of northern India, the Chola and Vijayanagar empires of southern India, and the Ottoman, Byzantine, and Safavid empires of Western Asia, insofar as they influenced the Mongol inheritance and Persian borrowings of the creators and builders of the Mughal empire in India.[27]

EXTRA-CONTINENTAL DIMENSIONS OF STATE FORMATION

The use in recent literature on state formation of 'international' forces, particularly market forces that link states and their economies, to explain the 'origins' and development of states is promising, even helpful, but ultimately unsatisfying. The conceptualization of 'international' economic

[25]See, for example, B.R. Grover, 'Nature of Land Rights in Mughal India', *Indian Economic and Social History Review*, 1 (4); Irfan Habib, *Agrarian System*; Tapan Raychaudhuri, 'The Agrarian System of Mughal India', *Enquiry*, n.s., 2 (1), 1965.

[26]See Habib, 'Examination of Wittfogel's Theory'; S.N. Eisenstadt, 'The Study of Oriental Despotism as Systems of Total Power', *Journal of Asian Studies*, 17, 1958; Burton Stein, *Peasant State and Society in Medieval South India*, New Delhi: Oxford, 1980.

[27]Haul Inalcik, *The Ottoman Empire: The Classical Age, 1300–1600*, translated by Norman Itzkowitz and Colin Imber, New York: Praeger, 1973; Norman Itzkowitz, *Ottoman Empire and Islamic Tradition*, New York: Knopf, 1972; Sir John Malcolm, *The History of Persia, from the Early Period to the Present Time*, London: John Murray, 1829. H. Franz Schurmann, *The Mongols of Afghanistan: An Ethnography of the Moghols and Related Peoples of Afghanistan*, Gravenhage: Mouton, 1962.

forces includes, for example, Wallerstein's evocation in the sixteenth century of the capitalist world economy of sixteenth-century Europe. Its 'core', 'semiperiphery', and 'periphery' were located in Northwest, Southern, and Eastern Europe, and its 'external arena' in Asia and other contemporary Third World areas. Wallerstein views external arenas much as Marx would have; they lack a meaningful history because they lack an economy that affects class or state formation.[28]

History is made by Europe, regardless of whether it is made by creation or oppression. There were no world systems before European capitalism created one. Buddhism and Islam fail to qualify as international systemic forces because of their superstructural nature. Nor do the diffusion of administrative and political forms by Byzantium and Persia qualify. South Asia's extensive international trade before the sixteenth century drops out of view because Asia is by definition peripheral. The European-oriented economistic view limits rather than enhances explanations of state formation because it too severely subordinates the cultural, political, and social domains to the economic. This is particularly true when nineteenth-century market forces based on industrial technology are read back into sixteenth and seventeenth-century historical contexts. Polanyi's seminal work, *The Great Transformation*, is more convincing because it claims less and explains better how different types of markets (local, national, and international) were both dependent upon and caused state formation.[29]

Other accounts of state formation suggest that existing European states joined in 'drawing the rest of the world into a system of states'.[30] In this reading, state formation in Asia is the result of European impact. No doubt the imperial penetration that began in the eighteenth century and accelerated in the nineteenth affected state formation in Asia. But attention to imperial penetration unduly emphasizes the role of imperialism and colonialism by exaggerating the discontinuities, and obscuring the continuities between alien imperial and indigenous state forms.

Durable Indian sources of stateness and state forms go as far back as the fourth century BC Mauryan Empire.[31] Mauryan rulers identified themselves as *chakravartin* (universal emperor), symbolically depicted as the centre of

[28]Emmanuel Wallerstein, *The Modern World-System: Capitalist Agriculture and the Origins of the European World Economy in the Sixteenth Century*, New York: Academic Press, 1974.

[29]Karl Polanyi, *The Great Transformation: The Political and Economic Origins of Our Time*, Boston: Beacon Press, 1957.

[30]Charles Tilly (ed.), *The Formation of National States in Western Europe*, Princeton: Princeton University Press, 1975.

[31]Romila Thapar, *Asoka and the Decline of the Mauryas*, London: Oxford University Press, 1961.

the great wheel that represented the political universe. Asoka, a devoted convert to Buddhism, ruled two-thirds of the subcontinent with the aid of an elaborate official hierarchy, an intelligence service, and a paid army. The imperial idea in India was not abandoned, even if it was only sporadically and indifferently realized. It was partially restored by the Gupta dynasty (320–535 AD) and powerfully restored by the Mughals (1556–1707/1857), whose Mongol Turkic origins and Persian borrowings brought external ideas, men, and practices to the process of state formation on the subcontinent. British rule, too, blended extra-continental ideas and institutions into indigenous state forms, even as it adapted and extended Mughal symbolism, ceremonials, and administrative arrangements. Utilitarian/autocratic ideas and practices that were unacceptable at home were applied in India to create a centralized and autocratic imperial state.[32]

THE NATION-STATE AND THE SUBCONTINENTAL EMPIRE IN EUROPE AND INDIA

The leading difference between European and Indian state formation is their historical outcomes, the nation-state in Europe and the subcontinental empire in India. The ideology and reality of the nation-state has been far less powerful in Asia than it has been in Europe. J.P. Nettl pointed out that 'if the entry of the third world onto the stage of modern socio-scientific consciousness has had one immediate result (or should have had), it is the snapping of the link between state and nation. What were awkward exceptions (Switzerland, the Soviet Union, empires generally, and so on) have now become also a rule of non-nation-states.'[33] India is a striking exemplar of the rule. It continued along the road Western Europe turned away from when it abandoned the Holy Roman Empire. India's historic concepts of stateness and collective representations of the political universe featured an imperial state. On the one hand, it aggregated diverse territorial, cultural, and functional communities. On the other, it featured a symbolic and institutional state domain. For Europe, the collapse of the Hapsburg, Tsarist, and Ottoman states after World War I seemed to confirm for the Atlantic world the atavistic nature of the multinational imperial state form. It is in the period after World War II that Europe sought once more, through economic and political means, to approximate a subcontinental political order.

[32]E.M.C. Stokes, *The English Utilitarians in India*, Oxford: Clarendon, 1959.

[33]Nettl, 'The State', For an important discussion of India as a multinational state, see Paul Brass, *Language, Religion and Politics in North India*, London: Cambridge University Press, 1974, pp. 14–20.

Unlike Europe, where internal sovereignty became the reigning state conception, in India a segmentary conception of state power prevailed. 'By 1300 it was evident that the dominant political form in Western Europe was going to be the sovereign state.'[34] By contrast, the doctrine and practice of the Indian state preserved subordinate jurisdictions. It included, rather than eliminated, layered and segmented social and political power, and created a socially constrained negotiated political order. This order was not merely a concession to the contingent and layered distribution of power among the regional kingdoms and local chiefs that prevailed through much of Indian history, or a consequence of limited technical means of control. It was also a principle of state formation and maintenance.

The doctrine of sovereignty, with its implied exclusive jurisdiction, was inimical to the sharing and layering of power among culturally diverse areas that made possible a multinational empire. 'Sovereign' European states (France, Spain) attempted to embrace and subsume diverse peoples even when they denied or resisted national assimilation. States in continental Western Europe preceded nations, and sought to create them through ideology and policy. By the nineteenth century, the nation-state had become so powerful an ideology that the existence of diverse ethnic communities was obscured, and their claims de-legitimized or repressed.[35] On the other hand, cultural diversity was translated into nationalism, and sought realization in states. The result of Woodrow Wilson's insistence on self-determination after World War I 'was the closest approximation that modern Europe has ever had to an ethnographic map coinciding with a political map'.[36]

The difference between state formation in Europe and India was affected by the relatively early stability state forms achieved in Europe, and the relative fluidity they retained in India through the eighteenth century. This fluidity was a product of the tension between the imperial state and the regional kingdom, and the mutual determination that affected system-level differences. Though the languages and symbolism of the Holy Roman Empire did not disappear nominally until 1806, or finally until the fall of the Hapsburg Austro-Hungarian Empire, its fate as a collective representation and as an institutional reality had been sealed live 100 years earlier. The sovereign national states that were evident in Europe by the fourteenth century became

[34]Joseph R. Strayer, *On the Medieval Origins of the Modern State*, Princeton: Princeton University Press, 1970, p. 10.

[35]Reinhard Bendix, *Kings or People: Power and the Mandate to Rule*, Berkeley: University of California Press, 1978.

[36]Thomas Andrew Bailey, *Woodrow Wilson and the Lost Peace*, New York: MacMillan, 1944, p. 316.

ascendant by the sixteenth when the reformation and national churches effectively denied the universalistic claims of the church in Rome and ushered in the age of absolutism.

State formation on the Indian subcontinent took a different course. The prevalent state form on the Indian subcontinent under Mughal and British rule from the sixteenth through the mid-twentieth centuries was the subcontinental empire rather than the regional kingdom. This outcome was by no means clear during prior, non-imperial eras, when the regional kingdom was the dominant state form. Literary and artistic creativity, as well as dynastic and territorial loyalties, are associated with both regional kingdoms and imperial states.[37] Nor were the Deccan states of Bijapur, Golconda, or the Chola and Vijayanagar southern empires necessarily destined to fail. If the subcontinental empire prevailed, it did so marginally rather than totally; the successor states of the British *raj* and the states in India's federal system are contemporary expressions of the regional state form.

A variety of elements created and sustained the universalism of the subcontinental empire. Mughal cultural policy featured Persian. It became the link language for a subcontinent of many tongues, and a mark of elite status. The emperor created a symbolic and cultural order. Akbar restored and benefited from the ancient and pervasive Hindu idea of a universal emperor (*chakravartin*), a *raja dhiraja* (raja of rajas) or *shahanshah* (shah of shahs), who turned the wheel (*chakra*) of the political universe and was the hub of its spokes. Akbar succeeded in sanctifying the person of the emperor in the face of an Islamic tradition hostile to such an enterprise. Iconography, rituals, and performances celebrated and elevated the emperor, who became an object of awe and wonder. Mughal miniature paintings featured the emperor with a penumbra. Because the loyalty and obeisance he commanded was at once intensely personal and abstract, it created a separate state domain that dissolved and displaced loyalties to place, king, and community.[38] Performances and exchanges amplified his presence: for the public, the daily royal audience in the *diwan-i-am* (hall of public audience); for the court attended by princes and nobles appearances in the *diwan-i-khas* (hall of private audience); and at frequent *darbars*; for the crown servants in the field, intimate personal exchanges—the gift of a *khilat* (robe said to have been worn by

[37]See exchange between R.S. Sharma, 'Problem of Transition from Ancient to Medieval in Indian History', and 'Methods and Problems of the Study of Feudalism in Early Medieval India', *Indian Historical Review*, I.(1), 1974; and S. Gopal, *et al.*, 'A Note on R.S. Sharma's Ideas on Indian Feudalism', *Indian Historical Review*, I (2), 1974.

[38]David Lelyveld, *Aligarh's First Generation: Muslim Solidarity in British India*, Princeton, N.J.: Princeton University Press, 1977.

the emperor) to mark an appointment as his agent, letters from the emperor's hand, and the reciprocation of gifts by subordinates.[39] Streams of exchanges kept the emperor's relations with service nobles at the far ends of the subcontinent 'thick'.[40]

The British used Mughal ceremonies and language to revitalize the universalism and mystique of the imperial state, reviving in Victoria's time the imperial grandeur and patrimonial ties in jubilees and coronation ceremonies, and in rituals of loyalty between the Queen and her subjects.[41] Their cultural policy featured English. Like Persian under the Mughals, it became the language of state administration, a mark of elite status, and the medium through which the political leaders of the subcontinent's disparate regions and communities deliberated and bargained.

Both the Mughal and British states formed alliances that recognized and legitimated the ordered heterogeneity of Indian society. Mughal marital, political, and military alliances with Rajput (Hindu) princes helped them to create and rule an empire. The Mughal court's patronage embraced Hindu aesthetic and literary products and, in the case of Akbar, Zoroastrian and Christian as well as Hindu religious practices. In turn, Rajput lifestyles, state administration, and art were infiltrated by Mughal forms and standards, even while Rajput rulers preserved their religious and political patrimony.

The inability of Mughal officials to recognize southern rulers as part of the system of ordered heterogeneity and incorporate them as collaborators in the task of ruling the imperial state was a significant cause of the deterioration and collapse of Mughal rule. The northern, Persian, and Persianized Mughal court nobility and officials had recognized without pain the geographically, ethnically, and linguistically adjacent Rajputs. Incorporating the Marathas proved troublesome yet possible, but Mughal nobles and officials lacked the cultural flexibility to treat as peers the 'hideous, black' and guttural sounding Poligars and other southern notables.[42] Together with overextended lines of communication, logistical

[39]John F. Richards, 'The Imperial Crisis in the Deccan', *Journal of Asian Studies*, XXV (2), 1976.

[40]See, for example, M.I. Borah, trans., *Baharistan-I-Ghaybi* (Mughal Wars in Assam, Cooch Behar, Bengal, Bihar and Orissa During the Reigns of Jahangir and Shah Jahan by Mirza Nathan), Gauhati: Assam Department of Historical and Antiquarian Studies, 1936, for numerous accounts of such exchanges.

[41]Bernard S. Cohn, 'The British and the Mughal Court in the Seventeenth Century', unpublished paper, University of Chicago, June–July 1977.

[42]John F. Richards, 'The Imperial Crisis'. For theories of the decline of the Mughal empire, see also M. Athar Ali, *The Mughal Nobility under Aurangzeb*, New York: Asian Publishing House, 1970; Satish Chandra, *Parties and Politics at the Mughal Court, 1707–1740*, New Delhi: People's Publishing House, 1959.

difficulties, and the exhaustion of resources, especially *jagirs*, to sustain an expanded and increasingly unproductive and ineffective army and bureaucracy, the inability to accommodate southern political elites helped to account for the Mughal failure in the south, and ultimately in the subcontinent. Ironically, British racial arrogance contributed to their superficial but comprehensive acceptance of Indian heterogeneity. All Indians became natives, an inferior species distinguished by a wide variety of esoteric and— for most—abhorrent beliefs and practices.

The instrumental and institutional variables that accounted for a viable state in India included centralized fiscal and administrative mechanisms in the hands of the Crown; patrimonial bureaucracies barred from control over the means of administration, and from appropriation and inheritance of office and estates; and military formations controlled by the Crown rather than by feudal lords or independent military entrepreneurs. These arrangements were already visible in the subcontinental, fourth-century (BC) Mauryan empire, and articulated in books of statecraft (*artha*) dating from that period and subsequently. Their actualization has varied over time. Revived in subsequent subcontinental empires and in regional kingdoms, they fade with the fragmentation of dominion under weak emperors or regional kings, whose servants under various guises and arrangements appropriate estates, offices, revenues, and military forces. Akbar and Jahangir followed the Sultanate in eliminating the principle of an hereditary state service, took control of revenue administration and its income, and exquisitely calibrated, depending upon performance, the honours and income associated with state service.[43] In the latter part of Aurangzeb's rule and under his successors in the eighteenth century, state autonomy and capacity markedly declined, but were restored under British rule.

In the last 100 years, new elements of political unity have emerged, grounded in the growth of an elite and popular consciousness of a national destiny free of external control. The Indian nationalist movement lent a sense of commonality to the separate communities of the subcontinent. At the same time, however, it gave a new meaning to the multinational aspect of the imperial state. Gandhi's strategy of nurturing popular consciousness through the medium of regional languages and symbols promoted regional identities.

At the cultural level, the prevalence of the Hindu religion and a Sanskritic language and civilization in India, like Christianity and Latin in Europe, provided favourable contexts for subcontinental empires. Yet, the cultural and organizational context of Christendom, which pointed towards an empire-state outcome for Europe, did not eventuate in one. In fact, the

[43]V.S. Bhatnagar, *Life and Times of Sawai Jai Singh, 1688–1743*, Delhi: Impex, 1974.

revolt against the universal church is usually seen as part of an explanation for the emerging national state.[44] The self-assertion of linguistic regions against Latin universalism, and the revolt of national churches in support of the reformation idea became the impetus for the emergence of the nation-state. In India, the outcome was different. Sanskritic Hinduism lacked organizational integration in a hierarchical bureaucracy capable of providing authoritative guidance for defining orthodoxy, and identifying and resisting heterodoxy and heresy. Most priests were Brahmins by caste, but neither the caste nor the priesthood was organized subcontinentally. Priests' authority and political influence varied enormously with place and time. The shapelessness of orthodoxy allowed heterodox *bhakti* (devotional) movements to infiltrate and transform Hinduism. They resembled the reformation in their pursuit of a direct relationship with God, their condemnation of priesthood and caste, and advancement of vernaculars against a sacred universal language (Sanskrit). Typically, the bhakti movements challenged the Brahmin priesthood without the benefit of alliances with states. The alliance between reformation and state, which advanced the nation-state in Europe, was not an element in Indian state formation.

THE SUBCONTINENTAL EMPIRE—MUGHAL AND BRITISH VARIANTS

The several major subcontinental empires that ruled large portions of the Indian subcontinent can be characterized in terms of two regime types, indirect rule by a master or masters, and direct rule based on a centralized patrimonial bureaucracy. Some empires incorporated aspects of both types. In the first regime type, lesser rulers occupied the space between the imperial master and his subjects. This arrangement preserved, within the empire, lesser political sub-units, that embodied distinct laws, customs, and sometimes religions. The second regime type, the centralized administrative state, tended towards the elimination of subordinate rulers, and the establishment of direct relations between the imperial master and his subjects. Both types entailed the creation of a distinct domain composed of an imperial language, culture, and elite. The Mughals attempted with mixed success to create a less constrained absolutist (or 'Sultanist') variant, and the British, after an initial attempt under Dalhousie to eliminate lesser rulers, created a version more constrained by indirect rule.

After six centuries, during which regional kingdoms and lesser segmentary units were ascendant, the Sultanate (thirteenth to sixteenth century) and

[44]Strayer, *Medieval Origins*.

the Mughal (sixteenth to eighteenth century) state resolutely attempted to displace them. They did so in part by opposing doctrines or practices that legitimized or institutionalized a prebendal or independent notability. Sultanate and Mughal state-building featured a sophisticated revenue apparatus. The Mughals added a more highly rationalized imperial service (the *mansabdari* system) under the direct command and control of the emperor. Sultanate and Mughal efforts were influenced by Abbasid and Saffavid models. Mughal literary, artistic, and ceremonial forms differentiated the state sector by elevating the emperor and his patrimonial bureaucrats, intellectuals, and cultural specialists above other elites. The heights attained by the state domain were unimaginable to the more God-fearing Arabic version of Islam. They were unimaginable too for Hindus accustomed to a kingship theory that interpreted the king's divinity through a cosmology that defined divinity as plentiful, and easily accessible.

The British subcontinental empire exploited Timurid (Mughal) descent ceremonials and doctrine to legitimize its authority. It also adapted the Mughal centralizing administrative practice, mingling it with Whig conceptions of feudal liberty. Out of these elements, it created a paradoxical state theory that featured an imperial viceroy and a limited liberal state. The Mughals had utilized a variable mixture of direct and indirect rule, relatively direct in areas such as Gujarat and Awadh, and indirect in Rajputana, where local rulers retained considerable autonomy. The British made the types manifest, separate, and stable when they distinguished direct rule in the British provinces from the (indirect) paramountcy relationship established with the princely states.

The similarities and differences in Mughal and British ideas about the state-society relation can be seen in their contrasting policies vis-à-vis rulers in Rajputana, whose north Indian regional kingdoms both sought to dominate. Mughal rulers attempted to impose upon Rajput kingdoms a centralized jagir system, and establish asymmetrical bonds of loyalty between themselves and Rajput rajas comparable to those that integrated master-servant relationships at the Centre. Centralized, hierarchical relations characteristic of the Mughal state stood in marked contrast to relations within Rajput kingdoms. Decentralization and horizontal bonds of clan and lineage brotherhoods sustained relatively symmetrical relations between rulers, and greater and lesser noble subjects. Maharajas stood above their brothers within dynastic clans, but did so as representatives of the clan's senior lineages. Over time, Rajput rulers emulated Mughal ideas and practice by trying to remodel their relations with their clan brothers into a more hierarchical master-servant connection. Their nobles' response recapitulated their own resistance to Mughal claims, that is, variable compliance punctuated by sporadic revolts.

Because language and symbols are often constitutive, they can enact or establish as well as characterize the political order. Variations in the language and symbols used by actors to designate the same resources and authority provide access to differences important for understanding and explaining conflict and change. Despite the common use of prevailing Persian terms, Mughal and Rajput language usage evokes the contrasting perspectives of empire and regional kingdom. Mughal patrimonial bureaucrats and chroniclers used the terms *mansabdar* or jagirdar to designate regional or local officials, and *mansab*, jagir, or *watan jagir* for estates, terms that made clear that offices and lands were granted in support of state service and held at the emperor's pleasure. Rajput rulers used other terms, raja (ruler) or zamindar (local lord), and *desh, raj, watan*, or *mulk* (a ruler's hereditary homeland) to express their sense of independence with respect to authority and land.[45]

The British exercise of 'paramountcy' over the princely states parallels in many ways Mughal doctrine and practice. At the same time, there are important differences. If the Mughal emperors thought of Rajput rulers as mansabdars (military and civil officials), dispensable servants dependent for their posts and perquisites on imperial will, the British thought of Rajput lords as a feudal landed aristocracy. Vassals of the Queen-empress, they were meant to be at the same time a governing class with rights and obligations. Mughal absolutist aspirations in Rajputana involved efforts to dissolve or displace local loyalties to kingdoms, homelands, and clans with the prestige and rewards of imperial service. Through paramountcy, the British recognized and legitimized the regional kingdoms of Rajputana in the form of semi-sovereign princely states. As a consequence, the British imperial state was more constrained than the Mughal one.

In India, successive waves of invaders, colonizers, and conquerors reinforced an already established process of social and state formation exemplified in caste and community compartmentalization, and regional kingdoms. Social and state formations were characterized by cultural syncretism, which included a stratified society in which the strata were said to be in harmony rather than in conflict. Laws and customs were thought to precede the state and to be protected by the 'good King'.

By this process, the imperial state, Mauryan, Mughal, British, absorbed indigenous ethnic groups, pre-eminently tribal peoples as well as external invading groups. The processes of social and state formation in India differ

---

[45]For a discussion of contrasting uses of these terms, see S.P. Gupta, 'Review' of V.S. Bhatnagar, *Life and Times of Sawai Jai Singh (1688–1743), The Indian Historical Review*, II (1), 1975.

in significant ways from the same processes in Europe. There, feudalism and the *Standes-Staat*[46] were subsumed or obliterated by sovereignty-seeking states, eventuating first in absolute and then in liberal states whose subjects or citizens related to them as equal individuals rather than via the medium of segmented communities and regional kingdoms. Social formation in India shaped a process of state formation characterized by a dialectical relation between the imperial state and the regional kingdom. When the imperial state prevailed, it invariably did so in a context where it preserved aspects of the regional kingdom, rather than obliterating it. Indian federalism is an expression of this process of state formation.

---

[46]A state based on status orders, such as the nobility, clerical orders, and the bourgeoisie.

2

State Formation in Asia

Prolegomenon to a Comparative Study*

SUSANNE HOEBER RUDOLPH

The dictionary says that a prolegomenon is 'a learned preface or preamble ... introductory or preliminary observations on the subject of a book'. And, indeed, the remarks I am about to make are preliminary to a volume on state formation that Lloyd I. Rudolph and I hope to produce one of these years. Such a prolegomenon is also a commitment to a path of action, a justification, a polemic in favour of what one proposes to do. Today, I want to speak for the domain of comparison.

The domain I speak of is not necessarily Immanuel Wallerstein's world system,[1] or William McNeill's world[2] as represented in this year's Association for Asian Studies (AAS) panels, or even Max Weber's world. I want to make a case for comparison that starts from below, when scholars study particular problems in particular areas and work their way up towards generalization, rather than a comparison that drops a deductive scheme from above down on the evidence. That kind of dropping not infrequently results in crushed data. I do not want to speak so much for what Paul Wheatley calls parallel comparison—for example, an AAS panel that offers women's literature in modern Japan, women's Bhakti poetry in Hindi, and women's short stories in Taiwan magazines—although this too calls our attention to contrasts and overlaps. The opposite of parallel is integral, referring to comparisons that

*Originally published as 'Presidential Address: State Formation in Asia—Prolegomenon to a Comparative Study', in *The Journal of Asian Studies*, XLVI (4), November 1987, pp. 731–45.

[1]Immanuel Wallerstein, *The Modern World System*, 2 vols, New York: Academic Press, 1974–80; see also Aristide R. Zolberg, 'Origins of the Modern World System: A Missing Link', *World Politics*, 33, 1981, pp. 253–81.

[2]William McNeill, *The Rise of the West*, Chicago: University of Chicago Press, 1963.

build, out of parallel instances, a general picture of women's literature as distinct from literature in general, which in turn informs investigation of particular Japanese or Indian forms. Such comparison lives in a realm between the generality of a *Naturwissenschaft* and the particularity of a *Geisteswissenschaft*.

The point of integral rather than parallel comparison is to formulate generalizations that allow me, while working on north Indian states, to understand their particularity by comparing them to the Chinese state under the Tang, Song, or Ming, each with its different strategies for sustaining empire. I want to specify the ways in which the Mughal/Rajput relationship, the relationship between an empire and component regional kingdoms, represents a unique and particular form of empire/regional kingdom integration, a form that both shares features with and expresses variants of the many forms of integration worked out by other Asian empires. Contrary to what some area scholars fear, comparison, when properly practised, is not a means for burying the particular configuration of a civilization under the gross categories of universal theories; it can be a way of featuring that particularity more powerfully against the backlighting of alternative expressions. It is only in the context of a general comparison among European states that one can recognize that Great Britain's absolutist phase differed critically from continental versions; that Great Britain's estates were never crushed as those on the continent were; that Britain had an early balance between parliament and Crown that mitigated its version of absolutism.[3] It is by comparing the Ottomans' timariot system with the Mughal mansabdari system that one recognizes that the seventeenth-century Mughal state penetrated its society far less than the Ottomans did in their prime.[4] This speech, then, is a prolegomenon to such a comparative project.

The project involves historically grounded analyses of what Charles Tilly has called big structures, large processes, and huge comparisons.[5] Such a project has provenance in nineteenth-century and some twentieth-century macro-history and macro-sociology, approaches that appear highly problematic to many of you—and for good reason. Most of the great practitioners of huge comparisons, among them Hegel, Marx, and Weber,

---

[3]See Perry Anderson, *Lineages of the Absolutist State*, London: New Left Books, 1974; Ernest Barker, *The Development of Public Services in Western Europe, 1630–1930*, Hamden, Conn.: Archon Books, 1966; Kenneth Dyson, *The State Tradition in Europe: A Study of an Idea and Institution*, New York: Oxford University Press, 1980; and Charles Tilly, *The Formation of National States in Western Europe*, Princeton: Princeton University Press, 1975.

[4]Douglas Streusand, 'Military Organization, Provincial Government, and Political Violence in the Ottoman and Mughal Empires', Unpublished paper, University of Chicago: Department of History, 1982.

[5]Charles Tilly, *Big Structures, Large Processes, and Huge Comparisons*, New York: Russell Sage Foundation, 1984.

have understood Asian social, economic, and political systems as flawed or degraded performances in a historical race in which all competitors run towards the same finish line—whether the finish line is nation-state, bourgeois capitalism, or universal rationalization. They attempted, by their grand comparisons, to grasp the cataclysmic social changes of their times. If we engage in macro-history, we do so with a similar motivation, to understand change in our time, but from a different perspective. Whereas for Hegel, Marx, and Weber there appeared to be but one race, and the West appeared to have strung the tape at the finish line for others to break, for us it has become apparent that there are multiple races and many finish lines, and the tapes are manufactured in Tokyo and Beijing as well.

For the nineteenth-century thinkers, the 'other' was culturally alien, but somehow would become like us as social change pulverized differences.[6] For us, the matter is far more complex. We find ourselves looking at an other that is increasingly becoming part of us. In business, culture, security, and ethnic amalgamation, the other and the self are becoming part of common systems. Turks are people who work in Stuttgart, Indians are people who staff American hospitals, Japanese are people who manage automobile factories in the United States, and Koreans are students who populate the graduate social science departments at the University of Chicago. When we look at Asia we no longer see, as nineteenth-century observers did, nations fated to be the historical losers. Post-Mao China is not the dowager empress's China invaded by the Allied Expeditionary Force; Rajiv Gandhi's India is not the India 'pacified' by the East India Company's army; the Japan that employs Americans in Columbus, Ohio, is not the Japan opened by Commodore Perry's threats. Even as it becomes apparent that the generalized other is less alien and more likely to become part of a system with the self, some 'others' grow more potent politically and economically. Future history is as much with them as it is with us. That changes scholars' questions, evaluations, and perspectives.[7] It becomes absurd to ask why Asian religions did not lead to the spirit of capitalism as we impose quotas on Japanese imports.

Comparativists are a guild. Guilds develop conventions. Comparativists have developed conventions about what is comparable. Units may be compared if they meet a certain minimum criteria of resemblance; otherwise the comparison appears quixotic. The criteria include similarity of time; similarity of cultural presumptions; similarity of what are perceived to be

---

[6]Ronald Inden, 'Orientalist Constructions of India', *Modern Asian Studies*, 20, 1986, pp. 401–46.

[7]Bernard S. Cohen, 'African Models and Indian Histories', in *Realm and Region in Traditional India*, by Richard G. Fox (ed.), pp. 90–113, Durham, N.C.: Duke University Monograph, 1977.

evolutionary stages; and similarity of structural forms. The units may be apples and oranges, but at least they should be fruit.

In the comparative study of the state in Asia, we are still very much at the beginning of formulating such conventions. Some years ago a group of historians at the University of Minnesota were driven by an Asian course requirement to sort Asian civilizations, including Asian polities, into one formidable format.[8] They found a certain temporal order in the rise of universal empires in the period 500 BC to AD 100 (the Achaemenid, the Mauryan, and the Qin), in the disintegration of empires into regional kingdoms in the period 700 to 1200, and in their reintegration. They invented a framework and situated states within it; they attempted to specify processes; they grounded their enterprise in particular histories, advancing the formulation of comparative conventions. The approach of the Minnesotans was driven, and ordered by time and processes of the sort to which historians are sensitive. The result was the handiwork of a group of area scholars with regional expertise working up from below to create a nonprocrustean schema.

Another kind of approach starts with a problem or a question. It is embodied, for example, in Rushton Coulborn's comparison of feudalisms,[9] that is, a search for the presence or absence of a significant syndrome of sociopolitical relationships. In retrospect, Coulborn's very interesting endeavour seems excessively driven by a European agenda, starting with a European historical phenomenon and asking if Asia has it too. Other examplars, although grounded in questions raised by European macro-sociology, are driven by a question or problem of trans-European significance. Such is Barrington Moore's search[10] for an explanation of democratic and authoritarian outcomes—ultimately found in the nature of alliances between agrarian and mercantile classes and the state. Such is Theda Skocpol's search[11] for an explanation of revolution, ultimately found more in the phenomenon of weak states than in that of strong classes. These efforts incorporate Asian states, China, Russia, Japan, into their comparisons.

Skocpol's and Moore's works are fruitful of hypotheses for the rest of us; they create conventions of comparison driven by a problem. But because their eyes are on the nineteenth and twentieth centuries, they do not help

---

[8]Edward L. Farmer, *Comparative History of Civilizations in Asia*, Reading, Mass.: Addison-Wesley, 1977.

[9]Rushton Coulborn (ed.), *Feudalism in History*, Princeton: Princeton University Press, 1956.

[10]Barrington, Moore Jr., *Social Origins of Dictatorship and Democracy: Lord and Peasant in the Making of the Modern World*, Boston: Beacon Press, 1967.

[11]Theda Skocpol, *States and Social Revolutions: A Comparative Analysis of France, Russia, and China*, Cambridge: Cambridge University Press, 1979.

us sort Asian states over time. It makes sense to compare Asian states across far longer periods than is conventional for European states. In Europe, what is called the modern period distinguishes itself from pre-Renaissance Europe at around 1500. What comes before and after seems incomparable. In Asia, on the other hand, eighth- and eighteenth-century states do not contrast sharply. Comparable units and processes encompass a longer time span.

There are other questions left unaddressed by problem-oriented comparisons, such as those of Moore or Skocpol. Shall we compare only subcontinental empires with each other,[12] and only in parallel times? The Mauryas, the Qin, and the Achaemenids? The Mughals, the Ottomans, and the Ming? Shall we compare the Mauryas and the Qin because they ruled empires, and Vijayanagar, the Tokugawa, and the Khmers of Angkor because they ruled regional kingdoms? Was the Tokugawa territory a regional kingdom? The answers are not obvious. The universes of regional kingdoms and subcontinental empires are not mutually exclusive. What sometimes appears as a regional kingdom is often an empire writ small, that is, a system composed of multiple subordinate political entities. Switzerland, in a manner of speaking, is an empire.

Students of the European state are well ahead of us in defining conventions for comparative state formation. Their task is simplified by the fact that they work within the boundaries of a single world civilization. An Asian comparison of the sort I envision must draw on several world civilizations, even when it compares only two polities, say the Ottoman and the Ming. European comparativists have further simplified their task by drawing the boundaries of comparison rather narrowly. Conventionally, one compares European absolutisms from the sixteenth to the eighteenth centuries. Bringing in Rome does not count, even if Rome shares cultural presuppositions with modern Europe, and even if its law proved helpful to continental centralization 1000 years later, as did the concept *quod Principe placuit legit habet vivant*.[13] Rome is, as it were, a different species, a vegetable, not a fruit. It is an empire, not a nation-state; it is out of sync temporally; it exists in a time when technology, especially war technology, was inferior to that of the age of absolutism.

Which definition provides the inclusionary and exclusionary rules for defining a state? The components of the standard definition of the state are relatively familiar: the state is a political entity that commands a monopoly

---

[12]S.N. Eisenstadt, *The Political Systems of Empires: The Rise and Fall of the Historical Bureaucratic Societies*, New York: Free Press, 1969.

[13]Edward N. Luttwak, *The Grand Strategy of the Roman Empire: From the First Century* AD *to the Third*, Baltimore: Johns Hopkins University Press, 1976.

over the legitimate use of force (*pace* Weber). A state is characterized by territoriality. It is characterized by centralization and by monopoly of sovereignty. The state is a political entity with staff. The state is differentiated from society—it is neither property nor family, but it partakes of trans-kin solidarities.[14]

This 'standard' conception of the state arose from a historical context in which significant changes in technology triggered other social changes. Military technology changed in ways that made obsolescent the small-scale military entrepreneur—the cavalry knight and his following—thus favouring that large-scale military entrepreneur, the state, and an organized military workforce that did not control the means of warfare.[15] This conception of the state appeared in contexts of expanded trade networks that altered the resource base of the state and gave it—where it could extract them—larger revenues that enhanced state control.[16]

What is the relationship between the standard definition of the state and the historical context to which it is related: did the definition have a virgin birth? Did it arise from the brow of Athena and then guide the scholar to the continental absolutist state? Or did the continental absolutist state arise, and then imprint its attributes on the emerging definition of the state, as Machiavelli and Filmer and Hobbes and Bodin began to describe and legitimize it? There is surely a circularity in the process. The European historical context dictated an emerging theoretical definition. The definition in turn narrowed the boundary of what a state is, of what may be considered comparable.

Why is it worthwhile to recite the European theoretical and conceptual dilemmas when my interest is, after all, in talking about Asian states? This is because the exercise is an essential preliminary to defining the universe in which we shall find comparables. It is preliminary to justifying the comparisons I would like to make.

[14]See Martin Carnoy, *The State and Political Theory*, Princeton: Princeton University Press, 1984; Ronald Cohen and Elman R. Service, *Origins of the State: The Anthropology of Political Evolution*, Philadelphia: Institute for the Study of Human Issues, 1978; J.P. Nettl, 'The State as a Conceptual Variable', *World Politics*, 20, 1968, pp. 559–92; Gianfranco Poggi, *The Development of the Modern State: A Sociological Introduction*, Stanford: Stanford University Press, 1978.

[15]See Eugene F. Rice, *The Foundations of Early Modern Europe, 1460–1559*, New York: Norton, 1970, p. 10; Samuel E. Finer, 'State and Nation-Building in Europe: The Role of the Military', in *The Formation of National States in Western Europe*, by Charles Tilly (ed.), pp. 84–163, Princeton: Princeton University Press, 1975.

[16]Rudolph Braun, 'Taxation, Sociopolitical Structure, and State-Building: Great Britain and Brandenburg Prussia', in *The Formation of National States in Western Europe*, by Charles Tilly (ed.), pp. 243–327, Princeton: Princeton University Press, 1975.

I want to create a boundary that will encompass not just apples and oranges, but cucumbers and artichokes as well, and to create a wider category that we might call organic edibles, of which fruit and vegetables are subtypes that may be compared. In short, I want to question the conventions of comparison that have governed definitions of the state and the process of state formation, and thereby suggest some new conventions. How do we do that?

My first step in this endeavour is to suggest that the heuristic type that has governed our consideration of states is so strongly skewed by the European absolutist experience that it has trouble handling even Western states—mostly arising out of the Anglo-American experience—which diverge on a number of the attributes encompassed in the idea of stateness.[17] The Anglo-American state is an aberration in European state theory.[18] It is too decentralized, and England's early traditions of political participation infiltrate and abort absolutism.[19] Its sovereignty is fragmented, and its jurisdictions multiple. King-in-Parliament is an untidy hybrid from the point of view of unified sovereignty. The federalisms of the United States, Canada, and other Commonwealth countries are even more untidy. The separation, division, and balance of power are designed to defeat the concentration of power that a monopolistic conception of sovereignty entails. If European state theory has trouble encompassing these instances and regards them as aberrations, what shall it do with the idea of universal empire in Asia? We shall probably have to begin with an assault on the definition of the state, refashioning it in light of the Asian experience, and providing markers, signs, and categories that can pick up and sort the phenomena Asian states exhibit. How do we do that?

My colleague Wendy O'Flaherty, initiating students into an Indian civilization course at the University of Chicago, tells them that in their texts they will not find narrative history of the sort they have learned from Herodotus. Nor should they attempt to extract from the *Puranas*, as some Indian historians have tried to do, the few kernels of positive truth that are wrapped up in mythic tales. You should listen, she tells them, to what the Indian texts *want* to tell you. Similarly, Clifford Geertz, initiating readers into his account of the theatre state in Bali, says, 'Most scholars of Indic Indonesia

---

[17]Shail Varma, 'The Absolutist State: An Inquiry into the Power Structure of England and France in the Context of a Critique of Perry Anderson's Lineages of the Absolutist State', M.A. paper, University of Chicago, 1981.

[18]See Dyson, *State Tradition in Europe*, and Nettl, 'The State as a Conceptual Variable'.

[19]Brian Downing, 'The International Order and Political Institutionalization in Early Modern Europe', Unpublished paper, University of Chicago: Department of Political Science, 1986.

have sought to write the sort of history for which they have not had, and in all likelihood never will have, the material, and have neglected to write precisely that sort for which they have, or at least might obtain, the material'.[20] O'Flaherty's exhortation is essentially a call for an ethnohistory, constructed out of the materials provided by the civilization.

I have a problem with that advice. It is not that I want to make Asian history appear just like all the other histories and fit it into European categories. The culture's medium is its message. The culture's categories are its culture. There is something macabre, for example, about dividing Indian history into ancient, medieval, and modern, when the consequence is to render a relatively centralized Mughal empire as 'medieval'. Fitting China into the cyclical conception of dynastic time developed by its own historians as part of its own ethnohistory seems much more plausible than fitting it into European teleological and unilinear models.[21] Fitting Ottoman history into the theory of decline that its own historians began to elaborate in the seventeenth and eighteenth centuries is more plausible than following the European evolutionary history model.[22]

At the same time, I find it hard to not look behind the texts that present themselves and ask who wrote them, and with what intent. I find it hard to sit still and just 'listen to what the texts want to tell me' without asking what that Brahmin, that Confucian scholar composing the story of the last realm, that Osmanli scholar speaking of the 'Ottoman way', does *not* want to tell me. One does not have to define social science as investigative journalism to suspect the dharmasastras of representing the worldview of dominant priestly intellectuals, and of legitimating an asymmetrical order that it was in their interest to preserve. The tradition of the sociology of knowledge mandates two ears, a first to hear what the authors of texts want to tell you, and a second to hear what they do not want to tell you.

The implication of this line of argument for the comparative study of states in Asia is that you cannot expect the Asian materials to spontaneously generate the categories of analysis. Let me illustrate the problem with Chinese materials. I do so not because I think the Confucian scholars obfuscate more than the Brahmins. Both have been extraordinarily successful in excluding inconvenient facts and dissenting values from their texts. But scholarship on India by Indians and by European scholars of India has

[20]Clifford Geertz, *Negara: The Theatre State in Nineteenth-Century Bali*, Princeton: Princeton University Press, 1980, p. 5.

[21]John K. Fairbank, *The United States and China*, Cambridge, Mass.: Harvard University Press, 1983, pp. 100–6.

[22]Norman Itzkowitz, *Ottoman Empire and Islamic Tradition*, Chicago: University of Chicago Press, 1972, p. 87ff.

probably gone farther in the last three decades to break the monopoly of the Brahminic worldview of Indian history than has the scholarship on China by Chinese and European scholars of China in breaking the Confucian monopoly over Chinese history. When I read Chinese history written by my American colleagues, I feel that, apart from some notable exceptions,[23] I read it through a screen that has been dropped over the subject by many generations of scholar-officials, who had an opportunity to structure their history and continue to shape the efforts of their twentieth-century successors.[24]

Was China so continuous? Is it true that culture was a far more potent instrument of control than military force? Is it true that a peaceable class of scholar-officials succeeded so well in establishing hegemony via a conciliatory ideology of loyalty to the emperor and that of universal filialism that it created the frictionless society celebrated in many scholarly accounts? Did the barbarians all internalize, via sinicization, control mechanisms that made external control less important? In studying the state, European scholars would start with the creation and financing of the military, and the extraction of taxes to support it. Shall we place those instrumentalities at the bottom of the inquiry schedule because they seem to matter less in the Chinese scheme of things? The difficulty is that in a social order where the scholar-official rated high on the scale of social and political significance, and the military and commercial orders low, the scholar-official controlled the means of historical production. He was in a position to delete through dynastic history those who could not be deleted in social reality. The virtue of importing external categories into the indigenous account is precisely that they raise questions that the indigenous accounts would like to let sleep.

One reason why the conventions of comparison developed in a European context serve us ill is because the European polities around which they developed became nation-states, whereas the Asian polities did not. The European polities approximate what in Asia we would call regional kingdoms. Asian polities reached for a greater comprehensiveness; except in Southeast Asia, they were continental polities, trans-ethnic empires. This distinction is so overwhelming and so obvious that it has to be the starting point of all comparative exercises. It suggests, to begin with, why the idea of a unified sovereignty, the idea of political monopoly so crucial to European definitions of the state, cannot be our starting point. A nation-state is a restricted territory in which there is a presumption, or at least an aspiration, of congruence

[23]For instance, Philip A. Kuhn, *Rebellion and Its Enemies in Late Imperial China: Militarization and Social Structure, 1796–1864*, Cambridge, Mass.: Harvard University Press, 1980.

[24]See Derk Bodde, *Essays on Chinese Civilization*, Princeton: Princeton University Press, 1981; Fairbank, *The United States and China*.

between the state and a nation or people. By contrast, an empire is an extended territory comprising a group of states or peoples under the control, or at least the suzerainty, of a dominant power. Historically, empires have been a more usual form of polity than nation-states. In Asia, tsarist Russia and later the Soviet Union, China, India, and perhaps Iran are polities that continue to embody imperial identities. Europe's nation-states were, in a sense, a sport. Had the Holy Roman Empire become the dominant polity in the twelfth century, Europe would have approximated the world 'norm' more closely.[25]

The idea of Oriental despotism, which was the most important concept Europeans employed to understand Asian polities, had the virtue of recognizing that what was happening on the other side of the line drawn by the Saracens was indeed different from what was happening in Europe. At the risk of repeating the familiar, I remind you of the main ingredients of this idea. The gross heuristic form of Oriental despotism encompasses five related elements: first, the all-empowered state, unconstrained by either ideal or institutional forces, and capable of pressing its instrumentalities into the furthest corner of the domain; second, the passive, localized, parochial society unempowered by property or ideas of entitlements, disarmed by its insulation from wider arenas and bereft of organizational forms that would or could resist the all-empowered state; third, an absence of relatively independent intermediary groups, such as classes, status orders, independent nobles, chiefs, guilds, or monastic and ecclesiastical establishments, which could act as meaningful centres of alternative power and authority; fourth, the whole overlaid with the whimsical arbitrariness that was the defining feature of what Weber called Sultanism; and fifth, the servile subject, dependent, infantilized, obedient, without public voice or identity.[26]

This model of an Asian state owes its original and its ever-renewed life as much to political didacts who wanted to teach Europe as to observers who wanted to understand Asia: Machiavelli praised the controllability of the Ottoman slave army to the Italian princes who needed a substitute for recalcitrant and independent feudal levies; Adam Smith wanted to frighten English monarchs out of mercantilism by means of the Ottoman ghost; Montesquieu used a horrendous image of supine Asian subjects to shame French absolutism into self-recognition; and Wittfogel[27] linked Asian

---

[25]Lloyd I. Rudolph, and Susanne Hoeber Rudolph, 'The Subcontinental Empire and the Regional Kingdom in Indian State Formation', in *Region and Nation in India*, by Paul Wallace (ed.), pp. 40–59. New Delhi: Oxford University Press and IBH, 1985.

[26]See Anderson, *Lineages of the Absolutist State*, p. 462; and Anne M. Bailey and Joseph R. Llobera, *The Asiatic Mode of Production*, London: Routledge and Kegan Paul, 1981.

[27]Karl A. Wittfogel, *Oriental Despotism: A Comparative Study of Total Power*, New York: Vintage Books, 1981.

autocracy to communist totalitarianism. The polemic purpose in each case overrode the complex realities.

The Oriental despotism model does not capture well even the states to which it allegedly refers, such as the Ottoman opponents at the gates of Vienna, and Bernier's Mughals. To be sure, the Ottoman state at its peak came close to eliminating intermediary classes, at least in Anatolia; the awesome central record-keeping of the *deftari* state did devise means for pressing its extractive mechanisms into the furthest corner of the realm, creating a direct tie between Porte and Reaya; its omnipresent officials, *sanjakbegs* and *beglerbegs*, could forcefully recruit the sons of the conquered to become imperial bureaucrats (*ghulam*) absolutely dependent on the state; and intermediary powers were few, except on the periphery.[28] However, the Ottoman state seems to have been at this uncharacteristic peak for no more than fifty to 100 years. Most of the history of the empire is the history of the reassertion of intermediary notabilities at the core, and hereditary outer lords on the fringes.[29] Even at the peak of the system, the *Kanunname* promulgated by successive rulers was a body of administrative law that subjected agents of the Porte to procedural regularity.[30] Allegedly, it worked well enough so that peasants often welcomed conquest by the Porte for the relative protection it afforded against avaricious landlords. Still, even if the Oriental despotism model does not fit the ideal-type case, it perhaps provides a helpful foil against which to erect more plausible alternatives.

Or perhaps it does not. The model has set back the project of state comparison. The very title, Oriental despotism, implies an undifferentiated condition from Constantinople to Edo. The polemical intentions of the users have resulted in rigid and homogeneous categories, and in a lack of subtlety. Wittfogel's theory imposed a common theoretical template fashioned out of the hard steel of ideological remorselessness on systems widely disparate in space and time. It pressed out standardized, uniform Leviathans. It provided a good example of what not to do.[31] All the world, from Incas to Babylonians, from Byzantines to the Zhou, became a Sovietized Manchu government.

[28]See Halil Inalcik, 'Ottoman Methods of Conquest', *Studia Islamica*, 2, 1954, pp. 103–29, 'Land Problems in Turkish History', *The Muslim World*, 45, 1955, pp. 221–9, *The Ottoman Empire: The Classical Age, 1300–1600*, trans. N. Itzkowitz and C. Imber, New York: Praeger, 1973, and 'Centralization and Decentralization in Ottoman Administration', in *Studies in Eighteenth-Century Islamic History*, by Thomas Naff and Roger Owen (eds), pp. 28–51, Carbondale: Southern Illinois University Press, 1977.

[29]Itzkowitz, *Ottoman Empire and Islamic Tradition*.

[30]Halil Inalcik, 'Suleiman the Lawgiver and Ottoman Law', *Archivum Ottomanicum*, 1, 1969, pp. 105–37.

[31]Irfan Habib, *The Agrarian System of Mughal India, 1556–1707*, New York: Asia Publishing House, 1963.

What we need to do is begin with more manageable comparisons, with a considerable degree of historical concreteness sensitive to variation in comparable functions or processes, sensitive to how wholes differ. At this stage we need fragile theoretical templates, made of soft clay rather than hard steel, which can adapt to the variety of evidence and break when they do not fit.

Oriental despotism assumes a degree of control by the state over society that is implausible, given the technologies of the time and the extent of the polities. It imagines degrees of control by reasoning backward from twentieth-century totalitarianism. Take the *Arthasastra*, the thoroughly real-political text that is often associated with the rule of the third-century BC Mauryas in India. Its first translator, Shamasastry (1960), was delighted to rescue India from the deplorable reputation it had acquired for otherworldliness. Hence, he created a language of translation that revealed the wily, cunning realism of the ancients—whose kings sent out spies among the multitude to ferret out treason, foment division among enemies, lie, cheat, and (not often) kill in pursuit of the state's interest. Our late and honoured colleague A.L. Basham (1969) describes the state of the *Arthasastra* as indubitably an example of ancient totalitarianism. Now, to be sure, the *Arthasastra* does show a certain enthusiasm for dirty tricks.[32] But look how much damage is done by a translation using the simple word 'spy'. Why spy? Why not agent? Writer? Were the 'spies' of the *Arthasastra* not like the omnipresent *vakils* of sixteenth-century India, sent by every court to every other court to represent its interests and send back faithful reports on daily events at the rival court? 'Spy' conveys the intended interpretation, that we are dealing with the KGBs and CIAs of bureaucratized absolutisms. And when this totalitarian text envisions the conquest of a neighbouring king, why does it recommend that his life be preserved, that he—or his son—be placed on the throne and local people's lives and customs protected? It is because these ancient states were not given, on principle, to *Gleichschaltung*, nor had they the capacity for it. One reason that the agent becomes a spy in translation and the considerable segmentation of the ancient state is suppressed in readings of the *Arthasastra* is that the metaphor of Oriental despotism has shaped the lenses, and thus the perception, through which the text is read.

However, Oriental despotism is not the only theory that leads us astray. I remarked before that the distinction between the European nation-state and the Asian empire should remind us that the idea of a monopoly of force, central to European definitions of the state, is problematic in Asia.

---

[32]R.P. Kangle, *The Kautiliya Arthasastra*, 3 vols, Bombay: T.V. Chidambaram for the University of Bombay Studies, 1960–5.

Samuel Finer has noted that attempts to apply this very exigent standard even to Europe, for which it was intended, is difficult.[33] If the definition does not fit the relatively unified nation-states of modern Europe, it is sure to be problematic with respect to Asian empires.[34] Some years ago, Lloyd I. Rudolph and I wrote a paper in which we conceived of the Indian polity along the lines offered by the *Dharmasastra* and *Arthasastra* texts.[35] These texts envision the king presiding over and sustaining the elements of a self-regulating society—castes, guilds, religious communities, regions, and sub-kingdoms.[36] This is a promising path to a counter-model, and on this path we have some respectable company.

Burton Stein, in his construction of the ninth-century Chola state, is fairly sure there were no monopolists of force around.[37] The conventional wisdom previously shaped by Nilakanta Shastri[38] saw the Cholas as a Byzantine monarchy (somewhat modified by a Lockean state and participatory democracy, an unlikely collection of metaphors not uncharacteristic of early conceptualizations of the state in Asia). Stein pretty well turned around the Shastri metaphor. Now the state is seen as custodial; elements of Aidan Southall's segmentary state are even imported from Africa.[39] The Chola state makes no attempt to seize or even to regulate the coercive functions of the non-political institutions of society, the territorial Brahmadeyas and the guilds. Stein depicts a federal world of self-regulating groups, barely linked to the centre by any mechanism of taxes, armies, or charities. Insofar as the centre had any links to the self-regulating society, it was to extract tribute and perhaps to exercise a weakly specified ritual suzerainty. Stein probably goes too far.[40] One cannot imagine what the Cholas did to overawe the self-

[33]Finer, 'State and Nation-Building in Europe'.

[34]See also Paul Brass, *Language, Religion, and Politics in North India*, London: Cambridge University Press, 1974.

[35]Rudolph and Rudolph, 'The Subcontinental Empire and the Regional Kingdom in Indian State Formation'.

[36]Georg Buhler, *The Laws of Manu*, Delhi: Motilal Banarsidass, 1975.

[37]Burton Stein, 'Review of Sangam Polity', *Indian Economic and Social History Review*, 5, 1968, pp. 109–15, 'The State and the Agrarian Order in Medieval South India: A Historiographical Critique', in *Essays on South India*, by Burton Stein (ed.), pp. 64–91, Honolulu: University of Hawaii Press, 1975, 'The Segmentary State in South Indian History', in *Realm and Region in Traditional India*, by Richard G. Fox (ed.), pp. 3–51, Durham, N.C.: Duke University Monograph, 1977.

[38]K.A. Nilakanta Shastri, *The Colas*, revised edition, Madras: University of Madras, 1955.

[39]Aidan W. Southall, *Alur Society: A Study in Processes and Types of Domination*, Cambridge: W. Helfer, 1956.

[40]Ravi Arvind Palat, 'Structures of Class Control in Late Medieval South Asia: Construction of an Interstate System (Circa 1300–1600)', Paper presented at the meeting of the Association for Asian Studies, Boston, 10–12 April 1987.

regulating society sufficiently enough to persuade it to pay tribute—there must have been some military and/or bureaucratic exercises out in the provinces to display a Chola presence. Stein, in some of his incarnations (not in 1978), is enough of a dedicated empirical social scientist to find it hard to credit the significance of the symbolic realm, to conceive of the Chola king as chakravartin, or universal emperor, conquering in four directions to manifest and enhance his stateliness. Stein wants to see the king's *defters*, his account books.

Stanley Tambiah's galactic polity,[41] like Stein's version of the segmentary state, is grounded in a deep scepticism about the totalist construction of the Asian state. Tambiah's galaxy consists of a powerful sun-like object at the centre, the leading king, the Rajadhiraj, the Shahenshah. Its gravitational pull keeps in orbit, at some distance from itself, an unspecified number of lesser rulers, each a simulation of the leading king, their courts a simulation of the central court. The whole is unified by a field of force characterized by both repulsion and attraction. In this system, the light of the centre loses strength as it approaches the periphery. The galactic polity is compatible with Stein's conception: it posits that there is a system, to wit, ritual sovereignty, even when one cannot locate the specific 'mechanism'—taxes, armies—as Stein cannot for the Chola state. The Mauryan state, as outlined and defined by Asoka, may or may not have had the means to extract taxes and tribute in a regularized fashion from the Oxus to the Narbudda; it may or may not have been able to control military commanders in Orissa and in Malwa; probably it could do both, sporadically. But it extracted from such instrumental activities a capacity to express itself symbolically, to assert, through rock inscriptions and pillars, that a chakravartin, a beloved of the gods, had created a conceptual realm, as the Guptas, Harshavardhana, the Mughals, and the British were to do again and again over another two millennia.

Somers, in a recent assessment of the early Tang dynasty (617–700), speaks of relationships between the emperor and his subjects that suggest that galactic or segmentary models may be relevant not only to South and Southeast Asia, but also to the apparently more unitary structures of China. Contrary to Wittfogel's and Balázs's conceptions, Somers argues that:

the emperor claimed formal status at the head of a hierarchical order in which all subjects were encompassed. This did not require any direct contact between the sovereign agents and the ordinary subjects of the empire, but only that the existing social and political hierarchies be subsumed within a single, all-

---

[41]S.J. Tambiah, *World Conqueror and World Renouncer: A Study of Buddhism and Polity in Thailand Against a Historical Background*, Cambridge: Cambridge University Press, 1976.

encompassing structure of order, whose summit might have either a great deal of power, or very little.[42]

Both Stein and Tambiah develop two ideas: units in such a system are replications of each other, and sovereignty, such as it is, is ritual sovereignty. The notion of replication is a cultural one related to ideas of diffusion, a process independent of the degree of penetration achieved by an overlord's account books, his bureaucratic formations, and his army garrisons. When I look at a painting produced at the Mughal court in 1700 and at another painted at the Rajput court of an Alwar raja 100 miles away and 100 years later, I find that the raja's horse faces in the same direction, the raja rides with a similar contingent, and he is whisked or flapped at by similar ritual implements.[43] When I look at the way a Jodhpur raja has organized his revenue-collection apparatus and the way he has reconstructed in a hierarchical fashion the previously more egalitarian relations to his lineage brothers, I find he is replicating the Mughal at Delhi, 400 miles away.[44] And these replications are 'caused' as much by processes of cultural, social, or political emulation as by the application of force or bureaucracy.

Replication is a manner of constructing a system, of creating a common domain independent of the centre's degree of formal control. It is a notion that is helpful in understanding other Asian states. Even when central power in China is weak, the scholar-official in his rural locale sustains a replica of the administrative conceptions of the Beijing centre. These replicas represent a potential that can evolve in one of two directions—a potential ruler can move in by force, marriage, or guile and utilize the forms of the replication to establish a state, or the replication can become an autonomous unit. Neither outcome is preordained; each depends on other historical conjunctures. In Tokugawa Japan, replications may even have worked in reverse, whereby the bureaucratic mechanisms and ideas developed by the daimyo bureaucracy in vassal lands moved to the centre.[45] What replication does not do is give us support for the idea of a state definition that features the idea of a monopoly of force, or indeed any sort of monopoly.

[42]Robert Somers, 'Time, Space, and Structure in the Consolidation of the T'ang Dynasty (AD 617–700)', *Journal of Asian Studies*, 45, 1986, pp. 971–94, esp. p. 973.

[43]Daniel J. Ehnbom, *Indian Miniatures: The Ehrenftld Collection*, New York: Hudson Hills Press, 1985, see Plates 29 and 79.

[44]Norman P. Ziegler, 'Some Notes on Rajput Loyalties During the Mughal Period', in *Kingship and Authority in South Asia*, by J.F. Richards (ed.), pp. 215–51, Wisconsin: South Asian Studies, University of Wisconsin, 1978.

[45]John Dower (ed.), *Origins of the Modern Japanese State: Selected Writings of E. H. Norman*, New York: Pantheon Books, 1975.

The other idea implicit in a segmentary state or galactic polity is that of ritual sovereignty. By 'ritual sovereignty', we designate cultural activities, symbols, and processes which, in the absence of instrumental mechanisms, nevertheless create a domain, a realm. Ritual sovereignty has ceremonial, aesthetic, and architectonic aspects, as well as historically grounded, genealogically perpetuated elements. Cultural processes, emphasizing adherence to a common form of life, affect ritual sovereignty. Clifford Geertz, in *Negara* (1980), focuses on the ceremonial and theatrical ways in which the monarch is established, on the pomp and display and infinite care with which a god and a king are created. Similarly, John Richards stresses Mughal courtliness, and the layout and symbolic significance of tent capitals. He also stresses the way the gift of a *siropao* (ceremonial robe) and the exchanges of gifts with generals at the very ends of the empire 'thicken' personal ties.[46] Ron Inden focuses on the king as *digvijayan* (conqueror), riding in the four directions to establish his dominion or loosing a horse to define his universal kingdom. These are the ceremonial, aesthetic, and architectonic aspects of ritual sovereignty. They are processes and signs by which a universal monarch is gradually elevated into a species distinct from the more accessible chiefs and kings of tribal confederacies and lineage states.[47]

The genealogical provenance of monarchies is a way of grounding sovereignty in selectively preserved history and, ultimately, in a cosmology. Genealogies have an ethnobiological aspect that certifies the transmission of a true charismatic substance across generations. They also have a historical aspect. They are the precipitates of contextual activity, of historical possibilities previously realized and then lost, of memories of capacities to dominate that could again be deployed. The Zhou emperors retained the mandate of heaven long after they had lost all semblance of empirical power.[48] When Iranian monarchies from the Sassanids through the late Shah repaired to Persepolis to attach their dynasties to Cyrus, Darius, and the Achaemenids, they were rehearsing earlier historical possibilities. They were also replicating the Mughal effort to stretch their genealogical connection from Timur to Chenghis Khan, to the princess who conceived a

[46]See John F. Richards, 'The Formulation of Imperial Authority Under Akbar and Jahangir', in *Kingship and Authority in South Asia*, by John F. Richards (ed.), Madison: University of Wisconsin Press, 1978, pp. 252–85; and Mirza Nathan, *Buharistan-I-Ghaybi*, trans. M.I. Borah, Gauhati: Assam Department of Historical and Antiquarian Studies, 1936.

[47]See Richards, 'The Formulation of Imperial Authority'; and Romila Thapar, *Lineage to State*, Bombay: Oxford University Press, 1984.

[48]Denis C. Twitchett and Michael Loewe (eds), *The Cambridge History of China. Vol. 1, The Ch'in and Han Empires, 221 BC–AD 220*, Cambridge: Cambridge University Press, 1986, p. 728.

child after being entered by a beam of light.[49] Both genealogical accounts certify the transmission of a true substance, and resurrect a historical past that can serve as a legitimizing model for the present.

A third element in ritual sovereignty has to do with larger social processes that demonstrate that the king and his people are part of a common social architectonic, and assure that barbarian conquerors are made of the material appropriate to kings. Sanskritization and sinicization are two forms of such a social process.[50] The absorption of the *ghazi* into the urban civilization of High Islam is a third. All three derive their importance initially from the relationship between the steppe and the sown or the forest and the sown, whereby the nomad invader or the forest hunter is naturalized into the fabric of sedentary society and its institutions.[51] The expansion of a Chinese core on the Yellow River into barbarian territory is accompanied by the diffusion of a central pattern that combines cultural style—the literary skills of the scholar-official, the gentlemanly culture of deference and appropriate relationships—with instrumental structures that place central bureaucratic and military agencies on the periphery.[52] The barbarian invaders, whether thirteenth-century nomadic Mongols known as Yuan or seventeenth-century Manchu hunters and fishers, acquire legitimacy as they adopt Chinese values, forms, and practices.

The process of Sanskritization has a pattern both similar and different. Indian society elaborated in the dharmasastras a distinctive way of absorbing the *mlechas*, what the Chinese would call the barbarians, both the external barbarians from central Asia and the internal barbarians, the forest dwellers and tribals.[53] India absorbed invading peoples at different levels of the four-fold *varna* (social order) structure, the triumphant conquerors as *kshatriyas*, or warrior rulers, their vans and camp followers as a variety of agricultural and artisan castes. Both systems had a sorting process that ranked conquering leaders high in the social order, provided they absorbed the dominant values of the pre-existing order and respected Brahmins or scholar-officials. Sanskritization differs from sinicization in that it is a more pluralistic, less

---

[49]Paul Hanson, 'Sovereignty and Service Relationships in the Timurid Corporate Dynasty Under Babur: The Continuing Legacy of the Chinghis Khanid Political System', Ph.D. dissertation, University of Chicago, 1984.

[50]M.N. Srinivas, *Caste in Modern India and Other Essays*, Bombay: Asia Publishing House, 1962.

[51]Cohen and Service, *Origins of the State*.

[52]Herrlee G. Creel, *The Origins of Statecraft in China: The Western Chou Empire*, Chicago: University of Chicago Press, 1970.

[53]Romila Thapar, *Ancient Indian Social History: Some Interpretations*, New Delhi: Orient Longman, 1978.

unitary process. New groups are encapsulated at different levels of society; their deviant practices are designated as appropriate for them.

The ritual domain, then, consists of a number of realms—the ceremonial, aesthetic, and theatrical; the genealogical and historical; and the cultural processes of assimilation that create a common form of life. These realms constitute the other half of the process of state formation, which is revealed when we emphasize mechanisms, instrumentalities, and their control by social coalitions.

The idea of ritual sovereignty attaches to a cosmological conception of kingship: the Chinese mandate of heaven, the Mongol lord of the wide blue sky,[54] the beloved of the gods, the shadow of God, the chakravartin.[55] The king, as upholder of the social order, fits into a cosmos. There are temporal aspects of the cosmos, eras, mythical time frames, the infinitely extensive *kalpa*s or eons of the Indic polities of South and Southeast Asia; or the more limited, quasi-historic time extending forward from Moses through Muhammad and Timur for the Mughals. There are spatial aspects of the cosmos constructed through *mandala*s in court and temple that connect the order of the person, the society, the king, and the world to the gods, as in Hinduism, or to a transcendent state of being, as in Buddhism—cosmologies that construe a ruler as mediating between forces 'here' and 'there'.

Convincing a class of students of comparative politics, who have been shaped in a world of neo-Marxian or positivist political economy, of the significance of a cosmological view, I can tell you, is a real feat. Cosmologies were what they had in ancient Asia. Cosmologies were helpful in understanding the proto-states of Southeast Asia before we acquired the superior analytic tool of political economy, before the world became demystified and rationalized. Cosmologies live in the mysterious East. Surely the states of nature invoked by Hobbes, Locke, and Rousseau, realms of being prior to society, are not cosmologies. The constructions that lie behind an Anglo-American view of society and polity, and behind both neoclassical and Marxist economics, are not cosmologies. They cannot be, because persons living in the post-rationalist societies of nineteenth and twentieth-century Europe had given up cosmologies.

For Clifford Geertz, the state is constructed by constructing a king, and a king is constructed by constructing a god.[56] The king is an incarnation of the holy; the ceremony creates him; the state draws its force from the symbolic

[54]Hanson, 'Sovereignty and Service Relationships'.
[55]Tambiah, *World Conqueror and World Renouncer*.
[56]Geertz, *Negara*, p. 124.

capacity to enchant. But that does not mean that the dignified and ceremonial serve the efficient. The king is not constructed in this way to awe and terrorize the gullible, as Hobbes would have it, or to mystify them, as Marx would have it, or even to legitimate the realm, as Weber would have it. He is at the still centre of the world. The ceremonial realms are autonomous, 'neither illusions nor lies, neither sleight of hand nor make-believe. They were what there was.'[57]

That kind of instruction is very hard for my political-economy-oriented students—and most of us—to understand. We have all, or almost all, lost the inner states that would make such outer states 'real'. Robert Bellah argues in *Habits of the Heart* (1985) that Americans do not have a language to convey the collective or the communitarian, only the individualist. Most post-eighteenth century social science has lost the language to convey, let alone take seriously, the ceremonial and symbolic as anything but instruments of the efficient. And you do not have to be a positivist to have that deficiency. Living as we do in democratic and Protestant American society, in a poverty of stateliness and regal ceremony, we underestimate the power and reality of these forces. It is a lacuna in our historical and theoretical imagination.

When empiricists or structuralists or political economists look at what they consider the mere flimflam of the symbolic realm, they want to know where the real stuff is: the village, the irrigation network, the coalition between king and noble, the extractive mechanism. They ask, 'How many divisions does the pope have?' I also want answers to those questions. But as we address the state in Asia, we must treat the symbolic as a phenomenon. We must try to create theoretical frameworks that combine a demystified, rationalist worldview with an understanding of the phenomenology of the symbolic in societies where the gods have not yet died. And we must combine it with the understanding that we, too, construct and act within cosmologies, and that we only deny the myths we live by because we cannot see or articulate them.

SELECT REFERENCES

Balázs, Étienne, *Chinese Civilization and Bureaucracy* by Arthur Wright (ed.), New Haven: Yale University Press, 1964.
Basham, A.L., *The Wonder That Was India*, New York: Grove Press, 1969.
Bellah, Robert, *et al.*, *Habits of the Heart: Individualism and Commitment in American Life*, Berkeley and Los Angeles: University of California Press, 1985.
Bendix, Reinhard, *Kings or People: Power and the Mandate to Rule*, Berkeley and Los Angeles: University of California Press, 1978.

[57]Ibid., p. 136.

Butterfield, H., *The Statecraft of Machiavelli*, London: G. Bell and Sons, 1940.

Fox, Richard G., 'Avatars of Indian Research', *Comparative Studies in Society and History*, 12, 1970, pp. 59–72.

Habib, Irfan, 'An Examination of Wittfogel's Theory of Oriental Despotism', *Enquiry*, 6, 1961, pp. 54–73.

Halbfass, Wilhelm, 'India and the Comparative Method', *Philosophy East and West*, 35, 1985, pp. 3–15.

Hall, John Whitney, *Japan: From Prehistory to Modern Times*, New York: Dell Publishing Co., 1968.

Heitzman, James, 'Segments, Centralization, and Modes of Production in the Cola State', Paper presented to the South Asia Conference, Wisconsin, 1984.

Ho, Ping-Ti, 'The Significance of the Ch'ing Period in Chinese History', in *Modern China*, by Joseph R. Levenson (ed.), pp. 17–25, London: Macmillan and Co., 1971.

——, The Paleoenvironment of North China—A Review Article', *Journal of Asian Studies*, 44, 1984, pp. 723–33.

Keightley, David N. (ed.), *The Origins of Chinese Civilization*, Berkeley and Los Angeles: University of California Press, 1983.

Lovejoy, Arthur O., *The Great Chain of Being: A Study of the History of an Idea*, Cambridge, Mass.: Harvard University Press, 1976.

Marshall, T.H., *Class, Citizenship, and Social Development*, Chicago: University of Chicago Press. 1977.

Min, Byung-Il, 'Formation of the First Empire in China', M.A. paper, University of Chicago, 1986.

Schram, Stuart R. (ed.), *The Scope of State Power in China*, New York: St. Martin's Press, 1985.

Shamasastry, R. (trans.), *Kautilya's Arthasastra*, 6th edition, Mysore: Mysore Printing and Publishing House, 1960.

Stein, Burton, 'All the King's Mana: Perspectives on Kingship in Medieval South India', in *Kingship and Authority in South Asia*, by John F. Richards (ed.), pp. 115–67, Madison: University of Wisconsin Press, 1978.

——, *Peasant State and Society in Medieval South India*, New Delhi: Oxford University Press, 1980.

Twitchett, Denis C., 'Provincial Autonomy and Central Finance in Late T'ang', *Asia Major*, n.s., 11, 1965, pp. 211–32.

Wakeman, Frederic, Jr., *The Fall of Imperial China*, New York: Free Press, 1975.

Wan, Gungwu, *The Structure of Power in North China During the Five Dynasties*, Kuala Lumpur, Malaysia: University of Malaysia Press, 1963.

Wang, Yu-Ch'uan, 'An Outline of the Central Government of the Former Han Dynasty', *Harvard Journal of Asiatic Studies*, 12, 1949, pp. 134–87.

3

State Formation in India
Building and Wasting Assets*

LLOYD I. RUDOLPH AND SUSANNE HOEBER RUDOLPH

I f India's relatively stable democracy and slow but steady economic development in the 1950s and 1960s seemed exceptional, they were in part due to the legacies of stateness and state formation that distinguish India from most Third World countries. Their proximate determinant was the viceregal state of the British raj.[1] Their more distant determinants included the Mughal empire, from whose ideas and practice the British benefited, and which they also assimilated, and the imperial states and regional kingdoms of ancient and medieval India. The troubled history of Third World countries since independence following World War II has revealed that state-building must precede and parallel nation-building and economic development. Contrary to prevailing assumptions of scholarship and policy in the generations since decolonization, states create nations and economies more than nations and economies create states.

Political economy encompasses two powerful paradigms, liberal and Marxist. Until recently, both depicted the state as reflexive of social forces. Liberal pluralists construed the state and its actions in terms of successive

*Originally published as 'State Formation in India: Building and Wasting Assets', in Lloyd I. Rudolph and Susanne Hoeber Rudolph, *In Pursuit of Lakshmi: The Political Economy of the Indian State*, Chicago: University of Chicago Press, 1987, pp. 60–102, and 425–36.

[1] For recent, comparative discussions of state formation in Western Europe, see Charles Tilly, *The Formation of National States in Western Europe*, Princeton: Princeton University Press, 1975. For a theory of viceregal versus parliamentary traditions, see Keith Callard, *Pakistan: A Political Study*, London: Allen and Unwin, 1958. For an account of European views of Asian state formation, see Perry Anderson, *Lineages of the Absolutist State*, London: NLB, 1977, especially the appendix.

equilibriums that followed from the play of organized interests. At best, liberal states could umpire contests among competing interests and execute outcomes, but could not independently determine policy or set goals. Marxists construed the state and its actions in terms of a struggle among classes formed and motivated by the mode and relations of production. The state was the agent of a ruling class, or of a hegemonic class coalition. Both paradigms depicted a reflexive state, whose nature and actions mirrored equilibriums of either organized interests or classes.

Both now hold that under certain historical conditions or, in particular, policy arenas, the state in both developed and developing societies can be autonomous as well as reflexive. For liberals, the revisionist position arose from experiences with the post-World War II welfare states that, until the mid-1970s, had successfully managed economies and provided rights and entitlements for citizens. For Marxists, revision arose from Marx's observation, in *The Eighteenth Brumaire of Louis Bonaparte*, that under the second Bonaparte the state made itself completely independent, with the result that the executive power subordinated society to itself. This observation seemed more germane under a wide variety of historical circumstances than his reflexive view of the state as an 'executive committee of the ruling class'.

For us, the heuristic for the state-society relationship can be located on a continuum ranging from complete state domination of society to complete societal domination of the state. We identify four potential positions on the continuum: *totalitarian*, in which the state completely dominates society, creating and controlling social formations, maintaining a closed milieu, and using force and terror without restraint; *autonomous*, in which the state can be self-determining because it is relatively insulated from societal forces, the only limits on its freedom to act being legitimacy and consent; *constrained*, in which the state's freedom to act is limited not only by legitimacy and consent, but also by the representation of organized social forces; and *reflexive* or *heteronomous*, in which the state lacks self-determination because it is dominated by society, whose organized interests or classes appropriate state authority and resources. A state's location on the continuum depends on historical circumstances, including ideology, leadership, conjunctural effects, and the balance of public and private power.

State formation and maintenance is a continuous process located in history; the nature of the state cannot be known a priori from theory. Since state-society relationships vary with historical circumstances, the continuous process of state formation and maintenance produces polymorphous entities; that is, states occur in a variety of forms, characters, and styles. Peter Nettl captured this polymorphous nature of the state when he introduced the term 'stateness', and argued that high and low stateness varied with historical experience, institutional legacies, and political culture.[2]

The Indian state is the residual legatee of a long tradition of high stateness that reaches back to India's ancient subcontinental empires and medieval regional kingdoms.[3] It has been more directly shaped by the relatively recent Mughal and British empires of the sixteenth through the twentieth centuries, which, like European absolute states of the seventeenth and eighteenth centuries, established internal sovereignty. The Mughal and British states made terms of high stateness, such as *sarkar* (government) and raj (rule), an integral part of popular consciousness that, like the monsoon, were perceived as an aspect of nature. After independence, the Indian state has been located in the middle positions of the continuum, autonomous or constrained, rather than at its extremes, totalitarian or reflexive. In this chapter, we analyse the ideas and forces that shaped the post-independence state, and provide some explanation for why the Indian state was relatively autonomous in the 1950s and early 1960s when Jawaharlal Nehru was prime minister, but subsequently became more constrained.

In Chapter 1 of *In Pursuit of Lakshmi*, we introduced a reason for the Indian state's being autonomous or constrained rather than reflexive: its superordinate relationship as a 'third actor' to the historic adversaries of class politics, private capital, and organized labour. The state as third actor began its autonomous career in independent India as a creature of Nehruvian socialism. India's ideological consensus and constitution featured socialism along with secularism and democracy. For Nehru, socialism meant using the planned development of an industrial society to eliminate poverty, provide social justice, create a self-reliant economy, and assure national independence and security in world politics. In a mixed economy, the state would occupy the commanding heights. The socialist state would serve society by providing collective and public goods, from which everyone would benefit. Equally importantly, concentrations of private economic power were to be eliminated or controlled so that they could not appropriate state authority or resources, or unduly influence the choice and implementation of state policy.

The successful practice of command politics and the rise of the state as third actor created conditions for a powerful state sector of the economy. The state sector brought into being a potentially privileged political class whose interests were defined by and associated with it. Public-sector

---

[2]We take the term 'stateness' from J.P. Nettl's seminal article, 'The State as Conceptual Variable', *World Politics*, 20, 1968, p. 566.

[3]For a historical and analytic account of state formation in India, see our 'The Regional Kingdom and the Subcontinental Empire in Indian State Formation', in *Region and Nation in India*, by Paul Wallace (ed.), New Delhi: Oxford and IBH, 1985.

employees and managers, petty and high-level officials, and professionals and elected politicians became a class defined by their ownership or control of state property, resources, and authority. Although the political class associated with the state sector shared common interests when it entered competitive relationships with political classes defined by other economic sectors, it was not necessarily or always unified. Both horizontal cleavages, between politicians and officials and among different levels of officials, and vertical cleavages, among ministries and other functionally defined units, from time to time created tensions and even violent conflict within the state sector's political class.

Another variant of the state as autonomous third actor was the 'state for itself', self-justifying and self-serving as well as self-determining, which arose when the socialist state was appropriated by its own functionaries. Building a socialist state required means. Resources had to be extracted, and capital accumulated for planned investment to occur. State services and production required employees. The state expanded as well as reproduced itself. The state sector, which burgeoned and flourished on the way to socialism, began to acquire and vest interests. Means began to become ends. Those in the pay of state firms became the beneficiaries of monopoly profits and administered prices; petty bureaucrats and senior officials became the beneficiaries of rents, the petty and grand larceny made possible by administrative discretion in the application of rules. The third actor spawned interests that increasingly diverted it from its socialist objectives.

The Indian state also appeared in a constrained variant. In Chapters 9 through 13, we show how, after 1964, rising levels of mobilization and the ascendancy of demand politics modified state autonomy. In doing so, we argue that the 1975–7 emergency regime's attempt to re-establish an autonomous state based on command politics met with only temporary success.

Which version of the state as autonomous third actor is at work at particular times and circumstances, whether the socialist servant of the public interest or the self-serving political class associated with the state sector, depends in part on how actions are interpreted. When the state raises the pay and benefits of some section of its fifteen million employees, is it being a model employer, buying labour peace, investing in political support, or serving the interests of a state class? If public-sector managers insist that the state buy their industrial goods rather than an imported version, are they supporting self-reliance or sheltering the high-cost and/or low-quality production on which their jobs and incomes depend? In an economy that is still building its industrial base, should the goal of an industrial relations regime that severely restricts collective bargaining and the right to strike be to maintain production and protect the public, or to hold down wages and coerce commitment? Do permits and licences ensure socially justifiable investments and production, or provide rents to those who issue them?

Which of its faces the polymorphous Indian state reveals is determined by policy as well as by ideology, historical circumstance, and the balance of public and private power. In this chapter, we discuss the historical forces and policy choices that initially provided the institutional assets for state autonomy, but subsequently put them at risk.

HISTORICAL LEGACIES: THE SUBCONTINENTAL EMPIRE

The state in India was not a European import, an ideological and institutional transplant from foreign climes rooted in India's exotic and alien soil. British rule profoundly influenced state formation and the level and quality of stateness in India, but it in turn built on Mughal rule and incorporated many of its features.[4] Regional kingdoms were the principal state form that had characterized the history of the Indian subcontinent until the sixteenth century. However, the subcontinental state conception had already been realized in pre-classical times in the Mauryan empire, particularly under Asoka (312–185 BC), and under the imperial rule of the Guptas (AD 319–540). At their apogee, India's ancient empires established hegemony over diverse regional kingdoms. Such kingdoms stood in tension with the subcontinental empire, and forced a recognition of their standing on the imperial forms that triumphed after the sixteenth century. As a state form, the regional kingdom has remained in a dialectical relation with the subcontinental empire throughout Indian history. Today, the dialectical relationship is expressed through Indian federal forms. The history of Indian state formation is more comparable to that of Russia and China, where empires became multinational states, than to that of Western Europe, where regional kingdoms were transformed into absolute monarchies, and then into nation-states. India is the state Europe would have become had the Holy Roman Empire embodied itself in a modern polity. On the subcontinent, the regional kingdom and the national state became the recessive, the multinational subcontinental

---

[4]See, for example, A.L. Basham, *The Wonder that Was India: A Survey of the History and Culture of the Indian Sub-Continent before the Coming of the Muslims*, New York: Grove, 1959, Ch. 4; Romila Thapar, *Asoka and the Decline of the Mauryas*, Oxford: Oxford University Press, 1961; R.C. Majumdar, and Amant Sadashiv Altekar (eds), *The Vakataka-Gupta Age (circa 200–500 AD)*, Banaras, India: Motilal Banarsi Dass for Bharatiya Itihas Parishad, 1946. For a perspective that challenges the notion that ancient and medieval empires wielded centralized power, see Burton Stein's account of the Chola kingdoms, 'The State and the Agrarian Order in Medieval South India: A Historiographic Critique', in *Essays on South Asia*, by Burton Stein (ed.), Honolulu: University of Hawaii Press, 1975.

empire, the dominant form of the state. The Mughal, British, and Indian states of the modern era incorporate the dialectical tension between these two pervasive state forms.[5]

India's subcontinental empires created means of penetration and control comparable to those developed by European absolutism in the seventeenth and eighteenth centuries: centralized fiscal mechanisms in the hands of the ruler; patrimonial bureaucracies barred from control of the means of administration and from inheritance of office and estates; and military formations funded and controlled by the ruler rather than by feudal chiefs or independent military entrepreneurs. Such arrangements were already known in the subcontinental fourth-century BC Mauryan empire, and articulated in books of statecraft (*artha*) dating from that period and subsequently.[6] Their actualization, however, has varied over time. Revived in later subcontinental empires and in regional kingdoms, they fade with the fragmentation of dominion under weak emperors or regional kings, whose servants—under various guises and arrangements—appropriate estates, office, fisc, and army.[7]

The Mughals (sixteenth to eighteenth century) succeeded in constructing a centralized military-revenue arrangement, the mansabdari system, which extracted the resources and provided the military with the force to conquer and hold in stable fashion an extensive empire. Comparable in size to the domains of Charles V, the Mughal empire probably controlled its area more securely.[8] The emperor's dominion was exercised through a centrally

[5]The Mughal period began with Babar in 1526 and is often considered to have 'ended' with the battles of Plassey and Panipat in 1757 and 1761, when the ascendancy of British power begins. The literature on the Mughal empire is well-developed and varied. For a guide, see Satish Chandra's bibliographic essay, 'Writings on Social History of Medieval India: Trends and Prospects', in his *Medieval India: Society, the Jagirdari Crisis and the Village*, New Delhi: Macmillan India, 1982; M. Athar Ali, 'The Mughal Empire in History', Presidential Address, Thirty-third Session of the Indian History Congress, Section 2, Medieval India, Muzaffarpur, 1972, 'Towards an Interpretation of the Mughal Empire', *Journal of the Royal Asiatic Society*, 1, 1978; and Irfan Habib, *Agrarian System of Mughal India*, Bombay: Asia Publishing House, 1963.

[6]Centralized fiscal mechanisms are described in detail in R.P. Kangle (ed. and trans.), *The Kautiliya Arthasastra*, second edition, 3 vols, Bombay: University of Bombay, 1960–5, a translation of a work that is generally dated at approximately 300 BC. Habib, *Agrarian System of Mughal India*, Ch. 7, deals with the ways in which the Mughals prevented *mansabdars* from inheriting estates and wealth, and also with the system's economic consequences.

[7]See M. Athar Ali, *The Mughal Nobility under Aurangzeb*, Bombay: Asia Publishing House, 1970.

[8]There was one great struggle in protest from the nobility and the theocracy—the revolt of 1518—but once it had been quelled, the empire never really faced a serious revolt from within the ranks of its own bureaucracy. However, in the latter half of the eighteenth century, rebellions by subordinate chiefs multiplied (Habib, *Agrarian System of Mughal India*, pp. 317–18). See also Abdul Aziz, *The Mansabdari System and the Mughal Army*, Delhi: Idarah-I Adabiyut-I Delli, 1952.

appointed court nobility, the mansabdars, and not through decentralized prebendiaries as in European feudalism. Mansabdars were dependent on the emperor; the lands allocated to support their foot and mounted troops and pay their expenses reverted to the emperor at his pleasure or at their death. Noble estates were not hereditary. The emperors exquisitely calibrated, depending on performance, the honours and income associated with state service.[9] Ottoman models probably influenced the administrative and revenue systems of the Mughals and their predecessors, but the Ottomans penetrated further and eliminated intermediary classes more ruthlessly than was done in India. The local rulers and chiefs beneath the mansabdari system survived, creating intermediary layers of economic, political, and cultural autonomy that contrast with Russian absolutism and the model of 'oriental despotism' expressed in the Ottoman empire.

The administrative system of the Mughals provided the network, units, and conceptions of revenue obligation on which the British system was modelled. The division of the country into *subahs*, *sarkars*, and *parganas* was reflected in British administrative divisions. The *zabt*, measurement of land for revenue purposes, migrated from the administrations of Sher Shah Sur and Akbar to Cornwallis and the British raj. In the latter part of Aurangzeb's rule and under the last Mughal rulers in the eighteenth century, state autonomy and capacity markedly declined, only to be restored under British rule, which fell heir to and reformulated the imperial state's ideas and practices.

Indian empires also created a symbolic and cultural order that emphasized the overarching significance of rulership, if not the state. Akbar restored and benefited from the ancient and pervasive Hindu idea of a universal emperor (chakravartin), who turned the cosmological wheel (chakra) and was the hub of its spokes.[10] The chakravartin or emperor was raja dhiraja (raja of rajas) or shahanshah (shah of shahs), conceptions that signified his primacy in a layered and aggregative, as well as a centralized state. Akbar succeeded in sanctifying the person and office of the emperor in the face of an Islamic tradition hostile to such sanctification. Iconography, rituals, and performances celebrated and elevated the emperor, who became an object of awe and wonder.[11] Since the loyalty and obeisance he

[9]V.S. Bhatnagar, *Life and Times of Sawai Jai Singh, 1688–1743*, Delhi: Impex, 1974.

[10]Heinrich Zimmer, *Myths and Symbols in Indian Art and Architecture*, by Joseph Campbell (ed.), New York: Pantheon, 1946. For an account that pays strong attention to the symbolic realm, see John F. Richards, 'The Formulation of Imperial Authority under Akbar and Jahangir', in *Kingship and Authority in South Asia*, by John F. Richards (ed.), Madison: University of Wisconsin Press, 1978.

[11]For a summary of the imperial idea as revived by the Mughals, see Percival Spear,

commanded were at once intensely personal and abstract, they created a separate state domain that dissolved and displaced loyalties to place, kin, and community.[12] The void left by this dissolution 'was unconsciously sought to be filled by the special position of the Mughal emperor as spiritual guide, and the self-conscious view of the Mughal empire as a great new polity, essentially just and humane'.[13]

Performances and exchanges amplified the emperor's presence: for the public, the daily royal audience in the *diwan-i-aam* (hall of public audience); for the court attended by princes and nobles, appearances in the *diwan-i-khas* (hall of private audience) and at frequent durbars; for the crown servants in the field, intimate personal exchanges—the gift of a *khilat* (robe said to have been worn by the emperor) to mark appointment as his agent, letters from the emperor's hand, and the reciprocation of gifts by subordinates.[14] Streams of exchanges kept 'thick' the emperor's relations with service nobles at the far corners of the subcontinent.[15] Here, too, there was continuity between British and Mughal empires. The British used Mughal ceremonies and language to revitalize the universalism and mystique of the imperial state. Through ceremonial enactments that closely emulated Mughal patterns, they revived in Queen Victoria's time imperial grandeur and patrimonial ties in durbars, jubilees, and coronation ceremonies, and rituals of loyalty between the Queen-Empress and her subjects.[16]

The actualization of the subcontinental state has waxed and waned over the centuries. The regional kingdom ceased to be the dominant state form with the rise of the Mughal Empire in the sixteenth century, although it revived briefly in the eighteenth. After the collapse of Mughal power with the death of Aurangzeb in 1707 and the failure of Maratha rulers to establish a successor state, British power, followed by British rule, revived and restored the subcontinental imperial state. The formation of India and Pakistan in 1947 and Bangladesh in 1971 left the subcontinent with two latter-day

---

'The Mughals and the British', in *A Cultural History of India*, by A.L. Basham (ed.), Oxford: Clarendon, 1975.

[12]David Lelyveld, *Aligarh's First Generation*, Princeton: Princeton University Press, 1977.

[13]Ali, 'Towards an Interpretation', p. 47.

[14]John F. Richards, 'The Imperial Crisis in the Deccan', *Journal of Asian Studies*, 25 (2), 1976.

[15]See, for example, M.I. Borah (trans.), *Baharisthan-I-Ghaybi* (Mughal wars in Assam, Cooch Behar, Bengal, Bihar, and Orissa during the reigns of Jahangir and Shah Jahan by Mirza Nathan), Gauhati: Assam Department of Historical and Antiquarian Studies, 1936; Henry Beveridge (ed.), and Alexander Rogers (trans.), *The Tuzuk-i-Jahangiri*, or *Memoirs of Jahangir*, second edn, Delhi: Munshiram Manoharlal, 1968.

[16]Bernard S. Cohn, 'The British and the Mughal Court in the Seventeenth Century', University of Chicago, 1977, typescript; W.H. Moreland, *India at the Death of Akbar: An Economic Study*, Delhi: Atma Ram, 1961.

representatives of the regional kingdom, and one of the subcontinental imperial state.

In contrast with European nation-states, whose strength rested on the extinction of regional cultures and identities, subcontinental empires in India have made accommodations where regional kingdoms are concerned. The strategy propounded in the fourth-century *Arthasastra*—that subordinate rulers shall be preserved and respected in their customs and territorial jurisdiction if they acknowledge, via respect and tribute, the superior authority of a ruler of rulers—governed the statecraft of subcontinental empires in Mughal and British times.[17] After independence, India's federal system became its modern embodiment within the twentieth-century subcontinental empire.

Indigenous Hindu and imported liberal state theory have also made substantial contributions to state formation, and to the level and quality of stateness. At first glance, they seem to differ sharply on key issues. Liberal theory posits the individual as the basic unit of society; Hindu theory emphasizes family, caste, and tribe. The theories also differ with respect to the primacy of consent and force for obedience, with liberal theory stressing the voluntary and contractual basis of individual obedience and Hindu theory stressing *danda*, the rod of punishment, as the indispensable requisite of order.[18] The severe realpolitik of might making right in the *Arthasastra* contrasts sharply with the liberal conception that natural law and right reason are the sources of morality and order.

Yet the two theoretical traditions converge with respect to the priority of societal values over state goals. Both see society as preceding and limiting the state (and for liberalism, unlike Hindu theory, the individual precedes and limits the society). The society displayed in the *Dharmasastras*, the classical texts of good conduct that constitute the fundamental prescriptive canons of Hindu culture, is one whose reality and legitimacy co-originate with the king, but are not his creation. Its units are self-regulating within a larger architectonic. The state in India did not constitute a community of feeling; the state-society relationship was primarily instrumental. The state upheld and protected society and its values rather than itself constituting the highest form of community and the means for realizing value. The Indian state was constrained by a society whose ordered heterogeneity was

[17]Kangle, *Kautiliya Arthasastra*.

[18]See, for example, J. Duncan Derrett, 'Social and Political Thought and Institutions', in Basham, *Cultural History*, quoting Narada 'with the rod of chastisement (*danda*) he is to control all his subjects' (p. 132). On Hindu state theory, see also Charles Drekmeier, *Kingship and Community in Early India*, Stanford: Stanford University Press, 1962; Louis Dumont, 'The Conception of Kingship in Ancient India', *Contributions to Indian Sociology*, 56, 1961; U.N. Ghoshal, *A History of Indian Political Ideas*, New York: Oxford University Press, 1959.

prescribed and legitimized in the *Dharmasastras*. This doctrine implied restraints on the state that stood in tension with the more absolutist doctrines of *dandaniti*, just as doctrines of state sovereignty and reason of state stood in tension with liberal doctrines of consent and natural rights.

The good Hindu king is meant to protect the laws of the self-regulating orders of society. The liberal state is meant to protect individual rights and interests. Insofar as a liberal state has goals and policies, they are to be determined by the outcomes of interest group and party competition that organizes and represents individual preferences. At the extreme, both liberal and Hindu state theory countenance anarchism, as the convergence of Thoreau and Gandhi on the legitimacy and importance of civil disobedience suggests, and discountenance reasons of state to justify acts that violate procedural norms and societal values.

The founders of modern India's constitution benefited from the legacy of stateness bequeathed by the Hindu, Mughal, and British subcontinental empires. They combined centralized rule with a parallel state form, the regional kingdom. The ideas and practice of the subcontinental imperial state from Mauryan to British times, and the Hindu conception that social order requires the state's force, left a legacy of high stateness. On the other hand, the sovereignty-limiting ideas and practice of the regional kingdom, and of the Hindu and liberal conceptions that society is prior to and autonomous of the state, created a legacy of low stateness. These paradigms and parameters structured the possibilities and choices of those who created independent India's state.

HISTORICAL LEGACIES: LIBERAL AND AUTHORITARIAN OPTIONS IN THE FOUNDING PERIOD

Models for the founding of states and for political change arise in both domestic and international environments. When a liberal theory of the state became the principal ideological determinant of the 1950 constitution, it drew on both domestic and international exemplars. It expressed the liberal obligation to recognize the civil and political rights embodied in the Westminster model, which had been gradually introduced from 1909 by the British raj.[19] It also included a more traditional Indian understanding—

---

[19]The motives and objectives of Englishmen at the beginning of the century were mixed, as often controversial or contradictory as consensual, with high Tory imperialists and liberal reformers disagreeing over the meaning of the empire and the capacity of Indians for self-government. Reginald Coupland's *India: A Restatement*, Oxford: Oxford University Press, 1945, provides a succinct statement of the issues and outcomes.

that claims on state sovereignty and monopoly over public and national interest were constrained by the traditional obligation of the ruler to recognize and uphold the jurisdiction of prior social groups. At independence, democratic, parliamentary, and constitutional government had become a form familiar to Indians, who had fought as nationalists for four decades to make it their own. A variant of Hindu state theory advocated by Mohandas Gandhi in the Constituent Assembly was little attended to.[20] It held that that society's dharmically ordered heterogeneity was prior to, and to a considerable degree autonomous of, state authority, and that local communities were capable of self-rule. Arguments were also offered in favour of the viceregal variant of the imperial administrative state. Like Gandhi's ideas, they were not endorsed by the small group of Congress leaders who managed the Constituent Assembly and its eight standing committees.[21]

That a liberal state should have triumphed was strongly determined, but by no means preordained. Fortuitous conjunctures and long-range secular trends collaborated in the outcome. The partition of India into two successor states, India and Pakistan,[22] and the integration of the autocratically constituted princely states[23] spared independent India the grapple with several divisive and recalcitrant state issues that had plagued British efforts at state building. The creation of an Islamic state in Pakistan removed the principal challenge to Congress's secular state ideology. The weak federalism that alone by 1946 could have kept the Muslim-majority areas from leaving India would have been a significant obstacle to planned

[20]For a careful, detailed discussion of the failure of the Gandhian option, see Austin, *Indian Constitution*. As Austin observes, 'Great as Gandhi's influence had been ... he had not succeeded in converting either the country or his own party to his view of how Indians should ... govern themselves' (p. 39).

[21]The key figures were Prime Minister Jawaharlal Nehru; Deputy Prime Minister Vallabhbhai Patel; Rajendra Prasad, the Constituent Assembly's presiding officer and India's first president; and Maulana Abul Kalam Azad, education minister, Congress's most prominent Muslim leader and a Nehru confidant (Austin, *Indian Constitution*, p. 19).

[22]Announced by the viceroy, Lord Mountbatten, on 3 June 1947, after having obtained the reluctant consent of Nehru. Gandhi, who was strongly opposed to it, was observing a day of silence when Mountbatten 'discussed' the decision with him. For a narrative account of the historical background of partition and the events surrounding it, see H.V. Hodson, *The Great Divide: Britain, India, Pakistan*, London: Hutchinson, 1969. Nicholas Mansergh (ed.), *The Transfer of Power, 1942–1947*, 12 vols, London: Her Majesty's Stationery Office, 1970–83, provides in published form the official records bearing, *inter alia*, on partition. See also C.H. Philips and Mary Doreen Wainwright (eds), *The Partition of India: Policies and Perspectives, 1935–1946*, Cambridge: MIT Press, 1970.

[23]For the most authoritative account, see V.P. Menon, *The Story of the Integration of the Indian States*, New York: Macmillan, 1956. Menon was secretary to the States Ministry under Vallabhbhai Patel.

development and social transformation. The incorporation of the princely states, whose territories covered about a third of the subcontinent and whose subjects encompassed about a quarter of its people, eliminated from serious contention the monarchical alternative that had for so long characterized regional kingdoms.[24]

The Gandhians in the Constituent Assembly were disarmed with minor concessions. The constitution's directive principles of state policy made commitments to *panchayati raj* (decentralized local government), and to certain cultural values dear to some upper-caste Hindus, such as the abolition of cow slaughter.

The liberal state created at independence was not merely the result of four years of deliberation in the Constituent Assembly, nor the political legacy of four decades of gradual parliamentary growth. The historical circumstances and accidents that made Nehru the principal founder of the state, and that enabled him to shape its conventions, also played an important part in determining its character. The historical outcomes we know seem natural only because we repress the memory of possible alternatives. The deaths of Subhas Chandra Bose in August 1945 and of Vallabhbhai Patel in December 1950[25] removed not only Nehru's principal competitors for national leadership, but also powerful spokesmen for authoritarian state ideologies. On the eve of World War II, Bose successfully challenged Gandhi's hold on the Congress by being elected its president in 1938, and again in 1939. Bose, like Nehru, had been shaped by a Cambridge education and exposure to European events in the 1930s. For a time they worked together in Congress's socialist left. By 1938, they diverged on the prospects and value of fascism, and on political means. Bose thought that Hitler and Mussolini represented the wave of the future and would win the war they both anticipated. Nehru believed that the Soviet experiment provided economic lessons for independent India, fascism should be opposed and would be defeated, and Gandhi and the liberal state's concern for right means was essential.

[24]Partition, Mountbatten's authority and persuasion, and Patel's accomplishments at the states and Home Ministries made what had seemed a most unlikely prospect, integration of the princely states, become a reality. As late as December 1945, integration was not anticipated even by so committed a nationalist as Nehru. See S. Gopal, *Jawaharlal Nehru: A Biography*, vol. 1, 1889–1947, Cambridge: Harvard University Press, 1967, p. 321.

[25]The best biographies of these two departed leaders are Hugh Toye, *The Springing Tiger: A Study of a Revolutionary*, London: Cassell, 1959, and N.D. Parikh, *Sardar Vallabhai Patel*, 2 vols, Ahmedabad: Navajivan Press, 1953–6. Howard Spodek's 'Sardar Vallabhai Patel at 100', *Economic and Political Weekly*, 13 December 1975, provides a new assessment of Patel's early career and explains some of the reasons for the Patel revival that accompanied the disillusionment with Mrs Gandhi, which began in 1973.

In April 1943, Bose arrived by German submarine in Singapore where, with Japanese support, he formed a government in exile (*Azad Hind* or Free India) and took command of the Indian National Army (INA), composed of 20,000 of the 80,000 Indian officers and men captured by the Japanese when Singapore fell. Styling himself *Netaji* (leader on the Fuhrer model), he declared his objective to be the liberation of India by military means.[26] 'I am convinced more than ever before,' he wrote to the German government in May 1942, when first proposing that it support his plan to shift his efforts to the Orient, 'that the Tripartite Powers [Germany, Italy, and Japan] and India have a common destiny.'[27] Writing in *Wille and Macht* in August 1942 on the subject of 'Free India and Her Problems', he found one thing clear: 'There will be a strong Central Government. ... Behind this Government will stand a well organized, disciplined all-India party, which will be the chief instrument for maintaining national unity.'[28] Earlier in his career, Bose had identified with and come to represent the realpolitik and extremist versions of Indian nationalism that flourished in Bengal and Maharashtra. He ended by being an apologist for national socialism. Nehru came to represent the liberal moderate version, whose lineage ran from Mahadev Ranade to Gopal Krishna Gokhale to Gandhi, with an essential detour via democratic socialism.[29]

[26]See Mansergh, *Transfer of Power*, vol. 4, 'The Bengal Famine and the New Viceroyalty', 15 June 1943–31 August 1944. Document 37, note by M.I. 2(a) gives the formation of the INA as 8 July 1943. It reports that Rash Behari Bose, the interim president of the Indian Independence League, presented Subhas Chandra Bose to the League as its new president 'who has adopted the title of "Mehtarji [Netaji] or Leader"'. Bose immediately announced the formation of a provisional government, declared his sincere belief in Japan's good intentions, and stated that India's hope for freedom lay in an Axis victory (p. 75). For a superb account of the military and political fortunes of the INA in its abortive attempt to free India in the wake of Japanese forces, see Philip Mason, *A Matter of Honour: An Account of the Indian Army, Its Officers and Men*, Harmondsworth, England: Penguin, 1967.

[27]Subhas Chandra Bose, *The Indian Struggle, 1920–1942*, Bombay: Asia Publishing House, 1964, p. 460.

[28]Ibid., p. 454. Bose, like the early Hitler, proposed to protect labour and promote its welfare rather than create a state that represented its class interests and ideology: 'The Azad [Free] India State will look after the welfare of the labourer ... [and] the peasant will have to be given relief ... In this connection, institutions for the welfare of labour, like "Arbeitsdiense" (services for labour), "Winterhilfe" (winter welfare), "Kraft durch Freude" (strength through joy) will be of great interest to India' (Bose, 'Free India and Her Problems', in ibid., p. 457).

[29]The young Bose's patron was C.R. Das, the Bengali trade unionist and democratic socialist who died in 1925. In time, his spiritual forefathers came to be Balwantrao Tilak and Bipin Chandra Pal, who allied in 1905 when the abortive partition of Bengal provided an issue around which extremists could rally at the national level. Their call for immediate independence and willingness to use violence and terrorism distinguished them from the moderates, who believed that representative government and independence could be won with British help and cooperation. Mahadev Govind Ranade, the father of social reform, and his intellectual heir

The fate of state formation in independent India depended also on the outcome of a related historical event, the trial of arms between the (British) Indian Army and Bose's Japanese-supported INA. Had the Japanese and the INA succeeded in reaching Calcutta or beyond and had Bose's government been established on Indian soil even for a time, or had Bose lived to return to independent India, the determinants of state formation in India would have included elements like those in Indonesia, where a Netaji and a political army gained independence by military means. The maintenance of a non-political, professional army was a close thing in 1946. Even Nehru, in November 1945, put on his barrister's gown for the first time in twenty-five years to help defend the three INA officers being tried by the British raj at the Red Fort, symbol of Delhi's empires.[30] As independence became increasingly imminent, Nehru and others came to accept another view, articulated by Lord Mountbatten to Nehru in 1946, that 'The I.N.A. were not politically conscious heroes fighting for their country but cowards and traitors who betrayed their loyal friends. The people who will serve you well in your national army of the future are those who are loyal to their oath [to the head of state, whether the king emperor or an Indian head of state]; otherwise if you become unpopular a disloyal army may turn against you.'[31] In the event, India opted for a professional army loyal to its oath and to the honour of its traditions and calling.[32] The INA trials were curtailed, but INA officers and men were barred from joining the Indian Army. Unlike in many Third World countries where armies have become political and governing institutions, the Indian state and Indian politics have been notably free from military control or

---

Gopal Krishna Gokhale, the greatest of the Indian liberals, represent a different strand from Tilak and B.C. Pal. Gokhale in turn became the young Gandhi's political guru and sponsor, and Gandhi played the same role for Nehru. See Stanley A. Wolpert, *Tilak and Gokhale; Revolution and Reform in the Making of Modern India*, Berkeley and Los Angeles: University of California Press, 1962; John R. McLane, *Indian Nationalism and the Early Congress*, Princeton: University Press, 1977; B.R. Nanda, *Gokhale: The Indian Moderates and the British Raj*, Princeton: Princeton University Press, 1977; and Michael Brecher, *Nehru: A Political Biography*, Oxford: Oxford University Press, 1959. For the larger Bengali context of Bose's ideas, see Leonard Gordon, *Bengal: The Nationalist Movement, 1876–1940*, New York: Columbia University Press, 1974.

[30]B.N. Pandey, a Nehru biographer, concludes that 'their trial by court martial aroused the country [then in the midst of the 1946 election campaign] as nothing else could'. They represented, for Nehru, India's fight for freedom (*Nehru*, New York: Stein and Day, 1976, p. 254).

[31]Pandey, *Nehru*, p. 254, citing Rajendra Prasad Papers, Report by Nehru on his visit to Malaya, 28 March 1946. See Gopal, *Nehru* 1: 309–11, for an account of Nehru's visit to Malaya and the immediate rapport that was established between Nehru and Lord and Lady Mountbatten.

[32]See Mason, *Matter of Honour*, pp. 513–22, where he describes Auchinleck's essential role. Paul Scott's *Raj Quartet*, particularly *A Division of the Spoils*, London: Heinemann, 1975, provides a subtle account of raj and nationalist attitudes toward the (British) Indian Army and the INA.

even influence. This reflects in part the success with which constitutional democracy has been pursued by Indian parties and leaders, but is also a consequence of the events and decisions of 1944–6.

An authoritarian alternative to India's state formation had other voices and legacies in the critical period of gaining independence and writing a constitution for the new state. If he had not had to share power with Nehru at independence, Vallabhbhai Patel, the 'iron sardar', might have oriented the Indian state in a Hindu revivalist, economically conservative, and authoritarian direction. The Bismarckian adjective 'iron' was not inappropriate. Patel was not a charismatic ideologist or master of words and crowds like his rivals for national leadership, Bose and Nehru. He despised political rhetoric and pleasing the multitude. His forte was control of the many by the few through command of the party organization, intelligence, police, and mass media. He was a past master at manipulating party factions and political elites.

Patel was a man of action rather than words, and his state theory must be inferred from what he did and how he did it. He was committed to Hindu tradition and interests as much out of convenience as out of conviction; they were key elements of the political forces that supported his leadership. As a Hindu traditionalist, he understood and appreciated the viceregal state's use of danda, the rod of chastisement, to ensure order and obedience. Patel's voice was essential for saving the ICS, the 'steel frame' of the imperial administrative state, and, until independence, the masters and jailers of India's political classes. His greatest accomplishment was integrating the princely states, but his success in quelling the naval mutiny of Bombay in 1946, and in directing 'police action' against a recalcitrant nizam of Hyderabad, also project a state that makes order and obedience a necessary, if not a sufficient, condition for legitimacy.

Patel was not a committed or convinced secularist. His call for Muslims to pledge their loyalty to India as a condition of citizenship after partition, his one-sided defence of Hindus during the communal rioting and carnage that accompanied partition, and his refusal to honour India's commitment to turn over to Pakistan the assets due it occasioned Gandhi's last fast in January 1948. The riots in Delhi abated; Patel, after being told by Gandhi on the verge of death, 'you are not the Sardar I knew', turned over the assets and deferred to Gandhi's call for brotherhood and forgiveness. Subsequently, he honoured his pledge to Gandhi to cooperate with Nehru, inter alia, supporting a secular state in the Constituent Assembly.[33]

Patel's death in December 1950 left Nehru as India's unchallenged national leader, free for a decade or more to shape the Indian state in a liberal

---

[33] For a full account, see Parikh, *Patel*.

direction. His doing so was not a foregone conclusion. In 1937, when his second term as Congress president was drawing to a close and there was talk of drafting him for a third, Nehru wrote an anonymous article revealing that he had authoritarian fantasies very close to the kind his daughter, Indira Gandhi, acted out. It was the decade of dictators; fascism seemed to be ascendant. Bose, who followed Nehru as Congress president, had begun to turn from democratic to national socialism.

'He calls himself a democrat and a socialist,' Nehru wrote of himself, 'but every psychologist knows that the mind is ultimately slave to the heart and that logic can always be made to fit in with the desires and irrepressible urges of man. A little twist and Jawaharlal might turn dictator, sweeping aside the paraphernalia of a slow moving democracy ... we all know how fascism has fattened on this language and then cast it away as useless lumber. ... Jawaharlal ... has all the makings of a dictator in him.'[34]

However, it was the liberal state of the moderate nationalists and Gandhi's commitment to right means that became Nehru's historical option. He shaped the liberal state in ways that accommodated it to the 1950 constitution's new commitments to universal suffrage, a federal system, and socialist objectives. He and like-minded colleagues in the Congress had been weaned on the parliamentary version of the liberal state, including its concern for a government of laws and civil rights.

The Government of India Act, 1935, became the text of reference and emulation for India's constitution. About 250 of its 395 articles are taken from the 1935 Act verbatim, or substantially intact. Nehru and his colleagues preferred the liberal state to the untried and utopian Hindu or administrative state alternatives advocated by leaders of minority factions in the Constituent Assembly: a Gandhian state, later elaborated by Jayaprakash Narayan,[35] which favoured radical decentralization and the inversion of the pyramid of power; a Hindu state that repudiated Congress's secular commitment and confirmed Muslim fears of becoming second-class citizens or worse; and a highly centralized, authoritarian state on the viceregal model. Nehru had the votes in the Constituent Assembly and, subsequently, the national support to establish a liberal state in India.

[34]Nehru wrote as 'Chanakya', sometimes known as Kautiliya, the famous Mauryan (c. 320–185 BC) statesman to whom is ascribed the authorship of the *Arthasastra*, a text often characterized as Machiavellian in its depiction of statecraft. He entitled the essay, 'The Rashtrapati' (father of the nation). The text, reproduced in Norman, *Nehru*, 1: pp. 498–501, appeared in *Modern Review* (Calcutta).

[35]See Jayaprakash Narayan, *A Plea for the Reconstruction of Indian Polity*, Kashi, India: Sarva Seva Sangh, 1969, and W.H. Morris-Jones's trenchant critique in 'The Unhappy Utopia: JP in Wonderland', *Economic Weekly*, 25 June 1960.

Had Bose or Patel lived into the independence period, highly divisive state issues would have created a very different history of state formation and building. As it was, Nehru had more or less a free hand, a historical circumstance that goes a long way in explaining the initial success of the liberal state and constitutional democracy in India.

The proximate causes of the 1970s struggles over democracy and authoritarianism were contests for power and political survival. But, to summarize, there were also more distant determinants, struggles over the kind and degree of what Peter Nettl called 'stateness'.[36] India was advantaged by the fact that the subcontinental empire had effectively established its hegemony over the regional kingdoms, and that this hegemony was institutionalized in administrative practices. But India's historical legacies and leadership at independence pointed to a variety of possible outcomes. The authoritarian variants of the Hindu, Mughal, and British empires, and the rise of fascism in the 1930s created one broad option. The liberal variants arising out of a means-oriented nationalism, the parliamentary features of the Westminster model, and Nehru's leadership of Congress created another.

High stateness in India is associated with its imperial legacies and the contemporary requirements of an interventionist, managerial state pursuing welfare and socialist objectives. However, unlike the high stateness of continental Europe, which is based on the era of monarchical absolutism, claims to state sovereignty and monopoly over public and national interests in India were constrained by the traditional obligation of the ruler to recognize and uphold the laws of prior social groups, and the liberal obligation to recognize civil and political rights. The claim that the state has a special relationship to the public good, that the state's interest is uniquely identified with the public interest, and that the interests of social groups are narrow, partial, and selfish dates from the early 1970s, and finds its analogues in theory.

State formation is never finished. It is a continuous process. Nehru's capacity to shape India's traditions in the first two decades of Indian independence greatly strengthened a liberal and constitutional state, but did not foreclose other options. When Indira Gandhi introduced an authoritarian state in 1975, some observers considered such an outcome natural. A reviewer surveying Barrington Moore's magisterial *Social Origins of Dictatorship and Democracy* wrote, 'India's move toward authoritarianism in 1975 confirms Moore's thesis that democracy can not survive without social revolution'.[37]

[36]Nettl, 'The State as Conceptual Variable', p. 566.

[37]Barrington Moore Jr., *Social Origins of Dictatorship and Democracy: Lord and Peasant in the Making of the Modern World*, Boston: Beacon, 1966. The quotation is from Jonathan M. Wiener, 'Review of Reviews', *History and Theory*, 5, 1976, p. 169, n. 124.

And yet it is possible that India's social revolution will take a form different from the European and Asian models Moore surveyed. Social revolution from below may work itself out in an incremental fashion. Upheavals scattered rather than concentrated in time and space can reorder society, even as they interrupt processes of economic development and state building.

The struggle between liberal and authoritarian versions of the state in India has featured opposing arguments. One asserts that institutions and processes representing organized interests in society are the best means to reach approximations of the public interest. Another claims that the state knows best because it speaks for a disinterested, long-run view of the public good and national interests. Such issues played a central role in the politics of the 1970s. The stage was set by Indira Gandhi's authoritarian regime, when the arguments for India's version of high stateness were rehearsed by those who justified the regime. The climax of the drama was the victory of the Janata Party in 1977, when the virtues of the liberal state were recalled and in considerable measure restored. But party alternation in control of the state after the 1977 and 1980 elections, when the principal contestants made state issues the central themes of their campaigns, have kept these issues at the fore. In the 1980s, Nehru's grandson sought to revitalize a Nehruvian constitutional settlement. The process of state formation continues.

THE STATE AND ITS PERMANENT GOVERNMENT

A leading state issue during the founding period, which reappeared in the 1970s and will affect the course of events in the 1980s, is the kind of policy-level bureaucracy India requires. India became a republic, casting aside the autocratic monarchical doctrines and administrative state of king-emperor and viceroy; a democracy, where for the first time the political masters, those who would represent and govern, were chosen on the basis of universal suffrage; and a welfare and socialist state, committed not only to economic growth and self-reliance, but also to social justice and national power. The ICS, which had governed and administered the British raj, was available. Acting within the imperial and viceregal tradition, British civil servants under the raj had not only represented state interests, but had also governed directly; they constituted a colonial version of bureaucratic absolutism. A distant king-emperor and his secretary of state, and a viceroy close at hand were political masters of a sort, but the British raj approximated bureaucratic more than monarchical absolutism. The steel frame and the guardians needed and took little political or policy direction. Was such a service suitable for the new state and nation? If yes, what changes in orientation were required of its successor service, the IAS, and could they be realized?[38]

At a time when many Third World states were struggling to build qualified and effective career services, the standing of India's senior bureaucracy was exceptional. It gave the post-independent state an autonomy and continuity that has persisted in times of uncertainty and unsteady political control at the national and state levels. In the era of Patel and Nehru and, after 1950, in the Nehru era of Congress-party dominance, the services were relatively sheltered from challenge and attack. The policy-level bureaucracy returned to the centre of controversy and political debate with the onset of party alternation, a new development for the Indian political system. It began with the election of 1967 and its aftermath, when opposition coalitions governed half of India's sixteen large states, and became more pronounced with the elections of 1977 and 1980, when the central government changed hands. States issues focusing on the senior civil service were brought to the top of India's political agenda by the temporary sharpening of socialist objectives after the Congress split of 1969 and the ensuing demands for commitment, the strain on the constitutional and legal obligations of civil servants created by the emergency, and the penetration of IAS state cadres by state politics and regional nationalism.

A variety of issues were debated but unresolved. The doctrine of 'neutrality' was challenged by the doctrine of commitment; the meaning and operational consequences of commitment were disputed. The rise of personal loyalty as the test of commitment threatened the viability of career services and a government of law.

The doctrine of neutrality was the product of an era of partisan party competition. In England, such an era followed the coming of political stability in the early eighteenth century, and the concept of loyal opposition in the early nineteenth.[39] The doctrine was exported to India when, at the provincial level in the 1920s, Indian party politicians took charge of a limited range of ministerial portfolios, and it became a central doctrine of state theory at independence when India embarked on its experiments with parliamentary democracy. It was a convenient doctrine. Of the approximately 1,000 ICS officers serving at independence, 453 were Indian, and became

[38]For autobiographical accounts that provide insights into the problematics of this transition, see that of an ICS officer whose experience spanned the British and Indian period, E.N. Mangat Rai, *Commitment My Style*, New Delhi: Vikas, 1973, and of a civil servant who joined in the special recruitment just after independence, Mohan Mukerji, *Ham in the Sandwich*, New Delhi: Vikas, 1979.

[39]See, for example, Ernest Barker, *The Development of the Public Services in Europe*, New York: Oxford University Press, 1944.

the policy bureaucracy of the successor states.[40] Neutrality served not only to explain and legitimize their role in the context of party government, but also provided a cover for their translation from political masters and jailers of Congress leaders to loyal servants of the new state.

Congress members of the Constituent Assembly were not easily convinced that the ICS should continue. As yesterday's nationalists, democrats, and reformers, they preferred to rid the state of an imperial legacy known for its elitism and conservatism. However, more statist counsel prevailed. Patel, referring to the interim government that took office in November 1946 and the Government of India that came into being on 15 August 1947, warned the Constituent Assembly in 1949: 'I have worked with them during this difficult period. ... Remove them and I see nothing but a picture of chaos all over the country.'[41] Nehru, who had been unconvinced, changed his stance as he had done with respect to the INA and the Indian Army: 'The old distinctions and differences are gone. ... In the difficult days ahead our Service and experts have a vital role to play and we invite them to do so as comrades in the service of India.'[42]

Nehru's remarks were premature. 'Distinctions and differences' from the colonial era were not so easily forgotten. The most powerful metaphor for the services, the 'steel frame', lingered on. The ICS was the vehicle of the colonial administration, which featured law and order and the collection of revenue. For nationalists, law and order meant repression; for nationalists and socialists, revenue collection meant a failure to promote economic growth and social justice.[43] The steel frame was a negative metaphor until,

[40]For the shift from the ICS to the IAS, see B.B. Misra, *The Bureaucracy in India: An Historical Analysis of Development up to 1947*, New Delhi: Oxford University Press, 1977, pp. 299–308. Misra, citing Home Department file no. 30/28/47-ESB(S), reports that there were 980 ICS officers on 1 January 1947. Of these, 468 were Europeans, 352 were Hindus other than 'depressed classes', and 101 were Muslims. The balance was from other religious and social communities (p. 306, n. 163).

[41]As quoted in W.H. Morris-Jones, *The Government and Politics of India*, third revised edn, London: Hutchinson, 1971, p. 26. Patel insisted, on pain of his own and the entire ICS's resignation, that the Drafting Committee of the Constituent Assembly include constitutional guarantees protecting conditions of service for the ICS comparable to those enjoyed under the raj. Patel told Constituent Assembly members opposed to guarantees for the ICS, 'If you decide that we should not have the service at all, in spite of my pledged word, I will take the service with me and I will go. I will tell the servicemen, "Let us go. The nation has changed." They are capable of earning their living' (T.V. Kunhi Krishna, *Chavan and the Troubled Decade*, Bombay: Somaiya Publications, 1971, p. 273, as quoted in Francine R. Frankel, *India's Political Economy, 1947–1977*, New Delhi: Oxford University Press, 1978, pp. 80–1, n. 24).

[42]Nehru, Jawaharlal, *Independence and After*, New York: John Day, 1950, p. 9, as quoted in Robert L. Hardgrave Jr., *India: Government and Politics in a Developing Nation*, third edn, New York: Harcourt Brace Jovanovich, 1980, p. 71.

[43]Stanley Heginbotham has disaggregated four organizational ideologies of civil servants,

in the face of the difficulties of governing the country, it lost its pejorative meaning. A new question emerged: was the steel frame strong enough and neutral enough? It became apparent in the late 1970s, even as the position of the services was subject to buffeting from all sides, that a steel frame was useful for maintaining continuity and stability, and sustaining national integration. In the face of their dramatic deterioration, maintaining law and order acquired a new standing—as an administrative virtue, rather than a colonial vice.

'The guardians' was another image from the colonial era that lingered on after independence to provide a target for nationalists, democrats, and socialists. Philip Mason, a leading scholar of the ICS and himself one of its members, used the phrase to characterize it. He explicitly compared its self-image and outlook to those of the rulers in Plato's *Republic*, whose special knowledge of the good made them superior to ordinary men and justified their rule over them.[44] Translated into vulgar imperial relations, the guardians were the bearers of the white man's burden, the 'heaven-born' superior beings whose duty it was to civilize the lesser breeds without the law, and to enlighten the benighted. The guardian and heaven-born mentality lingered on, providing that special sense of calling that fortified IAS officers against the often philistine and populist onslaughts of democratic politicians, the elected representatives, and ministers, who were their newly-installed masters. It lingered on, too, in the mistaken belief that amateur generalists were equipped to perform the technical and expert tasks involved in managing a vast and complex industrial and financial public sector, and in an ideology that stated that state servants were uniquely equipped to speak for the public interest.

The guardian mentality also provided ample ammunition to those who demanded that the civil service shed its superior airs and become more socially representative, on the mistaken premise that those who were of the people would, ipso facto, be for the people. It is doubtful whether a more

---

among which the 'colonial' is one. See his *Cultures in Conflict; The Four Faces of Indian Bureaucracy*, New York: Columbia University Press, 1975.

[44]Philip Woodruff, *The Men Who Ruled India*, 2 vols, New York: Schocken, 1967. Mason used Woodruff as a pseudonym when he published his remarkable, if apologetic, biographical and historical study of raj administrators. Also useful are B.B. Misra, *The Administrative History of India, 1834–1947*, Oxford: Oxford University Press, 1970; and David C. Potter, 'Bureaucratic Change in India', and Bernard S. Cohn, 'Recruitment and Training of British Civil Servants in India, 1600–1860', in *Asian Bureaucratic Systems Emergent from the Imperial Tradition*, by Ralph Braibanti (ed.), N.C. Durham: Duke University Press, 1966. W.H. Morris-Jones's chapter on governance in Government and Politics of India (Ch. 4) still provides the best short account of the services. Henry Hart has provided a thoughtful recent assessment of governance: 'Political Leadership in India: Dimensions and Limits' Paper presented at the Conference on India's Democracy, Princeton University, 14–16 March 1985.

socially representative IAS composed of the children of middle and small cultivators, or of urban petty traders, would be more socialist, secular, or democratic than the children of the English-educated professionals who have been disproportionately represented in the senior and central services.[45] In much of the furore about representativeness, class style and more equal opportunities for social mobility were as often the issue as ideological orientation. In any case, as ministers and elected representatives became more rural and less professional, educated, and anglicized, they found their role as political masters threatened and compromised by state servants cut from the very different cloth of elite colleges and high-income urban and professional families.[46] Noting that 80–95 per cent of India's higher civil service, as in most other countries, was drawn from the professional middle classes, they called for a more socially representative bureaucracy.[47]

At the national level, the disparity in educational levels and cultural styles was less marked, and caused less difficulty than at the state level. During the Nehru era, the ICS and the IAS were Nehru's allies as well as state servants. The shared objective of national power through the creation of a modern society and economy overrode whatever differences there may have been with respect to socialist commitment.[48] As Nehru's co-authors

[45]V. Subramaniam reports that 89, 81, 77, 80, and 79 per cent, respectively, of entrants to the Indian Foreign Service, IAS, Indian Police Service, Audit and Accounts Service, and Customs and Postal Services between 1957 and 1963 were from families whose father's occupation was 'professional middle class', (for example, higher or lower civil servant, employee of a private firm, schoolteacher, professor, doctor, and lawyer). See his *Social Background of India's Administrators*, New Delhi: Government of India, Publications Division, 1971, Table 6. See also David C. Potter, 'The Indian Civil Service Tradition within the Bureaucratic Structures of State Power in South Asia: 1919–1978', Paper presented at the Sixth European Conference on Modern South Asian Studies, 1978; published as a pamphlet by the Centre National de la Recherche Scientifique (Paris), 1978.

[46]For an insightful discussion of the strains between state servants and their political masters in India, see Richard P. Taub, *Bureaucrats under Stress*, Berkeley and Los Angeles: University of California Press, 1969.

[47]For the original use of the term 'representative bureaucracy', see J. Donald Kingsley, *Representative Bureaucracy*, Yellow Springs, Ohio: Antioch Press, 1944; for an able critique see V. Subramaniam, 'Representative Bureaucracy'. For a more recent restatement, see Samuel Krislov, *Representative Bureaucracy*, Englewood Cliffs, N.J.: Prentice-Hall, 1974. Subramaniam presents data for six countries for 1957–63, showing the middle-class origins of their higher services (p. 1016). He also notes that such origins make a civil service more representative in a society where the middle classes compose 60 per cent of the workforce (for example, the United States), than in one where they constitute 9 per cent (for example, India) (p. 1015).

[48]At the state level, see, for example, Mangat Rai's discussion of the administrative-political collaboration in constructing the Punjab's contributions to economic development, including the Bhakra Dam and the Punjab Agricultural University at Ludhiana. He also provides microdata, of which much more is needed, to support or discredit the unproven proposition that the IAS is not development-minded. His instances tend to fall fairly evenly on the pro

and implementors, civil servants were the vanguard of the lobby for an industrial strategy, collaborating in the creation of basic and heavy industry under the second and third Five-Year Plans. They brought into being the third actor in the Indian economy, the state sector, which rivalled and then surpassed private capital and organized labour. As the 'new class' of a semi-socialist state, they were among its principal beneficiaries. In Marxist terms, the policy bureaucracy of the permanent government was a leading element of the progressive national bourgeoisie, dominating state policy and being rewarded for it. Its members shared a common lifestyle: they talked the same languages, not only the king's English, but also state capitalism, science and technology, and secularism. And they were 'committed' to the government's policies and programmes.

A distinguished member of the ICS entitled his administrative autobiography *Commitment My Style*. He found that the services were 'infinitely more efficient' following the departure of the British at independence. The reason was the enormous challenge and 'bursting promise' of administration at that time. 'It is policy and direction, integrity and depth, that give [the civil servant] cohesion and knit him, in spite of heterogeneity, to the thrust of effective, massive organization, pursuing and achieving difficult and complex tasks. ... It is in the failure of policy, direction and integrity' that 'our present [1973] malaise' is to be located.[49]

After Nehru's death (May 1964) and two successions (1964 and 1966), the alliance forged between a prime minister and a policy bureaucracy to build a powerful nation fell on evil days. It was shaken by the weak direction and confused initiatives of less able and confident national leadership and by the onset, even before Nehru's death, of Congress's decline, followed by the first signs of party alternation (in 1967).

Neutrality as a doctrine was a suitable rationalization for the transition from imperial rule to party government. It posed few problems so long as the one-party dominance put no strain on the loyalty of civil servants.[50] However, it began to be questioned when civil servants were asked to serve a variety of party masters in the states after 1967, and at the Centre after 1977. Mrs Gandhi successfully challenged the old guard state bosses by backing radical policies such as bank nationalization, split the Congress in November 1969, and

---

and con sides of the argument. See, for example, *Commitment My Style*, p. 133. For a detailed account of development work at the local level by senior officers, see Heginbotham, *Cultures in Conflict*.

[49]Rai, *Commitment My Style*, pp. viii, ix.

[50]For an account and explanation of bureaucratic responsiveness in the 1970s, see Dennis J. Encarnation, 'The Indian Central Bureaucracy: Responsive to Whom?' *Asian Survey*, 19 (11), 1979, pp. 1126–45.

then twice led the Congress to victory—first early in 1971 with the slogan 'abolish poverty', then in the 1972 'khaki election' that followed the Bangladesh war. It was in this context—of a weak and divided Congress organization and the striking early success of the plebiscitary politics that were to become her hallmark—that Mrs Gandhi called for a committed civil service. Speaking to the Congress parliamentary party, she referred to the administrative machinery as a stumbling block, adding that 'the country would be in a rut' if it followed the British system, in which civil servants were not supposed to be concerned with which political party was in power. Her then colleagues but future political opponents, the Congress's left leaders Chandra Shekhar and Mohan Dharia, joined her call for the 'creation of an administrative cadre committed to national objectives and responsive to our social needs'. 'The present bureaucracy, under the orthodox and conservative leadership of the ICS with its conservative upper-class prejudices can hardly be expected to meet the requirements of social and economic change along socialist lines.'[51] In 1972 the Gandhi government, in the name of equality, abolished by amendment the constitutionally protected perquisites of the ICS. The gesture was not only vindictive, but also gratuitous since only eighty ICS officers remained in service, but it had high symbolic payoffs for a leader professing socialism and egalitarianism.[52]

Mrs Gandhi was not satisfied when civil servants and public figures argued that neutrality meant giving one's best to the government of the day, from policy advice to ministers to programme implementation. For her, commitment went beyond active support for Congress programmes to belief that she, as party leader, carried a personal mandate from the people. She wanted a style of commitment more suited to a bureaucracy serving a single party and its leader than to one serving alternating-party governments.[53]

[51]Cited in C.P. Bhambhri, *Administrators in a Changing Society*, New Delhi: National Publishing House, 1972, p. 24. For a series of case studies that illuminate the relationships between senior bureaucrats and politicians, see also his *Bureaucracy and Politics in India*, New Delhi: Vikas, 1971.

[52]In September 1972, in a renewed effort, this time successful, to eliminate the guarantees Sardar Patel had insisted on putting in the 1950 constitution, the parliament passed the Former Secretary of State Service Officer (Conditions of Service) Bill. It became the Twentieth Amendment Act, 1972, revoking Article 314 of the constitution, which had committed the Indian state to maintain the same conditions of service and rights as those enjoyed by ICS officers under the British raj. As a result, ICS officers served under the less favourable terms applicable to IAS officers.

[53]D.P. Dhar, planning minister and a Gandhi loyalist, 'pleaded for a civil service which is committed not only to the policies and ideas enshrined in the Constitution but also the policies and programs of the ruling party which was backed by a majority of the people in the country' (quoted in Vishnu Sahay, 'What Does it Mean', *Seminar*, cited by K.K. Tummala, *The Ambiguity of Ideology and Administrative Reform*, Bombay: Allied, 1977, p. 177).

In the face of party deinstitutionalization and the rise of plebiscitary politics, she attempted to substitute state bureaucracies for party-based organizational support.

Mrs Gandhi also wanted commitment of the sort patrimonial rulers command: personal loyalty to herself and, from 1975, to her son Sanjay. This view of commitment fed and grew first on prudence, then on opportunism and, under the emergency, on fear. Better to show loyalty even to the extent of bending or breaking the law than risk disfavour or punishment by too principled a conduct.

When the Janata Party swept the Congress emergency regime from office in 1977, it further muddied the doctrinal waters, complicating and compounding the issue of appropriate behaviour for civil servants. It meant to restore the doctrine and practice of neutrality. In fact, it began to discipline or put on trial the civil service loyalists of the emergency era who had engaged in excesses. The Janata government favoured not just upright professionals, but also those committed to its own people and measures. Some of its ministers confused good ends with partisan advantage and correct procedure with victimization. When Mrs Gandhi returned to power in 1980, her party government, often invoking Janata examples and precedents, restored to office and favour those whom Janata had found most culpable.[54] As India

[54]The roster of national-level reassignments in 1975, 1977, and 1980 is long and complex, and they were by no means all *mala fide*. Illustrations of some widely considered to be so are the following: the abrupt removal of N.K. Mukherjee, ICS, as Home Secretary when the emergency was declared; Mukherjee was posted to the Department of Tourism. T.C.A. Srinivasavardhan, due to retire, was replaced as home secretary by M.H. Burney when Congress returned to power in 1980. Burney had been secretary, Ministry of Information and Broadcasting, a critical emergency department, and was considered an emergency stalwart. Burney was sent back to Orissa, to whose cadre he belonged, when Janata came to power. His next in line at the Ministry of Information and Broadcasting, M.K.N. Prasad, who handled press censorship under the emergency, was transferred by Janata to the relatively harmless Police Research Bureau. The director of the Central Bureau of Investigation under Janata was transferred by Congress in 1980 to his home state of Tamil Nadu. The most widely criticized 1980 Congress appointments were the promotion, over the seniority claims of many others, of P.S. Bhinder to police commissioner of Delhi, and the promotion of Jag Mohan, Delhi Development Commissioner under the emergency, to lieutenant governor of Delhi (a union territory). Both were close to Sanjay Gandhi and figured centrally in the Shah Commission's examination of emergency excesses. They were associated with Sanjay's beautification programmes that led, *inter alia*, to the highly controversial clearance of Muslim quarters around the Jama Masjid and Turkman Gate. Bhinder, in particular, was responsible for the police arrangements when many poor Muslims who rioted at Turkman Gate against slum clearance and vasectomy camps died as a result of police firing (*The Statesman*, 13 April 1980, and Government of India, Ministry of Home Affairs, *Shah Commission of Inquiry: Interim Report II* [Delhi, 1978], Chs 8 and 9, particularly pp. 96–101, 120–46). For a close account by a craftsmanly administrator in the emergency, see Mohan Mukerji, *Non-story of a Chief Secretary During Emergency, Etcetera*, New Delhi: Associated Publishing House, 1982.

entered the 1980s and victims became heroes and heroes victims, all three doctrines—neutrality, commitment, and loyalty—had to be reargued in the light of a transformed historical context.

With the rise of alternating-party or coalition governments, the need for a politically 'neutral' but *professionally* committed policy bureaucracy that can shift masters has become more pressing. India's interventionist, managerial state can no longer pretend that its policy bureaucracy is neutral in the sense of being anonymous and voiceless.[55] At the cabinet level, effective policy coordination and guidance requires officials who are loyal to the responsible minister, and committed to the minister's policies. But it also requires that ministers themselves be professional. In France, prime ministers and cabinet ministers have for some time drawn directors and chiefs of ministerial 'cabinets' from senior civil servants who seemed loyal to them personally, as well as committed to their policy objectives. It is assumed that if senior officials are to help a minister make and coordinate policy, they must loyally share the minister's interests, a mix of policy and politics distinct from and often in conflict with both the interests of the permanent bureaus, and the organized interests in relevant policy arenas.[56] In America, at least since the creation of the executive office of the president in 1939, loyal as well as committed president's men have been a legitimate feature of policy bureaucracies at the cabinet and subcabinet, as well as at the presidential level. Often drawn from outside the ranks of the senior civil service, policy intellectuals and professionals are chosen both for personal loyalty and for their special knowledge and policy commitment. They become members of a responsible political official's team, and are vital to that official's ability to make and control policy.[57] In Britain, the Fulton Commission recommended that civil servants publicly explain and defend government policy. India's Administrative

[55]Rajni Kothari believed that the cure for a rule-bound and routinized bureaucracy characterized by lack of trust, confidence, and spontaneity was a radical restructuring of the relationship between bureaucracy and party: 'The point of all this is to politicize the administration' (*Democratic Polity and Social Change in India*, Bombay: Allied, 1976, pp. 67–9). In the perspective of the 1980s, such a critique and cure need to address the balance between the legal obligations and programmatic obligations of civil servants on the one hand, and demands for purely partisan resource and patronage allocation on the other. In 'Where Are We Heading', *Express Magazine*, 29 November 1981, Kothari wrote a powerful polemic along lines similar to those advanced here. He argued for 'an institutional framework that protects the country from both the cult of personality and the politics of survival'.

[56]See Ezra N. Suleiman, *Politics, Power and Bureaucracy in France: The Administrative Elite*, Princeton: Princeton University Press, 1974, Chs 8 and 9, pp. 181–238.

[57]For an extended discussion of loyalty and team spirit in bureaucracies, see our 'Authority and Power in Bureaucratic and Patrimonial Administration: A Revisionist Interpretation of Weber on Bureaucracy', *World Politics*, 31, 1979.

Reforms Commission of 1966 failed to deal with the issue, recommending only that the present arrangements be properly adhered to.[58]

Policy innovation and coordination require an Indian version of the French and American institutional arrangements that will mitigate, if not eliminate, the struggle over neutrality, commitment, and loyalty. However, in the early 1980s, commitment and loyalty were not being interpreted in policy and professional terms. Instead, many ministers, behind a façade of policy concerns, were more interested in patronage that served partisan and personal interests. Loyalty and commitment became willingness on the part of civil servants to accommodate themselves to ministerial manipulations of this kind. Rajiv Gandhi's managerial orientation towards government, his reluctance to use the services for political and personal ends to the extent that his mother had done, and the resuscitation in 1985 and 1986 of the Administrative Reforms Commission's recommendations favouring professionalization and specialization of the services provided a more favourable climate for dealing with this issue.

The demand that the IAS shed its superior airs and become more 'socially representative' has been fulfilled in ways not anticipated by its proponents. The real salaries of senior officials both in the public services (IAS, Indian Foreign Service, Indian Police Service) and in public-sector enterprises declined significantly in the 1970s. The highly differential levels of 'dearness allowance'—the inflation equalizer in government salaries—had the effect of eroding the emoluments of lower-level clerks by 2 per cent, while those of higher officers and public-sector executives eroded by as much as 37 per cent. The ratio between the highest and lowest paid in government shrank from 15: 1 in 1973 to 10: 1 in 1978.[59] Only in 1986 was this erosion halted and reversed by the report of the pay commission.

The more socially representative political milieu of state governments also weakened the IAS' national orientation and professional ethos.[60] The ways in which civil servants are posted have enabled local politicians to

[58]The Administrative Reforms Commission found that the principal weakness of India's higher civil service (IAS) was the supremacy of the generalist and 'generalism'. Its solution was to recommend that specialists and experts be given more senior posts, and to call for more professionalism in the outlook and training of the senior bureaucracy (Government of India, Ministry of Home Affairs, Administrative Reforms Commission, *Report of the Study Team on the Machinery of the Government of India and Its Procedures at Work*, New Delhi, 1968), pt 2, vol. 1, pp. 106–7. See also Shriman Maheshwari, *The Administrative Reforms Commission*, Agra, India: Lakshmi Narain Agarwal, 1972. For an account that argues that professionalization leads to rigidity, and that criticizes insulation of bureaucracies, see Encarnation, 'Indian Central Bureaucracy'.

[59]Government of India, Ministry of Finance, *Study Group on Wages, Incomes and Prices: Report*, Delhi, 1978, Tables 14, 15. (This is generally referred to as the Boothalingam Report.)

[60]For an early intimation of this problem, see Taub, *Bureaucrats under Stress*.

appropriate administration to partisan and personal ends. Frequent transfers, which render the life of a civil servant more difficult by disrupting the schooling of his or her children as well as the routines of their lives, have long been used by influential politicians to bring to heel or oust inflexible officers who resist inappropriate requests for resource allocation.

The 1984 crisis in the Punjab made it clear that civil and police services were incapable of maintaining public order. One cause was the capture of the services by local factions and communities. The formula for allocating officers of the centrally recruited but state-assigned IAS required that persons from the state not make up more than 50 per cent of the state cadre. The rationale for the formula was 'to insure that officials were not subject to local pressures and took a more objective and national view'.[61] When Prime Minister Gandhi addressed an extraordinary meeting of secretaries to the Government of India soon after the Indian army had battled its way into the Golden Temple in June 1984, she 'voiced concern over the growing tendency on the part of state government to dilute the original formula by not only reducing the proportion of officers hailing from other states but also making a systematic effort to remove them from key administrative positions'.[62] She revealed that the fifty-fifty rule had been breached to the extent that 70 rather than 50 per cent of IAS officers were serving in their state of origin.

The public services have not always strengthened the state as entrepreneur. The inability of the IAS to manage undertakings in the enormous public sector efficiently and profitably has contributed to the erosion of the Indian state. But for a few exceptional years, India's public sector has been in the red. Over the thirty-year period between 1950 and 1980, the incremental capital-output ratio for India as a whole has deteriorated, but in the public sector the position is considerably worse. For the economy as a whole, the ratio has roughly doubled (from 2.79 to 6.22), while in the public sector it has more than tripled (from 3.12 to 10.58).[63] We have discussed in Chapter 1 the disputes over the meaning of these figures. Many critics have attributed some portion of this failure to the role of generalist IAS officers in public-sector undertakings. This role is played at two levels, policy guidance and the management of firms. Public-sector firms, instead of being allowed to operate autonomously, have been brought de facto under the close supervision of government ministries, whose IAS officer-secretaries to government not only guide long-term policy—which is appropriate—but also intervene in

---

[61]*The Hindu*, 23 June 1984.
[62]Ibid.
[63]P.R. Brahmananda, *Productivity in the Indian Economy*, Bombay: Himalaya Publishing House, 1982, Table 19.02.

day-to-day decisions. As a former chairman of the Food Corporation of India, one of the largest public-sector undertakings, has observed, 'Generally the ministries adopt a superior fatherly attitude, trying to run the whole show. The autonomy of [public-sector undertakings] is reduced to a myth, since all decisions of importance and magnitude are taken by them.'[64]

The management of public-sector firms requires career professionals who combine technical knowledge with long-term experience in particular technologies and industries, such as steel, oil, transportation, and mining. The IAS officers do not possess such knowledge and skills, and their career experience fails to develop it. The insulation of IAS generalists from an understanding of their relevant specialties is illustrated by the career patterns of the officers in the Ministry of Information and Broadcasting, charged with overseeing Doordarshan, India's state-run television. In 1983, all three of the ministry's senior officers left before completing two years of service in that post. One had come from the chairmanship of the State Electricity Board of Madhya Pradesh and gone on to become secretary in the Coal Department; one had come from being commissioner of a division in Maharashtra and returned to manage that state's State Finance Corporation; and another had come from district administration and left for a training course abroad. 'It is hardly to be expected,' wrote the Joshi Working Group on Doordarshan, 'that the problems of Doordarshan ... can be appreciated and resolved by such birds of passage.'[65]

The generalist traditions of IAS officers and the frequency with which they are transferred militate against their performance as managers of the still-expanding public sector. At the level of the states, IAS officers occupy 75 per cent of the posts of chief executive officers of public-sector firms, and their average tenure in such posts is fifteen months.[66] Occasionally, a good IAS officer is exempted from the rapid turnover characteristic of the service and can develop expertise via extended incumbency, but such experiences are the exception.

In 1986, the Rajiv Gandhi government introduced measures to address the professional quality of the services and insulate them from inappropriate

[64]R.N. Chopra, *Public Sector in India*, New Delhi: Intellectual Publishing House, 1983, p. 85. For an account of conflict between the IAS and technical officers in the public sector, see Howard Erdman, 'Politics and Industrial Management: The IAS in Joint Sector Fertilizer Companies', *Journal of the Institute of Public Enterprises*, January–March 1986.

[65]'An Indian Personality for Television: Report of the Working Group on Software for Doordarshan', pt 2, published unofficially in *Mainstream*, 14, 21, and 28 April 1984, and May 1984 (Nehru no.).

[66]K.S. Bhat, 'Tenure of the Chief Executives and Composition of the Board: Two Issues in SLPE Corporate Management', Hyderabad, 1984, mimeograph. The author is on the faculty of the Institute of Public Enterprise, Osmania University Campus.

political pressures. Many of these measures were based on the recommendations of the Administrative Reforms Commission of 1966. The government proposed to prevent frequent transfers of officers, protect them against appropriation by local interests, encourage specialization, and break the monopoly of the IAS on the highest positions by opening alternative recruitment channels for high-quality candidates from technical services and the non-government sector. Only time can tell whether these measures will survive opposition and achieve their goal.[67]

India was endowed at independence with a permanent government that surpassed that of other Third World countries and rivalled those of many industrial democracies. The forces that have challenged the services since independence, such as the call for partisan and personal commitment and regional loyalty, are powerful and long-term. They have taken their toll, but they have not as yet prevailed.

WASTING ASSETS: THE EROSION OF STATE INSTITUTIONS

The Indian state has experienced two contrasting political eras between independence in 1947 and the assassination of Prime Minister Indira Gandhi in 1984, one associated with Jawaharlal Nehru, and the other with his daughter, Indira Gandhi. When Nehru died in 1964, he had been prime minister for seventeen years. The national press used the twentieth anniversary of his death in May 1984—when Mrs Gandhi had been prime minister for sixteen years—as an occasion to compare the ideas and practices of these two eras. It found profound differences in ideals and conduct. Regardless of whether this judgment was warranted or had taken adequate account of different conditions, it was widely held. More importantly, perceptions construct reality by shaping expectations and behaviour. Public perceptions of the Indian state have changed dramatically since the mid-1960s.

Nehru's advocacy of scientific rationalism and of principled, purposeful politics, and his respect for persons and means influenced the conduct of

---

[67]In January of 1986, the Ministry of Personnel and Administrative Reforms proposed a scheme by which newly appointed IAS officers would have no more than three appointments in their first eleven years, including the two probationary years; new entrants would be encouraged to specialize; senior officers in their seventeenth year would be subject to 'data based performance assessment' before further promotion; officers would be selected into an 'integrated management pool' from the three all-India services (Indian Police Service, IAS, Indian Forest Service) and other central services on the basis of proven administrative ability to fill senior positions in the administration; and entrants to the all-India services would be assigned to one of five zonal cadres instead of the present practice of assignment to a state, to break up the locality-based cliques and factions into which officers are now frequently drawn (*The Times of India*, 29 January 1986; *The Statesman*, 18 and 29 January 1986).

politics in his day. For him, the procedures of parliamentary democracy and a federal constitution were both civilizing and a means to express and realize values in politics and society. He became teacher and mentor to the political class of his day. As Raj Mohan Gandhi wrote, 'As Prime Minister for seventeen years he strove hard to coach Chief Ministers, MPs, MLAs [member, (state) legislative assembly] and the masses in the norms of democracy. The letters he wrote to the Chief Ministers almost every fortnight are for the most part lessons in democratic procedure.'[68]

Indira Gandhi's political aspirations and practice made a striking contrast, a contrast which she recognized. Her father was, she once said, a 'saint strayed into politics'. As he never had to struggle, 'he lacked the necessary ruthlessness'.[69] This she was able to supply. She even acted out the negative identity that Nehru had depicted in his anonymous article when he said that with the adulation of crowds ringing in his ears, he could easily become a dictator.[70]

Unlike her father, Mrs Gandhi depleted India's political capital by eroding the autonomy, professional standards, and procedural norms of political institutions and state agencies. She tried to make those responsible for parliament, the courts, the civil services, and the federal system answerable to her. The effort succeeded, to varying degrees, in orienting their conduct to her personal will. A paradoxical consequence was to diminish the legitimacy and effectiveness of the state. Centralization based on personal loyalty and obedience to a monocratic executive lessened the state's capacity to amplify itself through multiple agencies extending beyond the limited control and attention of one person. Jawaharlal Nehru was the schoolmaster of parliamentary government, Indira Gandhi its truant.

The changing political environment between the nationalist era and the 1980s also contributed to the erosion of state institutions. Nationalist politicians were gradually supplanted by professional ones, who in turn were joined and to an extent displaced by condottieri seeking personal profit. The men and women of the nationalist era who continued to lead the country in the 1950s and 1960s had been socialized at a time when dedication to ideal goals and public service shaped political expectations and careers. In practical terms, there was nothing to gain and much to lose by becoming a nationalist politician. Under the raj, joining the nationalist movement meant sacrificing conventional career opportunities and risking jail. It meant pursuing goals that transcended self-interest and personal benefit. A

[68]*The Statesman*, 28 May 1984.
[69]Ibid.
[70]See n. 34 above.

generation of professional politicians emerged in the 1960s. They included Lal Bahadur Shastri, prime minister after Nehru's death; Kamaraj Nadar, the Congress president who presided over the 1964 and 1966 successions; and other state chief ministers and party leaders, including the members of the so-called syndicate that Indira Gandhi bested and 'purged' in November 1969. They pursued power, prestige, and sometimes wealth by serving and satisfying the status and economic demands of their diverse and expanding constituencies. By the 1980s, the era of A.R. Antulay and Ramrao Adik,[71] the erstwhile chief and deputy chief ministers in Maharashtra who came to epitomize the venality and degraded personal conduct to which Congress party 'loyalists' could descend, politics had become a lucrative career. On the one hand, MPs and MLAs, besides receiving substantial salaries and allowances, received extensive perquisites—housing, telephones, travel, medical care, and medicine—which they used not only for themselves and their supporters, but also for their families and friends.[72] Public facilities—from elegant modern guest houses to plain *dak* bungalows—were increasingly appropriated for the private comforts and pleasures of the families of legislators. Ministerial positions in the states—as many as one-third of the governing party's state legislators—and directorships of state public undertakings were now being used extensively to provide even greater benefits and opportunities for patronage and income. On the other hand, huge amounts of black (underground economy) money were collected for political and campaign expenses, and private gain.

Sanjay Gandhi's choices of legislators and chief ministers in the 1980 elections crystallized earlier trends by providing the new class of political condottieri with an institutional base. Politics became attractive to those unscrupulous enough to subvert, by corruption and violence, the procedures and institutions designed to protect civility and a government of laws. The effect on the system of government of Rajiv Gandhi's succession in 1984 to the prime ministership was considerable. His self-image as an advocate of technocratic and managerial solutions led him to address the long agenda of administrative reform and institution-building that his

[71]Antulay resigned from his post as chief minister of Maharashtra after the Bombay high court held him culpable in exchanging cement allocations for party funds. He was later tried for extorting funds from businesses for the Pratibha Pratisthan Maharashtra, a trust said to support deserving artists and performers. After one dismissal by the Supreme Court, the case was still in the courts in April 1985 (*Asian Recorder*, 2–8 July 1985, p. 18391). Deputy Chief Minister Adik resigned after allegations of drunken and lascivious behaviour to, from, and at an international trade fair in Germany. See *India Today*, 15 May 1984, pp. 20–4, for accounts of Antulay's and Adik's conduct.

[72]See, for example, 'Uttar Pradesh, Milking the State', *India Today*, 31 May 1984, pp. 76–9.

mother ignored in her struggles for political survival. He is not seen, as his brother was, as a leader of the condottieri, and he recognizes, as his mother did not, that India can only be governed by significant sharing of power. The question is whether he can convert his strong commitment to institutions and professionalization into policies and programmes.

State institutions and procedures were unevenly affected by the corrosive process that set in after Nehru's death, and the forces and agents were multiple. Our account in this chapter will attend to the armed services, the Election Commission's role in the conduct of free and fair elections, the police, legislatures (parliament and state assemblies), and the federal system. We have already discussed the civil service, especially the IAS, and the judiciary will be examined. One corrosive force has been the long-term trend towards higher levels of mobilization, which will be documented. An increasingly active electorate found agitational politics more accessible, and often more effective than parliamentary politics for making demands and shaping policy. Professional politicians were able to ignore crucial distinctions between public authority and private power in pursuit of partisan goals. To establish his leadership in the 1960s, Punjab Chief Minister Pratab Singh Kairon politicized the police and civil service in the name of rapid development. He succeeded on both fronts. By 1984, when Punjab was threatened by terrorism and civil war, it became apparent that the Punjab services, particularly the police, had lost the capacity to act as professionals. In Bihar, under the aegis of corrupt or ineffectual chief ministers, locally dominant caste and landed elites have de facto appropriated police power in their struggles with increasingly assertive and resistant dependent castes and classes. Bihar's jails have acquired a national and international reputation for political bias and official violence. High-minded politicians of left persuasion also contributed to the erosion of state institutions. Mohan Kumaramangalam and H.R. Gokhale, central ministers close to the prime minister, provided the ideology and techniques for politicizing the judiciary in the name of social justice. Anticipating Indira Gandhi's advocacy of the same doctrine, Mohan Dharia, then a Congress socialist, weakened the claims of civil-service professionalism by attacking neutrality in the name of 'commitment'.

These initiatives were not necessarily undertaken with the thought of weakening the state or eroding constitutional democracy and parliamentary government, but their effect was to subordinate institutional autonomy, professionalism, and impartial procedures to the partisan and personal pursuit of power. For Kairon, insistence on correct means and recognition of professional standards was the failing of ineffective politicians; for Kumaramangalam and Gokhale, judicial autonomy the hypocritical self-protection of bourgeois interests. The Westminster version of the golden rule that Nehru practised, to treat opponents as he would be treated by them, and Mohandas Gandhi's preoccupation with personal ethics, were declared unsuited to the conditions of Third World countries or India's genius. 'The dominant literati traditions of India' reasserted themselves, Ashis Nandy wrote, through a statecraft 'sanctified by the amoral, dispassionate politics preached in the Arthasastra ... the Brahmanic concept of politics has always been that of a zero sum game ... the Gandhian tradition in this sense is an aberration.'[73] The paradox is that politics pursued in the name of realpolitik and a hard state reduced state legitimacy and institutional capacity.

Institutional autonomy depends on the viability of professionalism, which has become increasingly at risk in the face of populist and personalistic politics. The quality of the military services, police, civil service, courts, and parliament depends on professional commitment. Professionalism implies a body of knowledge that is to be mastered by apprenticeship or formal education, control over recruitment and training, through the criteria of adequate and inadequate performance, of which the professionals themselves are the main judges, and an informal ethos as well as formal rules to govern what professionals regard as technically and ethically correct conduct in their relationship with their clients or superiors. Since the application of professional criteria can serve to control entry, exit, and professional standing, and thus to allocate status, power, and income, professional autonomy can promote monopoly and privilege. Professions require regulation—societal control—if they are to serve rather than merely profit by society. Even so, professionalism requires a certain insulation from societal demands and political pressures. Democratic politicians distrust professionalism, which they find inimical to the responsiveness appropriate to democratic institutions and popular sovereignty. So do politicians for whom personal loyalty and compliance count for more than professional performance. From the late 1960s, both kinds of politicians contributed to the erosion of professional and institutional autonomy.

THE MILITARY
The military services have been least affected by politicization, the call for partisan or personal political commitments to supersede professionalism, and the appropriation of state authority and resources on their behalf. However, even the military, in the last decade, has suffered from a dilution of professionalism as it has been called in 'in aid of the civil'. Two crucial

[73]'Indira Gandhi and the Culture of Indian Politics', in Ashis Nandy, *At the Edge of Psychology: Essays in Politics and Culture*, New Delhi: Oxford University Press, 1980, p. 114.

decisions were made at independence. Professional commitment was rewarded and political commitment discouraged when the British Indian Army was transformed into the Army of Free India, and when the officers of the INA, commanded by Subhas Chandra Bose, were excluded from appointment in it (see the section on liberal and authoritarian options).[74] Political commitment was again discredited in October 1962 when the allegedly politically motivated appointment of General B.N. Kaul to command the army corps on the border facing China became associated with the failure of Indian arms in the 1962 war with China.[75] The negative example of military rule in Pakistan may have helped bring home the importance of keeping the generals out of politics, and politics out of the army.[76] When Sanjay Gandhi—who occupied no official position but exercised power by virtue of dynastic politics—used his connection with Defence Minister Bansi Lal to insinuate himself into national security decisions under the emergency of 1975–7, senior commanders resisted the attempt.

The military, by being radically enclaved, is more insulated from its political environment than the permanent government. Military personnel undergo long courses of training in separate educational institutions; they live in cantonments, isolated from surrounding towns; they mess together; they are encouraged to develop a distinctive subculture and regimental loyalties. They are sheltered from the pervasive populist demands for democratic responsiveness that affect other state services.

Even so, the armed services are not immune to politicization and threats to their professional standing. Some military promotions in the 1980s have

[74] See Mason, *Matter of Honour*.

[75] Defence Minister V.K. Krishna Menon, who presumably saw to Kaul's appointment as corps commander, was forced to resign over the deplorable state of readiness of the forces and the poor military leadership and performance. There was sentiment inside and outside the army that the appointment of Kaul to command the forces facing China at the moment of imminent crisis was based on his connection with Menon and with his fellow Kashmiri, Prime Minister Jawaharlal Nehru, rather than on professional considerations. Some thought Kaul was being groomed to become the chief of army staff. Kaul was relieved from command of IV Corps on 20 November 1962 by Lieutenant General Chaudhuri, who had just been appointed chief of army staff, replacing General P.N. Thapar, who resigned on 19 November. Kaul resigned from the army rather than accept the training command Chaudhuri offered to him. See Llyod I. Rudolph and Susanne Hoeber Rudolph, 'Generals and Politicians in India', *Pacific Affairs*, 37, 1964; Lt. General B.N. Kaul, *The Untold Story*, Bombay: Allied, 1967; Neville Maxwell, *India's China War*, New York: Anchor, 1972; and J.P. Dalvi, *Himalyan Blunder*, Calcutta: Thacker, 1969.

[76] See Stephen P. Cohen, *The Indian Army: Its Contribution to the Development of a Nation*, Berkeley and Los Angeles: University of California Press, 1971, and the same author's more recent assessment, 'The Military', in *Indira Gandhi's India: A Political System Appraisal*, by Henry C. Hart (ed.), Boulder, Colo.: Westview, 1976. See also 'Using the Army', *Seminar*, 308, (April), 1985.

attracted criticism.[77] Since the military services are volunteer as well as professional bodies, they depend for their viability on the market for pay and prestige. In the *enrichez vous* environment of the new India, modest pay scales and the invitation to a career of service make it increasingly difficult to compete for talent with more lucrative and less rigorous career lines. In consequence, the class character of the Indian army has changed over the last decade. As middle-class students stayed away from officer careers and headed for private business, they left the officer corps to the sons of non-commissioned and junior commissioned officers who were themselves recruited from the peasantry. The army has always had opportunities for corruption, both in recruitment and in the negotiation of arms purchases. These have increased and been more exploited with the growth of personal and institutional corruption in Indian politics and, some say, as a consequence of the changing educational and class composition of the army.[78]

Most hazardous for the professional nature of the army has been its steadily increasing interventions 'in aid of the civil power'. Stephen Cohen has documented the increasing deployments of the army to aid the civilian government in communal unrest arising out of religious, cultural, linguistic, and caste confrontations. His account shows heavy use of the military in civilian disturbances between 1973 and 1975 (fourteen cases), and again between 1980 and 1984 (fourteen, excluding 'continuing' cases such as Assam and Punjab). His account also documents that, over the last eight years, the army has often been called in to pacify or disarm the forces of law and order, as in the police strikes in Gujarat, Tamil Nadu, and Bombay, or strikes by paramilitary forces such as the Central Reserve Police. The army's seizure of the Golden Temple, the Sikh holy shrine, in 1984 and its continuous role in Assam from 1980 onwards placed something like forty million people under army rule.

These interventions bear witness to the increased levels of mobilization and the irregular and extra-institutional protests of the last decade, and to the declining legitimacy of the state.

[77]There was, for example, some controversy over the retirement of General Krishna Rao as chief of army staff in 1983, when the succession was decided in favour of the less senior General A.S. Vaidya and against the more senior General S.K. Sinha, vice-chief of army staff and generally considered in line for the chief of staff position, who resigned. The appointment was said to have been affected by personal and political considerations, which was regarded as unfortunate by members of the service. (See *The Indian Express*, 18 July [editorial] and 29 July [letter], 1984; and see General Sinha's article in *The Statesman*, 2 May 1984.) The appointment of General T.N. Raina over more senior officers in 1975 was controversial for the same reason.

[78]Stephen P. Cohen, 'The Military and Indian Democracy', Paper presented at the Conference on India's Democracy, Princeton University, 14–16 March 1985. The next paragraph draws on this account.

'It is tempting,' writes Cohen, 'to ask the military to serve political ends—increasingly as saviors of the law and order situation—but each such request further politicizes the military by bringing them into too close contact with civilian society and by placing more and more civilian tasks in their hands.'

Yet, while the military services face difficulties, their professional standing and autonomy have been less seriously compromised than have those of other services and institutions.

THE ELECTORAL PROCESS

The electoral process has also resisted the trend towards erosion of state institutions. The record of free and fair elections in India stands comparison with any Third World and most First World countries. Counting the 1984 election, eight national elections have been held since independence in 1947, and incumbent governments have been turned out of office at the Centre and in the states. Complaints of intimidation, the buying of votes, and the unfair uses of incumbency are frequently heard and sometimes documented, but no one has suggested that electoral verdicts have not generally reflected voter preferences.

Free India started its electoral life with a constitutionally independent body, the Election Commission (Article 324), to supervise the entire procedure and machinery for national and state elections. The statutory provisions for the removal of the election commissioner make him independent of the government of the day, and help keep elections free from partisan political influence. The commissioner is supported by a small professional staff of career civil servants. The commission depends on thousands of local officials deputed by the several state governments for registering voters and conducting elections. In the mid-1980s, the commission began to search for ways to protect the conduct of elections from the increasingly partisan and factional encroachments condoned or encouraged by incumbent state governments.[79] The election commissioner proposed that president's rule be substituted for state government rule some months before scheduled elections to obviate such encroachments. So pervasive is the problem of partisan influence on state officials that critics immediately responded that the party in power at the Centre could use president's rule to assist its own state parties.[80] The criticism gained strength in 1984, when Indira Gandhi's Congress-I government toppled opposition governments in Sikkim, Kashmir,

[79]See reports of Commissioner R.K. Triveldi's conference in December 1983 of seven national, seventeen regional, and eight registered parties (*The Statesman*, 4 December 1983).
[80]*The Times of India*, 13 December 1983; *The Indian Express*, 15 December 1983; *Hindustan Times*, 15 December 1983.

and Andhra Pradesh, in preparation, it was alleged, for the upcoming eighth parliamentary election in December.

The commission is concerned not only with the integrity of the electoral process, but also with assuring that those elected act in ways that guarantee the meaningfulness of the choices made by voters. The most important issues here are floor crossing and defections based on questionable motives and problematic inducements. The 1983 uproar over the 'Moily tapes', which recorded an effort by a Congress party leader in Karnataka to bring down the incumbent government by buying off its supporters, publicly documented a widely practised offence.[81] Defections have frequently jeopardized the integrity of the electoral process by substituting perquisites of office and material gain for electoral choice in determining a legislator's political commitment.

The powers of incumbency have been used not only to influence state officials in their conduct of elections, but also to influence voters directly by the timely allocations of benefits. National commentators interpreted a series of moves by the Indira Gandhi government in 1984 as being designed to influence the upcoming eighth parliamentary election: a sudden and controversial nationalization of thirteen closed and 'sick' textile mills in and around Bombay that put their workers back to work, a 25 per cent wage increase for 500,000 government-employed coal miners, and the dispersal of unsecured loans to tens of thousands of educated unemployed at 'loan fairs' throughout the country.

The incumbent party at the Centre has taken advantage of the government's monopoly over radio and television broadcasting to portray itself in a favourable light.[82] In the name of promoting development, the electronic media has featured incumbent leaders and governmental programmes at the expense of opposition criticism and alternatives to them. Opposition and independent access has been both sparse and closely monitored. Central control of the electronic media makes it difficult for opposition governments in the states of India's federal system to use the radio or television to portray their personalities. Only during the three weeks of national and state election campaigns can the time allocated by the Election Commission to opposition party spokesmen modestly offset the incumbent government's monopoly position.

[81] Following the revelation of the taped conversations of Veerappa Moily, leader of the Congress Party in Karnataka, offering a Rs 200,000 bribe to C. Byre Gowda to defect from the Janata Party and join the Congress, the late Congress-I party secretary C.M. Stephen, an articulate defender of the doctrine that all means are justified in politics, asserted the right of his party to encourage defection (*The Times of India*, 20 November 1985).

[82] For a critique of the central control of the electronic media, see 'An Indian Personality for Television'.

In summary, the independent position of the Election Commission has enabled it to resist the general trend towards institutional erosion. However, its ability to maintain free and fair elections has become more difficult. The Rajiv Gandhi government's early moves in 1985 to protect the electoral process by enacting several measures long demanded by the Election Commission suggested a reversal in trends. A bill was enacted, which obliges legislators to forfeit their seats if they defect (with or without payoffs) from the party for which they were elected. Another bill legalized corporate party donations, thus driving the process of party and electoral finances above ground, where it can be regulated. While both measures are likely to have only an incremental effect, they suggest a new attention to institutional autonomy.

THE POLICE

The police are the principal agents of the state's internal sovereignty. Their capacity to ensure the security of persons and property, to maintain law and order, and to play an active yet fair role in the administration of justice are leading indicators of both the legitimacy and viability of the state. Insofar as the police have lost the capacity to do these things, the state is in trouble.

The erosion of the police as a professional force has been a long and gradual process. It is not clear whether the quality of the police at the middle and lower levels—among the almost 90 per cent who are constables—is different or worse than it was eighty years ago.[83] The Police Commission of 1902–3 'found strong evidence of widespread corruption in the police particularly among Station House Officers throughout the country'.[84] What is clear is that the performance of the higher ranks has declined since independence, and that organized public opinion as well as the 'weaker sections' in many villages now demand a higher standard of police performance at all levels.

Constitutional responsibility for public order and police is vested in the states of the federal system. They have the primary responsibility for recruitment, training, posting, transfer, pay, and conditions of service. The constitutionally drawn line separating the state from central responsibility for public order and the police is blurred by the existence of central police services such as the Border Security Force and the Central Reserve Police, and by the Centre's responsibility for the Indian Police Service, one of three all-India services. An elite cadre, members of the Indian Police Service occupy

[83]Government of India, Ministry of Home Affairs, *Seventh Report of the National Police Commission*, Delhi, 1982, p. 7 (supplement note). For a careful overall view, see David H. Bayley, *The Police and Political Development in India*, Princeton: Princeton University Press, 1969.

[84]*Third Report of the National Police Commission*, Delhi, 1980, p. 25.

the senior police posts in the states and staff certain specialized police organizations at the Centre, such as those concerned with intelligence. However, they constitute a miniscule fraction of the total number of police, and a small proportion of officers.[85] Much of the responsibility for the crisis in the police rests with the states.

Today's police must deal with a dissatisfied public, more than 70 per cent of which believed in 1978 that the police are corrupt as well as partial towards rich and influential people.[86] The higher ranks must also deal with politicians who use their power to protect personal, partisan, and factional interests. In the words of the National Police Commission, politicians weaken

the normal chain of command. ... Interference at the operational level in police stations, police circles, etc. results in the total by-passing of the supervisory officers in the hierarchy. ... The frequent by-passing of the normal chain of command results in the atrophy of the supervisory structure. It, therefore, fails to operate effectively even in matters which do not attract any such extraneous interference.[87]

According to a note circulated in June 1979 by the Ministry of Home Affairs at a conference of chief ministers convened in the wake of police insurrections in several states,

there is a feeling in all States that interference not only in the matter of postings and transfers but also in the matter of arrests, investigations and filing of charge sheets is widespread. The principal grievance of the policemen is that if there is any unwillingness to comply with unlawful or improper suggestions the persons concerned are harassed and humiliated.[88]

These remarks may attribute too much responsibility to the machinations of politicians in explaining the deterioration of police professionalism. There have been professional failures within the police force itself, failures that are in part due to state and national governments' failures to provide policy leadership, and the resources and attention required to maintain the professional capabilities of the police. At the same time, the National Police Commission's remarks about ubiquitous political interference reflect widely felt perceptions within and outside the police force. These developments are associated with a significant absolute increase in the number of police, especially those controlled by the central government. Between 1970–1

[85]The total number of Indian Police Service officers in 1978 was 2,344 (*Sixth Report of the National Police Commission*, Delhi, 1982, appendix, p. 59).

[86]*Third Report of the National Police Commission*, p. 26.

[87]*Second Report of the National Police Commission*, Delhi, 1979, p. 24.

[88]Ibid., p. 25.

and 1975–6, central expenditure on the police doubled from Rs 101.6 to 209.1 crore, and it doubled again to Rs 424 crore, by 1982–3.[89] Myron Weiner has estimated that in the mid-1970s the centrally controlled police numbered 600,000, and those under the control of state governments numbered 750,000.[90]

The increase in special police and paramilitary forces has threatened as well as promoted internal peace. Since the mid-1970s, police strikes or strikes by special constabularies have occurred almost on an annual basis, and often constabularies have been pitted against each other. In the 1978 strike by the Central Reserve Police Force in Tamil Nadu, the police were unwilling to act against them, and two battalions of the Border Security Force had to settle the matter. Police strikes occurred in Gujarat in 1979, in Tamil Nadu in 1979, and in Bombay in 1982; strikes by various special constabularies (Central Reserve Police Force, Central Industrial Security Force) occurred in 1979 and 1980.[91]

One of the purposes behind building up central police forces was to release the military from the civil responsibilities of maintaining the peace in difficult political circumstances that might compromise them professionally and politically. This purpose has been at best only partially realized; the army, after almost a year of martial law rule in the Punjab, was still used to quell civil strife. In June 1984 it stormed the Sikh's premier shrine, the Golden Temple in Amritsar, an action that resulted not only in heavy casualties, but also in revolts by Sikh recruits and, indirectly, in the assassination five months later of Prime Minister Indira Gandhi.

Ordinary politicization has made considerable inroads into the standing and professionalism of the police. Perhaps more important has been the 'higher politicization' associated with exploiting atrocities against the poor and oppressed to gain political advantage in national and state politics. One might expect that national attention focused on crimes against the poor and oppressed would benefit them by making local oppression visible, and thereby strengthen the hand of the police in combating such crimes. Instead, national attention has encouraged manipulation of both victims and the police.

Publicizing police failures at the Centre or state levels has become a way of incriminating one's political opponents. Paul Brass, in a close examination of the infamous Narainpur incident, shows how the political strategy of publicizing alleged atrocities for political gain was perfected. In

[89]Reserve Bank of India, *Report on Currency and Finance, 1983–84*, Bombay, 1985, vol. 7, statement 80, p. 107.

[90]Myron Weiner, 'India's New Political Institutions', *Asian Survey*, 16, 1976.

[91]For a complete account of police and constabulary strikes, see Cohen, 'Military and Indian Democracy', p. 40.

Narainpur, a Muslim village with a substantial Scheduled Caste population, villagers and police clashed after an old woman was hit and killed by a bus. Uttar Pradesh, where Narainpur is located, was controlled at the time by a Janata government, the Congress-I's electoral enemy. The events occurred shortly after the Congress-I comeback victory in the 1980 national parliamentary elections, but before the June state assembly elections in nine states. According to Sanjay Gandhi's account after he and his mother inspected Narainpur in a widely publicized visit: 'There was not a single girl or woman ... who was not raped.'[92] His remarks bore no relationship to the facts as ascertained by an investigative commission,[93] or to what Brass had learned at Narainpur: it is doubtful that anyone was raped, and no one was killed. These events set a new national standard in the political manipulation of alleged local violence by preparing the ground rhetorically for the dismissal of the Janata in Uttar Pradesh, an event that was followed by the dismissal of opposition governments in the remaining eight states and by Congress-I victories in the June elections.

After Congress-I's return to power at the Centre and in most states, it became apparent that atrocities occurred as much under the Congress as under opposition governments. Opposition politicians were able to exploit for a time the law and order failures of the 'government that works', but soon overuse so devalued the currency that public attention and concern faded. Politicization of atrocities further eroded police autonomy and professionalism, and thereby lessened the prospect of crimes against 'weaker sections' being prevented or punished.

In the interstices of these pressures, the public has come to believe that 'complaints at police stations will not be registered', and that investigations of those that are registered will be 'apathetic, dilatory and protracted'. In national politics, the police have acquired a reputation as being the prime instrument of a lawless state and of state violence. They are charged with the torture and illegal detention of accused persons,[94] the rape of poor women who are suspects or witnesses, the widespread use of 'encounter' killings to remove opponents of local political notabilities or inconvenient elements, the incapacity to control lawless gangs in several northern states and deal

---

[92]*Leader*, 1 February 1980, cited in Brass, Paul, 'National Power and Local Politics in India: A Twenty-Year Perspective', Paper presented at the Institute of Commonwealth Studies, University of London, 1982, p. 13.

[93]*The Hindu*, 9 February 1980.

[94]Thus, a random example of Bihar administration of the sort one used to hear from indifferently administered princely states such as Udaipur in the 1920s, is that of Rudal Shah, who suffered fourteen years of unlawful incarceration after being acquitted in 1968. Shah had the unique luck of having his case brought to the attention of the Supreme Court in 1982 by a law student (*The Times of India*, 4 August 1983).

with the increasingly frequent train and bus robberies, and, finally, the failure to deal with terrorism in Punjab. These charges brought the Indian police into disrepute in the late 1970s and early 1980s to an extent unparalleled in their history.

Some of the problems are due to the recruitment, structure, and conditions of the services, which were addressed at length by the police commission. The ordinary constables who make up the force are under-educated, under-trained, and underpaid. The structure of the force is weak at its middle and lower-middle levels, where a higher standard of professional training is needed.

However, the problems are also due to the fact that India is conducting its social revolution in an incremental fashion, through decentralized and sporadic disorder rather than a concentrated revolutionary act. The Indian social structure is being challenged from both below and above. The challenge from below comes from social classes that are no longer willing to bear their poverty and oppression compliantly, and who resist economic and social injustice. The challenge from above comes from legislation—agrarian reforms, provisions favouring untouchables and backward classes—that enables the demands of the underprivileged. The increase in riots between 1965 and 1977 from 33,000 to 80,000 per annum, the increase in incidents of student indiscipline from 271 in 1965 to 10,600 in 1980; and the increase in workdays lost by strikes from 6.5 million in 1965 to 29.2 million in 1981 are all indicative of the social turmoil the public must face. A weakened professional force must mediate sporadic class and community conflicts in which its own cadres have divided loyalties.

With all that said, even critical accounts acknowledge that there are honest, responsible officers, capable of inspiring ordinary police cadres with a sense of mission and obligation. Such officers have to cope with a maze of local and higher-level loyalties, interests, and powerful persons, and with poorly educated, poorly trained, and poorly equipped personnel. Elected politicians and their party governments have so far found it easier to misuse the police politically than to support them professionally. The Indian state is paying the price for these failures in declining legitimacy and effectiveness.

PARLIAMENT

Parliamentary life has deteriorated in Delhi, and even more so in the state capitals. The parliament in India at independence was an honoured institution, rooted in the 'moderate' stream of Indian nationalism. Its leading exponent and Mohandas Gandhi's political guru, G.K. Gokhale, was widely admired by his nationalist generation for his artful parliamentary practice and budgetary analysis. Nehru was as much committed to the ideas of the moderates as he was to socialist ideals. At independence, the Constituent Assembly overwhelmingly chose to reaffirm India's prior experience with parliamentary forms of representative government. To be sure, parliament was not the only institution that determined leadership and policy. The Indian National Congress, against Mohandas Gandhi's advice to dissolve itself at independence, continued instead as a political party contesting for power in the new state. As had been the case in nineteenth-century Britain, when elections based on expanded suffrage rivalled and then displaced King-in-Parliament, party overshadowed parliament in the making of governments, policy, and political careers. The states of India's federal system also created paths to power. From the beginning, careers in parliament counted for less than those in party politics at the Centre and in the states.

In the Nehru era, the parliament was effective in performing its contemporary role: defending and criticizing government policy, overseeing bureaucratic performance, and, perhaps most importantly, holding the government accountable by exposing its policies and actions to informed opinion and voter judgment. It was able to do so in part because many of the MPs who sat in early parliaments had, as leaders of the nationalist movement, acquired considerable political and legislative experience. Many were lawyers whose métier featured procedural sophistication, command of the fine print, and adversary exchange.

Legislatures in India have suffered some of the same setbacks as legislatures in advanced industrial democracies; that is, they have lost power and influence to the political executive and specialized bureaucracies in the formulation and control of policy. Like parties and legislators in many other industrial democracies, parliamentary parties and committees in India have not developed the specialized knowledge and staff needed to challenge the experts and bureaucracies of the political executive. Parliamentary opposition has often exposed malfeasance and corruption; it has found it much more difficult to challenge the government's policy agenda and mount credible alternatives. As Kuldip Nayar wrote:

The opposition can also make Parliament more purposeful, but its eyes are mainly stuck to the headlines in newspapers. It does not pursue any subject diligently or doggedly, much less study it in depth. Even when the government has been caught on the wrong foot it has been let off because of lack of preparation ... what the opposition lacks is persistence.[95]

There is no equivalent in India of the Labour or Conservative Party's research bureaus to prepare policy options for the opposition parties. Above all, the

[95]Kuldip Nayar, *Sunday*, Calcutta, 24–30 July 1983.

absence of a functional equivalent for Her Majesty's loyal opposition—that is, a politically viable alternative (whether as one party or a coalition) to the Congress party, with a recognized role not only in parliament but also in the media and among the electorate—has seriously impaired the effectiveness of parliament to dramatize national politics and shape public opinion.

To help halt the decline of parliament under the complex conditions of an industrial, welfare, and national security state concerned with planning and managing the economy, there have been calls for providing parliament with adequately staffed, independent specialized committees. Presently the standing committees are ex post facto, and less and less attended to by the government, parliament itself, and by the public. An emergency era committee of the Congress parliamentary party, headed by the late C.M. Stephen, proposed to subordinate parliamentary deliberations to a Congress party-dominated committee structure. As *The Indian Express* commented, 'The intention was clear: to dilute the authority of parliament and to close all forums at which the opposition could express its point of view.'[96] In 1984, Lok Sabha (lower house) Speaker Balram Jakhar proposed to establish less partisan, speaker-appointed subject area 'budget committees', but qualified this move towards a more independent parliament by arguing that the committee meetings should be held in camera and not be open to the press.

Unlike the decline of legislatures in other industrial democracies, which has been associated primarily with domination by more expert executive agencies, the decline of Indian legislatures has been accelerated by political forces. The front bench must collaborate with the members if parliamentary procedures are to retain their integrity and effectiveness. Since the mid-1960s and the death of Nehru, there has been a failure by both to honour each other's parliamentary role. The prime minister and cabinet colleagues have neglected the parliament: 'The single most important factor that has contributed to this slump in the prestige and influence of Parliament,' said opposition leader Atal Behari Vajpayee, himself a formidable parliamentarian, 'is Prime Minister Indira Gandhi's unconcealed disdain for Parliament ... Pandit Nehru stayed away from the house only when it was absolutely unavoidable. She attends Parliament only when she must.'[97] Rajiv Gandhi's civility towards the opposition and respect for parliament created a more favourable atmosphere after 1984.

The election to early post-independence legislatures of members without parliamentary experience and often with little education was compensated for by the parliamentary concern and skill of government and opposition

[96]*The Indian Express*, 20 May 1984.
[97]Ibid.

leaders in many states, as well as by Nehru and his colleagues of the nationalist generation at the Centre. The legislatures of the 1950s and 1960s had to constantly socialize newcomers into a parliamentary outlook and procedures. In the first parliament, half of those elected had never before served in a legislature.[98] In 1967, opposition gains brought a new influx of inexperienced members into the state and national legislature. In 1980, Sanjay Gandhi inducted young, ambitious, inexperienced rowdies, whose contempt for procedure and penchant for violent means further diluted the standard of parliamentarianism at the Centre and in the states. But by that time there was no compensating influence of a tutelary nationalist generation.

The changing social background of legislators is of some significance, but cannot by itself explain the decline of parliamentary life in India. The proportion of professionals—especially lawyers, but also scientists, doctors, teachers, journalists, and civil servants—has declined. The only category that has increased—and it almost doubled from 22 to 38 per cent between 1952 and 1984—was that of agriculturists.[99] By itself, this proportional increase does not explain why parliament has become less effective. Many agriculturists are educated and experienced parliamentarians. Speaker Balram Jakhar, for example, lists himself as an 'agriculturist', and represents parliamentary as well as agricultural interests.

Decline took a new turn after Indira Gandhi's declaration of an emergency in 1975. The Congress-I government arrested and sent to jail the principal opposition party leaders, and it encouraged its chief ministers and party leadership to address workshops and political science study groups that deplored the waste of time and unnecessary garrulousness of legislatures.[100] The Janata government, which returned in 1977, restored constitutional democracy, but no one could accuse Charan Singh of parliamentary punctiliousness or Raj Narain of parliamentary civility. Both Janata leaders lavishly contributed to bringing ridicule upon parliamentary government.

Deterioration of legislatures has advanced further in the states than at the Centre. Madhu Limaye, an experienced opposition leader and political commentator, has noted that the deterioration began in 1967 with opposition victories in the northern states. The legislators who supported the opposition governments were 'inexperienced and, being a rag tag coalition, could not

[98]Hardgrave, *India*, p. 64.
[99]Subhash Kashyap, 'The Eighth Lok Sabha: A Profile of Its Members', *Indian and Foreign Review*, 31 May 1985.
[100]For example, in a speech before the Rajasthan Political Sciences Association Meeting of Fall 1975, Chief Minister Harideo Joshi condemned the wasting of time in parliament, which detracted from the vital business to which ministers should attend (authors' notes of meeting).

enforce discipline. The legislators were an unruly lot, almost a rabble.'[101] Governments were afraid to face such legislatures, and legislators had no conception of their role. In Bihar, which in this as in other matters tends towards the lowest political denominator, first the opposition and then the Congress government began to circumvent the legislative process. The result was a reduction of legislative days from 179 and 263 in 1960 and 1961 to 57 (1967), 37 (1968), 33 (1969), 55 (1970), and 63 (1973). Governments, rather than risk the introduction of legislation, began to rule by executive ordinance, a procedure used when legislatures are not in session or for extreme emergencies. Ordinances were re-promulgated when they expired. Between 1967 and 1981, the Bihar government re-promulgated 256 ordinances.[102] The breakdown of the legislature in Bihar, while not typical, is suggestive of the atrophy that has beset most state assemblies.[103]

The quality of legislative life depends on the quality of parliamentary leadership and legislators and, more importantly, on the legislators' capacity to master and use legislative procedures. Parliamentary leaders have fled from the crisis of the legislature in India rather than come to grips with it. Baffled by policy complexities and legislative procedures, legislators have resorted to shouting matches, ceremonial profanations, and occasional physical violence. The government's refusal to address pressing and embarrassing issues is answered by opposition walkouts and the politics of the streets. Legislators are increasingly unwilling to play the parliamentary game or accept the possibilities this form of regulated conflict provides. Legislative debate is a highly stylized form of verbal combat. Legislators who cannot use their tongues fling shoes. Legislators who do not know how to use the rules to their advantage prefer chaos. It is apparent that training legislators is as important as training administrators if parliamentary government in the states is to remain viable.[104]

FEDERALISM

There are reasons to believe that India's federal system is in jeopardy, not least of which is the personal centralization of power during the Indira Gandhi era that we have discussed. On the other hand, there are powerful counter-

---

[101]*Illustrated Weekly*, 1 January 1984.

[102]See ibid. and D.C. Wadhwa, *Promulgation of Ordinances: A Fraud in the Constitution of India*, Bombay: Orient Longman, 1983.

[103]The atrophy that besets state assemblies is also evident in the fate of legislative committees. For a critical account of the inattentiveness of Uttar Pradesh cabinets to the reports of legislative committees, notably the committee on government assurances, see P.K. Srivastava, 'Legislature in Uttar Pradesh', Ph.D. dissertation, Lucknow University, 1983, Ch. 7.

[104]The Harish Chandra Mathur Institute at Jaipur provides such training.

currents to personal centralization, of which an important one is the growing strength of regional nationalisms and the success of regional parties. Both currents have put the federal system under severe strain.

Apart from academic disputation about the nature and even the 'authenticity' of India's federal system as defined in the constitution[105] is the reality of an enormous country whose cultural heterogeneity is expressed in the federal organization of power. The population of many of its twenty-three states ranks with those of the largest countries in Western Europe. India's largest state, Uttar Pradesh, has a population of over 100 million, which puts it just behind Indonesia, the world's seventh-largest sovereign state. America's federal system divides a population of 220 million into fifty units, whereas India's divides a population of 710 million into only twenty-two units, five of which are marginal.

Since state reorganization in 1953 and 1956, state boundaries have roughly coincided with historically rooted linguistic and cultural regions. These differences reinforce the effects of size and continue in the federal system the tensions between regional kingdoms and subcontinental empire that have characterized the history of the state in India. A spate of studies, conferences, and commissions—beginning in the early 1970s with the Rajamannar Committee (1971) in Tamil Nadu[106] and continuing into the 1980s—reflected the fact that Centre-state relations had become a major issue on the national agenda. The opposition and regional parties' deep concern for Centre-state relations forced Mrs Gandhi to appoint the Sarkaria Commission to reconsider the functioning of the federal system.

The deinstitutionalization of the Congress party contributed to the crisis of the federal system by dismantling the party's federal features. Most visible and devastating to party federalism was the surrender by victorious state parliamentary parties of the right to select their leaders. In the wake of the 'Indira wave' of 1972, an electoral surge powered by Mrs Gandhi's personal appeal that swept Congress to victory in all but one state, Congress state assembly parties asked the prime minister to name their chief ministers, a practice that has continued under Rajiv Gandhi. In the absence of the internal democracy that party elections represent, pradesh (state) Congress committees were also appointed by the party presidents, Indira and Rajiv Gandhi.[107] Those selected found it expedient to feature loyalty to the party's

[105]For an early critique, see Ivor Jennings, *Some Characteristics of the Indian Constitution*, Oxford: Oxford University Press, 1953. For a discussion of bargaining federalism, see Morris-Jones, *Government and Politics of India*, pp. 150–6.

[106]Government of Tamil Nadu, *Report of the Centre–State Relations Inquiry Committee, 1971*, Madras, 1971.

[107]'The party organization of the prime minister's Congress, instead of serving as an

president at the Centre rather than represent the interests and aspirations of their respective states. As a consequence, they lacked the support that chief ministers and committee presidents with autonomous networks of influence and mutual obligation could command. At worst, the nomination from Delhi of government and party leaders produced politically impotent loyalists held in contempt by their local constituents. Andhra Pradesh voters interpreted the nomination from Delhi of five chief ministers between 1978 and 1982 as contemptuous of Andhra Pradesh's standing, and they overwhelmingly voted in January 1983 to install a regional leader and party in preference to the Congress.

Another development that weakened federalism was the failure of the Centre to respect the integrity of state assembly elections, which determine which party and leader should form the government. The 1977 elections, in which the Janata Party defeated the Gandhi-led Congress, were parliamentary elections only. They did not affect the standing of state assemblies, whose terms of office were not synchronized with parliament's. However, the Janata government pressed the view that the Congress governments' legally dubious actions under the emergency and, more importantly, Janata's sweeping victories in nine northern states (in many of which it won all parliamentary seats) compromised the legitimacy of the Congress governments, that is, that the state assemblies had ceased to reflect the views of the electorate. After consulting the Supreme Court—which, in a procedurally and substantively controversial opinion,[108] endorsed its proposal—the Janata government advised the president to dismiss the nine governments. Subsequently, it held (and won) state assembly elections. In 1980, after Congress swept back into power at the Centre, it used the precedent of the Janata government's action to again breach the autonomy and integrity of state assembly elections by dismissing nine governments and holding elections in which it (like Janata) succeeded in replacing the opposition with Congress governments. Taken together, the two actions dealt a severe blow to the integrity of India's federal system.

The integrity of the federal system was also threatened by the actions of state governors. A governor serves two masters, the president of India who appoints governors on the advice of the central cabinet (which, in Indira Gandhi's time, meant the prime minister), and the state's council of ministers,

---

institution of recruitment and linkage between different levels of India's federal system, as it had before, became more unitary with control maintained by the Prime Minister. Presidents circulated almost annually, tickets for elections were allocated centrally' (Richard Sisson, 'Prime Ministerial Power and the Selection of Ministers in India: Three Decades of Change', *International Political Science Review*, 2 [2], 1981, p. 150).

[108] *State of Rajasthan vs Union of India*, 1977, A.I.R. 1361.

which acts in the governor's name, but in fact advises him on what to say and do. The two masters may be from different political parties. As envisioned in the Constituent Assembly, the governor would be an eminent public person, detached from the world of partisan politics and not beholden to it. Governors would 'naturally cooperate fully with the state government in carrying out the policy of the Government and yet represent before the public something above politics'.[109] Over time, and at an accelerating rate in the 1970s, governors acted in an increasingly partisan manner, as agents not of a detached and respected president, but of power-seeking party leaders at the Centre.

The ambiguity of the governor's role also arises from the constitutional provision (Article 163 [1]) that states that apart from an obligation to act on the advice of the state cabinet, a governor may 'exercise his functions or any of them in his discretion'. In using their discretion, governors have been less and less constrained by parliamentary and constitutional conventions, acting more at the behest of party governments at the Centre. Prior to the 1984 parliamentary election, governors in Sikkim, Kashmir, and Andhra Pradesh helped destabilize and then topple opposition governments. The possibility of gubernatorial independence was further weakened when the Supreme Court held that the constitutional provision stating that governors are to serve at the president's pleasure took precedence over another provision—that they serve for a fixed term of five years. For some time, it was assumed that the president's authority to dismiss a governor should 'be sparingly used to meet with cases of gross delinquency, such as bribery, corruption, treason, and the like or violation of the Constitution'.[110] Such expectations were belied when the Supreme Court held that the governor of Rajasthan, Gurukul Tilak, who had been appointed on the advice of the Janata government, could be dismissed before the end of his term on the advice of the restored Congress government.[111]

[109]*Constituent Assembly Debates; Official Report*, 12 vols, Delhi, 194650, 7:455, as quoted in Durga Das Basu, *Introduction to the Constitution of India*, 10th edn, New Delhi: Prentice-Hall of India, 1983, p. 213.

[110]Basu, *Introduction to Constitution*, 10th edn, p. 212.

[111]*Surya vs Union of India*, 1982 A. 1982 Rajasthan 1, with respect to Tilak, confirmed that the president's pleasure under Article 154(1) can be used by the prime minister to dismiss any governor for political reasons without assigning any charge. Prabhudas Patwari was similarly dismissed in Tamil Nadu in October 1980. See Durga Das Basu, *Constitutional Law of India*, New Delhi: Prentice-Hall of India, 1983, p. 164, n. 12; see also Basu, *Introduction to Constitution*, p. 219n, 8a. See Bhagwan Dua's critical remarks in 'India: Congress Dominance Revisited', Paper presented at the Thirty-seventh Annual Meeting of the Association for Asian Studies, Philadelphia, March 1985. See also his *Presidential Rule in India*, New Delhi: Chand, 1979, a severe indictment of the partisan use of this power, and 'India: A Study in the Pathology of a Federal System', *Journal of Commonwealth and Comparative Politics*, 19, 1981.

Governors use their discretion when they ask legislative leaders to form governments and when they dismiss governments that have lost their majorities, and they have abused their discretionary powers on both counts. When Congress leaders with unproved and doubtful majorities were asked to form governments in Rajasthan in 1967 and in Haryana in 1980, they were able to use the prospect of office and other benefits to gain the majorities they needed to govern. When Governor Gopala Reddy dismissed Uttar Pradesh's chief minister Charan Singh in 1967, and when Governor Ram Lal dismissed Andhra Pradesh's chief minister N.T. Rama Rao in 1984, neither waited for the verdict of the state assembly.

Governors have also abused their discretion with respect to the imposition of president's rule under Article 356 of the constitution, which allows governors to advise the president that the 'government of (a) State cannot be carried on in accordance with the provisions of the constitution'. Such advice enables the governing party at the Centre to take over the government of a state. In the words of D.D. Basu, a leading constitutional authority, use of this 'drastic coercive power' takes the substance away from the normal federal polity described by the Constitution.[112] B.R. Ambedkar, a principal architect of the constitution, told the Constituent Assembly that 'the proper thing we ought to expect is that such articles (as 356) will never be called into operation, that they remain a dead letter'.[113] Ambedkar's expectations were not met. Article 356 was increasingly used in a partisan and arbitrary manner. Instead of being a matter of last resort, Article 356 had been used sixty-five times by March 1982.[114] According to Basu, 'this extraordinary power has been too often [used] to serve the *political* purposes of the party in power at the Union',[115] a result that occurs when governors (and presidents) fail to observe their constitutional responsibilities.

Instead of becoming guardians of the federal system, governors became agents of its decline. However, Indira Gandhi's partisan centralization at the expense of the federal system generated counter-currents. The cases of Assam and Punjab, so prominent in the politics of the early 1980s, lie outside the framework of our analysis of the erosion of the federal system. There, perceived threats to cultural identity and survival could no longer be accommodated by conventional political processes. Elsewhere, counter-currents took the form of regional nationalism and regional opposition parties that gained power because they better represented the aspirations

[112]Basu, *Introduction to Constitution*, p. 311.
[113]*Constituent Assembly Debates* 9: 177, cited in ibid.
[114]Ibid., pp. 308–11, where Basu lists each case. Janata used the device nineteen times.
[115]Ibid., p. 312.

and interests of India's diverse peoples. After its return to power in 1980, the Congress government had to operate a federal system in which regional and opposition parties governed five of the sixteen large states (West Bengal, Kashmir, Andhra Pradesh, Tamil Nadu, and Karnataka), while the civil administrations and political process had broken down in two (Assam and Punjab). Regional politics and parties became a persistent aspect of India's political equations.

Such politics can be accommodated only if the federal system remains a viable and important aspect of the larger political system. Rajiv Gandhi as prime minister recognized this fact in his accommodating approach to opposition-controlled state governments. He initiated his government's federal policy in 1985 by accepting with good grace opposition victories in Punjab and Assam, where his mother's fear of sharing power had led to a stalemate. He also reinforced the governor's role as a non-partisan figure obligated to respect the wishes of state legislatures rather than the partisan interests of the governing party at the Centre. Federal systems are mechanisms for sharing power. Rajiv Gandhi's willingness to do so is likely to counteract the centralizing tendencies of the previous administration.

4

Religion, States, and Transnational Civil Society*

SUSANNE HOEBER RUDOLPH

TRANSNATIONAL RELIGION IN LIMINAL SPACE: ITS DEMOGRAPHY

Religious communities are among the oldest of the transnationals: Sufi orders, Catholic missionaries, and Buddhist monks carried word and praxis across vast spaces before those places became nation-states or even states. Such religious peripatetics *were* versions of civil society.[1] In today's postmodern era, religious communities have become vigorous creators of an emergent transnational civil society.

*Originally published as 'Introduction: Religion, States, and Transnational Civil Society', in Susanne Hoeber Rudolph and James Piscatori (eds), *Transnational Religion and Fading States*, Boulder, Co., Westview Press, 1997, pp. 1–24.

This essay was part of a project to redefine the meaning of security in international relations. It examines the role of religion in rethinking security in terms of fear of cultural extinction, shows how religions help define transnational civil society, and summarizes and interprets the findings of nine studies that approach the topic of transnational civil society by exploring the effect of religious organizations. Readers interested in the studies should refer to the original book.

[1]Churches may be the oldest creators of civil society in the West. One is reluctant to assert that they have universally had such a role because the very notion of civil society is often considered a product of liberal Western thought. Don Baker's essay, 'World Religions and National States: Competing Claims in East Asia', in *Transnational Religion and Fading States*, by Susanne Hoeber Rudolph and James Piscatori (eds), Boulder, Co: Westview Press, 1997, suggests that the society-state dichotomy is not a 'natural' or universal conceptualization. For a discussion of the uses of the concept of civil society, see my concluding essay in *Transnational Religion and Fading States*.

Modern social science did not warn us that this would happen. Instead, it asserted that religion would fade, and then disappear with the triumph of science and rationalism. But religion has expanded explosively, stimulated as much by secular global processes—migration, multinational capital, the media revolution—as by proselytizing activity. Contrary to expectations, its expansion has been an answer to and is driven by modernity. In response to the deracination and threats of cultural extinction associated with modernization processes, religious experience seeks to restore meaning to life.[2]

Religious communities are helping to shape world politics. The language of international relations and security studies on the one hand, and that of foreign policy and domestic politics on the other distinguish political life within states from the alleged imperatives of an imagined international system. This distinction and separation deploy a rich vocabulary for 'inside' and 'outside', to follow Rob Walker's language.[3] Until recently, there were no words and metaphors for designating and populating the liminal space that cuts across inside/outside, a space that is neither within the state nor an aspect of the international state system, yet animates both.

This liminal and cross-cutting arena is becoming more densely occupied by communities—environmentalists, development professionals, human rights activists, information specialists—whose commonality depends less on co-residence in 'sovereign' territorial space and more on common worldviews, purposes, interests, and praxis.[4] Peter Haas has theorized them as epistemic communities.[5] Such communities, including religious communities and movements, have implications for the international system. Their

---

[2] 'The new mass clientele for Protestant missionary activity ... [arises from] the creation of converging trends in demography, social mobility, and the continuing appeal of religions that stress an intense spiritual life. Dramatic population shifts and accelerated urbanization have drawn Latin Americans to the cities while opening rural life to the outside world via expanded transport and communications.' Daniel H. Levine, 'The Latin American Experience of Transnational Religious Activism', Paper prepared for the SSRC Conference on Transnational Muslim Missionary Movements, University of Aberystwyth, Wales, October 1992, p. 8.

[3] R.B.J. Walker, *Inside/Outside: International Relations as Political Theory*, Cambridge, England: Cambridge University Press, 1993.

[4] This formulation does not make a distinction between ideas and practice, but assumes that concept and praxis implicate each other.

[5] See Peter Haas, 'Introduction: Epistemic Communities and International Policy Coordination', Special issue of *International Organization*, 46 (1), 1992, pp. 1–35. The general omission of religious movements from the category of such epistemic communities is presumably a replication of the pervasive enlightenment conceit that draws boundaries between 'rationalist' and 'affective', between positive and imagined, between ascriptive and voluntaristic. For a theoretical critique of these distinctions, see my concluding essay.

existence has transformed the way we understand and explain 'international relations', that is, relations among sovereign states in an anarchic space. It is possible to theorize these new transnational communities as constituting a world politics that encompasses both transnational civil society and sovereignty-sharing states. The objective of *Transnational Religion and Fading States* is to create a space for religious groups and movements in the consideration of such transnational solidarities.

The communities that populate transnational civil society do not affect the state 'system' in the way some hope world governance might. They do not provide a statelike entity to impose order, and perhaps justice, 'outside' in anarchic space by monopolizing force and supplying universal arbitration and rule enforcement. They do not even supply what transnational regimes are meant to provide—predictable systems of rules that facilitate cooperation.[6] Instead, they create a pluralistic transnational polity. They shape perceptions and expectations that contribute to world public opinion and politics.

Their effects on transnational space are only beginning to be understood. Existential fright about 'the coming anarchy' is probably premature.[7] But because a plurality of transnational spaces entails difference as well as commonality with respect to epistemes, identities, and expectations, transnational civil society can be the site of both conflict and cooperation.

While the fluidity of religion across political boundaries is very old, recent migrations, communication links, and elite transformations joining East with West and North with South have generated unaccustomed flows: Hindus in Leicester, Muslims in Marseilles and Frankfurt, Pentecostals in Moscow and Singapore. Europeans found themselves in a minority at Vatican II, overwhelmed by 200 American, and 228 Asian and African bishops.[8] Since

---

[6]Stephen D. Krasner, 'Structural Causes and Regime Consequences: Regimes as Intervening Variables', in *International Regimes*, by Stephen D. Krasner (ed.), Ithaca: Cornell University Press, 1983; and Robert O. Keohane, *After Hegemony: Cooperation and Discord in the World Political Economy*, Princeton: Princeton University Press, 1984.

[7]Robert D. Kaplan, 'The Coming Anarchy', *Atlantic Monthly*, February 1994. The authors of this volume find the positive, motivating, and cooperative impact of religion as significant as it is negative, divisive, and conflictual. By contrast, Kaplan's undiscriminating view of ethnicity and religion, born especially of his perception of conflict in Africa, strikes a single note; all mobilizations are assigned to the negative column. Yet it is precisely the variable potential of religious and ethnic formations that needs to be investigated. For an account of Africa that is also pessimistic but more discriminating, and which does not assume that Africa is the world, see Zolberg, Aristide, 'The Specter of Anarchy: African States Verging on Dissolution', *Dissent*, Summer, 1992.

[8]Although Europeans no longer constituted a majority at the time of Vatican II, two-thirds of the college of Cardinals was still Italian. See Jose Casanova, 'Globalizing Catholicism and the Return to a "Universal" Church', in *Transnational Religion and Fading States*.

the mid-1960s, American evangelism has helped to raise the proportion of Protestants to 12 per cent of the population of Latin America, formerly a Catholic bastion.[9] In predominantly Chinese Singapore, the Christian population has doubled to one-fifth since 1985. In China proper, optimistic Christian estimates place the number of Christians at 80 million.[10]

It may surprise readers to learn that since the mid-1970s, Oklahoma City has acquired five mosques, four Hindu temples, one Sikh *gurudwara*, and three Buddhist temples; that Denver has a similar configuration; that there may be as many as seventy mosques in the Chicago metropolitan area and fifty temples in the Midwest Buddhist Association; and that Muslims outnumber Episcopalians in the United States at two to one, and are likely to outnumber Jews in the near future.[11]

This explosion of religious formations seems to have been facilitated by the very forces that were supposed to dissolve them: increased print and electronic media, increased literacy—including the higher literacy of post-secondary education—and urbanization. Explaining the increase and intensification of religious discourse in Oman and its entry into everyday life and politics, Dale Eickelman writes:

The most profound change is associated with the spread of modern literacy and the new media through which ideas can be communicated. Mass literacy came late to Oman. ... By the early 1980s Oman had a sufficient number of secondary school graduates, members of the armed services and civilian government with in-service training, and university students abroad ... to engender a transformation in what constitutes authoritative religious discourse. The shift to a print and cassette-based religiosity and the exposure of large numbers of young Omanis to a written, formal, 'modern standard' Arabic through schooling and the mass media have altered the style and content of authoritative religious discourse and the role this plays in shaping and constraining domestic and regional politics.[12]

[9]For recent figures, see James Brooke, 'Pragmatic Protestants Winning Converts in Brazil', *New York Times*, 4 July 1993. For accounts of this growth, see David Martin, *Tongues of Fire: The Explosion of Protestantism in Latin America*, London: Basil Blackwell, 1990; David Stoll, *Is Latin America Turning Protestant?* Berkeley: University of California Press, 1992; and David Stoll, and Virginia Burnett (eds), *Rethinking Protestantism in Latin America*, New York: Columbia University Press, 1993.

[10]Nicholas Kristof, 'Christianity Is Booming in China Despite Rifts', *New York Times*, 7 February 1993.

[11]Diane L. Eck, 'In the Name of Religions', *Wilson Quarterly*, 17 (4), 1993, p. 99. These figures and estimates were gathered by the Pluralism Project of Harvard University's Committee on the Study of Religion. See also James Brooke, 'Attacks on U.S. Muslims Surge, Even As Their Faith Takes Hold', *New York Times*, 28 August 1995. Philip Lewis provides an account for Britain in *Islamic Britain: Religion, Politics, and Identity Among British Muslims*, London: I.B. Tauris, 1994.

[12]Dale F. Eickelman, 'National Identity and Religious Discourse in Contemporary Oman', *International Journal of Islamic and Arabic Studies*, 6 (1), 1989, pp. 1–20.

These are the demographics of a new religious transnationalism. In an earlier transnationalism of Islam and Christianity, religion accompanied trade, conquest, and colonial domination. Versions of Christianity continue to flow outward from the West, but reverse flows are now conspicuous as well. Accustomed as we were to controlling the missionary terms of trade, we may be astonished to find 'their' products flooding 'our' market.

Much of this new transnationalism is carried by religion from below, by a popular religious upsurge of ordinary and quite often poor, oppressed, and culturally deprived people, rather than by religion introduced and directed from above. Well-known transnational structures—especially the hierarchical and bureaucratized Catholic Church, led by an evangelizing Pontiff with global aspirations—are an important component of the new transnational religion. But popular, populist, enthusiastic movements leavened by Pentecostals, Catholic charismatics, and 'fundamentalist' Muslims have spread more by spontaneous diffusion.

RETHINKING SECURITY

Transnational Religion and Fading States is concerned with the implications transnational religions have for conflict and cooperation, for security, for the future of the nation-state, and for the emergence of transnational civil society. It began as part of an effort by the Social Science Research Council's Committee on International Peace and Security to query the conventional significance of 'security'. The relevance of transnational religions to security, not obvious in the mid-1980s, came to seem more plausible with the approach of the 1990s as domestic tranquillity and international peace were increasingly disrupted in the name of religion. Religious formulations of political purposes proliferated, and the political activities of non-state religious actors became conspicuous. For some, religion promised to become the same kind of summary predictor for peace and war that ideology had been in the 1970s.

But what is security? Whose security, and from whom or what? In American social science discourses the significance of the word, when uttered in the 1960s through the 1980s, was relatively transparent. It had to do with the Western alliance and with the state. For the Western alliance, it denoted the security of the United States and its allies in a bipolar world in the context of nuclear threat. For non-Europeans and their states, ambivalent subscribers to bipolarity who doubted the equation of US interests with their own, the word acquired negative and coercive meaning. For the Latin American left, the security state was an authoritarian polity living on US aid and protection. Indians and Indonesians equated security with a bipolarity that reduced their international choices.[13] 'Security', then, was a code, at its narrowest, for US security interests, and at its widest for the Western alliance and its adherents.

Second, the dominant definitions of security were state-centric. States were the units of action, the definers and guarantors of security. They were the agents that would constitute the international system, entering into alliances or conflict with other state units in pursuit of the security they defined. The state was the critical agent in all transactions governing security. These meanings, security as Western interests in the nuclear balance in a bipolar world and security as a state monopoly, are now being increasingly challenged in social science discourses.[14]

Our reading of security turns the lens away from the state as prime actor, focusing instead on civil society as creator and guarantor, as well as threat to security. The historical experience of the 1990s provides an empirical backdrop for that different reading. In this decade, the balance of violence has shifted significantly from war 'outside', in the anarchic space between sovereign states to war 'inside', between the embodiments of difference in civil society. Whereas war had formerly been embedded in the imbalance of power among states, it now became related to imbalance of status in civil society among ethnic and religious formations. Refocusing on civil society as a locus of security problems is justified by the mortal threat that 'civil' wars pose. Even as political developments in advanced industrial democracies make it virtually impossible to engage in interstate wars that create domestic casualties, the fatality counts in civil conflicts rise to figures approximating or overwhelming those for interstate wars.[15]

Focusing on security as a matter arising in civil society invites a redefinition of the problems that qualify as security issues. Security problems centre on physical and cultural survival. The fear of death, Hobbes's ultimate *causans*, and calculations about the probabilities of survival, are implied by the threats of environmental degradation, famine, poverty, population density,

[13]Discussants from Latin America, participating in meetings held to produce *Transnational Religion and Fading States*, viewed the mission of this group suspiciously insofar as 'security' was said to be part of its interests.

[14]See, for example, David A. Baldwin's review essay and the volumes he reviews, 'Security Studies and the End of the Cold War', *World Politics*, 48, 1995, pp. 117–41.

[15]See Stockholm International Peace Research Institute (SIPRI) figures for casualties in domestic wars in twenty-nine countries. The figures are topped by wars in Sudan (37,000 to 40,000), Angola (122,000), Tajikistan (20,000 to 50,000), and Guatemala (46,000). The compilation does not cite years, but acknowledges that these figures are in some cases cumulative over decades. Cited in *Time International*, 9 October 1995, p. 20.

disease, and chaos-generating migratory flows.[16] These threats to the physical survival of individuals and particular communities and countries, as well as of the whole human species, loom as large in the 1990s as a nuclear exchange or nuclear Armageddon had in the Cold War era.

But the fear of cultural extinction rivals the fear of physical extinction. One doesn't have to carry a New Hampshire licence plate ('Live Free or Die') to recognize that physical survival is not enough in a world threatened by the death of meaning. Many of today's conflicts arise from groups' fears that they are a culturally endangered species, that enemies seek their cultural, if not physical, annihilation. Such fears drive militant Sikhs, Sinhalese Buddhists, Kurds, Hutus, Andean Indians, and Bosnian Serbs, and provide motive and fuel to domestic conflicts in Punjab, Sri Lanka, Guatemala, Turkey, Bosnia, and Rwanda. Identities and the esteem conferred by them are at stake. Religion is one of the prime sources of identity. Its significance has intensified in a post-rationalist world threatened by disenchantment, impersonality, and loss of meaning. Cultural survival, like physical survival, is a critical security problem for the 1990s and beyond.

RELIGION: VEHICLE OF CONFLICT OR COOPERATION?

The essays in *Transnational Religion and Fading States* problematize the role of religion with respect to conflict and cooperation. Under what circumstances does religion divide persons and groups? Under what conditions does it bring them together? Religion, as the term is used most of the time by our contributors, refers to practice more often than it does to belief. Although guided and sustained by the meaning systems of transcendent realms, religion as practised is embedded in everyday life. In countries of the Western as well as the non-Western world, the most significant form of social organization and source of worldviews for a growing number of people may be religious entities rather than trade unions, political parties, or interest groups. How are these entities related to conflict and cooperation?

Daniel Levine writes:

Much recent writing on transnational dimensions of religious change in Latin America has been concerned with overt political acts driven by fears about religion's possible links to revolution (especially in Central America), by false images of a repetition of the Iranian Revolution, or by hopes that religious change would somehow fuel a thoroughgoing cultural and social transformation.[17]

[16]The formulation of the security problems in terms of physical and cultural survival or extinction is borrowed from Lloyd I. Rudolph.

[17]Daniel Levine, 'Transnational Religious Regimes in Latin America: Social Capital, Empowerment, Symbols, and Power', Working draft presented at the SSRC Working Group

The conflict-generating potential of religious mobilizations has received much more attention than their potential for cooperation.

We must remind ourselves that Enlightenment rationalism gave religion a bad name. Religion was false knowledge, the kind of knowledge that Voltaire, Condorcet, and Comte foresaw as disappearing from human consciousness. For Marx, the lingering effects of religions were actively negative, shoring up exploitation and oppression.[18] Modernist social scientists cannot imagine religion as a positive force, as a practice and worldview that contributes to order, provides meaning, and promotes justice.

Now that modernity is on trial, or in crisis, or bankrupt, are there arguments for religion as having a positive role? It can be argued that how people understand their condition affects their sense of security as much as, or more than, their objective conditions do. If religion can be an opiate that reconciles humans to injustice, it can also provide the vision and energy that engender collective action and social transformation.

Daniel Levine and David Stoll, in *Transnational Religion and Fading States*, tell of the earnest liberationists and Pentecostal congregations of the Latin American poor empowered by religious self-teaching. It gives them 'new orientations, social skills, and collective self-confidence', though less of all of these than the most optimistic liberationism anticipated. Writing earlier of Guatemala, Stoll stresses the role of the new Protestantism among uprooted populations and recent migrants to cities. They construct new institutions and practices to negotiate the shock of transfer, while those living under the surviving Hacienda regime, for whom the old-time Catholicism suffices, remain passive.[19] Ousmane Kane tells of mobile West African Sufis who spawn

---

on Transnational Religious Regimes, New York, October 1993. This was an early draft of the chapter by Daniel Levine and David Stoll in *Transnational Religion*.

[18]The Communist Party of India (Marxist) is debating whether to censure its local cadres for participating in, and even organizing, the festival activities for Goddess Durga, which are a pervasive feature of the October festival season in Bengal, stronghold of the communists in India. The proponents of participation argue that not doing so is to lose a central means of communicating with the people, *The Statesman* (New Delhi), 9 October 1995. For interesting neo-Marxian approaches that read religion as a language articulating the life-situation of believers, see writings by Indian historians in the 'subaltern' tradition, who attempt a new understanding of nineteenth- and twentieth-century 'communalism': Gyan Pandey, *The Construction of Communalism in Colonial North India*, New Delhi: Oxford University Press, 1990; Shahid Amin, 'Gandhi as Mahatma: Gorakhpur District, Eastern UP, 1921–2', in *Selected Subaltern Studies*, by Ranajit Guha and Gayatri Chakravorty Spivak (eds), New York: Oxford University Press, 1988.

[19]David Stoll, *Is Latin America Turning Protestant?*, p. 13. For an earlier account, see Emilio Willems, *Followers of the New Faith*, Nashville, TN: Vanderbilt University Press, 1967. The same religious orientations may be associated with a variety of practices, from quietism to activism. Today's Pentecostalism, speaking in tongues and recommending faith healing, may recommend tomorrow the cultivation of self-discipline and the will to seize one's fate. Nineteenth-century

zawiyas, a familiar spiritual and social milieu, in new locations for the migrating faithful, which provide them with the security of identity, food, and education.[20]

Such accounts reveal how religious associations provide structure and meaning to human relations, and how they create communities and enable action. The fact that the ritual and belief systems of religious communities have a 'security' component, and that they make possible both physical and cultural survival, is sometimes not visible until they are destroyed. Kane's account of the peaceable transnational trading and kinship networks of West African Sufis provides a benign contrast to the chaotic horrors of Rwanda and Somalia, where both states and civil society contributed to the problem rather than the solution. As Habermas remarks, 'Sometimes it takes an earthquake to make us aware that we had regarded the ground on which we stand every day as unshakable.'[21] States cannot, without the means of society, construct the ties that bind humans together in obligation.

If the practice and belief of religious formations can, at various levels, orient and facilitate collective action and provide security, they can also generate conflict. Religions often provide not only the language and symbols, but also the motives for cultural conflict between and within states: Shiite Iran, Orthodox Serbia, Jewish Israel and Muslim Palestine Liberation Organization (PLO), Buddhist Sinhalese and Hindu Tamils in Sri Lanka, Protestants and Catholics in Ireland, Muslims, Hindus, and Buddhists in Kashmir, Sikhs and Hindus in Punjab, Front Islamique du Salut (FIS) Islamists and Secular Socialists (is rationalism a religion?) in Algeria. Rather than reflecting disequilibria in the balance of power, state conflict has taken on the aura of the jihad and the crusade. Holy war has joined self-help and ideology as a casus belli 'outside', and the confessionally defined 'other' has become the enemy within.

The notion that 'war' by definition is an encounter between 'states' has been shaken by a democracy of weapons that makes Weber's notion of states' monopolizing the use of force seem like a fairy tale of modernization. Increasingly, wars have been presenting themselves as conflicts among

---

Evangelical fundamentalism in Great Britain underwent a shift towards 'a social theology that made less of biblical doctrines of inherent personal sinfulness, guilt and divine punishment ... whilst making more of practical service to others through the discipline of hardwork as self-denial'. Studdert-Kennedy, Gerald, 'The Imperial Elite', review of Clive Dewey, *Anglo-Indian Attitudes: The Mind of the Indian Civil Service,* London: Hambledon Press, 1993, in *Economic and Political Weekly,* 9 July 1994, p. 1722.

[20]Ousmane Kane, 'Muslim Missionaries and African States', in *Transnational Religion.*

[21]Jurgen Habermas, *The Theory of Communicative Action,* Vol. 2, *Lifeworld and System: A Critique of Functionalist Reason,* Boston: Beacon Press, 1984–5, p. 400.

civilian populations where more civilians than soldiers die. Civil wars like that in Kashmir, which by 1995 was engaging 600,000 Indian troops, more than had been engaged in the 1965 Indo-Pakistan war, and those in Algeria and Bosnia, are likely to be the main sources of violent conflict in the foreseeable future.

Religion is an important component of the identities that define inside conflicts. Low-level conflicts can arise when the practices of an immigrant religious group challenge the prevailing religious conventions and constitution of the host country. This happened when Muslims in London demanded the enforcement of blasphemy laws and those in Marseilles challenged compulsory dress codes in public education. More serious conflicts can arise when a religious minority lays claim to a separate political identity, as Sikhs did in Indian Punjab or Catholics have done in Northern Ireland. Such conflicts are exacerbated when transnational brethren of local-religious minorities seeking political autonomy provide help—North American Sikhs in Punjab; Pakistan Muslims in Kashmir; Indian Tamils in Sri Lanka.

AVOIDING DOMESTIC CONFLICT: ASSIMILATION VERSUS DIFFERENCE

If modernization can no longer be counted on to erase religion from human consciousness and religion can be expected to trigger some conflicts, what are the possibilities for fewer rather than more domestic conflicts? Processes that foster domestic peace among religious groups have taken a number of forms. Homogenizing assimilation and multicultural pluralism represent contrasting cultural regimes. Neither has wholly succeeded, and neither has wholly failed. The stereotypical American story featured assimilating immigrants who 'Americanized', that is, became more alike, more homogeneous. Newcomers were encouraged to emulate the mores of the dominant Anglo-Saxon Protestant cultural forms and to be different in private—for example, to speak Italian or Yiddish at home and not take religious differences into political arenas.

In recent decades multiculturalism has challenged the notion of Americanization and assimilationist homogeneity. Numerous movements recognize and celebrate religious as well as ethnic and racial identities, and call for educational diversity. Threats of cultural extinction are increasingly driving identity movements. Although threatened in both the United States and Europe by the nativist fringe and mainstream backlash, political recognition of difference and pluralist settlements seem harder and harder to oppose or deny. The increase in migration to Europe and North America from non-Christian lands, or to the Middle East from non-Islamic ones, is enabled by the ease with which information technologies and jumbo jets allow immigrants to stay in touch with their home communities. We are likely to see 'the indefinite survival of separate collective identities even among groups living in the same place and exchanging goods and services on a daily basis'.[22]

In retrospect, the historical ubiquity of 'ordered heterogeneity' makes the nation-state's insistence on homogeneity—'one culture fits all'—seem quixotic. The 'high level of ethnic uniformity that modern European nations took for granted,' writes William McNeill, 'was very unusual. Religious pluralism, rather than homogeneity, was the starting point for older civilizations.'[23] Mobile peoples moving from rural to urban areas or arriving from distant lands relied on their religious identities and practices to secure them against the shocks of transition. Those who brought their religion with them were not perceived as disrupting the homogeneity of a host country.

The great cities of Asia and Eastern Europe adapted to this sort of permanent poly-ethnicity by allowing a series of religiously defined communities to exist side by side. ... Chinese and Indian cities also accorded extensive autonomy to enclaves of foreigners as a matter of course.[24]

McNeill's accounts suggest that homogeneity is not the only mode that can govern how religious communities live with each other.

When and why does religious pluralism foster civility and order, and when conflict and disorder? A consideration of the relationship between security and religion has to recognize both possibilities, that is, religious

---

[22]William McNeill, 'Project Report: Fundamentalism and the World of the 1990s', *Bulletin of the American Academy of Arts and Sciences*, 47 (3), 1993, p. 29. For earlier discussions of assimilation in American life, see Milton M. Gordon, *Assimilation in American Life: The Role of Race, Religion, and National Origins*, New York: Oxford University Press, 1964; Nathan Glazer and Daniel Patrick Moynihan, *Beyond the Melting Pot: The Negroes, Puerto Ricans, Jews, Italians, and Irish of New York City*, Cambridge, MA: MIT Press, 1963; and Will Herberg, *Protestant, Catholic, Jew: An Essay in American Religious Sociology*, Chicago: University of Chicago Press, 1983. For a discussion of the role of cultural extinction in separatist movements, see Lloyd I. Rudolph, 'India and the Punjab: A Fragile Peace', in The Asia Society, *Asian Issues 1985: Asian Agenda Report 3*, Lanham, MD: University Press of America, 1986.

[23]Religious pluralism may have thrived in part because religion was too serious an aspect of life to be assigned to the private realm, a condition that homogenizing solutions encourage.

[24]McNeill, 'Project Report', pp. 29–30. For an extended discussion of this type of pluralism, see Benjamin Braude, and Bernard Lewis (eds), *Christians and Jews in the Ottoman Empire: The Functioning of a Plural Society*, 2 vols, New York: Holmes and Meier, 1982, especially the introduction and the essay by Benjamin Braude. For a proposal to institutionalize a form of *millets*, or religious federalism, in India, see Partha Chatterjee, 'Secularism and Toleration', *Economic and Political Weekly*, 29 (28), 1994, pp. 1768–78.

communities as conciliatory components of viable civil societies, and as sources of mutual alienation, distrust, and conflict. The dominant path to religious and ethnic civility for most nineteenth-century nation-states was homogenization and assimilation. However, this is not the only way to peaceable settlements. The pluralistic guarantees of multinational empires, and the permanent polyethnicity of the older cities in Asia and Eastern Europe, represent an alternative cultural constitution. These approaches to conflict resolution are points on a continuum rather than opposites. Future negotiations about cultural security are likely to engage both alternatives.

WORLD POLITICS IN TRANSNATIONAL SPACE[25]

The challenge by non-governmental organizations (NGOs) to states in world political arenas is a special phenomenon of the 1990s.[26] World summits on human rights, the environment, population, and women brought states together with relevant and often obstreperous NGO forums, and created a new arena for world politics: transnational civil society. The society they began to create had precedents. In place of the anarchy posited by realist theory, Hedley Bull initiated a discussion of state cooperation with his 'Grotian' concept of 'international society'. Robert Keohane, Stephen Krasner, and others elaborated the idea of state cooperation via treaties, international organizations, and regimes. But these precedents differed significantly from the new transnationalism.

The older theoretical discourse of international relations had been carried on mainly via dichotomous oppositions, self-help/anarchy versus world government/order.[27] And it was carried on by dichotomous voices, neo-realists

[25]For formulations in this and the next two sections, I have drawn extensively on Lloyd I. Rudolph's discussion of civil society in *Political Science*, 518, 'Rethinking Sovereignty', Graduate Seminar, University of Chicago, Winter 1995.

[26]Stephen Toulmin, 'The UN and Japan in an Age of Globalization: The Role of Transnational NGOs in Global Affairs', Paper written for a forthcoming, as yet untitled volume of the Peace Research Institute of International Christian University, Tokyo, October 1994.

[27]Neo-realism emphasizes an institutional version of radical individualism in which each state relies upon its own devices and balances of power provide hope for stability. 'A state has to rely on its own devices, the relative efficiency of which must be its constant concern.' Kenneth Waltz, *Man, the State, and War: A Theoretical Analysis*, New York: Columbia University Press, 1959, p. 159. '[U]nits in a condition of anarchy ... must rely on the means they can generate ... for themselves. Self-help is necessarily the principle of action in an anarchic order.' Kenneth Waltz, *Theory of International Politics*, Reading, MA: Addison-Wesley, 1979, p. 111. This emphasis is challenged by liberal institutionalism's assertion of conventions and rules: 'Much behavior [in international politics] is recognized by participants as reflecting established rules, norms, and conventions, and its meaning is interpreted in light of these understandings.' Robert Keohane, 'Neo-Liberal Institutionalism: A Perspective on World Politics', in *International*

versus liberals who, despite their differences, were united by a belief that states are the only meaningful units of action in the global environment.[28] These categories became inadequate for capturing the experience of the 1990s. John Ruggie complained about an 'impoverished mindset at work here that is able to visualize long-term challenges to the system of states only in terms of entities that are institutionally substitutable for the state.'[29] Since the 1990s, there have been the makings of more complex, less dichotomous theorizations that focus on non-state actors and liminal phenomena, entities operating on the border of 'inside' and 'outside'. Ronnie Lipschutz, for example, writes of 'self-conscious constructions of networks of knowledge and action, by decentered, local actors that cross the reified boundaries of space as though they were not there', and of heteronomous networks, 'differentiated from each other in terms of specializations: there is not a single network, but many, each fulfilling a different function'.[30]

Discussions on neo-medievalism had earlier led to an exploration of liminal phenomena and shared sovereignty. Neo-medieval discourse drew attention to the possibility of multiple overlapping institutions, organizations, and practices in conjunction with cooperating states that limited and shared sovereignty.[31] As early as 1977, Hedley Bull had noted that neo-medievalism 'promises to avoid the classic dangers of the system of sovereign states by a structure of overlapping authorities and criss-crossing loyalties that hold all peoples together in a universal society'.[32] Though we need not romanticize

---

Institutions and State Power: Essays in International Relations Theory, Boulder: Westview Press, 1989. Keohane's analysis continues to focus on states as the main actors, but asserts a more rule-governed set of interactions than the radical statist individualism of the neo-realists suggests. For the neo-liberals, there is an immanent orderliness emerging from the experience of interaction and the convenience of expectable behaviour.

[28]For an interesting account of the new theoretical players on the epistemological scene of international affairs, see Alex Wendt, 'Constructing International Politics: A Response to Mearsheimer', *International Security*, 20 (1), 1995, pp. 71–81. See also Stephen D. Krasner, 'Power, Politics, Institutions, and Transnational Relations', in Thomas Risse-Kappen (ed.), *Bringing Transnational Relations Back In: Non-State Actors, Domestic Structures, and International Institutions*, Cambridge: Cambridge University Press, 1995.

[29]John G. Ruggie, 'Territoriality and Beyond: Problematizing Modernity in International Relations', *International Organization*, 47 (1), 1993, pp. 139–74. Ruggie's doomed flirtation with postmodernism in this essay is also theoretically interesting.

[30]Ronnie D. Lipschutz, 'Reconstructing World Politics: The Emergence of Global Civil Society', *Millennium: Journal of International Studies*, 21 (3), pp. 390–1.

[31]The medieval metaphor was launched by Hedley Bull under the title 'the New Medievalism' as he tried to imagine alternatives to the nation-state system. Bull, *The Anarchical Society*, New York: Columbia University Press, 1977, pp. 254–5. See also John G. Ruggie, 'Continuity and Transformation in the World Polity: Toward a Neorealist Synthesis', *World Politics*, 35 (2), 1983, pp. 273–4.

[32]Bull, *The Anarchical Society*, p. 255. However, adds Bull, the promise was imperfect: '[I]f it were anything like the precedent of Western Christendom, it would contain more ubiquitous

the medieval, the language and practice of medievalism reminds us that the modern state and the nation-state are recent inventions, neither immortal and universal entities independent of time, place, and circumstance, nor endpoints of a teleological historical process.[33]

Multiplicity of forms is not the only marker of medieval thought and practice. The medieval Catholic Church was the earliest, and has proved to be an enduring constraint on modern state claims to a monopoly on sovereignty and (reason of state) morality. José Casanova, in tracing the career of Catholic globalism in *Transnational Religion and Fading States*, shows how the Church's universalism, although eclipsed in the era of absolutism and the nation-state, has reappeared as part of the 'still undefined global system within which the papacy is attaining once again a central structural role'.[34]

Once a non-state arena is imagined, in which states are significant but are not the only players, it becomes possible to specify a space for transnational civil society in global politics. Civil society was a category elaborated in Western liberal thought by social contract theorists. Locke—but not Hobbes—spoke of two realms beyond the 'state of nature'—a societal bond that supported civil society and a state that, at the very least, provided a common judge and coercive power. Over the years, the role of civil society has been to legitimize a space for non-state associations, discourses, and practices that can limit or direct state actions. In its Lockean version, civil society has also stood for the idea that society has conventions and regularities that govern human conduct even in the absence of states—the idea that force and coercion are not the only guarantors of order. Finally, civil society is characterized by the way it contrasts with the state. It is the realm of contest, of dispute, persuasion, and mobilization, that is, the realm of politics, and the state is the guarantor of order, umpire, executor of force, the realm of governance.

Distinguishing civil society from the state is easier than distinguishing it from the private realm. If civil society does not encompass the family, does it encompass neighbours or friends? It probably does not. Conventionally,

---

and continuous violence and insecurity than does the modern state system.' Ubiquitous and continuous, probably, but body counts may be higher for modern warfare. Markus Fischer attempts to subsume the medieval model of international relations to the neo-realist paradigm by showing that church discourses and practices that characterized inter- and trans-kingdom relations in the Christian world merely disguise the continuity of self-interested and conflictual motives that always have and always will characterize humankind. Markus Fischer, 'Feudal Europe, 800–1300: Communal Discourse and Conflictual Practice', *International Organization*, 46 (2), 1992, pp. 139–74.

[33] Kenneth Pennington's discussions of shared sovereignty place the problem of state-centred monopoly sovereignty in perspective. See *The Prince and the Law, 1200–1600: Sovereignty and Rights in the Western Legal Tradition*, Berkeley: University of California Press, 1993, especially 'Epilogue: The Sixteenth Century and Beyond'.

[34] José Casanova, 'Globalizing Catholicism and the Return to a "Universal" Church'.

civil society has included 'organized'—and in that sense intentional—entities.[35] Are religious identities voluntary and chosen, or inherited and pre-determined? As I will suggest at greater length in *Transnational Religion and Fading States'* conclusion, the distinction between inherited and voluntary may itself be the product of a particular historical moment, and may have outlived its significance.

Transnational civil society resembles civil society, but also differs from it. First and foremost, civil society is located 'inside' states, and transnational civil society 'outside'. Both provide arenas for challenging states as well as cooperating with them.[36] Just as it is hard to know what should count as civil society, it is hard to establish criteria and parameters for transnational civil society. Candidates include multinational production, service, and financial firms; Sufi *turuq* and the Pontifical Council for the Promotion of Christian Unity; human rights NGOs; terrorist, drug, and Mafia networks; and satellite telecommunication companies.

The idea of transnational civil society, like the domestic variant, invokes resistant and polemical connotations, a space for self-conscious, organized actors to assert themselves for and against state policies, actions, and processes. It is this resistant and oppositional meaning that differentiates transnational civil society from the state cooperation that Hedley Bull designated 'international society'. International society, like liberal regimes, was seen as taming and transcending the anarchy posited by neo-realists, and creating the conditions for cooperation and conflict in world politics. It was a statelike entity, providing authoritative guarantees. Transnational civil society, by contrast, is a political realm, representing and mobilizing interests and opinions. The religious formations and movements that inhabit transnational civil society engage in the persuasion and collective action of world politics.

The sectors of transnational civil society—including the religion sector—and actors within sectors may conflict or cooperate. Stephen Toulmin invokes

[35]Some would sort religion with 'unintentional' entities. Weber provides an interesting introduction to this question when he allots 'sects' to the intentional side of the divide, and 'churches' to the unintentional side. Whether the member has to qualify and be selected is Weber's crucial marker of intentionality. 'The Protestant Sects and the Spirit of Capitalism', in *From Max Weber: Essays in Sociology,* by Hans Gerth and C. Wright Mills (eds), New York: Galaxy, 1958, pp. 302–22. But this is not an easy distinction to maintain in a day when old 'churches', such as Islam or Hinduism, are erecting new qualification boundaries, or when Catholics have the choice of construing their faith according to *Opus Dei* or Liberation Catholicism.

[36]In a pre-Grotian world, before political theorists diverged on whether they would regard states or individuals as *the* moral entities of international relations, it was ambiguous as to who the actors were that constituted international society princes, *res publicae, civitates*. Bull, *The Anarchical Society*, p. 29.

the British television serial *Upstairs, Downstairs* to characterize the situation at five major United Nations (UN) organized meetings, world summits, where NGOs formed parallel forums to the official gathering.[37] These occasions have displayed the new world politics on a well-lit stage. By its horizontal, global mobilization of opinion, the NGOs 'downstairs' have broken the monopoly the states had on the representation of domestic opinion. They bring world opinion to bear on 'upstairs', the assembly of official state actors. It so happens that at recent global summits they have cooperated more than they have engaged in conflict with each other.[38] The need for a common front were state-drafted resolutions to reflect NGO preferences provided a powerful incentive to find and articulate common positions.

However, we cannot assume that transnational non-state space, transnational civil society, will be 'civil'. Entities bound by differing norms and interests will not always have strategic reasons to cooperate. Religious formations and movements may share analytic membership in a 'religion' sector, but will have good reasons to differ. Transnational pluralism is likely to result in both benign and non-benign outcomes.[39]

THINNING OUT MONOPOLY SOVEREIGNTY

While communities constituting transnational civil society may have authority and even power, they do not claim sovereignty. They have authority in that a formally organized religious transnational entity such as the Roman Catholic Church is in a position to license and de-license the activities of its organizational units, in particular national sites such as the National Councils of Bishops. An informally structured movement like that of the West African Sufis is able to shape the transnational pilgrimages of its adherents across sacred territory; to satisfy, by negotiations with nation-states, its adherents'

[37]Stephen Toulmin, personal communication. See also his 'The Role of Transnational NGOs'.

[38]Professor Carolyn Elliott of the University of Vermont, in an unpublished report on the Beijing conference on women, contrasts the coordination and consensus at Beijing with the internal conflicts visible at Mexico City, the first UN conference on women.

> Women of the world have learned to work together. The shouting matches between women—Arabs and Palestinians, South Africans and Africans, American feminists and Third World critics—that dominated Mexico City were virtually absent in Beijing. Nor was there division between regions of the world. ('Elliott Travel Letter', unpublished personal communication, 1 October 1995).

[39]For an account that emphasizes the possibilities for incivility as well as for change arising out of 'a marked increase in the number of spontaneous collective actions', see James N. Rosenau, *Turbulence in World Politics: A Theory of Change and Continuity*, Princeton: Princeton University Press, 1990, p. 369. Also Sidney Tarrow, 'Eastern European Social Movements: Globalization, Difference, and Political Opportunity', unpublished manuscript.

expectations and claims for free passage; and to regulate, financial and tactical support networks; but they do not spawn sustained cooperation or significant formal coordination.

In a reversal of conventional expectations that education and mass media will be bearers of rationalism and secularism, both forms of communication have strengthened Islamic commitments and commonalities. The proliferation of mass higher education in the 1960s, visible in Muslim as in other developing and developed countries, has created a flood of first-generation students, many of whom have repaired to religion as a way of understanding and supporting their status as educated persons and *nouveaux arrivés*. These young people, says Eickelman, have reimagined religion in ways that replace traditional religious specialists and their formal representation of Islam with simple, easily accessible, attractive, and cheap books, magazines, and cassettes. They consume and communicate in colloquial Arabic rather than the formal medium of the older-style scholars.

In 'Bridging the Gap Between Empowerment and Power in Latin America', Daniel Levine and David Stoll report the shift from transnational religious initiative from the top to local structures and networks generated from below. Highly visible transnational actors—liberation Catholics of the left, Evangelicals of the right—transported religious formations to Latin America and across national frontiers within Latin America in ways that paralleled cleavages in the Cold War. For a time, these transnationally propelled activities led observers to underestimate the role of local and autonomous agency in the spread of religious doctrine and practice.

Latin American Catholicism rests on 500 years of a transnational proselytizing that was deeply intertwined with the colonial experience and the export of culture from Spain and Portugal. In the post-World War II era, the generous social message of Vatican Council II and the more liberal thrust of the Latin American Episcopal Conference (CELAM) effected significant changes in the social base of the Church. The translation into local languages of the liturgy and the encouragement of Bible reading and lay participation created conditions hospitable to the spread of liberation Catholicism, and the decentralized and self-ministering networks of base ecclesial communities (CEBs). Catholicism itself became not only a religion for below, but also from below.

The Protestant presence in Latin America, which has not only challenged Latin American Catholicism but also moved into the local spaces and religious habits created by liberationism, has grown strikingly, with the number of churches nearly doubling from 28,000 to 54,000 from 1953 to 1985. Whereas pre-war Protestantism grew out of European missions, the post-war expansion was encouraged by the entry of US evangelical and Pentecostal churches into the ground that mainline Protestantism had abandoned. Most of the new missions were North American, and they came to fight both communism and the 'whore of Babylon'. But a focus on televangelism and on US proselytizers can be misleading for attempts to evaluate the significance of the Protestant resurgence. Levine and Stoll write of religion from below as spreading through an 'available demography' of mobile persons moving from rural to urban settings and into literacy and education, or stationary rural peoples receiving soteriological communications together with economic intrusions. As Eickelman does in the case of Islam, Stoll and Levine emphasize the casual nature of organizational structures. Such informal networks are easy for amateurs to create, and serviceable for the immediate needs of the faithful. They give Evangelicalism its competitive strength and diffusionary power.

Levine and Stoll are more cautious than an earlier generation of social scientists who expected much from Latin American religion from below. This religiosity can create 'social capital', laying the foundation for further changes in society and politics. However, there are limits to the effectiveness of religion from below. Self-ministered religiosity can empower and spread easily. But without connections to higher and more formal policy levels in civil society and the state, these networks may fail to generate consequential social change.

In Ousmane Kane's 'Muslim Missionaries and African States', West African Sufis are found to occupy autonomous spaces in transnational civil society, but are also intertwined with states. Regarded by the French colonial state as the embodiment of dangerous pan-Islamic tendencies, the Tijaniyya *tariqa* nevertheless made its peace with that state. The marabouts, spiritual leaders of the Sufi orders, replaced earlier kings as intermediaries between the colonial state and society. They increased their economic power as well as the reach of Islam. The Tijaniyya spiritual influence stretches from Morocco across the Senegambia region and on to Nigeria, with regional and local zawiyas sending disciples to the parent zawiya in the holy cities of Kano (Nigeria) and Kaolack (Senegal). The movement's transnational sacred geography is concretized by pilgrimage, trade, markets, and marriage networks enabled by sacred cities, and by the birthday celebrations of the prophet and of a tariqa's spiritual leader. Its engagement with states is confirmed through the electoral support it offers ruling governments, support that is reciprocated through extraterritorial privileges like customs exemptions, autonomy of holy cities, scholarships to foreign universities for the faithful, and loans.

Sufi zawiyas, like other Islamic informal organizations, address issues of physical and cultural survival in contexts where the state infrastructure is uneven or weak. They provide both forms of security through centres that offer multiple services, for instance, the transmission of religious knowledge, refuge to fugitives, help to the indigent, and political support. Zawiya networks serve as civil society's hedge against personal insecurity, communal violence, and chaos. The predictable symbolic and economic sociability of the Tijaniyya presents a sharp contrast to the utter collapse of sociocultural networks in parts of East Africa in the mid-1990s.

In 'Faces of Catholic Transnationalism: In and Beyond France', Danièle Hervieu-Léger reveals the new, informal, homemade face that is displacing the formal, catechized, and bureaucratized visage of an older Catholicism. She points to a number of contradictory tendencies. On the one hand, we see the decline of the parish and the local *clocher*, of the intimate universe that organized the practising Catholicism of the French, marked by the diminution of church attendance and clerical vocations. Their place is taken by wide-ranging, loosely structured affinity groups of enthusiastic and emotional young people travelling across state borders to World Youth Congresses, dedicated at the doctrinal level to a bland, generalized ethical commitment. On the other hand, the Church is moving to strengthen its hold and universalize its organizational structure. What continental scholars call 'integralist' tendencies are on the increase, reasserting more conservative and stringent standards of canonical adherence. The two tendencies, the looser, self-made Catholicism of affinity groups and the growth of a more centralized pattern, represent alternative forms of globalization.

HIERARCHY: FROM A CENTRE AND FROM ABOVE

Ralph Della Cava's 'Religious Resource Networks: Roman Catholic Philanthropy in Central and East Europe' is the quintessential account of religious formation from the top, from a centre, and via formal organization. He not only demonstrates the workings of religion from above, but also argues that 'autonomous' and 'spontaneous' religious NGOs are heavily and increasingly dependent on sponsors in the developed world. His argument is buttressed by his representation of the ways in which the Holy See, a multiplicity of lay-directed European and American philanthropic organizations, and the German episcopate reached out to the East European churches before and after the decline of communism. The story reveals the Catholic Church's vast and intricately complex bureaucracies—the German *Kirche in Not* could alone function as the department of welfare of a respectable state. The complexity reflects the pluralistic world over which the See of Peter presides.

The conduct of Catholic Ostpolitik from the Danube to Vladivostok posed delicate diplomatic issues for the Church as its multiple but coordinated players approached the states of Eastern Europe and Russia after World War II. The iron curtain proved more porous to church exchanges, and communist states proved more inclined to make concessions, than was then admitted by a Church seen as single-mindedly opposed to godless communism. The more recent, post-1980 encounter in the former Soviet Union between an expanding Rome and Russian Orthodoxy raises questions concerning the relationship between religious and political territoriality. The monopoly of the Orthodox Church, promoted by its earlier alliance with the communist state, is threatened by the new openness to religious diversity. The Russian state, like the East Asian states reviewed by Baker, favours religions that are well-insulated from outside influences.

In 'World Religions and National States: Competing Claims in East Asia', Don Baker discusses the dirigiste efforts of East Asian states to deny and render invisible domestic religions from below, while privileging world religions from above. This policy derives, on the one hand, from an internationally available post-Enlightenment discourse that declares some religions to be superstitious and others not, and on the other, from the propensity of East Asian states to subsume religion. Baker reviews the ways in which external agency has forced Asian states to grant religious freedoms, and the uneven distribution of such freedoms across religions. The path to religious autonomy in China, Japan, and Korea was forged by imperialist intruders who established enclaves of extraterritoriality. At the end of the nineteenth century, the European powers extracted the privilege of non-interference with their religions and the right to proselytize. With the end of overt European domination, East Asian countries supported freedom of religion as a marker of modern respectability in the world system of states.

The religions that East Asian states are willing to register and recognize for purposes of religious freedom include 'world' religions and exclude 'unevolved' popular religions, those without high-culture trappings, 'scriptures', and recognizable organizational attributes. Thus, in China, Protestantism, Catholicism, Buddhism, Taoism, and Islam are acceptable, but 'shamanism' and 'folk religion' are not. Indigenous privileging of the religions of the intellectuals coincides with the evolutionary history and social science classifications that are the legacy of colonial and neo-colonial cultural transmission.

These principles of recognition give transnational religions ambiguous significance. They are viewed positively as the bearers of triumphant modern norms, and the doctrines and organization of consequential world orders. They are viewed negatively when they contest the monopoly of states accustomed to subsuming religion. The preference for organized religions from above, says Baker, over spontaneous and informal practices from below may be dictated by political prudence as much as by a cultural aesthetic. Organized religion is easier to keep track of and control.

In 'Globalizing Catholicism and the Return to a "Universal" Church', José Casanova, addressing the oldest of the Western transnational religions, emphasizes religion from above and the expanding space of transnational civil society. Central to the story is the history of the waning and subsequent revival of Catholic universalism. The claims of the medieval Church to articulate a universal moral realm fell victim to the rise of the nation-state, and the consequent nationalization of churches. The Church's adaptation to nation-states protected the faithful and their space to practice religion, but it did so at the cost of upholding universal norms. The settlements with Mussolini and Hitler represented extreme adaptations, whereas the relatively informal exchanges with the East European communist regimes revealed a more moderate accommodation.

The trend is now reversed, claims Casanova. In the post-World War II discourses of the Church, the increasingly robust Catholic defence of human rights contrasts with the earlier, narrow defence of the needs of the faithful. Vatican II's Declaration on Religious Freedom as well as John XXIII's vigorous espousal of universal human rights heralded a shift from *libertas ecclesiae* to *libertas personae*. The Church, Casanova argues, has shown itself prepared to assert the freedom of religion in the face of state sovereignty and *raison d'état*, as in its challenges to the authoritarianism of Franco, Marcos, and the rulers of Poland (although the pope's equivocal retrospect in June 1996 on the Catholic Church's inaction with respect to the fate of the German Jews suggests that a few older reticences persist). This process, Casanova argues, has not only made the Church the 'First Citizen of Global Civil Society', but has also returned Rome to what he calls the North Atlantic Protestant capitalist system, from which it had become alienated.

Cary Fraser's 'In Defense of Allah's Realm: Religion and Statecraft in Saudi Foreign Policy Strategy' is an examination of the strategies adopted by Saudi Arabia in its manoeuvres for leadership in the Middle East. Here, religion is treated as a resource in interstate competition rather than as a realm in civil society or an autonomous meaning system. Iran exploits the affinity feelings of the Shiite diaspora in Lebanon, Iraq, and Saudi Arabia, and the contagious enthusiasm for a radical Islam in order to enhance its international capacities. Saudi Arabia contests Iran's primacy by exploiting its control of Mecca, its standing as guardian of the holy places of Islam, and its representation, via Wahhabi Islam, of an older Islamic legitimacy.

The account is situated in the context of a familiar balance-of-power story in which civil society hardly makes an appearance. All the actors are maximizing states using whatever resources they can—oil prices, support for the PLO, pro- or anti-monarchical sentiments, alliances with superpowers, Shia or Sunni affiliation—to enhance their respective interests.

The 1950s and 1960s witnessed a cleavage in the Middle East between pan-Arabist powers and their opponents. The post-World War II modernizers, Gamal Abdel Nasser, Saddam Hussein, and Anwar Sadat, led the secular, anti-monarchical, 'socialist', anti-Western, and often pro-Soviet pan-Arabism. They faced Islamist, monarchical, anti-Soviet, often Western-allied forces led by the Gulf kingdoms, with Saudi Arabia at their head. The Iranian Revolution, Fraser argues, redefined the rules of play. The older cleavage was partly superseded by a new one between radical Islam, led by Iran, and conservative Islam, led by Saudi Arabia. These contestants fill the space left vacant by the decline of pan-Arabism's main exponent, Egypt, which suffered Nasser's death, defeat by Israel, and expulsion from the Arab League after signing the Camp David accords.

Fraser's is not an account designed to support the view that Islam is a solitary force marching against the West, or that religion is a variable capable of predicting alliances. The Saudi dependence on the West for arms and financing, the Iraqi forces' dependence on the West in the Iran-Iraq War, and the anti-Iraqi forces' dependence on the West in the war over Kuwait together suggest that Islamic states ally across religious/civilizational lines, and represent anything but a united civilizational front.

The contributions to *Transnational Religion and Fading States* do not forecast a more likely future or more successful prospects for hierarchy or self-organization. They suggest that transnational civil society is made up of highly diverse forms that need to be understood and theorized with the nuance and complexity appropriate to a crucial new arena of action.

5

Framing the Inquiry
Historicizing the Modern State*

LLOYD I. RUDOLPH AND J.K. JACOBSEN

This is a book about experiencing the state—not the state as thing, or a bureaucracy, an army, a police force, something as Wittgenstein would have it, which one can define ostensibly by pointing to it; neither is the state an idea, an abstraction, which is what Hegel seems to have had in mind.[1] We and the contributors to *Experiencing the State* mean to engage state and stateness as it is encountered in everyday life. Still, the question remains: what is being experienced in the essays that follow? In each case it is some kind of a construction that arises out of language and practice in context. Where the language and practice came from is a question that returns us to 'the literature'.

Much of the literature in political science and the social sciences treats 'the state' more generally as an abstraction by universalizing and standardizing what the state is, what it does, and what it means. States are discussed as if they were the same through time, space, and circumstance, a practice that often results in analyses and narratives that suffer from being either anachronistic or presentist. Sometimes the opposite happens: state analyses and narratives suffer from what Whitehead called the fallacy of misplaced concreteness.[2]

*Originally published as 'Introduction: Framing the Inquiry—Historicizing the Modern State', in Lloyd I. Rudolph and John Kurt Jacobsen (eds), *Experiencing the State*, New Delhi: Oxford University Press, 2006, pp. vii–xxviii.

[1] Hegel's theory of the state can be found in his *Philosophy of Right*, trans. T.M. Knox, Oxford: Oxford University Press, 1942. According to Shlomo Avineri, 'On no account can Hegel's theory be so construed as to refer to any existing state; it is the *idea* [emphasis in the original] of the state with which Hegel is dealing and any existing state cannot be anything but a mere approximation.' Shlomo Avineri, *Hegel's Theory of the Modern State*, London: Cambridge University Press, 1972, 1974, p. 177.

[2] For the fallacy of misplaced concreteness, see 'Lecture Three: Understanding,' in Alfred

For starters, we try to avoid naturalizing the term 'state' by historicizing it. By locating states in time, place, and circumstance, as most of the contributors to *Experiencing the State* do, we can be contingent and evocative rather than definitive and essentializing. We write in the first years of the twenty-first century, a time when it is frequently said that states are being compromised at home and abroad by globalization and terrorism, processes that challenge their sovereignty and capacities both domestically and internationally. In the nineteenth century, the heyday of the modern state, states were assumed to be the means by which to solve problems and realize progress. As the twentieth century gave way to the twenty-first, states were more often than not spoken of as the problem rather than as the solution.

Turning from what we may think or say about the state, what images, what hopes and fears, what expectations and anticipations does the word 'state' evoke in the minds of our fellow scholars and potential readers? In order to unpack the baggage the word 'state' may carry in their minds, we turn to the story of Europe's invention of the modern state. We start with absolutism as it was invented and practised in seventeenth-century France and Prussia.[3] We summon an image of Cardinal Richelieu (Armand-Jean du Plessis, duc de Richelieu) as it was recently portrayed in Montreal's Museum of Fine Art's 2002 exhibition, 'Richelieu: Art and Power', to help us imagine the construction and career of absolutism. From 1624 until his death at the age of fifty-seven in 1642, Richelieu was the imaginative and ruthless prime minister of France. He moulded the unlikely and unpromising Louis XIII[4] into his conception of a divinely sanctioned absolute ruler, tamed the feudal aristocracy, reined in post-reformation religious conflict, created, in Norbert Elias' phrase, a 'court society',[5] and brought into being one state governed from Paris that dominated Europe culturally and politically until

---

North Whitehead, *Modes of Thought*, New York: Capricorn Books/G. P. Putnam and Sons, 1958, pp. 58–87.

[3]For an effective and succinct historical overview of early modern state formation, see Eugene Rice, and Anthony Grafton, *The Foundations of Early Modern Europe, 1460–1559*, New York: W.W. Norton, 1994. Brian M. Downing's *The Military Revolution and Political Change: The Origins of Democracy and Autocracy in Early Modern Europe*, Princeton, NJ: Princeton University Press, 1992, and Perry Anderson's *Lineages of the Absolutist State*, London: New Left Books, 1974 provide differing versions of the formation of the absolutist modern state. Downing shows how variations in circumstances such as geographical location and class structure opened the way for constitutional alternatives to French and Prussian absolutism in Britain and the Netherlands.

[4]Son of Henry IV of Navarre and Marie de Medici. Having been raised a Protestant and led the Protestant (Huguenot) cause in France, he became a Catholic as that was a pre-condition of becoming king of France in 1589. (Henry is believed to have said that Paris was well worth a mass.)

[5]See Norbert Elias (trans. by Edmund Jephcott), *The Court Society*, New York: Pantheon Books, 1983.

1789.[6] His campaign 'to invent the state' started with French culture; he built the first theatre in Paris, established the Académie Française to codify and elevate the language, and became the protector of the Sorbonne. To exalt his state, 'Richelieu tapped the mythical glories of ancient Rome as well as the mystical faith of Christian Rome'. Deborah Weisgall says,

It was Richelieu's genius to transfer to politics the Counter-Reformation's tools— dramatic, immediate and often breathtaking images emphasizing the mystery, the compelling irrationality, of faith. For Richelieu, the state and the king, with their God-given authority, shared these mystic qualities. And he was the worldly priest, the master of mysteries.

Richelieu knew himself, Weisgall says.

In his bedroom he hung a painting by George de la Tour: The Penitent St. Jerome. The saint, clad only in loincloth, holds his cardinal's robe and a crucifix in his left hand. In his right, he grips a scourge. Its knot drips blood onto the floor. Jerome's sin was intellectual pride.

Richelieu's pride, achievements, and wars with Spain and the Hapsburgs 'cost the common man heavily. When he died ... he was immensely wealthy and almost universally hated.'[7]

We fast forward in our story of the formation of the modern state to a century and a half later, from the era of absolutism to the era of the French Revolution. The revolution had the effect of translating Rousseau's concept of the general will into a claim that it was the people, and not the king, who were sovereign. Popular sovereignty displaced the absolutist notion of monarchical sovereignty by embedding sovereignty in the nation. The modern state became a nation-state. The era of high stateness[8] had begun. The career of the modern state, Stephen Toulmin argues, runs roughly from

[6]Carl Friedrich credits Richelieu and Louis XIII with giving birth to the modern state in the following anecdote. 'I am more obligated to the state', Louis XIII declared on the famous 'Day of Dupes', 11 November 1630, when he rejected the Queen Mother [Marie de Medici, wife of Henry of Navarre or Henry IV] and her claims for family in favour of Cardinal Richelieu and his claims for the state. Friedrich says, 'More than any other single day, it may be called the birthday of the modern state.' Carl J. Friedrich, *The Age of the Baroque: 1610–1660*, New York: Harper, 1962, pp. 215–16.

[7]Deborah Weisgall, 'A Hard Man Who Saw Art as Power and Vice Versa', *The New York Times*, 20 October 2002. Weisgall's article reviews 'Richelieu: Art and Power', an exhibit curated by Hillard T. Goldfarb at Montreal's Museum of Fine Art, October 2002 through 5 January 2003.

[8]We take this term from Peter Nettl's seminal article, 'The State as a Conceptual Variable', *World Politics*, 20 (4), 1968. High stateness was given new meaning and new life in James Scott's *Seeing Like a State; How Certain Schemes to Improve the Human Condition Have Failed*, New Haven: Yale University Press, 1998.

the Peace of Westphalia (1648)[9] to World War I[10] when, *inter alia*, its claims to monopolize sovereignty and the legitimate use of force, and to provide security inside and outside[11] began to prove ineffective, counter-productive, or self-destructive.[12]

From feudal to modern to postmodern times, we see an inverse relationship between attention to stateness and attention to civil society: the more the attention to civil society, the less the attention to stateness; the more the attention to stateness, the less the attention to civil society. Starting with the early modern ideas advanced by Machiavelli, Bodin, and Hobbes in the sixteenth and seventeenth centuries and supplemented by Rousseau in the eighteenth, the claims for state sovereignty and the legitimacy of state institutions rose even as the claims for the legitimacy of the feudal institutions of medieval civil society, such as estates, parliaments, the church, guilds, and towns associated with parcellated and contested sovereignty, declined. Machiavelli made reason of state a ruler's supreme consideration.[13] Bodin

[9]Although he died in 1642, six years before the Peace of Westphalia, it represented the success of Cardinal Richelieu's policies and concepts.

[10]This is the view taken by Stephen Toulmin in *Cosmopolis: The Hidden Agenda of Modernity*, New York: The Free Press, 1990.

[11]Processes, institutions, and organizations that limit state sovereignty 'inside' and 'outside' were theorized and examined early on by R.B.J. Walker in *Inside/Outside: International Relations as Political Theory*, Cambridge: Cambridge University Press, 1993.

[12]Arguments supporting the view that thinking about sovereignty and the modern state has become obsolescent or anachronistic can be found in a wide variety of works, only a few of which can be mentioned here: Vaclav Havel, 'The End of the Modern Era', *The New York Times*, 1 March 1992; John Dunn, 'Introduction: Crisis of the Nation State?'; and Istvan Hont, 'The Permanent Crisis of a Divided Mankind: Contemporary Crisis of the Nation State in Historical Perspective', in *Contemporary Crisis of the Nation State*, by John Dunn (ed.), Oxford and Cambridge, MA: Blackwell, 1995; Susanne Hoeber Rudolph, 'Introduction: Religion, States and Transnational Civil Society', in *Transnational Religion and Fading States*, by Susanne Hoeber Rudolph and James Piscatori (eds), Boulder, Co: Westview Press, 1997; David Held, 'The Decline of the Nation State', in *Becoming National: A Reader*, by Geoff Eley and Ronald Grigor Suny (eds), New York: Oxford University Press, 1996. Alarmed by the consequences of the economic development of failing states and state collapse, the World Bank devoted its 1997 World Development Report to *The State in a Changing World*, New York: Oxford University Press, 1997.

[13]For our purposes here, the literature on Machiavellism, which is most often read as the theory and practice of reason of state, is more salient than the literature by and on Machiavelli. For reason of state, Freidrich Meinecke's *Machiavellism: The Doctrine of Raison D' Etat and Its Place in History*, Boulder, Co: Westview Press, 1984 remains the authoritative work. Three chapters in Ernest Cassirer's *The Myth of the State*, New Haven: Yale University Press, 1946, 'Machiavelli's New Science of Politics'; 'The Triumph of Machiavellianism and Its Consequences'; and 'Implications of the New Theory of the State' updates and adds valuable historical and analytic insights to Meinecke's work. The essays in a book edited by Jules Kirshner, *The Origins of the State in Italy, 1300–1600*, Chicago: University of Chicago Press, 1996, puts Machiavelli's transformatory thinking in historical context.

advanced monopoly claims for state sovereignty. For Hobbes' concept of Leviathan and Rousseau's of the general will, associations were anathema, at best worms in the entrails of the body politic, a source of competing values, interests, and identities that threatened state sovereignty, individual security, and the public good.

In our effort to situate the perceptions of the modern state that come up in the essays that follow, we turn from the story of the rise of the modern state to that of the modern state in decline. World War I was an important turning point. The meaningless deaths of ten million soldiers and the expenditure of vast amounts of national wealth in the war marked a watershed in the modern state's reputation as a vehicle for civilization and progress. That decline was reinforced by the rise of violent and racist, fascist states before World War II, and the collapse of the Soviet empire at the close of the Cold War.

Increasing awareness towards the end of the twentieth century of state pathology and failure directed attention to the possibilities of civil society. The success or failure of ex-colonial states after World War II, and of transitions to democracy and market economies after the end of the Cold War and the collapse of the Soviet Union, began to be attributed to aspects of civil society such as the viability of associational life and public spheres, and the availability of social capital and trust. In Poland during the 1980s, Solidarity's, and the Catholic Church's, ability to challenge, then help topple and displace a communist state, and contribute to jump-starting a market economy were used to support arguments for the centrality of civil society in transitions to democracy, and state and market viability. As states stumbled, foundered, and failed, the attractiveness of the civil society alternative grew. Renewed attention to Tocqueville's argument that democracy in America depended on the strength of its associational life and to Habermas' argument (in a book first published in 1962) for the civilizing effects of a public sphere[14] were the forerunners of a spate of academic writing about civil society and its cousins, social capital and trust, which emerged in the closing decade of the twentieth century. Robert Putnam, a political science professor at Harvard, struck celebrity pay dirt in 1995 with a jeremiad about civic disengagement

---

[14]Jurgen Habermas (trans. Thomas Burger and Frederick Lawrence), *The Structural Transformation of the Public Sphere: An Inquiry into a Category of Bourgeois Society*, Cambridge, MA: MIT Press, 1989 and 1991, first published in German under the title *Strukturwander der Offentlicheit* (Darmstadt and Neuwied, FRG: Herman Luchterhand Verlag, 1962). Similar arguments were made in Lloyd I. Rudolph, 'The Origin of Party: From the Politics of Status to the Politics of Opinion in Eighteenth Century England and America', Ph.D. dissertation, Harvard University, 1956.

in America, entitled 'bowling alone'.[15] However, if, at the turn of the twentieth century, the state was being challenged by civil society as a means for collective action, a source of identity and security, and the realization of public goods, the state's decline was relative. Its decline did not herald its demise.

At the close of the twentieth century, citizens still turned to the state not only for security at home and abroad, but also as a vehicle for societal self-protection from market forces. Karl Polanyi in his 1944 classic, *The Great Transformation*, spoke of a double movement. On the one hand there was the relentless and ubiquitous drive by market forces to commodify human beings and nature as wages and rent and, on the other, there were the efforts by organized societal forces such as parties and trade unions acting through the state to save forms of life and the biosphere from the dehumanizing and destructive effects of market forces. As Joseph Stiglitz put it in his introduction to the 2001 edition of Polanyi's 1944 book, 'self-regulating markets never work; their deficiencies, not only in their internal workings but also ... in their ... [societal] consequences are so great that government intervention becomes necessary'.[16] The context for these observations was Stiglitz's observation that Polanyi wrote *The Great Transformation* before 'modern economists clarified the limitations of self-regulating markets. Today, there is no respectable intellectual support for the proposition that markets, by themselves, lead to efficient, let alone equitable outcomes.'[17]

The essays in *Experiencing the State* explore how citizens at the turn of the millennium are affected by the double movement. How do state policies, actions, and speech affect their everyday lives? Do they find the state supportive, impartial, or hostile? Is it perceived as benign and helpful, a clumsy behemoth, a malevolent source of Orwellian surveillance, or 'a committee

---

[15]In an end piece to his 2000 book, *Bowling Alone: The Collapse and Revival of American Community*, New York: Touchstone, 2001, Robert Putnam recounts how his January 1995 article about 'bowling alone' in *The Journal of Democracy* made him famous. 'Until January 1995,' he writes, 'I was…an obscure academic. ... Although I had published scores of books and articles in the previous three decades ... none had attracted the slightest public attention. Now I was invited to Camp David, lionized by talk-show hosts and ... pictured with my wife, Rosemary, on the pages of People. The explanation [lay] ... in the simple fact that I had unwittingly articulated an unease that had already begun to form in the minds of ordinary Americans' (p. 506). It seems that what Americans sensed they were losing or lacking, for example social capital, trust, and civic engagement, was what American academics, policy intellectuals, and domestic bureaucracies and international organizations thought developing and transitional countries needed for state formation and economic growth.

[16]Karl Polanyi, *The Great Transformation: The Political and Economic Origins of Our Time*, Boston: Beacon Press, 2001, pp. vii–viii.

[17]Ibid., p. viii.

for managing the common affairs of the whole bourgeoisie'?[18] Rashomon-like, the truth of each essay is shaped by its location in time, space, circumstance, and epistemic community.

The contributors have produced situated knowledge about experiencing the state in a variety of arenas–regional planning, local and urban government, the colonial, welfare and developmental state, literature, cinema, education, and psychotherapy. Combining personal experience or observation with careful analysis, they tell us how state forms and manifestations are experienced by themselves or by citizens, and explore the consequences of those experiences for politics and society.

In an era of downsizing and relentless technological change, market solutions by private corporations are being presented as better suited than state bureaucracies to provide the services citizens require. This was the message of the 1980s that British prime minister Margaret Thatcher and US president Ronald Reagan brought to their people.[19] They revived an American version of Lockean liberalism that called for a distrust of state power; the least government was said to be the best government.[20] Thatcher and Reagan redistributed income in ways that favoured the rich by cutting taxes, and trying with some success to dismantle their respective country's version of the welfare state.[21] Yet states, for all their limitations and abuses, remain the means through which citizens as consumers and investors can attempt to regulate and perfect markets, protect their rights, and seek security.[22]

Insofar as states, like nations, are 'imagined communities', it matters who does and who does not do the imagining. Stuart Hall argues that it is important to ask who does the imagining because there are many

ways in which meaning about this world can be construed ... it matters profoundly what and who regularly and routinely gets left out; and how things, people, events,

[18]Robert Tucker, *The Marx-Engels Reader*, New York: W.W. Norton and Company, 1978, p. 475.

[19]See, *inter alia*, Joel Krieger, *Reagan, Thatcher and the Politics of Decline*, New York: Oxford University Press, 1986.

[20]See Louis Hartz' generative analysis, *The Liberal Tradition in America*, New York: Harcourt Brace Jovanovich, 1955, and the critical considerations in Michael Paul Rogin, *The Intellectuals and McCarthy: The Radical Spectre*, Cambridge, MA: MIT Press, 1967.

[21]Regarding Reagan and after in America, see Edward N. Wolff, *Top Heavy: A Study of the Increasing Inequality of Wealth in America*, New York: Twentieth Century Fund, 1995; Thomas Ferguson and Joel Rogers, *Right Turn*, New York: Hill and Wang, 1992; and David Stockman, *The Triumph of Politics*, New York: Harper & Row, 1986.

[22]In December 2003, when we were re-writing this introduction, the story of the collusion between Boeing, the Pentagon, and Senator Stevens [R-Alaska] with respect to an $18 billion order for 100 refuelling tankers for the Air Force was being publicly told. See *The New York Times*, 19 December 2003.

relationships are represented. What we know of society, depends on how things are represented to us and that knowledge in turn informs what we do and what policies we are prepared to accept.[23]

Henry Giroux takes a somewhat different tack when he argues that we should 'be conscious of how power and authority are secured in the language through which individuals speak and are spoken'.[24] But people are not trapped in material structures or linguistic prison houses either—at least, not always. Margaret Archer reminds us that although the prior development of ideas (from earlier interactions) conditions the current context of action, the

reflective ability of human beings to fight back against their conditioning [gives] them the capacity to respond with originality to their present context—either taking advantage of inconsistencies within it and generating new forms of syncretism or pluralism from it, or by exploring novel combinations of compatible elements.[25]

In *Experiencing the State*, we have asked writers from diverse disciplines and callings to look at 'how meanings are produced within relations of power': they have done so by addressing a wide array of topics and using their preferred modes of analysis. Commencing from different vantage points and arenas, they explore how they, or those whose stories they tell, have experienced some aspect of differently situated states. Their stories address overt policy aspects of the experience as well as the images and presuppositions built into the way a state is perceived. Readers will find that state policies are differentially enforced. Race, class, creed, and place matter. States are experienced in radically different ways by homeless persons offering tabloids for sale, poor peasants displaced by big dams, slum dwellers in Karachi, cultivators in north Indian villages, hospitalized mental patients, exhibitors dealing with philistine state sponsors, and a mahatma on trial for subversion of the colonial state in India.

The state, Polanyi argued, is the site where political communities decide where commodification ends (or is extended), where business has no business imposing a profit criterion. Neither firms nor citizens can accomplish much

[23]Stuart Hall, 'Media Power and Class Power', in *Bending Reality: The State of the Media*, by Jim Curran and Jake Eccleston (eds), London: Pluto Press, 1986.

[24]Henry Giroux, *Disturbing Pleasures: Learning Popular Culture*, London: Routledge, 1994, p. 113. Pierre Bourdieu reminds us that the 'most successful ideological effects are those which have no need for words and ask no more than complicitous silence': *Outline of A Theory of Practice*, Cambridge: Cambridge University Press, 1977.

[25]Margaret Archer, *Culture and Agency: The Place of Culture in Social Theory*, Cambridge: Cambridge University Press, 1988, p. xxiv. See also the Introduction to Lloyd I. Rudolph and Susanne Hoeber Rudolph's *The Modernity of Tradition*, Chicago: University of Chicago Press, 1967, 1983, pp. 3–14.

without the instruments and symbols of the modern state on their side.[26] The question, then, is: to what political purposes are such instruments and symbols put? Even if the scope and sovereignty of the modern state has been limited by the challenges that multilateral and international organizations, non-governmental organizations (NGOs), and the 'transnational civil society'[27] have posed, it is premature to compose its epitaph. For the foreseeable future the modern democratic state remains the leading institutional alternative for citizens wishing to exert a direct and compelling influence over those who govern them. Witness the rather intense concerns prevailing today over the 'democratic deficit' inside the European Union. As the struggle over globalization processes and their consequences make clear, transnational civil society and world public opinion are growing in importance, and states' capabilities, functions, and strategies are being modified accordingly. But, as we have argued and as the essays that follow illustrate, it would be wrong to suggest the imminent demise of the modern state. For the foreseeable future, experiencing the state will continue to occupy an important place in most peoples' lives.

Having placed the state in historical perspective and suggested the kinds of challenges it faces inside and outside, we turn to how the essays presented in *Experiencing the State* address our theme of experiencing the state. We have organized the essays in four thematic sections: I. Experiencing High Modernist States in America, India, and the Soviet Union; II. Experiencing the State from Below in Village Germany, India, Urban Karachi, and London; III. Experiencing the State from the Outside: Psychiatry, Film, and Art; and IV. Emancipatory Resistance. The thinking that went into the writing of James Scott's opening essay in Section I, 'High Modernist Social Engineering: The Case of the Tennessee Valley Authority', helped shape his influential 1998 book, *Seeing Like a State: How Certain Schemes to Improve the Human Condition Have Failed*.[28] The TVA essay keynotes our volume in the sense that it makes a case for the potentially oppressive nature of the modern state. It does so as a vehicle for what Scott characterizes as high modernism, not only its a priori, abstract, contextless rationality,[29] but also its increasingly ubiquitous

[26]See Polanyi, *The Great Transformation*, Boston: Beacon Press, 1944, 1957. See particularly Chapter 19, 'Popular Government and Market Economy', pp. 231–44.

[27]For an interpretation and application of the concept of transnational civil society, see Susanne Hoeber Rudolph's 'Introduction: Religion, States and Transnational Civil Society', in *Transnational Religion and Fading States*, pp. 1–24.

[28]James Scott, *Seeing Like a State: How Certain Schemes to Improve the Human Condition Have Failed*, New Haven: Yale University Press, 1998.

[29]An important aspect of the contextless rationality is the invocation by high modernists of the science trope. For a critique of this view, see Paul Feyerabend, *Science in a Free Society*, London: Verso, 1978.

surveillance[30] and control that limits human freedom and threatens citizens' rights. Scott's reading of the modern state as a potentially oppressive institution catches echoes from nineteenth-century anarchist thinkers like Proudhon, Kropotkin, and Bakunin,[31] Weber's tragic metaphor of modernity, the iron cage, and Foucault's (via Bentham) of the panopticon. High modernists shun politics because it can challenge the rationality of their abstract schemes.[32]

The state-sponsored 'high modernism' of the Tennessee Valley Authority, a 'multi-purpose' regional development scheme meant to transform Appalachia from rags to riches, is paradigmatic of the a prioristic, axiomatic character of high modernist thinking and practice.[33] Tennessee Valley Authority programmes and policies needed 'grassroots' support if they were to work. Instead, TVA was 'co-opted and domesticated by local power-holders': The state was the crucial site on which these battles were waged because only 'the state could represent the interests of the poor, of blacks, or of the larger society'. Scott examines the high-modernist reformer's dilemma where a vision of a more just society confronts democratic institutions controlled largely by the 'beneficiaries of these inequalities'. The TVA reflected internal tensions between its benign democratizing aims and short-term pragmatic accommodations. What people on the ground experienced were good intentions, but ultimately not policies and actions that incorporated their knowledge, needs, and aspirations.

Arundhati Roy's 'The Cost of Living' picks up America's TVA story half a century later. Soon after winning the Booker Prize in 1997 for *The God of Small Things*, Roy joined forces with Medha Patkar's Narmada Bachao Andolan to resist the Narmada Valley Development Project,[34] a prodigious effort that

[30]Even before 9/11 Anthony Giddens, like James Scott, noted the 'expansion of surveillance in the modern political order, in combination with the policing of deviance radically transforms the relations between state authority and the governed population, compared with traditional states. Administrative power now increasingly enters the minutiae of daily life and the most intimate personal actions and relationships.' Anthony Giddens, *The Nation-State and Violence*, Cambridge: Polity Press, 1985, p. 309. See also the essays in the more recent Kristie Bell, and Frank Webster (eds), *The Intensity of Surveillance*, London: Pluto Press, 2003.

[31]For an overview of anarchist thought and action, and of its leading personalities, see Barbara Tuchman's Chapter 2, 'The Idea and the Deed. The Anarchists: 1890–1914', in her *The Proud Tower: A Portrait of the World Before the War, 1890–1914*, New York: Ballantine Books, 1996, pp. 63–113.

[32]Bernard Crick, *In Defence of Politics*, London: Penguin Books, 1982, pp. 92–110.

[33]This is what Dahl and Lindblom call 'social engineering optimism' in high gear. See Robert Dahl and Charles Lindblom, *Politics, Economics and Welfare: Planning and Politico-Economic Systems Resolved into Social Processes*, 2nd edn, Chicago, University of Chicago Press, 1967.

[34]The Narmada Valley Development Project (NVDP) envisages building 3200 dams that will reconstitute the Narmada River. There will be thirty big dams, 135 medium dams, and the rest of them small. Two of the major dams will be multi-purpose mega-dams. The Sardar Sarovar in Gujarat and Narmada Sagar in Madhya Pradesh are nearing completion. Their height is still

continues to this day. Her excoriating essay challenges the worldview and practical claims of those bent on imposing big dams on unwilling citizens and a vulnerable environment.

Jawaharlal Nehru, India's first prime minister (1947–64), shared the TVA high modernist vision. Notoriously, he called big dams the 'Temples of Modern India'; the phrase, Arundhati Roy says, 'has made its way into primary school text books in every Indian language. Every school child is taught that Big Dams will deliver the people of India from hunger and poverty.' The Indian state's high modernist ambitions have imposed big dams upon local people in ways that sacrifice their ways of life and livelihoods. They become displaced persons, whose promised 'rehabilitation' consistently fails to materialize. Like the TVA's Appalachia region and like the record of earlier big dam multi-purpose river valley development authorities in India (and elsewhere), most of the benefits seem destined to go to distant, affluent city dwellers.[35]

In the third essay of Section I, the focus shifts geographically to the former Soviet Union. In his essay 'Reverse Double Movement', Hyung-min Joo links the collapse after 1929 in Western Europe and the United States of laissez faire market capitalism and the collapse in the Soviet Union at the end of the 1980s of the communist state, society, and planned economy by reconceptualizing the 'double movement' that Karl Polanyi featured in *The Great Transformation*. As a self-regulating market system, laissez faire capitalism produced massive social dislocations, and reduced man and nature to bargain-priced commodities that could be bought and sold without compunction. Various actors organized and intervened to protect themselves from blind market forces. The unfettered, destructive expansion of the market is ultimately countered, and to some degree harnessed, by the cumulative self-protective actions by societal forces such as trade unions, labour and socialist parties, and agrarian and environmental movements.

Joo uses Polanyi's double movement concept to develop a corollary concept, which he calls a 'reverse double movement'. As the Marxist high modernist Soviet state proceeded implacably to appropriate or subjugate every aspect of civil society, the public sphere, and the economy, the pressure on ordinary life became increasingly unbearable. Like protective action by

---

in dispute. The two dams will, between them, hold more water than any other reservoir in the Indian subcontinent. According to informed estimates, the NVDP will affect the lives of the twenty-five million people who live in the valley and alter the ecology of an entire river basin.

[35]For an evaluation of who has benefited from multi-purpose river valley development in the US and India, see Daniel Klingensmith's forthcoming study of the TVA idea in America and India. Gail Omvedt and Sharad Joshi support the NVDP, arguing that Narmada irrigation water will benefit commercial agriculture in Maharashtra.

organized social forces in the face of market-induced commodification, Soviet subjects unwilling to accept what was being forced on them by the Soviet party-state apparatus began a remarkable process of constituting a 'parallel society'. As a result, almost every aspect of the official system came to be accompanied by corresponding shadow formations, including thriving underground markets and lively intellectual and cultural networks. Bereft of 'voice' and 'loyalty', the ingenious denizens of the Soviet system, Joo argues, chose internal 'exit'.[36] They migrated en masse to various manifestations of a parallel shadow society, where they found they could freely and profitably invest their feelings, talents, and energies. What citizens could not openly laugh at, they stealthily evaded. As a result the foundation of the Soviet state edifice was undermined. The reverse double movement was not the only cause of the collapse of the Soviet Union, Joo cautions, but without it our understanding of it would be radically incomplete.

Paul Brass's article, 'India and the Political Science of Development', takes us into the realm of meta-experience; he writes about how political scientists based in American universities experienced the high modernist developmental state in India. He finds that, at best, they were complicit in legitimizing it. Like a growing number of political scientists dismayed by failing and failed states and economies and by the dark side of globalization, Brass finds this a wholly unsatisfactory state of affairs. The high modernist state that Jawaharlal Nehru brought into being and bequeathed to his country was, for Brass, a poisoned chalice. Its innovators and acolytes not only worshipped the false god of big dams that Scott and Roy depict, they also made themselves powerful and prosperous in the name of helping the poor.

Besides establishing himself as a leading scholar of Indian politics through a series of path-breaking and influential books, Brass has also cultivated a role as the *enfant terrible* of his fraternity. He enacts the role in *Experiencing the State*, scolding and berating his colleagues not so much for being taken in by the powers that be—because he too admits to having been taken in for a time—but for failing to recognize as the 1980s gave way to the 1990s the developmental state's false assumptions and dire consequences.

His text proceeds at two levels, one a scholarly level where he deploys inner and outer critiques of his colleagues' work, and the other a self-conscious and deliberate polemical level. He deplores the fig leaf of neutrality behind which scholars relying on the trope of science hide. Explanations, he argues, are situated in assumptions and have consequences. However, Brass has trouble keeping his levels apart and under control. There are no shades of

[36]Joo is drawing on Albert O. Hirschman's *Exit, Voice and Loyalty*, Cambridge, MA: Harvard University Press, 1970.

grey, no upsides to go with the downsides of the developmental state. 'I have been accused,' he writes, 'of being a prophet of doom and gloom, of painting a picture of an India heading seamlessly towards catastrophe. ... What I want to say here and now ... is that India is not heading for catastrophe: India is a living catastrophe and its people, including its intellectuals, know it.' So, too, he implies, should the leading scholars of the American establishment whom he criticizes. Instead of recognizing the disaster wrought by the developmental state in India, leading American scholars of India have been complicit in legitimizing it. Brass singles out the late Myron Weiner for the most attention, attends as well to two other senior figures, the co-authors Lloyd I. Rudolph and Susanne Hoeber Rudolph, and to Atul Kohli, and puts a number of other political scientists' feet to the fire of his critique of scholarship on the developmental state in India.[37]

Helmuth Berking's 'Experiencing Reunification: An East German Village after the Fall of the Wall' opens Section II. Berking writes about the moral economy of an East German village in the decade after the fall of the Berlin Wall. Once again an interventionist high modernist state, this time a western capitalist one, evokes a protective response to its market capitalist efforts at revolutionary change. The rich, powerful, triumphant West German state sets out to reunify Germany by making over the character and ideology, as well as the economy, of the newly reunited nation's poor relatives, the *ossis* (East German people). In West German eyes, the East German state was evil, its economy—even worse—antiquated, its people dupes. The East Germans, many of whom were proud of their exemplary standing in the erstwhile Soviet empire, experienced the sudden makeover as degrading. The reunification process opened rather than closed the perceptual gap that separated West from East Germany, and laid the groundwork for a smouldering politics of resentment.

Berking describes how the newly minted Germans experienced their ambivalent embrace by the West German state. They were, it seems, like natives being ruled by a colonial power; the *ossis* were depicted as backward and benighted natives who needed to be civilized by being assimilated into

---

[37]For example, Brass says that the Rudolphs argued that the state in India was strong enough to prevail against the organized interests of capital and labour, but doesn't mention the Rudolphs' further argument that the state, as a more powerful 'third actor' with respect to capital and labour, increasingly became self-interested, a 'state for itself', and the problem rather than the solution to economic development. And he has the Rudolphs writing about modernity and tradition as if they were dichotomous and opposed. They wrote about 'the modernity of tradition' by characterizing the relationship of modernity and tradition as dialectical, and by de-essentializing modernity and tradition, *inter alia*, by finding elements of tradition in modernity and elements of modernity in tradition.

the superior West German social character and symbolic order. In the decade after the wall fell, the cultural and symbolic orders occasionally clashed, but more often passed as ships in the night.

Berking found the village's institutional order embedded in routines and expectations that made life not only comprehensible, but also morally intelligible. Such intangible presuppositions were not visible, not part of a public sphere, but sometimes akin to what James Scott calls 'hidden transcripts'. Unlike the physical and monetary assets that flowed from the West to the East, the embedded routines and expectations could not be easily uprooted. Berking reveals the 'microcosms of life', a lingering 'really existing socialism', networks based on close personal relationships governed by norms of reciprocity, inconspicuous but shared modes of resistance, and pervasive power games. Such relationships avoided or evaded the more formal and grating relationships based on edicts or cash. Berking's effort to find the macro in the micro in an East German village suggests that in the decade following reunification, former East Germans more often experienced the high modernist West German state as subversive and alienating than as liberating and transformative. Not surprisingly, according to villagers, politics, as they conventionally understood it, played little part in everyday life.

Tasneem Siddiqui's 'personal view' of the 'Dynamics of Bureaucratic Rule in Pakistan' carries forward Section II's account of experiencing the state from below. His heterodoxical bureaucratic career, first as an agent of Pakistani high stateness, than as an agent of Pakistani civil society, equips him with a double reflexivity. He is an adept and purposeful juggler, at once a self-conscious, alienated bureaucrat and a self-conscious civil society activist. He narrates two stories, one about the 'corrupt and inept' developmental administration with respect to housing in Pakistan's largest city, Karachi, a sprawling, chaotic port-city on the Arabian Sea, and a second about a successful bottom-up people's alternative.

Karachi is a city where 40 per cent of the population lives in squatter settlements, and another 20 per cent in sub-standard housing. Siddiqui's account exposes the adverse consequences high modernist assumptions and a centralized, top-down administration (which he once championed) have for housing policy. He then shows why and how a 'pro-people, bottom-up approach' succeeded. The do-it-yourself approach to housing, which he propagated, engaged the energies and ingenuity of the poor, and foiled predators even while enlisting some state aid. The proliferation of *katchi abadis* (squatter settlements) in the urban 'informal sector' became 'the peoples' response to the government's inability to provide shelter'. He demonstrates how, once a few resources are made available to them, citizens can identify needs, design projects, and implement and maintain housing schemes. 'If the government is freed from providing the basic services on individual basis (which it can't do anyway),' he argues, 'it can take care of bigger projects and external development.' NGOs and popular movements are necessary ingredients for making sure housing schemes work. 'But they cannot do it alone,' Siddiqui says. 'The state, spurred on by civil society, must remain serious about its social responsibilities for housing and about revitalizing local governments that support and facilitate housing schemes.'

Like Tasneem Ahmed Siddiqui's essay about the Kachi Abadi Authority in Karachi, Philip Oldenburg's 'Face to Face with the Indian State: A Grasssroots View' locates the state experience locally in everyday life. Oldenburg provides vivid and telling descriptions in the context of analytic inquiries, whose answers explain even as they describe. Oldenburg's essay shows us a state that is ubiquitous and embedded, even natural, but one that is also autonomous and often serviceable. 'Village teachers and doctors are figures,' Oldenburg reports, 'who must look half public/half private in the eyes of citizens, employed by the state part-time and thus included in government but also using their government employment as base from which to build a private enterprise.' Corruption is common, but often functional.

His story about the state as it is experienced at the local level in Ghazipur, a district in eastern Uttar Pradesh, in the early 1990s, has a certain timeless quality. *Sarkar* (the Hindi/Urdu word for state in the sense of government), for the locals, has been, is, and will be. Yet new functions are added; the face of the developmental state that Brass warns us against seems in Oldenburg's telling more likely to be locally co-opted than to command and control the locals. 'The various programmes for rural development that have been implemented make an impressive list,' Oldenburg writes. '... The community development programme of the 1950s ... visible in Ghazipur in the form of a very large government tube well/water tank installation ... food for work programs and intensive; [or integrated] agricultural development programmes, etc., in the next decades and in recent years, the Jawahar Rozgar Yojana [Jawaharlal Nehru Employment Plan] (JRY) and the IRDP [Integrated Rural Development Programme]. ...' 'Rural roads,' Oldenburg continues, 'have been ... a major portion of the "assets" created by the JRY, along with housing for the "weaker sections" ... , and wells under the "Million Wells Scheme"'. Other assets include trees planted under social forestry programmes, school buildings, sanitary latrines, 'works benefiting scheduled castes and scheduled tribes ...'. The major difference [in the early 1990s] ... was that 'the major portion of the financial allocation is given to the gram panchayat [elected village councils] for planning and execution'. Oldenburg found that while the elected local government officials responsible for implementing development programmes siphon off as much as 30 per cent of the funds, 'corruption has not overwhelmed development programmes; the benefits outweigh the corruption'. 'There is no doubt,' Oldenburg concludes, 'that the state reaches into the furthest corners of Ghazipur and touches the lives of large number of Ghazipur's people in significant ways.'

In Section III, 'Experiencing the State From Outside', three essays expose readers to the way the state is experienced in the realms of psychotherapy, cinema, and art. Nick Temple, a psychiatrist and administrator, describes how perceptions and attitudes at the Tavistock Centre, a National Health Service facility in North London, were transformed by the 'organizational upheavals' that followed policy shifts by Conservative and then (the new) Labour governments. Market radicalism was brought to bear on what the core element of the Welfare State, established in 1948 by Clement Attlee's Labour government, was. With a psychoanalyst's eye, Temple sees in Tory behaviour and New Labour's acquiescence a worldview that needs to

attack dependency to fulfill greedy wishes while, at the same time, attributing badness and weakness to those who are vulnerable or needy. This transformed worldview informs and pervades changes at the Tavistock Institute and in the NHS more generally. It often takes the form of blaming NHS staff for wasteful or indulgent use of resources, with the result that NHS staff are treated as if they, like the patients they care for, are dependent and needy. Professionals at Tavistock found that they experienced the state in the antagonistic attitude of the ministerial staff with whom they were in regular contact.

J.K. Jacobsen's essay, 'In Cahoots?: Experiencing The State in American Cinema', explores the ways in which recent Hollywood films about the state cultivate a cynical attitude in the viewing public. The cultivation of a cynical response occurs regardless of whether the films engage in critiques, or in Capraesque treatments of politics (*JFK*, *Clear and Present Danger*, *Nixon*, *Dave*, *The American President*, and so on). Both arouse cynical responses by questioning the purposes of the American state—particularly whether it controls or is controlled by interests in the wider society and economy. The ambiguity latent in this dual possibility raises, in its turn, another question: to what degree do films shape or are shaped by the cultural expectations and political understandings of cinema-goers? How do films affect conversations in the public sphere? What lessons or views do they impart to a country's civic culture and moral reasoning? The ubiquitous framing of political legerdemain in terms of 'conspiracies' stems partly from Hollywood narrative conventions requiring identifiable heroes and villains, partly from an underlying cultural distrust of centralized public organizations, and partly from the personalized (and occasionally idiosyncratic) expressions of these preferences and attitudes by filmmakers themselves. Jacobsen highlights the special characteristics of American film conventions and their public consequences by comparing them with those characteristic of European cinema. The contrast highlights differences between American and Europe with respect to the way cinema reflects and inflects how citizens experience the state.

The last essay in this section by Patricia Bickers examines the relations between state funding, and the nature and content of the art that results. Her narrative features the British Arts Council, dispenser of national lottery money. She highlights the British case by drawing comparisons with France and the United States. Her essay addresses the way differences in forms of state mediation—particularly the source, amounts, and conditions of funding—affect how citizens experience art.

The theme of Section IV, 'Emancipatory Resistance', is first explored in an essay by Sudipta Kaviraj on Gandhi's trial for sedition in 1922. Kaviraj re-examines Gandhi's 1922 trial in ways that reveal how the man, who Winston Churchill once dismissed as a 'half-naked fakir', managed to turn his trial for sedition into a vindication of his resistance to colonial rule. 'Trials are spectacles of power,' Kaviraj argues, 'and thus bring to representation not only material aspects of political power, but also ideal, symbolic, and representational ones.'

Three major audiences who observed the trial 'tried to fit this new event into their narratives of colonial rule: the Raj administrators and British public at home, the Indian middle class and educated elites, and the Indian peasantry'. Kaviraj shows how Gandhi's rhetorical strategy contained skilful, implicit messages for each audience: to the British audience, prevailing notions of 'justice' and fair play; to the Indian middle-class audience, the prospect of nationhood; and to the peasants of village India, for whom 'everything was invested with meanings ... [an] ineradicable aura of mysteriousness ... [about] the small and finite acts of ordinary people'.

Gandhi appreciated the theatricality of the law, its high drama in which both sides are obliged to stage an 'unprepared play' whose exchanges are 'not fixed, but strategic'. Kaviraj's essay illuminates how Gandhi was able to dramatize his experience in a courtroom of the colonial state in India in ways that transformed the consciousness of both the rulers and the ruled.

Bruce Cumings' essay, 'Experiencing Repressive States: Resistance, Memory and Avoidance', offers a riveting 'subjective knowledge'[38] account

---

[38]For a theoretical account of the place of subjective knowledge in political science and the social sciences more broadly, see Lloyd I. Rudolph, and Susanne Hoeber Rudolph, 'Engaging Subjective Knowledge: How Amar Singh's Diary Narratives of and by the Self Explain Identity Formation', *Perspective on Politics*, 1 (4), 2003, pp. 681–94. Note also Bernard Crick's observation

of experiencing the American and Korean states, as a result of his personal involvement in the conduct of US relations with the Korean peninsula. He carefully underlines how the American, South Korean, and North Korean states are repressive in a number of senses.[39] One is in the James Scott sense of 'high modernism'. 'Among the many virtues of James Scott's recent work, *Seeing Like a State*', Cumings writes, 'is his unwillingness to distinguish between types of modern states. The industrial states were all gripped by 'high modernist ideology', yielding state practices that are best conceived as a strong, one might even say muscle-bound, version of the self-confidence about scientific and technical progress, the expansion of production—the mastery of nature [including human nature], and, above all, the rational design of social order commensurate with the scientific understanding of natural laws: There is an 'elective affinity', he continues, 'between high modernist ideology and the interests of state officials—whether they hark from formal democracies, like the United States ... totalized colonial states' like the Japanese colonial state in Korea, or the American military occupation regime in Korea. What unites the behaviour of officials in such states, Cumings argues, 'is a self-confident certainty that they implement a seamless "rational design" of "social order" amid a heterodox reality.'

Cumings begins his account of the repressive face of the American state by resuscitating what he suggests are deliberately buried historical records of several American atrocities in Korea, including a particularly cold-blooded massacre of Korean civilians at Nof'n-ri in July 1950.[40]

But his most telling accounts are of his own experiences over twenty-five years as a dissenting policy voice on Korea for mostly Republican administrations—'telling what he knows' about FBI efforts to intimidate him in his University of Chicago office, gumshoe CIA surveillance in Korea, seemingly punitive IRS audits, and the hostility displayed at the inauguration of Kim Dae Jung as president of South Korea by top US officials with CIA provenances who served as US ambassadors in Korea, James Lilley and Donald Gregg, and by former Reagan National Security Advisor Richard Allen.

---

that 'Every purported methodology of how to study the activity of government objectively, that is, every prefabricated set of rules for the discovery of knowledge in advance of experience is itself a doctrine'. Crick, *In Defence of Politics*, p. 102.

[39]South Korea's recent repressive political experience left in its wake multitudes of walking wounded to whom Cumings pays tribute—ordinary citizens of extraordinary courage who confronted the state and paid a price for it, but who manage to remain admirably human in their higher capacity for resistance, grit, and regeneration.

[40]This leads Cumings to quote a sentence from Barrington Moore's *Social Origins of Dictatorship and Democracy: Lord and Peasant in the Making of the Modern World*, Boston: Beacon Press, 1966. Moore wrote that to sustain state power, people are 'put up against a wall, beaten, shot, and sometimes taught sociology'.

Cumings concludes his gripping narrative of experiencing the American and Korean states by a playful but astringent critique of the scientific pretensions of Kenneth Waltz's neo-realist theorizing. Cumings then wryly denigrates what he has to say about the doyen of neo-realism and the scientific trope by 'confessing' to his readers that his spirited account 'would be chucked out of any "refereed" or "discipline conscious" journal of political science ... on the ground that ... my "experience" of the Korean and the American state is personal, "anecdotal", and ad hoc ... or that what I have said is not "theoretical". ... Yet the experiences that I have related are true, they all happened.'

After a critical exegesis of Waltz's scientific claims, Cumings concludes that Americans may filter their experience of the state through founding-father, Tudor-policy myths, but 'rarely if ever experience the American state in the ... arbitrary way' Waltz posits, that is, in which state action flows from an unmarked, empty structure. Their experience of the state can best be explained 'by arbitrary power or *force-majeure*'.

II

Processes of Institutional Change

The articles in this Section about institutional change span thirty-seven years of India's tumultuous independent history, 1965 to 2002. 'Generals and Politicians in India' (1964) was written in the aftermath of India's defeat in a war with China in 1962. 'New Dimensions of Indian Democracy' (2002) was written a decade after the momentous economic reforms launched in 1991 by Prime Minister Narasimha Rao, and then Finance Minister Manmohan Singh. India's defeat by China raised questions about its national identity, institutional arrangements, and policy priorities. The defeat had a shattering effect on India's self-conception as a peaceful and secure country, on its foreign and defence policies, and on its capacity to pursue planned economic development. It re-opened the question of civil-military relations. Had the Indian military invited defeat because favourites of the Congress party's leadership had been promoted and given commands without regard to qualification and seniority? How and why had India been able to maintain civil control of the military when Pakistan and many other new and developing nations had turned to the military for modernization?

How did the defeat affect the standing and viability of India's political leadership, in particular that of Jawaharlal Nehru, the prime minister, and Krishna Menon, the defence minister? Institutional changes also followed from the initiation of economic reforms in 1991. The reforms signalled the end of India's state-dominated economy, and the beginning of a market-oriented one. These processes of change were paralleled by major changes in the balance among India's political institutions. 'New Dimensions' and 'Redoing the Constitutional Design: From the Interventionist to the Regulatory State' examine the causes and consequences of the emergence of the Supreme Court, the Election Commission, and the President as effective and respected institutions, and the decline in the reputation and effectiveness of the political executive and parliament.

'Iconisation of Chandrababu: Sharing Sovereignty in India's Federal Market Economy', also published in 2001, shows how economic liberalization combined with the transformation of the party system from dominant to multiparty opened the way for India's federal states to take charge of their own economic fates. With Planning Commission public investment less available and each state increasingly a tub on its own bottom, state chief ministers were challenged to compete for domestic and foreign private investment if their states were to prosper.

In the years leading up to the publication in 1980 of 'The Centrist Future of Indian Politics', scholars had heatedly debated the role of class in Indian politics. Was India like China, where Mao had found class relations in the countryside that, he argued, fuelled revolutionary change? Was India like the countries of Western Europe where organized labour helped class parties to play a major role in politics and governance? Was India like the United States where, according to Alexis de Tocqueville and Louis Hartz, Americans were 'born free' and class consciousness and class politics were, at best, marginal?

We answered that India had a distinctive centrist dynamic. Its pluralist objective conditions were inhospitable to class politics. Its indigenous categories were more often those of caste, ethnicity, and religious community than they were of class. Its industrial workforce was proportionately small— in 1976 its five million factory workers constituted only 3 per cent of its total workforce of 180 million. The 67 per cent of the workforce in the agrarian sector lacked consciousness and organization. There was hardly a shadow of a peasant-worker alliance. And India's financial and industrial capitalist class was overshadowed by state firms, and rendered dependent by state regulation—the notorious 'permit licence raj'. We offered seven reasons for centrist politics to be and to remain for the foreseeable future dominant in Indian politics, one of which was the marginality of class politics, and another the electoral strength of upwardly mobile lower castes seeking status and benefits.

In our 1981 article, 'Judicial Review *versus* Parliamentary Sovereignty: The Struggle over Stateness in India', we addressed a central arena for institutional change, the relative standing of parliamentary sovereignty and judicial review in India's constitutional order. Was parliament's power to legislate, including its power to amend the Constitution, unlimited as Nehruvians tended to believe, or did the Supreme Court's power of judicial review allow it to set limits on parliament's power to legislate? In 1973 the court in *Keshavananda Bharati vs State of Kerala* ruled that parliament's power to legislate and amend is not the power to destroy. Parliamentary sovereignty is limited by the constitution's 'basic structure' or 'essential features', terms it was in the court's provenance to specify, define, and apply.

'Rethinking Secularism: Genesis and Implications of the Textbook Controversy, 1977–9', examined one of the most important arenas for defining who and what is Indian, the textbooks assigned in India's schools. The most influential textbooks are written by scholars commissioned by the National Council for Educational Research and Training (NCERT). Soon after Morarji Desai's Janata-led government assumed office in 1977, questions were raised about four textbooks. It was alleged that their 'controversial and biased material' would lead readers to acquire 'a prejudiced view of Indian history'. Written by prominent historians from a Nehruvian secular perspective, the books, *inter alia*, critiqued 'communal' history, that is, history that depicted India's Muslim minority as foreigners and interlopers in a Hindu nation.

The Desai-Jan Sangh sections of the Janata Party did not take kindly to such views, and moved to remove and replace the books at issue. The textbook controversy that followed renewed a century-old effort to articulate a national identity and public philosophy for India that came to grips with the role of Muslims in Indian history. The controversy anticipated the even more acrimonious and extended one that accompanied the rise in the 1990s of the Bharatiya Janata Party as a national and governing party committed to defining India as a 'Hindu nation'.

Our conception of institutional change encompasses non-state actors in civil society. Our 1986 article, 'Demand Groups and Pluralist Representation in India', introduced a distinctive form of political representation, what we called the 'demand group'. Unlike interest groups which feature formal organization and continuity and operate for the most part in the corridors of power, demand groups are more spontaneous and less formed versions of collective action, akin to movement and issue politics that operate 'out of doors' in the public square; their tactics and style draw on the political theatre of Gandhi's non-violent non-cooperation and civil disobedience campaigns. Demand groups' natural habitats are the agrarian producers of India's vast unorganized economy, and the lower castes of India's hierarchical social order.

6

Generals and Politicians in India*

LLOYD I. RUDOLPH AND SUSANNE HOEBER RUDOLPH

I ndia has been transformed from the leading exponent of peaceful
initiatives to a nation vitally concerned with military security.[1] Her
military defeat at the hands of China has led to large increases in defence
spending, and a substantial projected expansion of the military services. In
new states, the modern professionalism of the military, with its apparent
promise of order and efficiency—and the ineffectiveness of nationalist
political classes—has often led to military takeovers. This has not been the
case in India; but will it be so in the future?

*Originally published as 'Generals and Politicians in India', in *Pacific Affairs*, XXXVII
(6), Spring 1964, pp. 5–19.
[1]This chapter profited from a series of interviews conducted in India in the spring of
1963. We are grateful to Prime Minister Jawaharlal Nehru, Defence Minister Y.B. Chavan,
Defence Minister V.K. Krishna Menon, civil servants presently or formerly connected with the
Defence Ministry, and present and former members of the military establishment for their
comments and views.

The politics of the military, particularly in developing nations, has produced a considerable
amount of literature in recent years. We have tried here, among other things, to discuss those
factors that will facilitate a comparative analysis. See, for example, Samuel P. Huntington, *The
Soldier and the State*, New York: Vintage, 1957; Morroe Berger, *Military Elite and Social Change:
Egypt since Napoleon*, Princeton, Centre of International Studies, 1960; Edward Lieuwen, *Arms
and Politics in Latin America*, New York: Praeger, 1960; P.J. Vatikiotis, *The Egyptian Army in Politics:
Pattern for New Nations?*, Bloomington, IN: Indiana University Press, 1961; Samuel P. Huntington
(ed.), *Changing Patterns of Military Politics*, New York: Free Press, 1962; H. Daalder, *The Role of the
Military in Emerging Countries*, Princeton: Princeton University Press, 1962; Willm Gutteridge,
Armed Forces in New States, London and New York: Oxford University Press, 1962; John L. Johnson
(ed.), *The Role of the Military in Underdeveloped Countries*, Princeton: Princeton University Press,
1962; S.N. Fisher (ed.), *The Military in the Middle East: Problems in Society and Government*,
Columbus: Ohio University State Press, 1963; and Richard D. Robinson, *The First Turkish Republic:
A Case Study of National Development*, Cambridge: Harvard University Press, 1963.

How is it that Indian military services have played a limited professional role when in neighbouring Pakistan, also part of the old British Raj, the present regime is headed by a military man, General Ayub Khan? Both military and political leaders in India agree that the variable is not the army itself. Senior Indian officers who attended Sandhurst with their Pakistani counterparts remember a shared military past, and see little difference between themselves and Pakistani generals. Prime Minister Nehru and Defence Minister Chavan concur. They agree that it was not inordinate ambition or a special taste for politics, but the failure of the political classes to govern effectively that persuaded the Pakistani army under Ayub Khan to seize power. It took power, Mr Nehru believes, 'naturally', 'automatically', when politics failed. It seems reasonable to senior Indian officers that when politicians 'play ducks and drakes', as they did in Pakistan, rather than shoulder their responsibilities, the army should step in to 'put things right'. However, in the absence of a serious failure of politics, Indian army men will adhere to a standard learned under the British, to 'know their place'.

So far, Indian politics has by no means failed. Its relative success is the product of long experience with modern political ideas and practice, and the integration of these with traditional Indian values. The assimilation of modern political ideas began almost 130 years ago with the introduction of 'English' education. Indians have been electing legislators for over fifty years. Indian parties formed provincial cabinets, responsible to elected legislatures, twenty-five years ago.

Indian politics has profited from the experience of three nationalist generations: the generation which espoused Gandhi's statement of transformed traditionalism; its predecessors, the 'moderates', loyalist in their sympathies and committed to such liberal ideas as fundamental rights and parliamentary government; and its successors, the socialists, concerned with social and economic justice and planned development. If there was tension and conflict among these nationalist generations, there was no fundamental break, no alienation of the modern liberals and socialists from Gandhi's more traditional following. The adherence to Gandhi on the part of the Nehrus (Motilal, the liberal-moderate father, and Jawaharlal, the socialist son) illustrates Gandhi's ability to keep these generations in harness with him, even if he did not manage to convince them of the ultimate truth of his ideas. They followed him without fully believing, partly because of his extraordinary human and moral qualities, and partly because of his concern and ability to be heard by traditional India, the India of villages, castes and regional languages.

Nehru, too, unites the three nationalist generations, but not in the same way as Gandhi. He has governed in the spirit of the grandfathers and the sons, of the liberals and the socialists, yet he retains much of Gandhi's traditional support and authority as the Mahatma's political heir, if not his moral disciple. The gap between tradition and modernity, between village and city, oral and written communication, dhoti and trouser, so often found in other new states, has been closed not only by the amalgamation of traditional and modern ideas and generations, but also by the pervasiveness and depth of party and associational life. The dominant Congress party, heir to the nationalist movement and independence, has won large legislative majorities at the Centre and governed in most states, and yet has polled less than half the popular vote in India's three general elections. The four major opposition parties, along with an active and independent press, provide the lively and telling public dialogue that makes democracy meaningful. At the mass level, it is the caste associations and linguistic states that provide channels of communication and bases for leadership and representation, which have made political participation understandable and effective.

Though political democracy in India has steadily enlarged the chances of its continued existence by educating India's huge electorate in the skills and values of self-government, its fate is by no means secure. Of the many difficulties that persist, the propensity to popular authoritarian rule is most likely to play into the hands of military leadership. The authoritarian character created by the traditional family, the attraction cultural fundamentalism holds for the urbanized lower middle classes, and the appeal of order, discipline and efficiency for the professional classes, now marginal features of Indian political life, are susceptible to mobilization by military leadership under the right circumstances. However, the expressions of authoritarianism (the memory of Subhas Chandra Bose's efforts to identify Indian nationalism with fascism during World War II; the Rashtriya Swayamsevak Sangh [RSS], a uniformed cultural cadre behind the right radical Jan Sangh party; the Dravida Munnetra Kazhagam [DMK], the Tamilian fundamentalist and secessionist opposition in the state of Madras; and unreconciled elements of the old feudal order) show neither signs of common purpose nor military leadership. The efforts of General Cariappa, the first Indian to hold the office of commander-in-chief, to lead the forces of order and cultural fundamentalism have made little impression nationally or regionally.

The viceroy and the parliament, one autocratic, the other democratic, represent the two great traditions of modern politics that the subcontinent experienced under British rule. The differences between the role of the military in India and that in Pakistan are related to the fact that after independence, Pakistan, under Jinnah, identified with the viceregal tradition, while India under Nehru embraced parliamentarism. The English viceroy and governor-general headed an administrative state which, at its best, approximated the ideal of platonic guardians, paternal, benign, and efficient. The commander-in-chief stood second to the viceroy under the British raj, powerful yet subordinate to the Crown's civilian representative in India. Representative democracy developed side by side with the viceregal tradition; in Pakistan, a kind of viceregal government formed by civil servants in the guise of politicians was toppled by a general who has tried to rid the state of parties, politics, and politicians. In India, parliamentary nationalists might have yielded to the opposite temptation, ousting the remnants of the viceregal tradition, the military officers who had fought for England and the civil servants who had jailed the nationalists. Had they done so, they would have seriously jeopardized governmental effectiveness and created a potentially subversive political class. However, the Congress leaders recognized the value of these professional services to the new state. There was some readjustment of their status in state and society, but no purges.

At independence, India's new rulers were under some pressure to replace the 'military mercenaries' who had served the British raj with a political and nationalist army. Of the 60,000 Indian troops captured by the Japanese in Malaya, 25,000 went over to the Indian National Army (INA), a force built by the Japanese to aid its South Asia offensive, and described to Indian soldiers as a nationalist liberation force for India.[2] The army was eventually led by Subhas Chandra Bose, a prominent nationalist from Bengal who had been president of the Indian National Congress, and who thought well of Hitler's Germany. Bose was killed in a 1945 plane crash, but in the nationalist upsurge at independence, the INA and its leaders were given great prominence and glory. Their reputations were enhanced when the British tried to convict them in widely reported public trials of desertion, mutiny, and other serious crimes.[3] Bose had promised them that 'out of your ranks will be born the future General Stag of the Army of Free India'.[4] A less prudent leadership might have been pressed in the excitement of freedom to replace 'mercenaries' with 'dedicated fighters for freedom'. But this was not done. None of the INA's 'heroes' were retained as officers, a decision which not only cemented the loyalties of the old officers to the new regime, but also strengthened the

[2] Hugh Toye, *The Springing Tiger: Subhas Chandra Bose*, London: Cassell, 1959; and Stephen B. Cohen, 'Subhas Chandra Bose and the Indian National Army', *Pacific Affairs*, Winter 1963–4. For examples of the sentiments the INA leaders evoked, see Jag Parvesh Chander, *Meet the Heroes*, Lahore: Print Works, 1945.

[3] Selected Speeches of Subhas Chandra Bose, Government of India, 1962, p. 183.

[4] As a member of the Interim Government, Nehru probably gave a difficult speech supporting the Commander-in-Chief, Auchinleck, in resisting demands in the Legislative Assembly for the immediate release of former INA men still in prison. See John Connell, *Auchinleck: A Biography of Field-Marshall Sir Claude Auchinleck*, London: Cassell, 1959, pp. 869, 871; and Alan Campbell-Johnson, *Mission with Mountbatten*, Cassell, 1951, p. 53. For an officer's view, see Sir Francis Tuker, *While Memory Serves*, London: R. Hale, 1950.

idea that professional competence, not political initiative, was the first requirement of the Indian Army.[5] The INA was not dishonoured: for example, Shah Nawaz Khan, one of its leaders, is today deputy minister of railways, and the late J.K. Bhonsle, another leader, headed the National Discipline Scheme. However, unlike Indonesia and Burma, India did not start its independent life with a political army that claimed a share in the nationalist movement and the winning of independence.

Since India's political classes were able to master the civil and military services of the Viceregal tradition, and because they had the wisdom to reconcile them, they have benefited from certain of their 'English' prejudices. The senior civil servants and military officers were highly anglicized, the military perhaps even more than the civilians[6] A Sandhurst man accounted for the high number of dropouts in his generation of officers by describing the severe demands for English cultural assimilation, in large things as well as small. 'The Civil Servants could at least go home at five o'clock to their wives and children. But we went "home" to our messes. We ate, drank and lived with the British. We had more chances to make bloopers.'

Among Indian officers, the assimilation displays itself today not merely in the exquisitely tailored lounge suits of officers in mufti, or in a penchant for understatement, beautiful silver, and cavalry moustaches, but also in a belief that really civilized politics, like that of the Small Island, requires civilian control and parliamentary processes. Furthermore, under the raj, Indian officers learned how prudent it was to have no political views. Older officers recall complicated cat and mouse conversations with British superiors in which they averred they had no opinions about the Congress. That does not mean that a recessive belief that 'all politicians are scallywags' would not assert itself were the scallywag qualities of political leaders to become too apparent. British mess talk in the 1930s did not neglect to point out frequently that the leaders of Indian nationalism were no-account men. Retired General Cariappa has taken the view, it was alleged in parliament,[7] that India could stand two years of President's rule with army support, the civil administration being made subordinate to the army. 'Look at Pakistan,' he is said to have stated at a public meeting, 'people there are happy, and everything is clean.' But most Indian officers prefer to serve under a civilian

[5]The problems and consequences of assimilation are suggested in Humphrey Evans, *Thimayya of India: A Soldier's Life*, New York, 1960. Some of the concern as to whether the proper patterns are still being observed in the post-independence period emerges from Lord Birdwood, *India and Pakistan: A Continent Decides*, New York, 1954, Chapter V.

[6]*Lok Sabha Debates*, 1961. Second series, LIV, 41, p. 10589.

[7]When the Interim Government took office in 1946, Sardar Baldev Singh replaced Field Marshal Sir Claude Auchinleck, who had been War Member.

government, providing that it is sufficiently competent and effective for one to do so honourably.

The army's position has been downgraded both administratively and socially. In the days of British rule, the commander-in-chief of the Indian Defence Forces, a high-ranking military officer, sat as a member of the viceroy's executive council, the administrative state's equivalent of a cabinet. His position as number two man in the executive suggested that the circumstances of empire required a much more prominent position for the army in India than at home in Britain. The pre-independence army considered itself a very important part of the governing class. Immediately after the war, the process of down-grading began. The commander-in-chief was replaced in the cabinet by a civilian defence minister responsible to an elected legislature.[8] This, the Constituent Assembly believed, was no more than a logical consequence of responsible government. Thereafter the defence ministry, at least until Krishna Menon took over, did not count, as it generally does in the West, as one of the two or three key portfolios. The President of India became the Supreme Commander of the armed forces, a ceremonial supersession symbolizing civilian control. In 1955 the military office of commander-in-chief was abolished altogether, and now there are only three Chiefs of Staff, one each for the Army, Navy and Air Force. The move reflected some nervousness concerning the military's potential role, and a consequent desire 'to trim their tails'. Ceremonial rankings reflect these changes. Lieutenant-generals who were entitled to gun salutes are no longer. Only some lieutenant-generals are entitled to travel in saloon cars, and the democratic state encourages them to act. The Warrant of Precedence places the army chief of staff, the senior military officer in India, in twenty-fifth place, behind such offices as the comptroller and auditor general, chief justices of state courts, members of the Planning Commission, and state cabinet ministers.[9] Officers are moving away from the idea of a mess, from dressing for dinner, and wine and fine silver, to the idea of Officers' Clubs, where wives can be brought an evening to save cooking dinner.

The relatively modest standing of the military is a logical consequence of non-alignment. Some of India's most distinguished officers built up their reputations under the UN rather than Indian commands. Best known is former chief of staff Thimayya, who was in charge of the POW Repatriation in Korea. Others have served in Gaza, the Congo, and Cyprus. The present Chief of Staff, General Chaudhuri, built his reputation in limited engagements at home: the 'integration' of Hyderabad just after independence, and the

[8]Warrant of Precedence, in *India, 1962*, Government of India, 1962.
[9]*Asian Recorder*, 1962, p. 4911.

more recent Goa takeover. In India, one of the leading justifications of non-alignment has been that it permits India to devote her efforts and resources primarily to economic justice and growth, rather than to military weapons and personnel. Both Nehru and Menon see the failure of politics in Pakistan as in part a result of the opposite emphasis. Far greater resources, prestige, and national effort have gone into planned development than into the military establishment; both before and after the Chinese invasion, military security has been seen as a function of rapid and effective development. After reviewing the Third Plan in the light of the Emergency, the prime minister declared that it was 85 per cent defence-oriented, while the National Development Council stated that 'the country's Plans of development [are] an integral part of national defence'[10]

The reorientation of Indian foreign policy in light of the Chinese threat is apt to bring with it some changes in the political role of the army. Increased resources are likely to have similar effects on the standing of the Indian armed forces as large-scale US aid under CENTO and SEATO had on Pakistan's, raising their prestige and power vis-à-vis other social forces in the state. The fact that defence has become a desirable and eagerly sought-after portfolio already suggests a shift. So far the Emergency, however, has produced no men on horseback. Those who rode to the frontier returned as something less than heroes. Short of large-scale and protracted fighting, which at the moment seems unlikely, the scope for men on white horses is limited. There was some indignation among retired senior officers at the extent of the debacle. For a while it looked as if they might provide some direction to public indignation in a way that could affect the civil-military balance through demands for a public inquiry. But then two former chiefs of staff and another retired officer, the late Rajendrasingji, Thimayya and Thorat, were absorbed in the National Defence Council, set up to advise the government during the Emergency. The Council's Military Affairs Committee had not been very effective or active, but it did satisfy the generals and public that the available military talent was being consulted. Most of the retired officers declared themselves content with a confidential internal inquiry into the military reverses on the northeast frontier.

The public position of an army is not only affected by the strength of politics and the quality of foreign policy, but also by its relative status in society. While armies in the West still profit from historical traces of feudal honour and social standing, this is hardly true of the Indian Army. The historical eclipse of the kshatriya—the ancient warrior-ruler caste—has

---

[10]D.N. Rao, 'Disprities of Representation Among the Direct Recruits to I.A.S.', *Indian Journal of Public Administration*, IX (1), 1963, p. 91.

dimmed the traditional glamour associated with the fighting man, while his standing as a modern professional is still somewhat tainted by his association with British power and culture. Among India's three great caste cultures kshatriya (warrior-ruler), *brahmin* (priest, teacher), and *vaishya* (merchant), kshatriyas have lost the most in the transition to independence and modern times. They declined because they failed in their ancient duty: for centuries they were unable to prevent large sections of Hindu India from falling under alien rule. Brahmins, who had served the kshatriyas as priests and administrators, survived foreign rule better: some took to the new learning, whether Persian under the Mughals or English under the British. While brahmins adapted to modern culture and learned to turn liberal and nationalist ideas to Indian account, kshatriyas survived as rulers of princely states, who were frequently indifferent to the changes in society and in the political ideas occurring in British India. Having stood aloof from nationalism, kshatriyas at independence were identified with monarchy and feudalism rather than with nationalism and its major components, democracy, parliamentary government, social justice, and planned development.

The kshatriya ideal also survived among the 'martial races'—though not all 'martial races' are kshatriyas—those communities considered fit by the British raj to fight for the empire both abroad and, if necessary, at home. Not only did the 'martial races' serve the cause of British imperialism, but they were also least involved with, and frequently opposed to, the causes of nationalism and independence. The British recruited officers who came initially from 'loyal classes', from families known to support the raj. These officers often shared the British disapprobation for bookish, pen-pushing vaishyas and brahmins like Gandhi and Nehru, who formed the backbone of the modern middle classes who dominated Indian nationalism. By taste and culture they found themselves outsiders as Gandhi transformed traditional vaishya and brahminical non-violence for use in contemporary political settings. Nationalists considered the army an instrument of British imperialism, cultural as well as political. After independence, Nehru's peace policy, for quite different reasons, continued to emphasize non-violence.

In those new states where ambitious young men are blocked from politics, business and the professions because they are the closed preserves of entrenched elites, the army has become a significant outlet for talent as well as a revolutionary force. In India, alternative careers open to merit compete strongly with the army. Politics, in fifteen of India's states, has become a vehicle for ambitious men, offering them the opportunities American urban and state politics did to emerging ethnic groups at the turn of the century. The professions beckon talent: the senior civil service (IAS) attracts able youths from all backgrounds. There is an increase in bright but unpolished

IAS probationers (9 per cent over the past twelve years have come from families who earn less than $60 per month),[11] who learn upper middle-class social graces from the sophisticated wives their prestige can command on the marriage market. Other central and provincial services also recruit by merit. The modern professions, particularly engineering and, to a lesser degree, medicine, also attract a very substantial portion of the talented youth. Business, too, is offering increasing scope for ambitious young men. While traditional family firms still favour family and caste, modern firms, many of them the outriders of British and American companies—Lever, Burma Esso, Imperial Tobacco—recruit more by merit and to some extent by class style. In this career competition, the army comes a weak third, that is, if its position is that high. This is a considerable contrast to its pre-independence status, and is partly due to the fact that pay and perquisites are below those of the civilian all-India services. The marriage 'market', a reasonably faithful barometer of career status in a society where marriages are still arranged, ranks young men in the 'foreign firms' at the top, those in the Indian foreign and administrative services in second place, and then perhaps those in the defence forces. (The army's position in the marriage market registered a disastrous decline with the Chinese invasion; mothers prefer to see their daughters married into safe professions.)

The army has been complaining of difficulties in officer recruitment for some years. There is little by way of service traditions in officer families, although there is a strong tradition of this kind among enlisted men. Senior officers are as apt to send their sons to foreign firms, or modern professions, or coffee plantations as they are to the military services. To be sure, the position has been improving since the defence ministry initiated, in Krishna Menon's time, the so-called Sainik Schools which offer the equivalent of an English Public School education for boys wishing to enter the National Defence Academy at Khadakvasla. These schools should increase the supply of good material to the officer corps. But so far, the Indian military services, unlike those in many other underdeveloped countries, are by no means the most obvious path for the ambitious and talented in search of honour and power. Nor are officers socially isolated. Sons of business and professional men choose the military as a career, and military, professional and business families intermarry. The army is merely one honoured occupation among many.

But suppose that the military's built-in feelings of restraint should weaken, that it should receive more resources—as it will—and that the political policies and leadership should cease to command respect. Suppose

---

[11]See Benjamin Schoenfeld, 'Emergency Rule in India', *Pacific Affairs*, Fall, 1963, for the powers that may be exercised.

some leaders in the army wanted to seize power. One consideration that would restrain them is that of Indian federalism, a federalism that expresses the country's size, diversity, and diffusion of power. The fifteen states, eleven with populations larger than California and one with a population larger than any European country save Russia, are more powerful vis-à-vis the Centre—not perhaps on paper, but politically—than any American state, and as such constitute obstacles to military rule. Defence Minister Chavan, who knows the meaning of state power from his years as chief minister of Maharashtra, points out that while control over Karachi could mean control over Pakistan—and even here there are problems—Delhi could not so easily control unwilling states. Most of the state chief ministers are self-confident politicians and administrators enough to take a dim view of military claims that officers govern better.

Army organization itself militates against the possibility of a coup. The subcontinent is divided into four Commands (Southern, Western, Central, and Eastern), each reasonably self-sufficient, and each under a general officer commander-in-chief. An effective coup would have to bring in all commanders, a formidable concert that seems implausible even under the most difficult circumstances. The temptations of easy access to power do not presently exist in India.

On 26 October 1962, President Radhakrishnan, for the first time since independence, declared a state of Emergency under Article 352 of the constitution.[12] He did so of course on the advice of the government, as required by constitutional convention, and so far the government has used few of its extensive powers. However, it is not impossible to imagine an Indian president, when confronted by a weak, divided and ineffective government and a serious crisis, stretching or ignoring the convention to act on government advice, and declaring a state of emergency and calling upon the military services as well as the civilian administration to support him as supreme commander and head of state. If military or quasi-military rule is to come to India, it is much more likely to do so under the cover of legality than through a *coup d'etat*. But even with the possibility of legal justification, the same factors that inhibit a *coup* will also profoundly inhibit such a presidential-military venture. While it should not be ruled out as a future possibility, it as yet remains quite unlikely.

In post-independence India, few people worried about the army as a political force. The military services and their budget remained small, and the defence minister a relatively unimportant member of the cabinet. It was only after Krishna Menon took over as defence minister in 1957 that

---

[12]*Lok Sabha Debates*, 1961, Second series, LIV, 42, p. 10827.

the press, parliament, and public began to take political notice of the military establishment. Even though the new minister's responsibilities at the United Nations and at the Planning Commission (as Member for International Trade and Development) prevented him from concentrating all his time and energy on defence matters, he, from an early stage, began to draw public attention to himself and the services by hustling about the country inspecting installations, to the accompaniment of considerable photographic and written press coverage. His policies vis-à-vis defence production, and research and development, drew both praise and criticism as the ordnance factories turned their unutilized capacity to the manufacture of items for civilian consumption; as the supply of trucks from the private sector was supplemented by a defence sector venture in that field; and as defence research efforts were considerably expanded. Critics charged that a defence sector was being added to the public and private sectors of the country's economy, while friends argued that the defence establishment was for the first time receiving the imaginative and effective leadership it required. The critics were concerned that Menon was adding a new dimension to the power factors in Indian politics by identifying himself with the generals and building up the defence establishment. While it is difficult to assess the validity of these concerns, a combination of the Menon left, with its sources of strength both in and out of the Congress, and the military establishment was seen by some as a potential source of danger, particularly in the context of settling the succession issue.

Mr Menon's strategic doctrines concerning Pakistan and China, and the relationship of those doctrines to professional standards in the services, represent another important area of political controversy. In briefest form, the defence minister's speech and action reflected the view that Pakistan was the real and most likely enemy, while China was a friend who shared similar domestic and international concerns. Ideology and strategy combined to shape Menon's perceptions and attitudes towards Pakistan's military pact allies on the one hand, and China's great ally Russia on the other; on such key issues as non-alignment and Kashmir, the East seemed to be more favourably disposed to India than the West. That these strategic views were not universally shared in the defence establishment seems certain. The extent to which senior officers believed that their professional future depended on overt or passive adherence to these views is less clear. Under such circumstances, it becomes particularly difficult to judge Mr Menon's handling of promotion policy. Did he promote men who approved of his strategic and political views, disrupting the professional spirit of the army in the process, or did he recognize and encourage imagination and talent, refusing to adhere rigidly to the blind dictates of seniority?

The capacity to know and even anticipate his political chief's mind while maintaining an independent capacity to give professional advice is one of the tests of a good civilian or military officer. However, this delicate relationship requires sensitivity and an appreciation of responsibilities on both sides, from the chief as well as the subordinate. There is evidence to suggest that during Mr Menon's tenure at the defence ministry, this relationship broke down under the pressure of Menon's known and strongly held political opinions and personal evaluations. The fact that a number of senior officers now holding positions of the highest responsibility were placed on the retirement list, and managed to remain in service only because of Mr Menon's abrupt departure, supports this view. So too does the degree to which seniority was ignored in promotions. In parliament, Mr Nehru argued that it was proper that the top posts be filled by the political executive 'ignoring seniority—not ignoring it, but certainly not attaching too much importance to it',[13] while Mr Menon observed that officers like General Thimayya, the then chief of the army staff, had superseded several senior officers without difficulties being raised. The opposition held that retirement and promotion policies were being used in a way that went beyond a legitimate concern to recognize professional talent. In particular, opposition members charged that retirement and promotion policies were being used to clear the way for General B.M. Kaul, a man highly valued by both Nehru and Menon.

Like the Prime Minister, General B.M. Kaul is a Kashmiri brahmin, and is endowed with a good many of the intellectual qualities that such a background often produces. Even some conservative officers who resented his rapid advance respect him. It seems plausible that it is these qualities, plus his strategic and political views, which paralleled those of his political chiefs', that account for the preference that they showed him over his bluff, straightforward, and less brilliant colleagues. It is generally believed that his rapid promotion was designed to place him in a position from which he could succeed General Thapar in the top post as chief of the army staff and that, but for the events following upon the Chinese invasion, he would have done so.

In 1959, under rather dramatic circumstances, the then chief of the army staff, General Thimayya, offered his resignation on the issue of General Kaul's promotion to Lieutenant-General.[14] The president of Pakistan was about to pay a flying visit to India and, as it turned out, the prime minister

[13]*The Statesman*, New Delhi, 1–2 September 1959.
[14]See *Lok Sabha Debates*, Second series, remarks ranging from 31 August to 12 September in Volume XXXIV. See especially p. 5588.

had to deal with the resignation of his senior military officer on the very day that he was greeting General Ayub. It was rumoured that the air and naval chiefs were on the verge of following suit. The parliamentary opposition stated that Kaul's promotion over the heads of more senior officers was more a matter of personal and political preference than of professional merit.[15] According to the usual practice, the chief of the army staff, after consultation with the area commanders, had offered the names of three officers, Generals P.S. Gyani, P.P. Kumaramangalam, and B.M. Kaul, as fit for promotion to the post of Lieutenant-General. Of these, Kaul was the most junior. The chief of the army staff had placed Gyani first on the list, but Defence Minister Menon and his cabinet colleagues chose just Kumaramangalam and Kaul.

On its face, the decision was a legitimate exercise of civilian authority, but General Thimayya interpreted the action differently, which led him to submit his resignation to the prime minister. Mr Nehru quickly persuaded him that his action on behalf of the career service was ill-advised, and the general withdrew his resignation before the news reached the public and the parliament. In parliament, the Prime Minister justified Gyani's exclusion on the ground that he had not yet commanded an infantry division, a normal requirement for promotion to lieutenant-general. But Gyani was an artillery officer with extensive experience and senior commands in that branch; his professional colleagues apparently did not regard his not having held command of an infantry division as a bar to promotion and nor, eventually, did his civilian superiors. He was made a lieutenant-general a few months after the public outcry over General Kaul's promotion.[16]

While promotions were the immediate occasion of Thimayya's resignation, strategy was also an issue. *Link*, a popular weekly friendly to Krishna Menon, wrote about whispers regarding the inadequacy of defences in NEFA, whispers quieted, it said, by the prime minister's remarks in the debate that followed the Chief of Staff's resignation. 'The North East Frontier,' said *Link* in memorable prose, 'was safe as houses.' Finally, the events of 1959 raised questions concerning lines of communication and responsibility in the defence establishment. General Thimayya was in the habit of seeing the prime minister directly from time to time, and some say that at one time at least, he had had a special relationship with Mr Nehru. The Kaul promotion seems to have been an occasion for Thimayya to find out whether it was he or the defence minister, from whom he had become progressively estranged, who commanded the greater confidence of the prime minister.

[15]*Asian Recorder*, 1959, p. 2944.
[16]*The Statesman*, New Delhi, 20 and 28 February 1961.

At stake was an issue of some enduring importance for civil-military relationships in India: whether, as in Britain, chiefs of staff were to have direct access to the prime minister when they disagreed with their political superiors.

In 1961, when General Kaul was appointed chief of the general staff, the top staff appointment in the army, he again became an issue before parliament.[17] Promotions, it was said, took place 'according to the whims and fancies of the Defense Minister or what will suit his political or ideological purposes'. However, the opposition acquitted itself badly. Senior spokesmen, in their eagerness to beat Mr Menon with any stick that came to hand, had not taken the elementary precaution of reading General Kaul's biography in the standard references, and were duly caught short when they accused him of not having combat arms experience.[18] The debate became a test of a parliamentary review of appointments as the opposition fought for the right to canvass promotions case by case, naming names.[19] But the Speaker forbade the naming of military officers: 'If I allow this,' he said, 'there will be eternal lobbying. Member after member of the Armed Forces will come and catch hold of all the 500 odd members here. ...'[20]

In 1962, the Kaul affair came to an abrupt and tragic close. On 5 October, some weeks after the Chinese had intensified their military activity on the northern frontier but before they launched their main offensive, which took place on 20 October, General Kaul was appointed commander of a newly formed corps that was responsible for the Northeast Frontier area. This appointment confirmed that Nehru and Menon had great confidence in his abilities since the government, at the end of September, had decided to oust the Chinese from what it believed was Indian territory. When Mr Nehru left for Ceylon in the second week of October, he announced: 'Our instructions are to free our territory. I cannot fix a date. That is entirely for the army.'[21] The government seemed convinced that a determined but limited effort would deter the Chinese: General Kaul was credited with being an exponent of this forward policy as he believed, unlike some of his military colleagues, that army preparedness was commensurate with the risk.[22] In the event, the worst happened: instead of driving the Chinese back and deterring them

[17]Mr Kripalani in *Lok Sabha Debates, 1961*, Second series, LIV, No. 41, p. 10059.
[18]*Debates*, LIV, No. 42, p. 10829.
[19]*Debates*, LIV, No. 41, p. 10551.
[20]*Debates*, LIV, No. 42, p. 10812.
[21]*The Statesman*, New Delhi, 12 April 1963, and Indian Affairs Record, October 1962, p. 261.
[22]Romesh Thapar, 'Contemporary', in *Economic Weekly*, February 1963.

from further advances, the Indian advance probably precipitated China's well-planned attack, an attack that quickly overran India's surprised, poorly led, and ill-prepared forces. The Delhi casualties of the Chinese offensive included Defence Minister Krishna Menon, Chief of the Army Staff Thapar, and Corps Commander Kaul.[23] On 1 April 1963, Defence Minister Chavan disclosed to parliament the terms of reference for the investigation into the debacle to be conducted by senior army officers, terms that included 'the capacity of the commanders at all levels to influence the men under them'.[24] The inquiry eventually concluded that 'while commanders up to the brigade level had exercised command adequately, at higher levels ... shortcomings became more apparent'. Defence Minister Chavan stated 'that some of the higher Commanders did not depend enough on the initiative of the lower Commanders, who alone could have the requisite knowledge of the terrain and local conditions of troops under them'. The judgment suggests, in its own officially circuitous way, that the highest command, presumably including General Kaul, may have been more in touch with its political chiefs than with the lower commands, and had ignored professional advice that might have warned them that the troops and equipment were inadequate. Another finding of the inquiry strengthens the impression that professional criteria were inadequately consulted, so that the troops were committed to an enterprise which they could not successfully complete. 'Even the largest and the best equipped of armies need to be given proper policy guidance and major directives by the government ... these must bear a reasonable relation to the size of the army and state of its equipment from time to time.'[25] Among the lessons taught by the Chinese invasions seems to be the importance of respecting the professional integrity and independence of the military service.

Finally, Mr Menon's role as defence minister must be viewed in the context of the succession issue. In the spring of 1962, it was very much on the public mind because of Mr Nehru's illness. Any prominent and ambitious member of the cabinet is interested either in his own success, or in ensuring that the man who does is not unsympathetic to his views. Krishna Menon is not immune to such sentiments. When G.B. Pant, the deputy leader of the Congress Parliamentary Party, died in March 1960, those with ambitions and hopes for the first place, Finance Minister Morarji Desai and Transport and Communications Minister Jagjivan Ram, manoeuvred to fill

[23]*The Times of India*, New Delhi, 1 December 1962.
[24]*The Statesman*, New Delhi, 2 April 1963.
[25]Text of speech in *Hindustan Times*, 3 September 1963.

his party post while Home Minister Lal Bahadur Shastri stood ready in case of a stand-off. After several postponements, the prime minister decided to sweep the problem under the rug by abolishing Pant's old post. At the time of Mr Nehru's illness in the spring of 1962, then, there were at least three known aspirants for the succession, as well as a less visible consortium of well-established state chief ministers who were contemplating joining the central cabinet en bloc and establishing their collective leadership at the Centre.

Krishna Menon, who had never held a strong position vis-à-vis the professionals of the Congress party, was not even prospectively in the running. Nor was any possible aspirant particularly friendly to Menon either personally or politically. Menon's best hope for remaining influential after the prime minister left the scene lay in maintaining the Nehru family leadership, that is, the leadership of the Prime Minister's daughter, Indira Gandhi. He is not alone in this. The amorphous but visible Congress left, made up of ideologically self-conscious socialists, younger intellectuals with leftist leanings and disdain for what they regard as the parochial and philistine professional politicians, and some top men in the central party organization who see Indira Gandhi as the only person in the country popular enough to keep powerful state chief ministers in line, believe that the Prime Minister's daughter is their best hope. A part of this unassembled jigsaw puzzle could have been Krishna Menon, heading a powerful defence establishment with a sympathetic professional like General Kaul at its helm. No one believed that Kaul would have helped or supported Menon in furthering his personal political ambitions. However, that he would have been sympathetic to any of Menon's effort aimed at blocking some current contenders for the succession, and, as one close to the Nehru family, would have looked favourably upon those who might support Indira Gandhi for Prime Minister, was not out of the question. But the Chinese invasion changed the political climate, and destroyed the particular constellation of power on which these speculations were based.

Military rule is more the result of civilian political failure than the political ambition of military men. The Indian Army's traditions, unlike those of armies in some other Asian countries, are professional rather than political. The Indian government has been sufficiently effective, so the military has had little cause to question their place in the state. The future of the military will depend in part on the continued success of political leadership. It will also depend upon the conduct of political leaders where the military is concerned. If politicians, instead of exercising self-restraint, yield to the temptation to strengthen themselves by developing friends or allies among military men, they will inevitably draw the military into politics. The future course of Indo-Chinese relations will also have a bearing on the future standing of the military in Indian public life. Persistent tension will sustain large defence budgets and give added prominence to military opinion and leadership. And large-scale, sustained fighting will not only accentuate these trends, but also open the way for a re-orientation of Indian politics. Violence and chauvinism could strengthen existing authoritarian tendencies, and create opportunities for military heroes.

7

The Centrist Future of Indian Politics*

SUSANNE HOEBER RUDOLPH AND LLOYD I. RUDOLPH

The most striking feature of Indian politics is its persistent centrism. During the thirty-five years parliamentary elections in which the Indian National Congress was the dominant among India's several parties, it benefited from three interdependent characteristics: first, a national apex organization with national goals, leadership, and strategy; second, a centrist (for India) ideology and centrist policies; and third, a pluralist basis of support. Despite the country's notorious social, economic, and cultural diversity, the characteristics of the Janata Party, victor in the sixth parliamentary election in 1977, the Congress-I, victor in the seventh parliamentary election of 1980, and the several parties that split from the Congress and Janata between 1978 and 1980 resemble those of the Indian National Congress.

Why are India's national parties centrist and pluralist rather than left or right class parties? Why, in a country with prominent religious communities, are confessional parties like those of the Middle East or Western Europe, which appeal to religious sentiment and identity, ineffective and defensive?

There are several reasons as to why we expect national centrist parties to constitute the mainstream of party politics over the next decade: (*i*) the tenuous quality of national class consciousness; (*ii*) the fragmentation of the confessional majority; (*iii*) the electoral strength of disadvantaged confessional and social minorities; (*iv*) the increasing political consciousness and strength of 'bullock capitalists' and 'backward classes'; (*v*) the imperatives of capturing power in Delhi; (*vi*) the constraints imposed by cultural diversity

*Originally published as 'The Centrist Future of Indian Politics', in *Asian Survey*, XX (6), June 1980, pp. 575–94.

and social pluralism in the federal system; and (*vii*) the advantages that accrue to a centrist national party when parliamentary seats are won by pluralities in single-member constituencies.

CLASS POLITICS

A leading reason for centrism is the tenuous quality of national class consciousness. To many it may seem plausible, even inevitable, that the politics of a country with as much inequality, poverty, and injustice as exists in India will take the form of class conflict. However, class has not been and may not become the principal medium for representation. Consciousness and organization with respect to inequality, poverty, and injustice have been as much, or more, the provenance of other kinds of social groupings—such as status groups and cultural communities—as of class. Organizations representing language, caste, and territorial (sons of the soil)[1] interests, and those of disadvantaged minorities (backward classes, Scheduled Castes and Tribes, Muslims), have been more successful than class-based organizations in creating consciousness and guiding political action to deal with the economic interests of the poor and the oppressed.[2]

If class is to become a stronger determinant of political action, suitable objective conditions are required. Conventionally, this has meant a heightened conflict between capital and labour as capital accumulation accelerates, and larger proportions of the workforce enter wage employment in the industrial sector of the organized economy. The future of class politics in India, however, is likely to remain as tenuous as it was in the past.

Although India is a leading industrial country (fifteenth in world rankings), it has no national classes. Its industrial workforce is proportionately small and stationary, and poorly organized. India's five million factory workers in 1971 constituted 3 per cent of its total workforce of 180 million, and 28 per cent of the 18 million employed in the organized sector of the economy (10 per cent of all workers).[3] The proportion of workers employed

[1] Myron Weiner, *Sons of the Soil, Migration and Ethnic Conflict in India*, Princeton: Princeton University Press, 1978.

[2] See R.A. Schermerhorn, *Ethnic Plurality in India*, Tucson: University of Arizona Press, 1978, and Lloyd I. Rudolph and Susanne Hoeber Rudolph, *The Modernity of Tradition: Political Development in India*, Chicago: University of Chicago Press, 1967.

[3] For a good summary of organized-sector figures, see A.N. Agrawal, *Indian Economy*, 5th revised edition, New Delhi: Vikas, 1979, Chapter 32. Standard sources include Government of India, Central Statistical Organization Department of Statistics, Ministry of Planning, *Statistical Abstract, New Series*, various numbers; Government of India, Planning Commission, Economic Survey, annual, Delhi. The latest figures, which do not allow the range of comparison of the 1971 figures, are 5.7 million factory workers in 1975, total workforce 212 million in

in the organized sector (like those employed in agriculture and services) has remained constant between 1960 and 1977, and more or less constant from 1901. About 34 per cent of organized-sector workers in 1978 belonged to India's fragmented, competing, and locally oriented trade unions.[4] Unions, and leadership positions within unions, have proliferated much faster than membership. Between 1927–32 and 1974, the average membership per union declined steadily.[5]

Organized labour's apex organizations have little control over subordinate units or influence on national policy or politics. Their fragmentation along party lines and competitive relationship make it difficult for them to pursue common policy or political objectives.[6] There is no equivalent in India to Britain's or Germany's national trade union congresses, France's or Italy's rival but national apex labour organizations, or even America's AFL-CIO.

The closest approximations to national labour organizations in India are the unions representing workers in the public-sector industries and government departments that span the subcontinent. These include the railways (1.4 million employees in 1975), insurance (800,000 employees in 1974), posts and telegraphs (650,000 in 1975), banks (400,000 in 1975), and smaller but strategically placed industries such as oil, coal, steel, and airlines. Sixty-five per cent of the workers employed in the organized economy in 1974 were public employees. Federal and state government employees, including the police, have acted nationally on the basis of emulation and contagion rather than an all-India organization. The railway strike of May 1974, which Mrs Gandhi broke through massive repression and the arrest of union leaders, was an impressive demonstration of organized labour's potential for national action, and may be considered a harbinger of the future. However, the working-class consciousness of state employees is compromised by their status as public employees, the nominally non-antagonistic nature

---

1980 (applying a 2 per cent annual growth rate to achieve an estimate), and 21 million organized-sector employees. *Economic Survey*, 1978–9, pp. 87–8.

[4]Alak Ghosh, *Indian Economy; Its Nature and Problems*, 22nd revised edition, Calcutta: World Press, 1979–80, p. 429. Ghosh's figure of 34 per cent for the proportion of union members among workers in the organized economy has to be an estimate. The Labour Bureaus of many state governments do not submit any returns (presumably because they must rely on union cooperation, which is not forthcoming), and some of those that do submit returns report incomplete coverage. *The Statistical Pocketbook*, 1979, p. 171, relying on such state Labour Bureau figures, gives five million as the number of union members in 1971. Ghosh's 34 per cent works out to 6.1 million.

[5]Agrawal, *Indian Economy*, p. 584.

[6]See Rakhahari Chattopadhyay, 'The Political Role of Labour Unions in India: An Interstate Study of Labour Unions in West Bengal, Karnataka and Rajasthan', Ph.D. thesis, University of Chicago: Department of Political Science, 1975.

of their relationship with owner-managers who are 'socialist', and the common interests that many white-collar and skilled blue-collar workers share with the management. When the state controls the means of production and administration, conflict arises between workers' claims based on performance, and those based on equity. As wards of a nominally socialist state that aspires to be a 'model employer', India's thirteen million state employees tend to be dependent or rebellious rather than class conscious. Nor are they likely to make common cause with agricultural labourers and poor cultivators. Not only do they live as races apart, but they also live as beneficiaries of state exactions and investments. State employees can become rivals rather than brothers of their fellow workers in the unorganized economy.

India's blue and white-collar workers' limited and episodic capacity to engage in class politics is paralleled by the marginal capacity of the owners and managers of capital in the private sector to engage in class politics, or to overtly influence policy on their behalf. India's large private firms rarely approximate the national scope (in markets, employment, investment, and influence on consumption and political consciousness) that national firms in advanced industrial economies do. Furthermore, the conglomerates that replaced the British managing agencies have been placed on the defensive by the widely accepted ideological position that states that the profit motive produces antisocial consequences. Legislation and licensing procedures that regulate the kind and amount of commodities produced, as well as state control of credit and investment, reflect the limited capacity of conglomerate firms to insure their freedom of action by influencing politics and policy. The frequent statements and policy proposals of spokesmen for private capitalism find little public favour with party leaders, and with elected and appointed officials, because they want to avoid the political costs associated with legitimizing their views. Those who accept campaign contributions from private-sector donors and support their interests governmentally find it convenient to attack them in public.

In marked contrast to private capitalism, state capitalism, under the name of the public sector, is honoured and well-endowed. Planned investment over the past thirty years has created a public sector that, as Jawaharlal Nehru intended, occupies the commanding heights of the organized economy. From the Third Plan to the Sixth, the ratio of planned investment between the private and public sectors has been 40:60.[7] Public-sector industries and financial institutions are, more often than not, national in ways comparable to their counterparts in advanced industrial economies. Of India's twenty largest firms, the top ten are in the public sector. The sales of the largest

[7]Ghosh, *Indian Economy*, p. 312.

public-sector firm, Indian Oil Corporation, exceeded the combined sales of the top ten firms in the private sector, and the combined sales of the top ten public-sector firms exceeded the sales of the top 101 private-sector firms.[8]

The existence of state capitalism on this scale severely limits the objective possibilities for parties grounded in the class politics of industrial and finance capitalism. The public sector is of and within the state. Its apex industry organizations, firms, and multifarious credit institutions *ab initio* engage in bureaucratic rather than class politics. The organizational interests of state bodies are pursued more in the rooms and corridors of central secretariat buildings and in bargaining sessions with agents of competitive apex bodies and interest groups than in the parliament, on the hustings, or in the streets. The politicians and bureaucrats who articulate and pursue the interests of state capitalism do their best to avoid or escape class or interest group politics by making ideological claims that place agencies of the state above or outside the political struggle.

As the nation's largest employer, the state's claim to be above or outside class or interest group politics affects its relations with its own workers. On the one hand, state employees who provide public or essential services *de jure* or *de facto* are not expected to use strikes to make demands or bargain collectively. On the other hand, when state capitalist firms try to live up to the states' paternalistic claims of being a model employer or, like large corporations in the advanced industrial economies, increase prices in order to pass on the costs of buying the industrial peace that was achieved by granting increased wages and benefits, they not only contribute to inflation, but also, in a poor developing country like India, sacrifice the country's long-term collective interest by dissipating investment funds in present consumption.

The domination of the means and relations of production by state capitalism in the organized sector severely limits the objective conditions for industrial and financial capitalism in India to become a conscious, organized force in politics. State capitalism's ambiguous dual role as the representative of the public or people's interest, and as the nation's largest and most powerful holder of capital and employer of labour, radically diminishes the means available for the conduct of class politics.

CONFESSIONAL POLITICS

There are reasons why India does not have national class parties; but why does it not have confessional parties? Why not a national Hindu party? Moderate Christian parties play an important role in the politics of Western

[8] *India Today*, 16–31 May 1979, p. 83.

European states, where 'rationalist' culture and 'secular' norms are more advanced than in India. Why has India not been affected either by the religious revivalism that has swept the Islamic world, or by the confessional parties that had earlier played an important part in the politics of the Middle East and Southeast Asia? Why does 'centrism' in India include secularism as much as it does 'socialism' and democracy?

The support base for a national confessional party, the Hindu majority, is illusory, even as confessional minorities play an important role in national and regional politics. The overwhelming Hindu majority, 83 per cent according to the 1971 census, is in part an artefact of categorization. In addition to the 17 per cent (ninety-five million) of the population who are not Hindus, another 15 per cent (eighty million) are members of Scheduled Castes. Their categorization as Hindus is as much a result of census enumeration as it is of their choosing. Most are not susceptible to political appeals based on a Hindu identity or Hindu interests. Similarly, it is questionable whether the thirty million out of the thirty-eight million tribals classified as Hindus in the 1971 census share a Hindu identity. They, too, are not available for party appeals to Hindu nationalism and interests. Indeed, many are actively engaged in asserting a variety of cultural or sub-national identities, and in defending their interests against 'Hindu' encroachment and appropriation. Together, Muslims, other non-Hindus, and Scheduled Castes and Tribes counted as Hindus (11, 6, 15, and 5 per cent respectively) constitute 37 per cent of India's population.[9] Out of the 63 per cent of the population that is left, only a fraction of an uncertain magnitude shares a Hindu identity that also has political saliency. More importantly, the Hindu majority is more fragmented and competitive along class, caste, and regional lines than are India's minorities.

The potential support base for a Hindu confessional politics is located, for the most part, among the traditionally literate, spiritually initiated ('twice born') upper castes in the relatively backward, Hindi-speaking heartland states of northern India. In the nine large and more advanced states of southern, eastern, and western India, the kind of Hindu consciousness and social structure needed to support confessional party politics is marginal to non-existent.

Prior to the 1975 emergency regime, it was the erstwhile Jan Sangh— which was reduced to a fraction in the Janata Party—and its sister organization, the RSS, which articulated the ideology of a Hindu Rashtra (Nation), and the symbolic, cultural, and social policies that addressed Hindu interests

---

[9]These percentages are based on the table given in Ministry of Information and Broadcasting, *India, 1979: A Reference Annual*, Delhi: Government of India, 1979, p. 10. Tribal Christians are included among 'other non-Hindus'.

and values. A rough measure of the potential support base for a Hindu confessional party is the proportion of the vote captured by the Jan Sangh in elections before 1977—that is, 9 per cent in 1967 and 7.4 per cent in 1971.

MINORITY POLITICS

By contrast, India's important minorities—the Scheduled Castes, Muslims, Scheduled Tribes, and Christians—like the African Americans and the Spanish-speaking population in the US, have had a greater propensity, which is now declining, than the Hindu majority to vote en bloc.[10] Among the minorities, the Scheduled Tribes vote more than Scheduled Castes and Muslims combined. The minorities' community identity is more pervasive and politically salient than the Hindu majority's, and they share common economic and social conditions to a much greater degree than Hindus. Again, like African Americans and the Hispanic population, they suffer simultaneously from poverty, discrimination, and powerlessness, objective circumstances that have been translated into a subjective awareness of economic exploitation, status deprivation, and political repression. The objective conditions and consciousness of India's minorities have been less subject (than the Hindu majority's) to the cross-cutting or divisive effects of class, caste, and region.

Muslim and Scheduled Caste and Tribe support is particularly vital for electoral success in the five Hindi heartland states of northern India, where the undivided Janata enjoyed its greatest electoral successes, and where in 1980 the opposition to the Congress remained the strongest. In other words, minorities are most significant numerically in just those states where elections since 1967 have been most closely contested. In Uttar Pradesh, Bihar, Madhya Pradesh, Haryana, and Rajasthan, a group that includes India's two most populous states and that elects 40 per cent of the parliament's 542 members, the three minorities together constitute 37 per cent of the votes in the first three states, 34 per cent in Rajasthan, and 23 per cent in Haryana (see Table 7.1).

Since minority support is vital to electoral success, gaining or holding it has become a common feature of party strategy and ideology. Parties that rely primarily or exclusively on class appeal to reach the poor and the disadvantaged have been less successful than those that seek to represent

[10]For a careful examination of Muslim voting in Bihar, which shows, *inter alia*, increasing Muslim electoral cohesiveness, see Harry W. Blair, *Voting, Caste, Community, Society: Explorations in Aggregate Data Analysis in India and Bangla Desh*, New Delhi and Stockholm: Young Asia Publications, 1979.

Table 7.1: Parliamentary Seats and Minority Population Proportions
in India Heartland States, 1977

| State | No. of Seats | Minority Muslim | Percentage of Population | | Total of Three Minorities |
			Scheduled Castes	Scheduled Tribes	
(All India)	(542)	(11)	(15)	(7)	(33)
Uttar Pradesh	85	16	21	Negligible	37
Bihar	54	14	14	9	37
Madhya Pradesh	40	4	13	20	37
Rajasthan	25	7	15	12	34
Haryana	10	4	19	Negligible	23

Source: *India, A Reference Annual, 1979*, p. 10.

minority interests and identities. The electoral successes of the Congress party under Jawaharlal Nehru and Indira Gandhi were in large measure a result of the support from India's largest minority groups, Muslims and the Scheduled Castes, who regarded the Congress as their friend and protector. The Janata's success in the March 1977 election followed the alienation of these minorities from the Congress, and their support of the Janata. All three national parties contesting in 1980 tried to occupy the Centre by avowing that they were secular and socialist—that is, that they recognized the minorities' need for protection and help, and the state's obligation to eliminate destitution (or poverty) and provide economic opportunities to the poor and the disadvantaged. Each made symbolic and policy claims designed to gain the support of India's minorities: Janata's Scheduled Caste leader Jagjivan Ram and its Gandhian commitment to eliminate destitution and promote employment; Lok Dal's son-of-a-*kisan* (cultivator) leader Charan Singh and its commitment to promote secularism and the interests of the agrarian sector, which is where most of the disadvantaged minorities live; and Congress-I's Nehru legacy of friendship and protection for Muslims and the Scheduled Castes, personified in his daughter Indira, and its effort to eliminate poverty by promoting industrialization.

The nominal reason for Janata's three splits in July 1979 and March and April 1980 was the credibility of its commitment to secularism, a code word for the party's attitude towards the minorities and Hindu communalism. The Charan Singh, Jagjivan Ram, and Chandra Shekhar-led factions alleged that the former Jan Sangh faction's 'dual membership' in the Janata party and in the upper-caste dominated RSS was incompatible with the party's secular commitment. The RSS' ideology of a Hindu Rashtra, they argued, would exclude minorities from the benefits of citizenship, and inhibit policy initiatives on their behalf. Leaders of the former Jan Sangh depicted the Hindu Rashtra as an inclusive term that encompassed India's composite Hindu culture and plural society. They stressed that the Janata Party's founder, the late Jayaprakash Narayan, found no incompatibility between his commitment to secularism and to Gandhi's social philosophy, and Jan Sangh and RSS support prior to and after the formation of the Janata Party in May 1977. In April 1980, at the time of Janata's third split, Atal Behari Vajpayee, former Jan Sangh leader and president of the newly formed Bharatiya Janata Party (BJP), reaffirmed the new party's commitment to Jayaprakash Narayan's philosophy. Emphasizing that secularism and unity in diversity were the cornerstones of Indian nationalism, he said that his party would give foremost place to promoting the interests of minorities and the backward sections.[11]

By advocating secularism, the Janata Party and its successors could continue to bid for the support of Scheduled Caste and Muslim voters, many of whom had deserted the Congress to vote for Janata in 1977 as a result of emergency excesses. Indeed, the Janata in 1977 captured all 38 Scheduled Caste seats in the five Hindi heartland states (Table 7.2). Contrary to the impression conveyed by the 1980 outcome in seats when Congress-I won 62 per cent of the seats in the Hindi heartland states (see Table 7.2), the 1980 outcome in party vote shares there made clear that opposition inroads on Congress support from minority communities persisted at diminished levels. In 1971, the Congress-I won 65 per cent of the Scheduled Caste seats in the 17 large states, and in 1977 Janata almost reversed the result by capturing 58 per cent, but in 1980 Congress-I apparently regained its 1971 hold on Scheduled Caste support by winning 61 per cent (see Table 7.2). This aggregate result is misleading, however, because Scheduled Caste votes in Hindi heartland states were more closely divided in 1980 than they were in either 1971 or 1977, when we infer the minorities voted decisively for Congress and then for Janata. In UP, not only India's most populous state but also the state with the highest proportion (21 per cent) of Scheduled Caste voters, Janata and Lok Dal candidates in 1980 gained 58 per cent of the vote in Scheduled Caste constituencies, 6 per cent higher than their average vote in UP (52 per cent) and 22 per cent higher than the Congress-I's vote in UP Scheduled Caste constituencies and in the state as a whole, both of which averaged 36 per cent.[12]

[11] *The Times of India*, 7 April 1980.
[12] Constituency reports, 6–15 January, *Hindustan Times, The Times of India, The Indian Express, The Statesman*. Of the eight seats the Congress won in UP, all were by minority votes ranging

Table 7.2: Scheduled Caste Constituencies, Seats by Party, in the
1971, 1977, and 1980 Lok Sabha Elections

17 Large States								
1971			1977			1980		
Congress	Janata	Other	Congress	Janata	Other	Congress	Janata	Other
No. %	No. %	No. %	No. %	No. %	No. %	No. %	No. %	No. %
48 (65)	7 (10)	18 (25)	15 (11)	45 (58)	18 (23)	46 (61)	14 (18)	16 (21)
Total Seats 73			Total Seats 78			Total Seats 76		

Hindi Heartland

	1971		1977		1980	
	Congress	Janata	Congress	Janata	Congress	Janata
Bihar	5	1	8		6	2
Haryana	2		3		1	1
Madhya Pradesh	3	2	5		4	2
Uttar Pradesh	17		18		8	9
Rajasthan	2		4		4	
	29 (85%)	5 (15%)	0 (0%)	38 (100%)	23 (62%)	14 (38%)

Sources: Government of India, Election Commission, *Report on the General Election to the Lok Sabha, 1971*, vol. II; *Report on the General Election to the Lok Sabha, 1977*, vol. II. For 1980, G.G. Mirchandani, *The People's Verdict* (New Delhi; Vikas, 1980), p. 135.

Note: The number of Scheduled Caste seats has increased over time. Congress refers to Congress (R) in 1971; Congress in 1977; Congress (I) in 1980. Janata refers to the components that united in 1977; 1971 counts the premerger parties and 1980 counts Janata, Lok Dal, and Congress-U.

In Bihar, home state of the then Janata leader and potential prime minister Jagjivan Ram, himself a member of a Scheduled Caste community, Congress-I candidates in Scheduled Caste constituencies polled a higher percentage of the vote than they had in UP, and which was higher than their Janata and Lok Dal rivals, but still fell short of a majority. Mrs Gandhi's well-publicized efforts, which began as early as May 1977 at Belchi in Bihar, to recapture the confidence and loyalty of Scheduled Caste voters by rushing to the scene of atrocities against them, as well as the backlash among upper and Scheduled Caste voters against Bihar's Janata Chief Minister's successful effort to reserve 22 per cent of government jobs for the backward 'classes'

---

from 35 to 45 per cent. None would have been won had Lok Dal and Janata voted together. Of the six seats Congress-I won in Bihar, it would have lost two had those parties voted together.

(that is, castes), could help to account for the fact that Congress-I candidates in Scheduled Caste constituencies won 48 per cent, while Janata/Lok Dal candidates won 44 per cent of the vote. Both sets of candidates did better in Scheduled Caste constituencies than in the state as a whole, with the Congress-I polling an impressive 12 per cent and Janata/Lok Dal a more modest 4 per cent, higher than their statewide average.

Muslim seats and votes in 1980 were closely divided. Congress-I captured twenty-nine (45 per cent) of the sixty-five seats with 20 to 50 per cent Muslim voters, a result 22 per cent below its national average (67 per cent) of seats won. Similarly, Congress-I won only 36 per cent of the vote in the sixty-four 'Muslim' constituencies, 7 per cent less than its national average of 43 per cent. Clearly, its special relationship with the Muslim community had not been re-established. Out of thirty-two of the sixty-four 'Muslim' seats captured by other parties, twelve were won by the Lok Dal in UP, and 18 by the Communist Party-Marxist in West Bengal—which, from June 1977, has been the governing party in that state. Congress-I victories, in contrast, were spread over the country,[13] mainly in states where Muslims were smaller fractions of the statewide population, and thus are more isolated than they are in UP and West Bengal, which rank first and second with regard to the proportion of the Muslim population. Since a significant proportion of UP Muslims were small or middle-sized landholders and many Bengal Muslims poor labourers, there is reason to believe that Muslims who voted for the Lok Dal and the CPI-M in these two states respectively interpreted their interest more in class than in community terms, while Muslims who voted for Congress-I more often understood their interest in communal terms.[14]

Among the minorities, in 1980 only the Scheduled Tribe voters returned to the Congress-I fold in overwhelming numbers.[15] In 1971, the Congress-I won 68 per cent of the Scheduled Tribe seats, in 1977 Janata won 61 per cent, and in 1980 Congress-I improved substantially on its impressive 1971 margin by capturing 82 per cent (Table 7.3). Voting patterns confirmed that tribal voters, unlike Scheduled Caste and Muslim voters in 1980,

[13]G.G. Mirchandani, *The People's Verdict*, New Delhi: Vikas, 1980, p. 134; *The Times of India*, 26 January 1980.

[14]For an examination of long-term social factors at work shaping electoral behaviour in UP, see Francine Frankel, 'Problems of Correlating Electoral and Economic Variables: An Analysis of Voting Behaviour and Agrarian Modernization in Uttar Pradesh', in John O. Field *et al.*, *Electoral Politics in the Indian States: The Impact of Modernization*, New Delhi: Manohar, 1977. Frankel (p. 180) shows a modest positive correlation (.41) of BKD vote with the percentage of Muslim population in the West Plain (eighteen western districts) of UP.

[15]The Janata/Lok Dal average vote in tribal constituencies declined from 61 to 34 per cent, an enormous twenty-seven point decline. Constituency reports, *Hindustan Times*, *The Times of India*, *The Indian Express*, *The Statesman*, 6–15 January 1980.

Table 7.3: Scheduled Tribe Constituency Seats by Party, 1971 to 1980, Lok Sabha

	1971		1977		1980	
	No.	%	No.	%	No.	%
Congress	21	(68)	9	(29)	27	(82)
Janata	5	(16)	19	(61)	2	(6)
Communist Parties						
Other	5	(16)	3	(10)	3	(3)
	31	(100)	31	(100)	33	(99)

Sources: Same as Table 7.2.
Note: Congress means Congress (R) in 1971, Congress in 1977, Congress-I in 1980. Janata in 1971 means the components of the 1977 Janata; in 1980 it means Janata, Lok Dal, and Congress-U.

engaged in bloc voting for Congress-I, but only at the state level. In Madhya Pradesh, the state with the largest Scheduled Tribe population and the most Scheduled Tribe seats (nine), the Congress-I in 1980 won comfortable majorities or high pluralities in all but one. Its overall average in Madhya Pradesh tribal reserved seats was 55 per cent, eight points higher than its average in the state, and 12 per cent above its national average. Scheduled Caste and Muslim voters rarely exceed 30 per cent of the population even in reserved constituencies, and, as a result, often reflect by choice or intimidation the voting pattern of their constituency. Tribal voters, however, are more densely concentrated, typically constituting 50 per cent or more in reserved constituencies,[16] and vote more independently. Unlike ex-untouchables and Muslims, whose level of consciousness and organization are higher and whose constituency circumstances are different, tribals, as the most oppressed and disadvantaged minorities, turned to the Congress-I in 1980, and to a lesser but significant extent, to tribal parties.

The 1980 election results confirm that the need to win a substantial share of the minority vote is one of the essential determinants of centrism in Indian politics. Parties whose ideology, policies, and electoral strategy do not attend to representing minority interests and identities cannot compete for power at the national level. Centrist parties, in the coded language of Indian politics, espouse secularism and socialism in order to

[16]See Gopal Krishna, *Electoral Participation and Political Integration in Center for the Study of Developing Societies, Context of Electoral Change in India*, Delhi: Academic Books, 1969, p. 37. He shows that in 80 per cent of reserved constituencies, the Scheduled Castes constituted less than 30 per cent while Scheduled Tribes constituted 50 per cent of the population in two-thirds of the constituencies reserved for them.

signal their regard and concern for the 37 per cent of the electorate who make up the minority voters.

BULLOCK CAPITALISTS AND BACKWARD CLASSES

The centrist character of India's national parties is also determined by the balance of forces in the agricultural sector. Polarization and left and right class politics in the countryside are unlikely because the first wave of land reforms broke the power of the neo-feudal landlord class (zamindars and jagirdars), and because a centrist political class composed of bullock capitalists and backward classes had emerged as the leading representative of agrarian interests. The power of neo-feudal notables was initially limited by the first and largely successful wave of land reforms in the 1950s that abolished the 'intermediaries', India's landlord class. Without the first wave of land reform, neo-feudal landlords using attached (traditionally dependent) labour and/ or tractor capitalists using wage labour might have provided, as they have in Pakistan, the basis for a viable conservative politics.[17] The Swatantra party for a time created an alliance between neo-feudal and capitalist agricultural interests, and private industrial capitalism. Its demise ended India's only experiment with class politics of the right.

At the bottom of the agrarian pyramid, except in a few districts such as those in Kerala, the level of consciousness and organization among agricultural workers is too low to enable them to represent themselves effectively. India's 'proletariat' in the organized economy is in fact a labour aristocracy composed of white and skilled blue-collar workers. It is sufficiently separated by interest, lifestyle, and aspirations from unskilled rural wage labour to prevent urban and rural workers in the foreseeable future from becoming allies, much less comrades. This urban-rural gap may close as agricultural workers become more conscious and organized, as more members of their households are employed in the city, or, as rural producers, they become beneficiaries of the Green and White (milk) revolutions. Over the next decade, though, such linkages seem unlikely. In contrast with the objective circumstances and subjective orientations of the top and bottom of the agrarian pyramid that constrain class parties of the right and left, the circumstances and orientation of bullock capitalists and promote centrist politics.

[17]Ronald Herring and Charles Kennedy, 'The Political Economy of Farm Mechanization Policy: Tractors in Pakistan', in Raymond Hopkins (ed.), *Politics of Agricultural Development*, Boulder, Co: Westview Press, forthcoming; and (with M. Ghaffar Chaudhry) 'The 1972 Land Reforms in Pakistan and Their Economic Implications: A Preliminary Analysis', *Pakistan Development Review*, Autumn, 1974.

In the 1970s, the political influence of large landholders was successfully challenged by a new rural class we call bullock capitalists. Their political strategy was to challenge the Congress' alleged urban and industrial bias by generalizing the interests of independent agrarian producers to the agricultural sector and rural society as a whole. The victory of the Janata Party and the formation of a Janata government in 1977 marked the ascendance of a political coalition in which agrarian interests played the role of senior partner. Charan Singh's March 1979 pro-agrarian budget, like his six-month (July-December 1979) Lok Pal-led coalition government and 1980 campaign themes (for example, his attacks on organized labour as privileged, and on Nehru's urban-industrial bias),[18] created a backlash whose strength, *inter alia*, is a measure of his success. No party, including those on the left, has ignored Charan Singh's mass base among agrarian producers.

Eighty per cent of India's population is rural, 72 per cent of its labour force is agricultural, and 45 per cent of its national income comes from its agricultural sector. Independent agrarian producers constitute a plurality of the Indian workforce, but are even less effectively organized and represented at the state and national levels than industrial labour. Prior to 1977 they had partially overcome this apparent handicap when it came to influencing policy by direct representation in state legislatures and cabinets. After Janata's victory in 1977, they were for the first time directly represented at the national level by virtue of being the largest faction in the Janata Parliamentary Party, and through their influence in the cabinet planning commission and ministries.

The emergence of agrarian interests on the national political scene undid the political settlement of the Nehru era, which was based on a coalition of urban and rural interests united behind an essentially urban-oriented industrial strategy. Its senior partners were India's proportionately small (about 3 per cent) but politically powerful administrative, managerial, and professional English-educated middle classes, and big industrialists who welcomed the freedom from the foreign competition of import substitution and the industrial self-reliance strategies of the second and third Five-Year Plans. The English educated middle classes manned the bureaucracy, built and managed the state capitalist (public) sector, and staffed large firms in the modern private sector. The junior partners in the Nehru settlement were rural notables, mostly from the large landowner class. They consented to the import substitution, industrial self-strategies, and urban control of the

---

[18]Charan Singh articulated these themes while campaigning in Andhra Pradesh in October 1979. See the *Deccan Herald, Hindu,* and *Indian Express* (Bangalore) for 23 and 24 October 1979. We are grateful to V.K. Narasimhan, editor of *The Deccan Herald,* for providing these cuttings.

central government, and the advantages that accrued to the urban elites and organized workers, on condition that they themselves remain in charge of the state governments. Being in control of the state governments enabled them to allocate resources and control policy implementation for the agricultural sector and rural society in ways that protected their interests. One of the consequences of the 1977 election, which, however, was only partially intended, was that for the first time since independence agricultural interests were powerfully represented at the Centre as well as in the states. At the same time, bullock capitalists partially displaced large landowners in the agrarian power constellation. As a result, the Nehru era policies favouring cities, centralization, big dams, and capital-intensive industrialization were displaced by policies that favoured the agricultural sector and rural society, the decentralization of government and the economy, and small producers using labour-intensive technologies that promoted employment.

After the January 1980 mid-term parliamentary election, the Gandhi-led Congress-I government indicated that it intends to revive the Nehru settlement. Industry, rather than agriculture, is to be the principal means of growth and employment generation. Tenants, smallholders, and labourers led by neo-feudal notables and large landowners are likely to play a larger role than bullock capitalists and backward classes in the Congress-I's rural support, pointing towards a variety of Tory socialism.[19] If local notables and large landowners become junior partners in Congress-I's rebuilt Nehru-style urban-rural coalition, they may be willing to support the return of an urban-oriented industrial strategy in return for a partial restoration of their status and power in rural society and state politics. At the same time, Mrs Gandhi, whose party ridiculed Janata's agriculture-led employment strategy,

[19] In anticipation of assembly elections in nine states projected for late May or early June 1980, ex-Swatantra neo-feudal notables (mainly Rajput) in Rajasthan previously associated with the Janata Party, but badly treated by Janata Chief Minister Bhairon Singh Shekhawat and adversely affected by his redistributionist policies, were being encouraged by Congress-I state and national leaders to believe that they would be allocated a substantial number of tickets (nominations). Rajputs in Gujarat and to a lesser extent in Madhya Pradesh had already moved into top leadership positions in the Congress-I. His Highness Baria was coordinating Rajput-Congress-I negotiations. In UP, Rajputs played a significant part in the 1980 Congress-I parliamentary campaigns. In Amethi, the son of the Raja of Amethi, Sanjay Singh, managed Sanjay Gandhi's successful campaign. The Rajmata of Gwalior, Vijaya Raje Scindia, Mrs Gandhi's Janata opponent in Rae Bareilly constituency, fared badly, in part because the Rajputs whose support she expected voted instead for Mrs Gandhi.

In the 1980 state assembly elections in UP, 115 of the 334 Congress (I) candidates for general seats were Rajputs. Brahmins for the first time, ranked second with ninety-five. Brahmins, like Muslims and Harijans, are not likely to take well to Sanjay Gandhi's reliance on Rajput leadership. For details, see S.K. Tripathi's column in *The Indian Express*, 16 May 1980.

had not ignored the policy needs of middle-level agricultural producers, no doubt in the expectation that some support could be obtained from that quarter.[20]

Middle-level agricultural producers are one component of the ascendant political class in India's countryside. This component encompasses two overlapping categories: a producer group; the middle-level peasants we call bullock capitalists; and a status group, the backward classes, an administrative euphemism for backward castes. They constitute about 25 per cent of the population located in the lower reaches of the caste order, but above the untouchables. Backward castes began to mobilize politically in the south and west after World War I, but have only recently come to be a political force in the north.[21] The centrepieces of Janata's economic and social policies articulated political class interests, an agriculture-led employment strategy, and a new wave of reservation of seats, this time for backward castes in government jobs and educational institutions.

Bullock capitalists are advantageously placed by their objective circumstances to be the hegemonic agrarian class. As of 1971–2, they constituted a large proportion of agricultural households and controlled more land (35 per cent controlling 51 per cent) than any of the other three agrarian classes—the landless (27 per cent), smallholders (33 per cent controlling 10 per cent), or large landholders (6 per cent controlling 39 per cent). Large landholders, whose average size holding increased marginally, lost ground to bullock capitalists between 1954 and 1972 in terms of the proportion of households and area controlled, and, we infer, in their capacity to practice vertical mobilization. Along with the end of pro-Congress block voting by minorities (except tribals) in the Hindi heartland states, the absolute and proportional decline in the largely pro-Congress large landholder category, and the more effective political mobilization of bullock capitalists and backward castes contributed to the Congress' progressive loss of support, particularly in UP, Bihar, and Haryana. Congress' decline

---

[20]The Congress-I minister for agriculture, Rao Birendra Siugh, has pushed vigorously for more favourable prices for agricultural products and inputs. 'Appeasing the Rich Farm Lobby', in editorial, *Economic and Political Weekly*, 15 (9), 1980. Finance Minister K. Venkataraman's temporary budget of March 1980, which had virtually no relief for any category of taxpayer, did have one for the tax-paying farmers who are by definition rich, allowing them to take into account the previous year's losses in the current year's declaration. *The Times of India*, 12 March 1980. The two moves suggest appeals to both bullock capitalists and rich farmers.

[21]See Lloyd I. Rudolph and Susan Hoeber Rudolph, *Modernity of Tradition*, Part I; Robert L. Hardgrave Jr., *The Nadars of Tamilnad*, Berkeley: University of California Press, 1979; Eugene Irschick, *Politics and Social Conflict in South India: The Non-Brahman Movement and Tamil Separatism*, Bombay: Oxford University Press, 1969.

began in 1967, touched bottom in 1977, and made only a weak recovery in 1980.[22] This decline paralleled the rise of Charan Singh's BKD (a Janata faction and later the Lok Dal), the party *par excellence* of the bullock capitalists. This pattern may be interpreted in light of Paul Brass' investigations in UP, which show that the Congress' strength lay especially among operators of 30 acres or more and one acre or less, while the BKD's lay among the two to 20 acre holders.[23]

Bullock capitalists resemble 'yeoman' farmers in that they are independent agricultural producers. Self-employed and self-funded, their holdings are large enough to support the use of a pair of bullocks and the new inputs associated with the 'Green Revolution'. Typically, they operated between 2.5 and 15 acres. At the same time, their assets are not large enough to enable them to engage in capital-intensive agricultural production based on an extensive use of machines, or to require them to rely wholly or mainly on wage labour. We prefer the term 'bullock capitalists' to 'middle peasants' because of the mix of capitalist, pre-industrial, and non-capitalist features that characterize their economic circumstances. They operate family farms; the family, broadly defined, is the primary, if not the exclusive, source of capital management and labour. Bullock capitalists produce enough for the market to be oriented to and constrained by it, but not so much that consumption of their own products or non-monetized exchanges ceased to matter. The costs of their inputs, like the prices of their products, are powerfully but not wholly determined by market forces; state actions also affect agricultural prices and factor costs. They sometimes employ but do not depend on attached or casual wage labour. Since they are self-employed, they benefit from their own high quality, committed labour. While they use and pay for capital and participate in markets, they are 'non-capitalist' producers in the sense that, being self-employed, their relations of production remain relatively undifferentiated and non-antagonistic.

Most important for consciousness and politics is the fact that the economic circumstances of bullock capitalists unite the interests of capital, management, and labour. Bullock capitalists own the means of production, manage the productive unit, and themselves provide most, if not all, the labour. If there is exploitation involved in their relations of production, it is self-exploitation—for example, they benefit from the 'surplus value' of their labour. Their ideological propensities are individualistic rather than

[22]The Congress per cent of votes over three elections is as follows: UP—1971, 49 per cent; 1977, 25 per cent; 1980, 36 per cent. Bihar—1971, 34 per cent; 1977, 23 per cent; 1980, 36 per cent. Haryana—1971, 53 per cent; 1977, 18 per cent; 1980, 30 per cent.

[23]'The Politicization of the Peasantry in a North Indian State', (author anonymous), mimeo, 1978, p. 66.

collectivist or capitalist. Their objective interests do not place them in a necessarily antagonistic relationship with other agrarian classes. At the same time, to the degree that they supplement family labour with wage labour or compete for scarce land with tenants or landless labourers, their mainly non-capitalist relations of production are no bar to severe conflict with other agrarian classes. Nonetheless, they are freer than any other agrarian class to seek hegemony by appealing to the common interest of all agrarian classes, and by making upward and/or downward alliances to become the fulcrum of political centrism.

All these features conspire to make bullock capitalists not only a centrist class, but also the agent of a centrist politics equally opposed to collectivist and capitalist agriculture. As the bullock capitalists' most articulate ideologue put it:

A system of agriculture based on small enterprises, where the worker himself is the owner of the land under his plough, will foster democracy. For, it creates a population of independent outlook and action in the social and political fields. The peasant is an incorrigible individualist; his vocation, season in and season out, can be carried on with a pair of bullocks or a small machine in the solitude of nature without the necessity of having to give orders to or take orders from anybody. That is why the peasant class everywhere is the only class which is equally democratic without mental reservations. Further, the system of family-sized farms or peasant proprietorship ensures stability because the operator or the peasant has a stake in his farm and would lose by instability.[24]

The political coming of age of bullock capitalists runs parallel with and is strengthened by the first wave in the northern Hindi heartland states, and the second wave in the southern and western states of Karnataka and Maharashtra of the so-called backward classes movement. While the objective overlap is hardly perfect, the backward castes that were and are now being mobilized represent the status aspect of the economic category represented by bullock capitalism. Bullock capitalists are an economic category grounded in the means of production; the backward castes are defined by the traditional ritual ranking of caste, modified by the British and Indian states' 'official' sociological ranking of India's disadvantaged.[25]

[24]Charan Singh, *India's Economic Policy: The Gandhian Blueprint*, New Delhi: Vikas, 1978, p. 16.

[25]For an account of the complex ideological and legal aspects of the backward classes movement, see Marc Galanter, 'Who are the "Other Backward Classes"? An Introduction to a Constitutional Puzzle', *Economic and Political Weekly*, 13 (43 and 44), 28 October 1978. Also Lelah Dushkin, 'Backward Class Benefits and Social Class in India, 1920–1970', *Economic and Political Weekly*, 14 (4), 7 April 1980. Today the term backward classes loosely refers to lower 'shudras', about half the castes located below the upper 'shudras'—for example, Jats—and the

Both the British government and the Government of India's Backward Classes Commission designated as 'backward classes' those castes whose ritual rank and occupational status were above the untouchables, but otherwise in the lower reaches of the caste order of traditional society. The fact that in 1977 both 'backward classes' and bullock capitalists had caused and benefited from the electoral victory of the Janata coalition bears witness to their substantial overlap. The chief ministers of Janata-governed northern states were themselves from, or spoke for, the Yadava (Ahir), Kurmi, Koeri, and other prominent backward classes who have traditionally worked the land, but now aspire to higher social status and improved occupational opportunities.[26] The demand by 'backward classes' for reservation of posts in government service and seats in educational institutions is partly an expression of the upwardly mobile lower-caste cultivators' efforts to challenge the hold traditionally literate upper castes have on clerical positions. They hope to place family members in white-collar service jobs and thus improve the family's social standing, income, and security. In Bihar, UP, and Karnataka, and later at the Centre, the demands of 'backward classes' became a divisive political issue as it generated a backlash among upper-caste Hindus and untouchables. Just prior to the 1980 election, abortive efforts were made by the Charan Singh caretaker government to have the central government follow Bihar and UP in reserving jobs in government service for 'backward class' members.[27]

The interests and ideology of the political class formed by bullock capitalists and backward castes strengthen centrism in Indian politics. This composite class encompasses more voters than any other agrarian class taken by itself (34 per cent of households), and any other status group taken by itself (about 25 per cent of the total population). Though imperfectly

---

traditionally literate upper 'twice-born' castes—for example, brahmins, kshatriyas, vaishyas, and the para-twice born such as kayasthas and khatris—but above the untouchables.

[26]Ram Naresh Yadav and Karpoori Thakur, the chief ministers of UP and Bihar, were from backward classes. Studies that deal with specific 'backward classes' include Bhatt, Chandrasekhar, 'The Reform Movement among the Waddors of Karnataka', in *Social Movements in India*, vol. 1, M.S.A. Rao (ed.), New Delhi: Manohar, 1978; Mark Franda, *Small is Politics*, New Delhi: Wiley Eastern, 1979, which deals with 'backward classes' in Bihar; M.S.A. Rao, 'Political Elite and Caste Association', *Economic and Political Weekly*, 3, 18 May 1968, an account of the Yadavas; and K.K. Verma, *Changing Role of Caste Associations*, New Delhi: National Publishing House, 1979, a study of the Kurmis.

[27]These efforts reflected the commitment in the Janata manifesto of 1977 and the Lok Dal manifesto of 1979, which provided that 'at least 25 per cent of Groups A and B ... jobs in the Central Government services will ... be reserved for young men and women coming from ... [the socially and educationally backward classes ... both Hindu and Muslim] as recommended by the Backward Classes Commission appointed in the fifties by the Union Government itself, under Article 340 of the Constitution'. *Lok Dal Election Manifesto*, 1979, New Delhi: Shyamal Basu, Publicity Secretary, 1979, p. 29.

mobilized and far from homogeneous in political outlook and behaviour, on both counts this group compares favourably with other agrarian classes and status groups. As self-employed agrarian producers, their relations with capitalist farmers and agricultural labourers are less antagonistic than the wide appeal of its agrarian ideology and policies would suggest.

The prospects for bullock capitalist leadership depend on the recognition in their alliance strategy and policy agenda of the mixed class character of India's rural economy. If the parties under bullock capitalist influence make alliances with lower ranking classes and status groups and credibly pursue policies that promote redistribution, growth, and the collective good of the agrarian sector, bullock capitalists will improve their chances to play a leadership role. Alternative strategies such as forming alliances upward with large landowners or pursuing only its own class interests are viable, but foreclose the possibility of hegemony. In the world of day-to-day political struggles, where personal ambition, group self-interest, and short-term calculations often govern the course of events, all three strategies are evident at different times and in different contexts.

THE IMPERATIVES OF NATIONAL POWER

The goal of capturing power in Delhi or wielding political influence there also strengthens centrism. Power in Delhi requires a party majority or opposition standing in parliament. As a result, the powerful tendency towards party fragmentation is met by a countervailing tendency towards party consolidation. Factions and personalities motivated by short-run calculations designed to exploit the main chance deflect from and split parties, even while India's political elites seek homes in national parties in order to exercise power and influence at the national level. Governing in Delhi means access to the advantages of incumbency. India's federal system gives the Centre initial or residual control over most of the resources and rules that affect state governments, and leaves a substantial portion under the Centre's direct authority. The governing party gains bargaining advantages with its own and rival state-level party units seeking to influence policy choice and implementation. Even though a national party may lose an election, belonging to it may be a more attractive possibility than going into the political wilderness at the head of a minor party.

THE CONSTRAINTS OF PLURALISM

India's cultural diversity and social pluralism provide another reason for parties seeking national power to adopt centrist ideologies and policies. Issues and symbols highly salient to one or a few states are irrelevant to others.

For example, Madhya Pradesh, one of India's more backward states because of its marginal agricultural economy, predominantly rural society, large and backward tribal population, and residual princely state loyalties, is very different from its neighbour Maharashtra, whose productive, market-oriented agricultural economy, numerous industrial complexes, large urban centres, and advanced and well-organized ex-untouchable castes make it one of India's most advanced states. National parties must adopt ideologies and advocate policies that articulate and represent the formidable range of economic, cultural, and social differences that exist among and within India's twenty-two states and eight union territories [as of 1979]. The result has bedevilled efforts by scholars to establish significant correlations between socioeconomic variables and party voting.[28] For example, in 1977 the Janata Party may have got a substantial portion of its support from poor and uneducated labourers in Bihar, in Delhi from upper income and educated commercial and professional classes, and in Rajasthan from middle-income traders and cultivators. Associations between socioeconomic status and party preferences have been found at the district and, to an extent, at the state level, but they wash out at the national (all-India) level. In consequence, electoral pluralities and parliamentary majorities depend on articulating policies that reconcile contradictions among conflicting interests, yet avoid consensual formulas that by speaking to everybody, speak to nobody.

THE ELECTORAL SYSTEM AND CENTRISM

Finally, the formal rule governing electoral competition among parties has favoured centrism. Regardless of the number of candidates and the division of the vote among them, the candidate first past the post (plurality) wins the seat. Given the absence of national classes, communities, and interest groups, and the presence of cultural diversity and social fragmentation, it is not surprising that no party has won a majority of the vote in seven parliamentary elections over a thirty-year period. What may be surprising is that (with the exception of the November 1969–February 1971 and the July–December 1980 periods) parties with comfortable parliamentary majorities have governed the country since the first election in 1952. Without a majority party, India has regularly produced majority governments.

The first past the post rule rewards the party with the highest plurality by inflating its seat over its vote percentage by 20 to 25 per cent. Conversely, the rule penalizes competing national centrist parties by deflating their seat

---

[28]Biplab Das Gupta and W.H. Morris-Jones, *Patterns and Trends in Indian Politics: Art Ecological Analysis of Aggregate Data on Society and Elections*, New Delhi: Allied Books, 1976.

as against their vote percentages. Given the high proportion (46 per cent in 1980) of plurality victories and the predominance of multi-cornered contests (518 of 525),[29] two phenomena that reflect the attempts by some candidates to represent narrow confessional, caste, tribe, and other diversities, the first past the post rule has given the advantage to parties appealing to a wide spectrum of classes, communities, regions, and interests.

The Centre may not hold. There is a limit to how many parties can aspire to be national and centrist. Multi-cornered contests involving several centrist parties open the way to levels of vote fragmentation that can advantage parties with more focussed appeals to class, community, or special interests. If three centrist parties (or electoral coalitions), having failed to agree on seat adjustments, face each other in 300 to 400 of the parliament's 542 constituencies, their average vote per candidate could decline sufficiently for the first past the post rule to reward candidates of narrow rather than broad-gauged parties.

A centrist multiparty system may self-destruct by failing to produce a parliamentary majority. That possibility was implicit in the 1980 election. One hundred seats won by Congress-I pluralities would have gone to Janata or Lok Dal if they had made seat adjustments. For the first time, an Indian national election would have failed to produce a parliamentary majority. But Mrs Gandhi's Congress-I won 353 rather than 253 seats, a two-thirds majority with less than 43 per cent of the vote. For the seventh time a minority vote produced a majority government. (Janata and the Lok Dal alliance, with 33 per cent of the vote, won 15 per cent of the seats.) The first past the post (plurality wins) rule once again supported centrism.

Despite the de facto regime changes of the 1975–7 period, when the Indian state changed from democratic to authoritarian and back again, the long-run character of political ideology, electoral politics, and public policy has remained centrist. More recently, since 1977, the transformation of the party system by alternation of party control of the national government has led to a perceptible decline in the level of procedural consensus. The result has been an increased conflict over state issues such as the nature of the federal system, and the independence (or 'commitment') with which judges and higher civil servants interpret the law and carry on the administration.

[29]Both figures are for 1980. See Mirchandani, *People's Verdict*, p. 127, for plurality victories in 1980, and p. 103 for the number of multi-cornered contests, 1980 and 1977. In 1977, 438 of 540 contests were multi-cornered, but 473 of 540 contests were won by a majority, a result reflecting the Janata's sweep in the northern states. For the 1977 majority/plurality win figures, see Election Commission, *Report on The Sixth General Election to the House of the People ... 1977*, vol. II (Statistical), p. 16.

Significant as the changes since 1975 have been, they are not likely to change the centrist character of Indian politics in the foreseeable future. In the absence of state fragmentation, revolution, or international cataclysm, which we consider unlikely, the social and institutional determinants of centrism are likely to prove more powerful and durable than those supporting class or confessional politics at the Centre. Even if India returns to a one-party dominant system or comes under a dynastic one-party rule, the determinants of centrism will shape party strategy and policy.

8

Judicial Review *versus* Parliamentary Sovereignty
The Struggle over Stateness in India*

LLOYD I. RUDOLPH AND SUSANNE HOEBER RUDOLPH

The consensual framework for the Indian state created by its Constituent Assembly did not settle or foreclose future state issues. The struggle between parliamentary sovereignty and judicial review, a struggle at once institutional and substantive, became acute in the 1970s, and promises to remain at the forefront of debate in the 1980s as well. The state created by the 1950 constitution was more liberal than viceregal. With Jawaharlal Nehru's support and blessing, it manifested more low than high 'stateness', to invoke Peter Nettl's suggestive noun.[1] The introduction of universal suffrage and parliamentary democracy was designed to make party governments accountable to the people through open and free electoral competition, legislative deliberation, and public discussion. Judicial review of a written constitution guaranteed that fundamental law, a federal system, and the liberties of citizens would be essential features of the liberal state.

At the same time, Nehru and like-minded colleagues believed that a viceregal-like strong Centre was a necessary condition for the realization of their substantive goals: national power based on a modern and independent

---

*Originally published as 'Judicial Review *versus* Parliamentary Sovereignty: The Struggle over Stateness in India', in *Journal of Commonwealth and Comparative Politics*, XIX (3), November 1981, pp. 231–56.

[1]Nettl's concept of 'stateness' refers to the saliency of the state. It implies a strongly developed concept of the state and powerful state structures, and a concentration of power in the hands of a central authority at the national level. In a society with a high level of 'stateness', state structures possess the strength to be their own 'engines of authority legitimation' and conflict management, rather than relying on political parties to play that role. J.P. Nettl, 'The State as a Conceptual Variable', *World Politics*, 20, 1968, pp. 559–92.

economy, and socialist transformation of India's society and economy. The sufficient condition for the realization of their goals, strong party government in a parliamentary and federal system, became a reality when the Congress party gained and held through three general elections a dominant position among its competitors.

Even so, during India's first decade as an independent state, successive Congress governments bent on carrying out social and economic reforms, particularly land reforms, confronted successive Supreme Courts bent on upholding fundamental rights, particularly property rights. The court's reliance on legal solipsism and formal and technical interpretations of the constitution inhibited the efforts of Congress governments to effect social and economic change. The confrontations became more conflictual after Nehru's death in 1964, and the Congress' near loss of the fourth general election in 1967. They intensified further in the 1970s when the Congress, under Mrs Gandhi's leadership, won impressive legislative majorities in the 1971 parliamentary and 1972 state assembly elections.[2] The failure of diverse and divided opposition parties to provide an effective check on an increasingly autonomous and powerful executive had opened the way for the Supreme Court to play an opposition-like role in India's parliamentary system. The conflict reached its height during the emergency, when the abolition of a Supreme Court capable of judicial review was under serious consideration. As India entered the 1980s, the state issue of parliamentary democracy versus judicial review, although no longer a likely occasion for state transformation or breakdown, remained a principal line of political cleavage.

The country is divided and uncertain about the question of parliamentary sovereignty versus judicial review. It has not yet assimilated the implications for the claims of parliamentary sovereignty of authoritarian rule and political repression under the emergency. Nor has it grasped the implications for judicial review of the flawed Janata attempt to restore a liberal state, liberty, and the rule of law. So long as the Indian state remains committed to both constitutional government and social transformation, the political cleavage over judicial review and parliamentary sovereignty will remain a source of political tension and institutional ambiguity. In the shorter run, dilemmas and threats abound. A court that has learned that its authority, if not its survival, depends on reading the election returns must also find ways and means to protect and maintain judicial review and the constitution's essential

[2]One index of the intensified struggle is the fact that fourteen of thirty-seven amendments (the twenty-fourth to the thirty-seventh) prior to the emergency (25 June 1975) occurred in the period beginning after the 1971 parliamentary election. Among the fourteen was the twenty-fourth, an attempt to reverse *Golak Nath*, discussed below.

features. Can the court be counted on to do so when for two years under the emergency it countenanced political repression, including depriving citizens of liberty without known cause or legal resources? Can the law of the land, as interpreted by the court, accommodate the legislative actions of a party government bent on economic and social transformation? Can the court maintain a government of laws when law has become a conventional weapon in the partisan political struggle?

The pendulum of doctrinal and institutional controversy over constitutionally defined state issues swung wider in the eleven years between 1967 and 1977 than it had in the first twenty years of independence. Several dimensions of constitutional interpretation were at issue: the amending power, property rights, particularly the acquisition of property, and citizens' liberties.[3] The pendulum swung to its furthest points in 1967 and 1976. At one extreme, the court in *Golak Nath*[4] restricted the parliament's amending power. It barred the parliament from using its constituent authority to amend the fundamental rights protecting the liberties of citizens. At the other extreme, the parliament barred the Supreme Court's power to review. Under a provision of the omnibus forty-second amendment passed during the emergency (1976), it laid down that there was 'no limitation whatever on the constituent power of parliament to amend' the constitution.[5] For good measure it added another provision, that no law declared by the parliament to be giving effect to the directive principles of state policy[6] could be called into question by the court as abridging fundamental rights.

Between these extremes, court decisions and parliamentary amendments kept the pendulum swinging, but within narrower limits. The most notable of the decisions was that of *Kesavananda Bharati* (1973).[7] It reversed *Golak*

[3] Articles 368, 31, 31a, 31b, and 19, 20, 21, and 22.

[4] *Golak Nath vs State of Punjab*, AIR, 1967, SC 1643. It reversed *Shankari Prasad vs Union of India*, AIR, 1951, SC 458, which held that no part of the constitution was unamendable, and *Sajjan Singh vs State of Rajasthan*, AIR, 1964, SC 845.

[5] For a discussion of the forty-second amendment and other constitutional developments under the emergency, see Michael Henderson, 'Setting India's Democratic House in Order; Constitutional Amendments', *Asian Survey*, 19, 1979.

[6] Part IV, Articles 36–51.

[7] *Keshavananda Bharati vs State of Kerala*, 4 SCC, 1973, 225; AIR, 1973, SC 1461. The eleven opinions of the case run to over 700 pages. They have been abridged in M.C.J. Kagzi, *The Kesavananda's Case*, Delhi, 1973. Surendra Malik (ed.), *The Fundamental Rights Case: The Critics Speak!*, Lucknow: Eastern Book Co., 1975, provides a summary of the arguments (pp. 1–52); six articles interpreting the decision and its eleven opinions by N.S. Bintha, N.A. Palkhivala, K. Subba Rao, P.K. Tripathi, Upendra Baxi, and Joseph Minattur (pp. 53–158); and an 'Analytical Summary of the Case' in seven parts prepared by Surendra Malik (pp. 225–304Y), who also supplies an 'editorial' introduction. The book is self-confessedly misnamed: 'Though the case primarily involved the validity of Constitution Amendments and should

Nath's bar to parliamentary amendments affecting fundamental rights, but protected judicial review by limiting parliament's amending power to matters that do not destroy the constitution's 'basic structure' or 'essential features'. After Janata's 1977 electoral victory, doctrinal controversy and institutional rivalry abated somewhat as a result of a legislative stalemate, and the caution of a chastened court. However, the pendulum continued to swing between extremes wide enough to ensure that the state issue of parliamentary sovereignty versus judicial review will continue to divide parties, the court, and the country in the 1980s.

THE CHANGING MEANING OF PARLIAMENTARY SOVEREIGNTY

In Nehru's time, parliamentary sovereignty took on a meaning that distinguished it from the meaning it had had among India's founding political generation. The Westminster model that furnished their understanding tempered the unlimited power of parliament and the absence of judicial review with a keen sense for the conventional restraints of the unwritten constitution, and of court interpretations of the common law. For Nehru and his like-minded colleagues, parliamentary sovereignty opened the way to legislate social transformation and a planned economy. The primacy of parliamentary will over a judiciary bent on protecting citizens' rights, particularly property rights, was a necessary condition for realizing a socialist society. Nehru's strongest statement on parliamentary sovereignty came during the course of the Constituent Assembly's debate on compensation for property, particularly landed property. 'No Supreme Court and no judiciary,' he said, 'can stand in judgment over the sovereign will of Parliament representing the will of the entire community ... ultimately the whole Constitution is a creature of Parliament.'[8] At the same time, however, he remained silent during the debate that took place a few weeks later (17 September 1949) on the amending article. Known to favour amendment by a simple majority, he did not offer a motion to that effect. Instead, he acquiesced to a statement by B.R. Ambedkar, chairman of the assembly's Drafting Committee and Law Minister, which stated that 'The Constitution

have been so popularly named, the name "Fundamental Rights Case" was popularized by the daily newspapers apparently because *Keshavananda Bharati* was a sequel to *Golak Nath* which had held the Fundamental Rights unamendable.', (p. 5). Upendra Baxi observes that 'although ... [*Keshavananda Bharati*] is in the ultimate analysis a judicial decision, it is not just a reported case on some Articles of the Indian Constitution. Indeed, I believe that it is, in some sense, the Indian Constitution of the future' (p. 130).

[8]Constituent Assembly Debates: Official Report, IX, 1195, cited in Michael Brecher, *Nehru: A Political Biography*, London and New York: Oxford University Press, 1959.

is a fundamental document', and that 'utter chaos' would follow if it could be amended by a simple majority.[9]

A careful student of the Constituent Assembly concluded that, despite the diversity and relative ease with which the constitution it created could be amended, 'it must not be assumed ... the Assembly favored parliamentary sovereignty. The members believed that the [Constituent] Assembly had superior status and that its product should be the supreme law of the land.'[10] The Constituent Assembly also rejected an effort by Sir Benegal Rau, its Constitutional Adviser and a Nehru intimate, to give the directive principles of state policy precedence over fundamental rights in case of conflict.[11] Nehru and the Congress left were deeply concerned that the judiciary would create obstacles to the realization of socialist objectives, while hard state advocates led by Patel were concerned that the courts would jeopardize the state's capacity to maintain law and order.[12] Nevertheless, Nehru himself was sufficiently committed to a liberal state to accept a constitution whose Supreme Court could interpret fundamental law and protect fundamental rights and the federal system.[13]

[9]Constituent Assembly Debates: Official Report, IX, 1662–3, cited in Austin, Granville, *The Indian Constitution*, New Delhi and New York: Oxford University Press, 1966, p. 263.

[10]Ibid., p. 264.

[11]See articles by Kuldip Nayar and Nani A. Palkhivala in *The Indian Express*, 14 May 1980, and 16 May 1980. A.K. Ayyar and K.M. Munshi were the strongest advocates in the Constituent Assembly's rights subcommittee of limitations on fundamental rights. They were supported by a galaxy of members of the assembly's senior advisory committee, including K.M. Panikkar, G.B. Pant, C. Rajagopalachari, and Sardar Patel. The rank and file of the assembly resisted and blocked the substantial limitations favoured by the leadership. Rao's proposal, that directive principles should override fundamental rights, was supported by K.T. Shah, K.M. Munshi, and Dr Ambedkar. See Austin, pp. 68–78, for the debate on fundamental rights and pp. 77–8 for the discussion of directive principles.

[12]According to Granville Austin,

The desire to restrict the purview of the courts in certain matters was not restricted to 'liberals' like Ayyar and Rau. Patel led the way in giving the Executive authority, largely unsupervised by the courts, to impose preventive detention. He had also opposed the inclusion in the Constitution of rights to secrecy of correspondence and to inviolability of an individual's person and home.

In the Advisory Committee's discussion of 'due process' limitations on the abolition of zamindari (agrarian intermediaries), Patel's strong state views converged with Nehru's on the state as an agent of social transformation: '"There is a danger," Patel said, "that a certain old type of judges may misinterpret this new process of law."' Austin, p. 175.

[13]The fears of the socialists were realized when early state acts abolishing intermediaries ('feudal' landlords) were subject to long delays from frequent appeals to the courts. Nehru forced through the first constitutional amendment in 1951, which removed such acts from court review by placing them in a ninth Schedule of the constitution under newly inserted clauses, 31A and 31 B of Article 31 dealing with the acquisition of property by the state, and with the amount of compensation. Further amendments to Article 31 followed in 1955 (fourth

In his time and in the early years of his daughter's prime ministership, the struggle between parliamentary sovereignty and judicial review was carried on in terms of the legislative authority required for progressive social policies, particularly land reform, versus the court's efforts to protect the principle of meaningful compensation against attempts to render it nominal. As Mrs Gandhi's support ebbed, as she was threatened by Jayaprakash Narayan's movement to remove her from office, and as the executive democracy of 1971–4 gave way to emergency rule in 1975, the struggle took on a new cast reminiscent of Patel's efforts to create a strong state. Parliamentary sovereignty eventually became a means of protecting those in power from accountability and competition, and a doctrine to legitimize authoritarian rule and repressive government. In the end it was used to strengthen the executive's power of preventive detention—under the Maintenance of Internal Security Act (MISA)—and then, under the emergency, to remove all restraints on the state's authority to deprive citizens of their fundamental rights.

The question for the courts and the prime minister became, who spoke for the people? Judges of state high courts and of the Supreme Court claimed to speak from the authority of the written constitution, which expressed the people's will as well as the fundamental law of the land. Ruling Congress governments claimed to speak with the authority of constitutional majorities in parliament, based on electoral mandates that expressed the people's will. N.A. Palkivala, one of India's leading constitutional lawyers and an opponent of the emergency, while recognizing that the parliament's claim to possess unlimited powers of amendment rests on its representation of the people's will,[14] argued that judicial review of parliamentary acts had a higher claim because the constitution is a superior expression of the will of the people: 'Where the will of Parliament, declared in an amendment, stands in opposition to that of the people, declared in the Constitution, the will of the people must prevail.'[15] It may be argued, and was argued in 1975, that the latter view of the will of the people includes the prior existence in a 'state of nature', or in human nature, of individual rights not contracted away in the formation of civil society and/or the state.[16] However,

---

amendment), 1964 (seventh amendment), 1971 (twenty-sixth amendment). On four more occasions after the first amendment and prior to the emergency (June 1975), additional state acts were placed in the ninth schedule as a result of the fourth, seventeenth, twenty-ninth (1972), and thirty-fourth (1974) amendments. Wholesale use of the ninth schedule was resorted to under the emergency. These uses by parliament of its amending power provided a less direct but effective procedure for limiting judicial review.

[14]N.A. Palkhivala, *Our Constitution Profaned and Defiled*, Delhi: Macmillan, 1974, p. 135.

[15]Ibid., p. 137.

[16]The Gandhi government's brief in the *habeas corpus* case of 1976 argued that under an emergency, there were no constitutional, statutory, common law, or natural law restraints on

advocates of both parliamentary sovereignty and judicial review repaired ultimately to democratic rather than statist or natural law grounds to legitimize their positions.

JUDICIAL REVIEW: PROTECTION OF PROPERTY OR PROTECTION OF LIBERTIES?

'Progressive' opinion in India often accused the court of using judicial review to protect the interests of propertied classes from the Congress government policies that threatened them. The most effective advocate of this view from 1966, when he left the Communist Party to join Madras Congress Chief Minister Kamaraj Nadar as advocate-general, until his death in an air crash in May 1973, was Mohan Kumaramangalam. He was an old friend of Indira Gandhi's from their student days in London, leader of the Congress Forum for Socialist Action, the progressive faction of the Congress parliamentary party that played a key role in shaping Mrs Gandhi's strategy and policies between 1969 and 1973, and minister for mines and steel in her 1971 government.[17] His Marxist legal theory shaped the Gandhi government's counter-attack against the Supreme Court after it gained a two-thirds parliamentary majority in 1971. Kumaramangalam conceived the twenty-fourth, twenty-fifth, and twenty-sixth amendments, which struck back at *Golak Nath* and other decisions, as 'a single whole' that would, by establishing the parliament's supremacy, enable it to enact progressive measures endorsed by the people. It was Kumaramangalam who formulated the doctrine of a 'committed judiciary', the legal counterpart of the doctrine of a committed bureaucracy.[18] Together, these efforts anticipated the forty-second Amendment Act enacted under the emergency. The progressive view of the law and the

---

the state in depriving citizens of liberty, or even life. See Kuldip Nayar, *The Judgment: Inside Story of the Emergency in India*, New Delhi: Vikas Publishing House, 1977, p. 123, for Attorney-General Niren De's brief on behalf of the government. A more detailed account of doctrines at issue in the *habeas corpus* cases is given in David Selbourne, *An Eye to India: The Unmasking of Tyranny*, Harmondsworth and Leadon: Pelican Books, 1977, pp. 145–50.

[17] For an excellent discussion of the political significance of Kumaramangalam, see Francine Frankel, *India's Political Economy, 1947–1977*, New Delhi: Oxford University Press, 1978, Chs 10 and 11.

[18] For Kumaramangalam's legal theory, see his *Constitutional Amendments: The Reason Why*, New Delhi: All India Congress Committee, 1971. In it, he argued that the twenty-fourth, twenty-fifth, and twenty-sixth amendments (reasserting the amending power of parliament, asserting the primacy of directive principles over fundamental rights, and abolishing the privy purses of the princes), and the substitution of the word 'amount' for the word 'compensation' in Article 31 C to ease acquisition of property, gave parliament the power to determine where the line is to be drawn between 'the preservation of private property rights on the one hand, and the assertion of the rights of the community on the other' (p. 29).

court's role had, until November 1980, at least one voice on the bench itself, Justice V.R. Krishna Iyer. 'Even after thirty years of independence,' he argued, 'the Indian judicial system followed the path of the Anglo legacy left behind by the British. The law, framed by the British to suit their class interests, has no relevance to the present Indian social conditions.'[19] The court had also at least one justice whose admiration for Mrs Gandhi transcended the decent respect due to a prime minister:

Dear Indiraji,
    May I offer you my heartiest congratulation on your resounding victory in the elections and your triumphant return as the Prime Minister of India. It is a most remarkable achievement. ... Your party has been voted to power with an amazing outburst amounting almost to an avalanche, of affection and enthusiasm. ... You have become the symbol of the hopes and aspirations of the poor, hungry millions of India who ... are now looking up to you for lifting them from dirt and squalor and freeing them from poverty and ignorance. ... I am sure that with your iron will and firm determination, uncanny insight and dynamic vision, great administrative capacity and vast experience, overwhelming love and affection of the people and above all, a heart which is identified with the misery of the poor and the weak, you will be able to steer the ship of the nation safely to its cherished goal. ...[20]

According to the progressive view, the struggle between parliament and court for supremacy in interpreting the constitution pitted proponents of the oppressed many without property against the privileged few with property. The court's rejection in February and December 1970, just before Mrs Gandhi's upset victory in March 1971, of her minority government measures nationalising the fourteen largest commercial banks and depriving the princes of their privileges and privy purses were only the newest examples of its efforts to maintain the viability of property rights. The court found it difficult to devise means to distinguish the civil and political from the property rights of

[19]*The Statesman*, 7 April 1980.
[20]*The Indian Express*, 23 March 1980, gives the full text. Public fears about the independence of the Supreme Court were exacerbated when this letter, dated 15 January 1980, from Justice B.N. Bhagwati to Mrs Gandhi congratulating her on her recent electoral success, was leaked to the press. The letter was thought by many members of the Supreme Court bar association to raise problems not merely of taste, but also of constitutional propriety. At a special meeting convened to consider the matter, however, a majority declined to adopt formal measures indicating that body's disapproval (interview with a senior member of the Supreme Court bar, 2 April 1980). Justice V.D. Tulzapurkar, speaking at the Indian Law Institute on 22 March 1980, remarked that 'the recent news item ... has caused great anguish and pain to me and many of my colleagues ...'. Hovering round the seats of power, he said, was 'dangerous to the independence of the judiciary', and damaging to its image. He continued that the need for vigilance was particularly acute at that time, as there were seven vacancies to be filled on the Supreme Court (*The Statesman*, 23 March 1980).

citizens.[21] Yet, even in the era from *Golak Nath* (1967) to the amendments of 1971 and 1972, the congruence between the interests of the propertied classes and the proponents of judicial review on the one hand, and the interests of the poor and Parliamentary sovereignty on the other, was far from complete. The congruence began to lose what meaning it had when the consequences that an unrestrained parliament and a committed judiciary had for constitutional government and the rule of law became more apparent. Congress socialists, such as Chandra Shekhar and Mohan Dharia, who had supported the progressive view of law, recognized that 'progressive' was becoming a code word for Mrs Gandhi's partisan interest. It became increasingly clear that liberty was a collective good. With the death of Mohan Kumaramangalam in 1973, his left doctrine increasingly gave way to Sanjay Gandhi's free enterprise and anti-left convictions.[22]

In May 1973, Jayaprakash Narayan, whose socialist credentials included Marxist, democratic, and Gandhian variants, wrote a personal letter to Mrs Gandhi, pointing out the need to provide constitutional safeguards to prevent parliament from 'abrogating the fundamental freedoms of the citizens', and to ensure the independence of the judiciary. Without these limitations, the proclaimed aim of national leaders to establish socialism by peaceful means would be defeated, and 'the very foundations of our democracy will be in danger of being destroyed'.[23]

As the emergency era (1975–7) and its Janata aftermath (1977–9) demonstrated, the struggle was as much over the continued existence of the 1950 constitution, the meaning of constitutional government, and the standing and enforcement of citizens' rights against the state, as about the capacity of the state to enact socialist measures. Although the struggle between parliamentary sovereignty and judicial review is often animated by conflicts among classes and interests, it cannot be reduced to them, and for that reason is not merely 'superstructural'. The 1977 election demonstrated

[21]For a detailed discussion and critique of the Supreme Court's positions on land reform, see George H. Gadbois, Jr, 'The United States and Indian Supreme Courts as Political and Policy-Making Institutions', paper delivered at the Conference of the Research Committee on Comparative Judicial Studies of the International Political Science Association, Oxford: Mansfield College, 6–8 April 1981. See also Mohammed Ghouse, 'The Right to Property and Planned Development in India', in *Indian Constitution: Trends and Issues*, Rajeev Dhavan and Alice Jacob (eds), Bombay: N.M. Tripathi, 1978.

[22]See Uma Vasudeva's interview with Sanjay Gandhi of 6 August, as published as appendix to her *Two Faces of Indira Gandhi*, New Delhi: Vikas Publishing House, 1977, especially pp. 201–7. For a tactical retreat on his anti-Russian and anti-communist views in that interview, see interview in *Surya*, July 1979, p. 32.

[23]Narayan's letter of 16 May 1973 is reproduced in Kuldip Nayar (ed.), *The Supersession of Judges*, New Delhi: India Book Company/Hind Pocket Books, 1973, pp. 69–72.

that the poor, like other citizens, appreciated the connection between a government of laws, and their welfare and material interests. Left as well as right activists valued the liberty both had lost under the emergency.

ARENA OF STRUGGLE: THE POWER TO AMEND AND THE POWER TO DESTROY

The actual struggle between the Supreme Court speaking for a liberal state and the executive speaking for a more authoritative, if not authoritarian, one had begun soon after the commencement of the constitution in 1950. This struggle is manifest in the fact that an extraordinarily high proportion (about two-thirds) of cases heard before the Supreme Court involved government, and that the government, to a remarkable extent (40 per cent) lost these cases.[24] One of the principal substantive grounds on which the battle was fought was the meaning of and limitations on the right to property.[25] The principal formal arena was the amending power of parliament. Congress, as a nationalist movement and as a governing party in the provinces (1937–9), had given very high priority to agrarian reform. Immediately after independence, when state legislation abolishing 'feudal' intermediaries (zamindars and jagirdars) was passed, it was blocked in the courts by cases brought under Articles 14, 19, and 31,[26] protecting fundamental rights. The parliament responded in 1951 by passing the first amendment. It protected legislation acquiring the 'estates' of intermediaries against the application of these articles, and for good measure, added a new (ninth) schedule to the constitution that immunized any state or union legislation placed in it by parliament from judicial review.[27] However, the struggle continued in a

[24]See George H. Gadbois, Jr, 'Indian Judicial Behavior', *Economic and Political Weekly*, 5 (3, 4, & 5), 1970,, p. 153. Gadbois' universe is made up of cases reported in the Supreme Court Reports between 1950 and 1967.

[25]Article 19 (f) and Article 31.

[26]Article 31 governs state acquisition of property, providing that it be acquired by law and for public purposes. After three amendments, the first, fourth, and seventeenth, failed to preclude a judicial review that enforced the payment of adequate compensation (market value), the twenty-fifth amendment (1971) substituted the word amount for compensation. Even so, the majority in *Keshavananda Bharati vs State of Kerala* (1973) held that the amount fixed by the legislature cannot be arbitrary or illusory. Articles 14 and 19 guarantee equal protection of the laws and fundamental rights.

[27]The amendment added Article 31 A, which holds that no law providing for the acquisition by the state of any 'estate' shall be deemed void on the ground that it is inconsistent with the rights conferred by Articles 14, 19, or 31; it also added 31 B, which established the ninth schedule, 10, note 23 (addition). See G.G. Mirchandani, *Subverting the Constitution*, New Delhi: Abhinav Publications, 1977, Ch. 7, 'The Ninth Schedule', for an analysis of the history of its use and abuse. Of the 188 laws protected from judicial review by the ninth schedule, 102 were

series of cases about the meaning of compensation. The courts held that it meant, in effect, market value. The government responded with new constitutional amendments, notably the fourth and the twenty-fifth,[28] which attempted to protect from judicial review the amount it paid for compulsorily acquired property.

The issue of the scope of parliament's authority to amend the constitution and its relationship to judicial review and fundamental rights was most seriously joined in the momentous *Golak Nath* case decided in 1967. It held that the fundamental rights provided for in Part III of the constitution could be amended only by a new constituent assembly, not by the parliament. The parliament responded with the twenty-fourth amendment, which overrode *Golak Nath* by making fundamental rights amendable by parliament. In 1973, the battle was rejoined in the equally momentous *Keshavananda Bharati* case. It may prove to be India's *Marbury vs Madison* by establishing an acceptable ground for judicial review. *Keshavananda* legitimized constrained versions of both principles, parliamentary sovereignty in the service of state purposes and interests, and judicial review in the service of fundamental law and a government of laws. *Keshavananda* provided a framework for accommodating a hard and/or socialist state with a liberal one. The court embarked on a path that continued to characterize its strategy in the late 1970s and early 1980s, firmly protecting its own jurisdiction and prerogatives while yielding to the executive and parliament on substantive issues. It conceded that legislation and amendments giving effect to state purposes and interests may take precedence over fundamental rights and a government of laws, provided that the court has an opportunity to review their bona fides and compatibility with the constitution's essential features.

While upholding the twenty-fourth amendment and thus reversing *Golak Nath*, *Keshavananda* nevertheless limited the parliament's amending authority. According to *Keshavananda*, parliament's authority to amend is not the authority to either destroy the 1950 constitution, or make a new one. The amending authority[29] is limited by the constitution's 'basic structure' or

---

placed there by the thirty-ninth and fortieth amendments passed under the emergency. See ibid., pp. 162–73 for the titles of all acts placed in the ninth schedule, including the Prevention of Publication of Objectionable Matter Act, which made possible the censorship of parliamentary debates.

[28]The fourth amendment added Article 31(2), making the adequacy of compensation nonjusticiable. When the courts responded in *Cooper vs Union of India*, AIR, 1970, SC 564, that the very word compensation implied full monetary value, that is, market value, the twenty-fifth amendment substituted the word 'amount' for the word 'compensation' in Article 31(C), and provided that laws implementing certain Directive Principles of State Policy (Part IV) calling for a redistribution of resources could not be voided for inconsistency with Articles 14, 19, or 31.

[29]Article 368.

'essential features', which include judicial review, the sovereignty and territorial integrity of India, the federal system, free and fair elections, and other disputed or as yet unspecified features. Amendments attacking the constitution's essential features or basic structure would be held unconstitutional. Nor can judicial review be eliminated or compromised, as it was in the twenty-fifth and twenty-sixth amendments, by parliamentary professions that particular laws give effect to the directive principles of state policy generally (twenty-fifth amendment), or to those particular ones (twenty-sixth amendment) providing for state ownership, control, or redistribution of 'the material resources of the community' (Article 39[b] and [c]). On the other hand, *Keshavananda* recognized what the court reaffirmed seven years later in *Minerva Mills*, that in certain specified areas of stipulated state purposes, those that provide for control or redistribution of 'the material resources of the community', the directive principles might override fundamental rights (twenty-fifth amendment), *subject to the court's review.*[30] And it in effect upheld the 'Kumaramangalam package' of the twenty-fourth, twenty-fifth, and twenty-sixth amendments, the twenty-fourth (reversing *Golak Nath)* and the twenty-sixth (abolishing the privy purses of princes) wholly, and the twenty-fifth insofar as it could short of yielding up judicial review.

While the court was willing to accommodate state purposes, it continued to resist property being made nominal by reopening the question of meaningful compensation for property compulsorily acquired by the state. The twenty-fifth amendment's substitution of the word 'amount' for 'compensation' did not, according to *Keshavananda*, open the way for legislatures to fix 'arbitrary or illusory' sums, or lay down irrelevant criteria. Although *Keshavananda* represented a retreat from *Golak Nath* and some accommodation to Congress' post-1971 election amendments, it clearly

---

[30]*Keshavananda* upheld the validity of the twenty-fifth amendment, Article 31 (C), which provided that no act of parliament which includes a declaration that it is designed to give effect to Directive Principles 39 (b) and (c) would be declared void 'on the ground that it is inconsistent with, or takes away or abridges any of the rights conferred by Article 14, 9, or 31'. Under 39 (b), the state is enjoined to direct its policy towards securing that the 'ownership and control of the material resources of the community are so distributed to subserve the common good', and under 39 (c) that 'the operation of the economic system does not result in the concentration of wealth and means of production to the common detriment'. Both tests seem to provide substantial policy space for a 'socialist' parliament. See report on *Minerva Mills* case in *The Times of India*, 10 May 1980. For the view that *Keshavananda* did not preclude a court review of the constitutionality of legislation passed under the provisions laid down by 31 C, see Durga Das Basu, *Introduction to the Constitution of India*, 6th edition, New Delhi: Prentice Hall of India, 1976, p. 103. For an extended discussion of *Keshavananda*, see Rajeev Dhavan, *The Supreme Court of India and Parliamentary Sovereignty: A Critique of Its Approach to the Recent Constitutional Crisis*, New Delhi: Sterling Publishers, 1976.

limited parliament's amending and legislative authority by re-establishing firm grounds for judicial review.

Keshavananda (1973) was the law of the land when the emergency was declared on 26 June 1975. Neither the courts nor the executive seemed able to separate the legislative pursuit of social transformation, particularly compensation for property compulsorily acquired by the state, and restraints on the state through judicial review. Even though Sanjay Gandhi, who once described the CPI leadership as rich and corrupt, and who thought de-control of the economy would produce growth and equity,[31] had replaced Mohan Kumaramangalam as Mrs Gandhi's political adviser, she continued to claim that those who accused her of using the doctrine of parliamentary sovereignty to undermine constitutional government were opposed to her progressive policies. By 1974 her political support in the country and the party had deteriorated markedly in the face of failed policies, party factionalism, and political repression. By June 1975 she was fighting for survival. The electoral defeat of the Congress in Gujarat and her conviction by the Allahabad (UP) High Court for corrupt electoral practices rendered her situation precarious, even desperate. Pending her appeal to the Supreme Court, she was barred from sitting in parliament for six years. In the meantime, the opposition parties, now led by the JP movement, as well as elements within her own party, were clamouring for her resignation. A desperate situation called for desperate measures. On 25 June 1975 a presidential declaration put the country under emergency rule on the grounds that an 'internal disturbance' threatened the security of India. With fundamental rights suspended for the duration, parliamentary leaders from both the opposition and her own party, as well as Jayaprakash Narayan and hundreds of others throughout the country, were arrested and press censorship imposed.

Having successfully imposed a constitutional dictatorship on the country, Mrs Gandhi could still be barred from parliament if her appeal to the Supreme Court failed. Further, as long as *Keshavananda* remained the law of the land, judicial review could be used to protect the constitution's essential features. Mrs Gandhi moved quickly to protect her personal and constitutional position. In August, a depleted and intimidated parliament passed the thirty-eighth and thirty-ninth amendments. The first made the emergency proclamation non-justiciable.[32] The second removed from the jurisdiction

---

[31]See n. 22.

[32]It explicitly excluded the courts from entertaining questions relating to the ground or reasons for the president's 'satisfaction' in issuing an emergency proclamation on the advice of the council of ministers, and allowed the president to make multiple (concurrent) declarations.

of the Supreme Court the authority to review on appeal election petitions involving the prime minister and speaker. It also retroactively amended the Representation of the People Act (1951) to remove the provisions under which Mrs Gandhi had been convicted.

For a time it seemed that Mrs Gandhi's emergency government meant to rely on the Supreme Court itself to enhance the authority of the executive and legislative branches by helping to keep her in office, and establish the clear supremacy of parliament in constitutional matters. In 1937 a similar crisis in America pitted the president's executive leadership and reform legislation against the use of judicial review by the United States Supreme Court to declare New Deal measures unconstitutional. Franklin Roosevelt, after his massive electoral victory in 1936, tried unsuccessfully to 'pack' the court with men sharing his views. The country was spared further struggle by the 'switch in time that saved nine', the re-alignment of the court's majority favourable to New Deal measures. Mrs Gandhi may have expected a similar 'switch' as a result of the highly controversial and much disputed 'supersession of judges' engineered by Mohan Kumaramangalam a month before his death, and one day after *Keshavananda* was handed down on 25 April 1973. In the face of the well-established seniority convention,[33] her government had superseded the three most senior judges to reach A.N. Ray, and appoint him Chief Justice. He had established his qualifications according to Kumaramangalam's doctrine, which stated that judges should be committed to the outlook and philosophy of the government that appoints them by voting Mrs Gandhi's way in three significant decisions.[34] There was hope that as Chief Justice he would provide a lead to the court through his stand on cases, the selection and ordering of business, and appointment of the members of the benches before which particular cases are heard.

[33]See Nayar, *Supersession of Judges*, articles by Nayar, Justices J.M. Shelat, K.S. Hegde, and A.N. Grover, M.C. Chagla, and N.A. Palkhivala.

[34]Kumaramangalam's defence in parliament of the supersession of the three senior Supreme Court judges to appoint A.N. Ray Chief Justice on the retirement of Chief Justice S.M. Sikri, is reproduced in Nayar, *Supersession of Judges*, pp. 78–92. Kumaramangalam argued that it was the government's 'duty ... to come to the conclusion whether a particular person is fit to be appointed the Chief Justice of the Court because of his outlook, because of his philosophies expressed in his ... opinions'. See also his *Judicial Appointments: Analysis of the Recent Controversy Over the Appointment of the Chief Justice of India*, Oxford and New Delhi: Oxford University Press, 1973. George Gadbois, after an extended analysis of judicial attitudes and behaviour, concludes that there was real disagreement between Ray and three superseded judges, Shelat, Hegde, and Grover. 'We cannot effectively measure the magnitude of these apparent attitudinal differences [but] ... we can be somewhat more confident in concluding that Ray's attitudes and values are more consistent than those of the superseded with Mrs Gandhi's conception of what is best for the nation.' *Banaras Law Journal*, special issue on 'Supreme Court of India: Some Aspects of Its Contributions', 1978, pp. 42–4.

Indeed, on 7 November the court gave a preliminary indication that it too was prepared to switch by unanimously reversing Mrs Gandhi's June conviction by the Allahabad High Court of two electoral offences, and quashing its order barring her from elective office for six years. It took its decision by recognizing as valid the August election law amendment that retrospectively removed the offences at issue. But the court was not prepared to be fully committed. At the same sitting it upheld *Keshavananda* when it struck down the clause of the recently enacted thirty-ninth amendment (adding Article 329A), which removed election petitions against the prime minister and speaker from the courts' jurisdiction. The immunity jeopardized free and fair elections which, the majority suggested, was an essential feature of the constitution, and one not susceptible to constitutional amendments.[35] The decision had in common with *Keshavananda* the propensity to save judicial review while yielding substance. At least one leading scholar of the court thought that this decision precipitated the move evident by the end of November to bring in a new constitution, in which, *inter alia*, the judiciary would be subordinate to the executive.[36]

Despite the court's ruling, informed opinion expected Chief Justice Ray to find a way to accommodate the government's request that the Supreme Court review *Keshavananda*. With a proposal already in circulation to scrap the 1950 constitution, it seems reasonable to suppose that the government anticipated a ruling that would repudiate *Keshavananda*'s basic structure justification for judicial review of parliamentary legislation, including constitutional amendments. On 10 November Chief Justice A.N. Ray, on an oral request from the attorney-general, convened a full bench (all thirteen justices) to reconsider *Keshavananda*. Three hundred writ petitions were pending before state high courts, challenging a wide range of acts on the grounds that they violated the basic structure of the constitution. Using an unprecedented procedure, the chief justice asked the court whether the power to amend the constitution was limited by the doctrine of 'basic structure', and whether the bank nationalization case had been correctly decided. But when court proceedings began, none of the state attorneys-generals present were prepared to offer a case to test the meaning or validity of basic structure; other justices questioned Ray's purpose in convening the bench, indicating that a majority was unwilling to reverse *Keshavananda*;

[35]The invalidating was supported by all five judges, Ray, Beg, Khanna, Chandrachud, and Mathew. The basic structure argument was that of the last three, *Keesing's Contemporary Archives*, 16 January 1976, p. 27525. See also Basu, *Introduction to the Constitution*, pp. 325–6, particularly n. 3.

[36]Upendra Baxi, *The Indian Supreme Court and Politics*, Lucknow: Eastern Book Co., 1980, p. 193.

the attorney-general of India, who had orally asked for the review, virtually yielded to objections raised by eminent counsel N.A. Palkhivala; and the chief justice, after the third day of the hearing, suddenly dissolved the bench. The government's attempt to use the court to rid itself of *Keshavananda* ended in inaction, not to mention confusion.[37] It was a reverse for the government, but not an entirely surprising one, given a court interested in survival and reluctant to destroy itself.

While the court was struggling with the legal and constitutional dilemmas posed by the emergency, unofficial documents that contemplated scrapping India's British-style parliamentary system for a French style presidential one began to circulate in government circles in October and November. They soon leaked down to the underground opposition as well. The 1975 proposals would have subordinated the parliament and a cabinet only partially chosen from it to a directly elected president, whose time 'should not be allowed to be frittered away in fruitless debate and discussion'.[38] Particularly vital, given the battles raging over judicial review and parliamentary sovereignty, was the proposal to subordinate the hitherto independent judiciary to a presidentially and ministerially dominated judicial council. The council was to be more oriented towards state than citizen interests, and distinctly corporatist in selection and membership. The document explicitly cited an annexed article of the French constitution, which dealt with France's state-dominated superior council of the judiciary.[39]

[37]Interview with a senior member of the Supreme Court Bar Association, 2 April 1980. *Keshavananda* was a confusing decision because it failed to define basic structure or provide an agreed list of its components. The government wanted not merely a clarification for the sake of some thirty-one writs pending in various courts challenging laws for violating basic structure, but also a reversal of the doctrine because of the limitations of the amending power. But an Andhra Pradesh case, which was selected to test the doctrine and which was heard by a partial ('constitution') bench, was not pursued by the full bench (all thirteen justices) convened by Justice Ray, and was later dismissed by a constitution bench of the court. See Baxi, *Indian Supreme Court*, pp. 70–6; *Keesing's Contemporary Archives*, 16 January 1976, p. 27526; Nayar, *The Judgment*, p. 94, which claims that Chief Justice A.N. Ray 'came to know that the majority of judges were not in favour of reviewing the case' (that is, *Keshavananda*); and Dhavan, *Supreme Court*, pp. 189–90.

[38]'A Fresh Look at Our Constitution; Some Suggestions', mimeo, New Delhi, 1975. See also Nayar, *The Judgment*, p. 115. Nayar attributes authorship to B.K. Nehru and Rajni Patel.

[39]Article 83 of the Constitution of the Fifth Republic, cited as source, does not deal with the judiciary, but with the community of French ex-colonial countries. Article 64, Chapter VIII, 'The Judicial Authority', deals with the Supreme Council of Justice. That article coincides roughly with the description attached to 'A Fresh Look':

Composed of fourteen members, its president is the president of the republic and its vice-president is the justice minister. It also includes twelve persons chosen for six year terms, six from outside the national assembly but elected by two-thirds majorities within it, four elected judges representing each category of the judiciary, and two members of the legal profession appointed by the president from outside the membership of the national assembly and the judiciary.

The document also proposed to undo *Keshavananda Bharati* by withdrawing jurisdiction over fundamental rights from the courts,[40] introducing language that makes the parliament's judgment 'conclusive' in disputes between the government and the courts, and barring the courts from calling into question restrictions on any of the rights provided for in Article 19, which specifies the fundamental—or civil—rights.[41] In consequence of these proposals, 'the Court was faced for the first time in its history ... with a credible threat to its survival as a major institution of the Government', a fact of political life that Upendra Baxi urged its critics to take into account when they found that the court, like 'those who were at the helm of other major institutions of the society ... yielded in substance to the regime's demand in the interests of self-preservation'.[42]

Indeed, if in November the court found ways to avoid jeopardizing its institutional interest, in April it found ways to placate the emergency executive. On 28 April the court upheld the government's authority under the emergency to jail its political opponents without court hearings or subsequent review. The court, with only Justice Khanna dissenting,[43] agreed that under an emergency, not only fundamental rights, but all safeguards protecting individual liberty are also suspended. A five-member constitution bench had been convened in November 1975 to hear the union attorney-general challenge decisions by seven state high courts allowing *habeas corpus* petitions. The bench's subsequent decision in April held that the state high courts were wrong in believing that courts could look into the *bona fides* and accuracy of preventive detention orders, or decide whether they conformed to principles of natural justice or the common law. No person could move the courts for a writ petition challenging the legality of a detention order. Further, the 29 June 1975 ordinance amending MISA, an act reviving preventive detention in 1971, validly removed the requirement that a prisoner be informed of the reason for his detention. According to Chief Justice Ray, the emergency provisions themselves were the rule of law under an emergency. Khanna, dissenting, held that the constitution did not provide for any authority to suspend *habeus corpus*. If life and liberty were not protected by

---

[40]By deleting those sections of Article 13 of India's present constitution that make fundamental rights justiciable.

[41]The rights specified are freedom of speech and expression; peaceable assembly; association; free movement; freedom to have, hold, and use property; and to carry on an occupation.

[42]Baxi, *Indian Supreme Court*, pp. 34–5.

[43]Justices Chandrachud, Beg, Ray, and Bhagwati constituted the majority. *Keesing's Contemporary Archives*, 18 June 1976, p. 27781. According to Kuldip Nayar, the decision 'came as a surprise and disappointed many people because it was believed that Chandrachud and Bhagwati would support *habeas corpus*'. *The Judgment*, p. 124.

law, the distinction between a lawless society and one governed by laws would cease to have any meaning.

When a reconstituted court, purged of the three dissenting judges, led by a committed chief justice, and surrounded by emergency pressures, nevertheless failed in late 1975 to abrogate *Keshavananda*'s doctrine of judicial review, Mrs Gandhi took a more direct path to disestablish judicial review. Instead of finding a way to create a Constituent Assembly to write a new 'presidential' constitution, the Congress' annual session meeting in Chandigarh at the end of December appointed a committee chaired by Swaran Singh, a veteran minister and party stalwart, to recommend constitutional amendments that would make the fundamental law more responsive 'to the current needs of the people and the demands of the present'.[44] Its recommendations formed the basis of the forty-second amendment, a sweeping fifty-nine clause constitutional revision. Tantamount to a new constitution, the amendment was accepted by a compliant parliament fettered by censorship and intimidated by arrests of leading members.[45] It purported, *inter alia*, to undo *Keshavananda* by barring the court from reviewing parliamentary amendments, declaring 'that there shall be no limitation whatever on the constituent power of parliament to amend ...' the constitution. The 'amendment' limited the court's authority in a variety of ways, and added provisions that vastly strengthened the executive. It completely subordinated the fundamental rights of Part III to parliamentary legislation giving expression to any of the directive principles of state policy in Part IV,[46] and severely restricted the courts' capacity under Article 226 to issue writs to public authorities for the enforcement of rights conferred by Part III and 'for any other purpose'.[47]

[44]Quoted in Norman D. Palmer, 'India in 1975: Democracy in Eclipse', *Asian Survey*, 16, 1976, p. 104.

[45]For a significant challenge on these and other grounds by Indian intellectuals, see M.C. Chagla *et al.*, *Nationwide Demand for Postponement of Constitution Amendment Bill*, New Delhi, 4 December 1976, which contains a 'Statement by Intellectuals', pp. 51–2, signed by 375 of India's leading academics, journalists, writers, and professionals.

[46]By stipulating that legislation stated to give effect to the directive principles could not be impugned as violations of Articles 13 and 19 (fundamental rights). The twenty-fifth amendment had attempted to do this. See n. 26. For useful contemporary accounts, see S.P. Sathe, 'Forty Constitutional Amendment', *Economic and Political Weekly*, 23 October 1976; S.V. Kogekar, 'Constitutional Amendment Bill', *Economic and Political Weekly*, 16 October 1976.

[47]Another provision of the forty-second amendment that weakened judicial review and the court's capacity to 'balance' parliament was one that raised from five to seven the number of judges for a constitution bench, and required a majority of five to validate decisions. For further analysis of the forty-second (initially forty-fourth) amendment, see references in 41 above; Mirchandi, *Subverting the Constitution*, which deals with the thirty-eighth amendment denying the courts the power to review a presidential proclamation of emergency, and the

The electorate's massive repudiation in March 1977 of Mrs Gandhi's authoritarian regime and emergency excesses, and its affirmation of Janata's commitment to a liberal state that respected judicial review, citizen rights, and the rule of law raised the question of how the new government would 'restore' the constitution. In particular, how would it redeem its pledge to re-establish judicial review of parliamentary legislation and amendments, and right the balance between the executive and the Supreme Court?

Prime Minister Morarji Desai began by taking a difficult and controversial decision in favour of an independent judiciary. On the retirement of Chief Justice A.N. Ray soon after the Janata Party assumed office, eminent members of the Supreme Court bar and other opponents or victims of the emergency called on a sympathetic Janata government to make a one time and only exception to end exceptions by superseding Y.V. Chandrachud, the senior justice who had voted with the majority in the notorious *habeas corpus* case. But Prime Minister Desai chose to protect the independence of the judiciary by reinstating the seniority rule rather than appointing a chief justice with the right legal philosophy.[48]

Conflict over state issues was at the centre of the Janata government's policy concerns, and its relationship with the Gandhi-led Congress-I opposition in parliament. Choosing the level and quality of stateness, and framing and passing amendments that institutionalised hard-fought cabinet decisions, proved difficult and frustrating. Now that Janata faced the responsibility of ruling the country, it could not easily or automatically redeem the pledges of an opposition party struggling against a tyrannical government and an authoritarian regime. Even if it had known its own mind about what it meant to restore to the constitution, doing so would have proved difficult and complex. As it was, the staggered terms of the upper house

---

thirty-ninth, which retroactively barred the courts from examining electoral disputes involving, *inter alia*, the prime minister, as well as the forty-second; and our 'To the Brink and Back: Representation and the State in India', *Asian Survey*, 18, 1978, pp. 397–9.

[48]*The Times of India*, 12 February 1978. The prime minister took his decision in the face of strong pressure by 'a veritable Who's Who of the legal profession'. A *Statesman* editorial called for a 'supersession ... to end all supersessions', or 'a third "ultimate" supersession'. See Henry J. Abraham, '"Merit" or "Seniority"? Reflections on the Politics of Recent Appointments to the Chief Justiceship of India', *Journal of Commonwealth and Comparative Politics*, 16, 1978, p. 305. For a critique of the Abraham article, see George H. Gadbois, Jr, 'The Perils of Non-Contextual Analysis: The Contexts of Judicial Appointment in India', mimeo, Oxford, 1981. Gadbois argues that the issue was not merit versus seniority, but a 'politicized, independent Court v. a politicized dependent Court' (p. 23). The controversy is covered in some detail in Rajeev Dhavan and Alice Jacob, *Selection and Appointment of Supreme Court Judges: A Case Study*, Bombay: N.M. Tripathi, 1978, Appendix IX, 'Appointing the Chief Justice of India: The 1978 Controversy', pp. 119–25.

(one-third elected every two years) deprived the Janata government of a majority, much less the constitutional majority (two-thirds of those present and voting) required for amendments. In the lower house it had to rely on friendly and/or opposition parties to muster a constitutional majority. The Janata government's forty-fifth amendment bill (later the forty-fourth Amendment Act), which cleared both houses in December 1978, twenty-two months after Janata assumed office, and received the president's assent in May 1979, just two months before its government fell, reflected the limitations of Janata's parliamentary situation, and the compromises and bargains required by the diverse preferences of influential actors within and outside the Janata government.[49] As a consequence, the forty-fifth amendment bill failed to reverse the emergency (forty-second) amendment asserting the primacy of directive principles over fundamental rights, and the immunity of parliamentary amendments from review by the Supreme Court.

Though the forty-fifth amendment bill did not restore a liberal state, it did go to considerable lengths to prevent the recurrence of an authoritarian one. Mrs Gandhi, on 26 June 1975, had invoked the language of Article 352, authorizing the proclamation of an emergency by the president if the country's security was threatened by an 'internal disturbance', to repulse and repress political and legal threats to her power and authority.[50] In doing so she may have abused power in two ways, wrongly identifying such threats as an 'internal disturbance' that constituted a threat to the security of India, and asking the president *ab initio* to act on her advice rather than, as the constitution requires, the advice of the council of ministers.[51] The forty-

[49]For details see *The Times of India*, 1 January 1978; *The Hindu*, 21 April 1978; *The Indian Express*, 8 August 1978; *Overseas Hindustan Times*, 14 September 1978; *Asian Recorder*, 1979, pp. 14685–6 and 14919–20.

[50]Mrs Gandhi's formal case for the proclamation of emergency being 'a Constitutional step' is given in *Shah Commission of Inquiry, Interim Report I*, Delhi, 1978, paragraphs 5.61 and 5.62, pp. 26–9. Mrs Gandhi explicitly denies that 'the Emergency was declared for personal reasons, namely, to stultify the judgment [of the Allahabad High Court] by extra-legal means and to maintain my position as Prime Minister by extra-constitutional methods' (p. 29). She charges that there was an 'internal disturbance' that threatened India's security: '... the Judgment of the Allahabad High Court was ... seized upon by the opposition', she stated in a written reply to the Shah Commission, 'to whip up political frenzy against me.' Critical evaluations of the declaration of emergency and its use can be found in Nayar, *The Judgment*; Vasudev, *Two Faces of Indira Gandhi*; Nayantara Sahgal, *Indira Gandhi's Emergence and Style*, New Delhi: Vikas Publishing House, 1978; and Selbourne, *An Eye to India*. The most scathing, and historically and philosophically informed, interpretations of the emergency can be found in Arun Shourie's *Symptoms of Fascism*, New Delhi, 1978. For a generally positive interpretation, see Mary C. Carras, *Indira Gandhi: In the Crucible of Leadership*, Boston: Beacon Press, 1979.

[51]For an authoritative and detailed account of the abuses of power or 'excesses', see *Shah Commission, Interim Report I*, Chapter V, 'Circumstances Leading to the Declaration of Emergency on June 25 1975', pp. 17–32. The Shah Commission report was withdrawn from the market

fifth amendment bill provided remedies for these potential abuses of power by substituting 'armed rebellion' for 'internal disturbance', and prohibiting the president from issuing a proclamation of emergency 'unless the decision of the Union Cabinet ... that such a Proclamation may be issued has been communicated to him in writing'. The clause also required that parliamentary resolutions approving declarations of emergency be passed by constitutional (two-thirds) rather ordinary majorities. Other remedies of the forty-fifth amendment bill for abuses of power under an emergency were guarantees: that the media can report freely and without censorship the proceedings in parliament and the state assemblies;[52] that citizens' access to the courts on matters that touch their rights to life and liberty cannot be suspended; that protection against self-incrimination, retroactive laws, and double jeopardy cannot be suspended, and that writs will be available from the high courts to enforce these protections; that persons arrested under laws authorizing preventive detention (for example, MISA and DIR) cannot be held for more than two months without court-supervised review procedures;[53] and that one-

---

in March 1980 after Mrs Gandhi returned to power, and government booksellers were ordered to return their copies to the government. The second paragraph of Prime Minister Gandhi's midnight letter to the President of India recommending that he declare an emergency states:

> I would have liked to have taken this to Cabinet but unfortunately this is not possible tonight. I am, therefore, condoning or permitting a departure from the Government of India (Transaction of Business Rules, 1961), as amended up-to-date by virtue of my powers under Rule 12 thereof. I shall mention the matter to the Cabinet first thing tomorrow morning, (p. 25).

Paragraph 5.66, p. 29, deals with the validity of Mrs Gandhi's use of Rule 12. For a defence of Mrs Gandhi's use of Rule 12 to justify her failure to submit the emergency decision to her cabinet colleagues (Council of Ministers), see Carras, *Indira Gandhi*, pp. 218–23. Carras reports that Mrs Gandhi told her she did not 'consult the ministers' prior to the decision because 'she was fearful of leaks and felt that secrecy had to be maintained at all costs' (p. 221). See Arun Shourie, *Symptoms of Fascism*, pp. 212–15, for an account of Mrs Gandhi's premeditation in declaring the emergency.

[52]The provision sought to remedy and prevent one of the most significant restrictions of civil and political rights during the emergency: the censorship of press reports of parliamentary debates and proceedings under the Prevention of Publication of Objectionable Matters Act. The fortieth amendment, also passed during the emergency, placed the Act in the ninth schedule, where it became immune from judicial review.

[53]See clauses 42, 40, 3, and 37 of the forty-fifth amendment bill (later forty-fourth amendment) and *Overseas Hindustan Times*, 10 May 1979. Also see Henderson, 'Setting India's Democratic House', p. 953. The *Shah Commission, Interim Report 1*, paragraph 5.80, 5.81, pp. 31–3, refers to the 'gross irregularities by which the provisions of the Maintenance of Internal Security Act and provisions of the Defence of India Rules were misused to the detriment of political opponents'. Their provisions

> ... were not complied with, either at the behest of Smt. Indira Gandhi or her aides and orders were made without any grounds, without any satisfaction or maintenance of any record regarding the satisfaction of competent authorities; and personal liberty of many citizens was taken away and they continued to remain deprived of liberty for substantial periods even in the face of safeguards which were incorporated against misuse of section 16A of MISA. ...

tenth of the total number of members of the lower house can call for a special sitting to consider disapproving the continuance in force of an emergency.[54]

In a surprising, even daring, decision four months after Mrs Gandhi was swept back into power, the Supreme Court in May 1980 restored through judicial review what the Janata government was unable to restore by parliamentary amendment. In the *Minerva Mills* case the court invoked *Keshavananda Bharati* to declare invalid, because they attacked the basic structure of the constitution, the two clauses of the forty-second amendment meant to reverse *Keshavananda Bharati*. The first prohibited court review of laws that contravened fundamental rights if parliament declared that they gave effect to directive principles of state policy; the second proscribed judicial review of constitutional amendments.[55] The court's decision was reminiscent of its actions in November and December 1975 when it struck down the thirty-ninth amendment's attempt to immunize the prime

---

On 23 September 1980, the Gandhi Congress-I government via presidential ordinance (the National Security Ordinance) reinstated preventive detention. It authorized the detention of persons to prevent them from acting in a manner prejudicial to the defence or security of India, as well as on the grounds of the security of a state and the maintenance of services essential to the life of the community. Since 1950, there have been only two brief periods February 1970–May 1970 and March 1977–22 September 1980—when India has been without central authority to use preventive detention. The September ordinance, unlike the notorious MISA used during the emergency, is subject to provisions of the forty-fifth amendment, such as the requirement that a detained person be informed of the reason for his arrest, that an advisory board composed of sitting or former high court judges review the circumstances of arrest within two months, and that individual acts as well as the ordinance (or subsequent legislation) can be challenged in a court of law. Another ordinance issued in September amended the Criminal Procedure Code by substituting the executive for judicial magistrates to enforce provisions of Section 108 barring attempts to bring into hatred and contempt the government established by law, preaching disaffection, including disloyalty and feelings of enmity towards it (but not comments disapproving of the government's action), imputations of lack of patriotism on the part of religions or linguistic groups' preaching of communal or religious disharmony, and deliberate and malicious acts intended to outrage religious feelings. The danger is that overzealous executives intent on pleasing higher authorities may treat allegations about expression as proof. For an analysis of both ordinances, see S. Sahay, 'A Close Look: That Law Again', *The Statesman Weekly*, 4 October 1980, p. 12, and 'MISA in Another Garb', *Economic and Political Weekly*, 27 September 1980, which argues that loopholes in the NSO appear to have restored 'all the hateful provisions' of the emergency period of MISA (p. 1602).

[54]The forty-fifth amendment reduced from two months to one the period, if parliament is not sitting, for which an emergency proclamation is valid before approved by a (now) two-thirds parliamentary vote. The 1950 constitution had already stated that approval of a proclamation of emergency could be given by parliament for six months only, with six-month extensions thereafter, and for special measures to guard against emergency proclamations if parliament is dissolved.

[55]*The Statesman, The Times of India, The Indian Express, Hindustan Times*, of 10 and 11 May 1980.

minister's election from review by a competent tribunal, and refused to follow the chief justice in his attempt to reverse *Keshavananda Bharati*. Without returning the pendulum to the extreme of *Golak Nath*, the court returned it to a position between *Keshavananda Bharati* (1973) and the twenty-fifth amendment (1971) by recognizing in *Minerva Mills* the limited primacy of directive principles created by the twenty-fifth amendment (Article 39[b] and [c] only), but challenged by *Keshavananda Bharati*.[56] Buffeted by the constitutional storms of the emergency period and the alternation of Janata and Congress governments, the court seems to have adopted a dual strategy to assure its survival as a co-ordinate branch of the government: it protected judicial review by asserting its special responsibility for defining what was constitutional; and it practised self-restraint with respect not only to legislative, but also to executive action.

SELF-RESTRAINT: WILL SAVING THE COURT SAVE A GOVERNMENT OF LAWS?

The political innocence that accompanied the court's era of legal solipsism produced *Golak Nath*. Since then it has learned to read the election returns in ways that attend to long-run political currents, as well as short-run opportunities. Its conduct since 1977 suggests a politically responsive and self-restrained strategy that seeks to protect the principle of judicial review while recognizing that the executive, acting through or with the support of parliamentary majorities and in the name of state purposes and interests, can make claims that constrain citizens' rights, the federal system, or even the rule of law.

When the 1977 election ended Congress' emergency regime and installed a Janata government in Delhi, the court showed its responsiveness in an advisory opinion (Article 143).[57] The Desai government proposed to dissolve the assemblies and hold mid-term elections in nine states with Congress

---

[56]The court's opinion specifically mentions that Article 31 (c), as it stood prior to the forty-second amendment, that is, when it provided that directive principles of state policy 39 (b) and (c) could override fundamental rights, is compatible with the basic structure argument. It is the much wider 1976 effort to extend the precedence to any law 'containing a declaration that it is for giving effect to' directive principles, which is struck down. *The Times of India*, 10 May 1980. The rationale for the May decision to strike down Article 368 (4) and (5) and Article 31 (c) was issued at the end of July. Four of the five judges fully supported the decision; Justice Bhagwati concurred in the decision striking down Articles 368 (4) and (5), protecting the absolute amendment power of parliament, but dissented with respect to Article 31 (c). *Hindustan Times*, 14 August 1980, and *Economic and Political Weekly*, 9 August 1980.

[57]Basu, *Introduction to the Constitution*, pp. 249–50, lays out the nature of the advisory process and describes its use up to 1975.

governments. The Congress had captured no parliamentary seats in some and one or two in others, and its share of votes had declined precipitously in all. The Janata government in Delhi held that the parliamentary results made clear that the Congress governments in the nine states no longer represented the people. In any case, their involvement in emergency excesses made it difficult for them, because of the people's hatred and their loss of legitimacy, to maintain law and order. The Supreme Court advised the president that dissolution was justified. It was an unprecedented act that significantly undermined the constitution's federal arrangements.[58]

While acquiescing to the wishes of the country's new political masters, the court failed to specify adequately the special electoral and legal circumstances that could distinguish the Janata's dissolution from similar ones that might arise in the future. It failed to give sufficient consideration to the consequences of the precedent. In March 1980 Mrs Gandhi's newly elected Congress government, despite patent differences in electoral outcomes and extant legal and political circumstances, justified the dissolution of nine state assemblies with non-Congress majorities and governments by invoking the court-sanctioned Janata precedent.[59]

The court again acquiesced to the purposes of the Janata government by providing a second advisory opinion that upheld the legality of legislation that would create special courts to try Mrs Gandhi, Sanjay, and others for their alleged abuse of power, excesses, and criminal acts under the emergency.[60] After Janata's defeat and Mrs Gandhi's return to power, the two special courts set up by the Janata government followed the election returns by invoking 'improper procedures' in their creation to dismiss summarily the cases against Indira and Sanjay Gandhi pending before them.[61]

When Mrs Gandhi returned to power in January 1980, the courts in other ways accommodated themselves to the interests and needs of the

[58] See ibid., pp. 294–9, for an account of the provisions and use of Article 365 (1), which provides that the president, by proclamation, may impose president's rule when he is satisfied that a state's government cannot be carried on in accordance with the provisions of the constitution. 'It has been strongly urged,' Basu writes, 'that the power under Article 356 cannot be used to dismiss a Ministry so long as it commands the confidence of the majority in the State Legislature. But since the use of the power rests on the subjective satisfaction of the President, its propriety cannot be questioned by the Courts' (p. 298).

[59] For an account of the parliamentary debate, including Home Minister Zail Singh's statements that 'his Government was merely following the precedent set by the Janata Government in 1977', see Hindustan Times, 28 March 1980.

[60] The special courts bill, contrary to Janata's original intent, was amended in parliament to give such courts jurisdiction over all abuses of power, not merely those committed under the emergency. Overseas Hindustan Times, 17 May 1979.

[61] See The Indian Express, 20 February 1980, for a critical editorial, 'End of Special Courts', which decried their demise on 'an obscure technicality'.

country's new political masters. Not only did the courts find ways to wind up the special courts trying emergency offences, but also they found ways, between January and June 1980, to dismiss all the cases pending against Mrs Gandhi and her emergency associates. Mrs Gandhi dismissed them in her own way by characterizing all prosecutions against her and her political associates as being merely politically vindictive. In June, the Supreme Court seemed to agree when it held in the Baroda Dynamite and Bansi Lal cases that the state need not prosecute criminal cases when it finds that the motives involved were political.

Before its decision was handed down, the country was treated to a spectacle of cavalier dismissals that jeopardized the rule of law. Four cases against Bansi Lal, emergency defence minister, former chief minister of Haryana, and a close associate of Sanjay Gandhi, were dropped when the then Lok Dal chief minister of Bansi Lal's home state, Bhajan Lal, found that he needed the political support of a co-defendant close to Bansi Lal.[62] The Delhi High Court dismissed an important defamation case against Maneka Gandhi, Sanjay's politically active and ambitious wife who edited *Surya*, a political weekly, on a minor procedural detail.[63] The Central Bureau of Investigation (CBI) found that it had 'insufficient evidence' to proceed with its case against Jag Mohan, the Sanjay intimate who, as Commissioner of the Delhi Development Authority, had played a key role in the demolition of 'slums' such as those near the Jama Masjid and around Turkman Gate.[64] On the same grounds of insufficient evidence the CBI stopped work on a case against R.K. Dhawan, the private secretary to Mrs Gandhi who had handled many of the repressive acts under the emergency, and who was being investigated for misuse of party funds.[65] The special courts, trying the procurement without payment of 139 jeeps, and Mrs Gandhi's harassment of officials charged with investigating why and how five state chief ministers purchased equipment from Sanjay's Maruti firm without proper bidding,[66] found that they themselves had been improperly constituted.[67] A hit-and-

---

[62]*Hindustan Times*, 23 September 1979; *The Indian Express*, 25 September 1979. Arun Shourie's 'Haryana Cases: What Next?' in *Institutions in the Janata Phase*, Delhi: Popular, 1980, pp. 52–7, discusses the purely political nature of the Haryana government and the public prosecutor's decision. Soon after the dismissal of the case, Bhajan Lal's government defected *en masse* to Congress-I to save itself from dissolution.

[63]After repeated and protracted delays to accommodate Maneka Gandhi or her counsel, a single non-attendance by the plaintiff, the noted journalist Romesh Thapar, was used to dismiss the case.

[64]*The Statesman*, 24 February 1980.

[65]*The Times of India*, 15 March 1980.

[66]*Hindustan Times*, 13 September 1979.

[67]The justices presiding over the special courts appointed six months earlier under the

run case lodged at Dehra Dun against Sanjay Gandhi in September 1979 was adjourned after the election when the injured victim discovered that he, rather than Sanjay, was at fault, and witnesses changed their testimony.[68] These are only a few of the nearly twenty cases to be dropped after Congress-I's electoral victory in January 1980.[69]

The Supreme Court directly confronted the problem of the balance between a government of laws and executive discretion in two cases handed down in May 1980. It skilfully paired its review of the two cases: the withdrawal by the Janata government of the Baroda Dynamite case brought against Janata sympathizers under the emergency by a Congress government, and the withdrawal by Congress of the Bansi Lal case lodged by the Janata government against the Congress government's defence minister under the emergency. The court asserted the principle of the non-political nature of state prosecutions even while erecting a commodious shelter for governments wishing to withdraw cases on purely political grounds. On the one hand Justice Reddy asserted that 'criminal justice is not a plaything and a court is not a playground of politicking'. The court's function is to ensure that the public prosecutor 'had applied his mind as a free agent', and did not allow himself to be the 'stooge' of the executive. On the other hand, in sanctioning the withdrawal of cases by both the Congress and Janata governments, the court's opinion offers special protection to politically motivated offences.

The Janata government, the court notes, withdrew the Baroda Dynamite case because 'the motivating force of the party [Janata] which was formed to fight the election in 1977 was the same as the motivating force of the criminal [the Baroda Dynamite] conspiracy'. The court then poses a question: 'To say that an offence is of a political character is not to absolve the offender of the offence, but the question is, is it a valid ground for the government to advise the public prosecutor to withdraw from the prosecution?' Indian history suggests that it is indeed a valid ground: 'A political offence is one which is committed with the object of changing the government of a state or inducing it to change its policy', and these are 'the kinds of offences with

---

Janata government, discovered on 15 January and 14 February, shortly after Mrs Gandhi was elected, that the Home and Law Ministries were not specifically allocated the function of setting up such courts under their rules of business at the time of setting up the special courts (20 May 1979), but only in September. *The Times of India*, 19 February 1980; *The Indian Express*, 20 February 1980.

[68]*The Indian Express*, 27 April 1980. Abdul Ghani, the victim, declared in September of 1979 that the Matador by which he was hit and injured was driven by Sanjay Gandhi. On cross-examination in April 1980, he reported that the accident was his own fault, and the Matador was driven by one Chattar Singh.

[69]Kuldip Nayar in *The Indian Express*, 30 April 1980.

which Mahatma Gandhi and his spiritual son, the first prime minister of India', as well as the present prime minister and president were once charged. In consequence, 'One cannot say that the public prosecutor was activated by any improper motive in withdrawing from prosecution.'

Is it then all right, under this doctrine, to commit crimes, provided they are politically motivated? Apparently so. Three days after the Supreme Court handed down its judgment, the metropolitan magistrate of Delhi used it to dismiss the Janpath riot case involving Sanjay Gandhi and his Youth Congress followers. They were charged with mayhem and window smashing in New Delhi's central shopping area. Since the acts occurred during a political demonstration protesting against the Janata government policies—special courts, unemployment, and corruption—they fell under the authoritative judgment of the Supreme Court protecting such offences. The magistrate cites the court: 'To persist with prosecution where emotive issues are involved, in the name of vindicating the law may be utter foolishness tending on insanity.'[70]

In the midst of the wholesale withdrawal of emergency cases, a prominent Indian journalist argued that 'we have not reached the stage of maturity in our development as a democracy' to make it possible for the Indian government to enquire into the transactions of close aides to the executive. Judges who have collaborated in the evaporation of cases 'should be recommended for their common sense and realism' in avoiding a confrontation between the concepts of popular sovereignty and an independent judiciary, if only because they cannot hope to win it'.[71] Many leaders of India's legal profession do not deserve this judgment, written in any case before *Minerva Mills* was handed down. It does, however, suggest the fashion in which the positive norm of judicial self-restraint towards the politically responsible executive can be converted into a defence of judicial abdication in the interest of judicial survival.

STATE ISSUES IN THE 1980s

As India enters the 1980s, state issues remain at the centre of the political struggle. Institutional rivalry between parliament and court; constitutional controversies over the relative standing of judicial review and parliamentary

---

[70]*The Times of India*, 7 May 1980. For accounts and citations from the two cases, see *The Indian Express*, 25 September 1979, 3 May 1980; *The Times of India*, 19 January 1980, 3 May 1980, 7 May 1980; and Arun Shourie's extended critical analyses, 'Preaching High, Practising Low—I & II', *The Indian Express*, 22 and 23 May 1980.

[71]Girilal Jain, 'Authoritarian or Indecisive', in *The Times of India*, 23 April 1980.

sovereignty; and conflict between citizens' rights and state interests continue
to orient leaders and parties seeking power. Constitutional doctrine in India
is not explicit about a government based on a balance of powers, and does
not feature the pursuit of institutional self-interest as a restraint on power.
Yet India in the 1980s will test whether the prescription offered in *The Federalist*
for the successful working of a division and balance of powers among several
branches of government is viable. According to Federalist 51,

... The great security against a gradual concentration of the several powers in the same
department consists in giving those who administer each department the necessary
constitutional means and personal motives to resist encroachments of the others.
... Ambition must be made to counteract ambition. The interests of the man must
be connected with the constitutional rights of the place. ... In framing a government
which is to be administered by men over men, the great difficulty lies in this: you
must first enable the government to control the governed; and in the next place
oblige it to control itself.[72]

The Janata government (1977–9), via the provisions of the forty-fifth
amendment, and the Supreme Court, in reaffirming in *Minerva Mills* the basic
structure doctrine of *Keshavananda Bharati*, have restored a balance between
judicial review and parliamentary sovereignty that gives the court and the
parliamentary executive 'the necessary constitutional means and personal
motives to resist encroachments by the other'. Whether the court, in the
face of seven forthcoming vacancies available to the Gandhi government
during its expected term in office (1980–4),[73] will continue to be manned
by judges whose personal motives will connect with the constitutional rights
of the place remains to be seen. Chastened by the shocks and pressures of
the emergency and alternating party governments, the Chandrachud court,
to accommodate the political interests of governments of the day, has
circumscribed the meaning of the federal principle and of a government of
laws. At the same time it has protected the doctrine of fundamental law
and the practice of judicial review. Whether balances struck over the next
decade will reflect judicial self-restraint that protects the constitution and
fundamental rights or judicial abdication that sacrifices both awaits the
course of historical events and the country's judgement of them.

---

[72]Alexander Hamilton, James Madison, and John Jay, *The Federalist Or, The New
Constitution* (with an Introduction by Professor W.J. Ashley), London: Everyman, 1911, p. 264.
[73]See *Statesman Weekly*, 27 September 1980, for the names and dates of retiring justices.
We are grateful to L.M. Singhvi for discussing various aspects of judicial conventions with us.

9

Rethinking Secularism
Genesis and Implications of the
Textbook Controversy, 1977–9*

LLOYD I. RUDOLPH AND SUSANNE HOEBER RUDOLPH

M any factors contributed to the Janata's demise just two years after its stunning victory in the 1977 elections. At the ideological level, the principal cause was the party's inability to resolve its orientation towards the meaning and practice of secularism and its perceived opposite, communalism. At the level of intra-party policy, the ideological struggle raised the question of whether, or perhaps how, to allow 'dual membership'. Should party members be allowed to belong to a doctrinaire Hindu nationalist organization, the Rashtriya Swayamsevak Sangh (RSS)? Conflict over these ideological and organizational questions renewed debate over cultural policy. Since at least 1885, when only two of the seventy-three persons who met in Bombay to reform the Indian National Congress were Muslims,[1] differences over secularism and communalism have affected nationalism and state formation on the Indian subcontinent. Janata's inability to resolve satisfactorily the dual membership and secularism/communalism controversies provides the historical backdrop for our analysis of the textbook controversy.

The textbook controversy began in May 1977, less than three months after the Janata government assumed office. V. Shankar, principal secretary to Prime Minister Morarji Desai, sent a note to Education Minister P.C. Chunder about some textbooks whose 'controversial and biased material' would lead readers to acquire 'a prejudiced view of Indian history'.[2] Shankar did not say

*Originally published as 'Rethinking Secularism: Genesis and Implications of the Textbook Controversy, 1977–79', in *Pacific Affairs*, 56 (1), Spring 1983, pp. 15–37.
    [1]For the founding of the Indian National Congress, see Briton Martin, Jr, *New India*, Berkeley and Los Angeles: University of California Press, 1969.
    [2]Note, dated 28 May 1977, PM's [Prime Minister's] Office U/O No. 40 (277) 77 PMS [Prime Minister's Secretariat], Rudolph personal files.

who had sent the four books (together with critical comments) to the prime minister. 'PM thought,' Shankar's note continued, 'that the Education Ministry might consider withdrawing these books from circulation, particularly those which are intended to be textbooks in schools'. Shankar signalled that the prime minister intended to go further along the path of historical rectification: '[S]imilar publications that may have been issued by the ... Education Ministry might be examined from the same point of view and suitable steps taken to ensure that readers do not get wrong ideas about various elements of our history and culture'.

What textbooks say about history is not esoteric lore. They help define who and what is Indian, and clarify the meaning and value of secularism. After the Shankar note was leaked to interested parties and the press, the controversy became a public and political debate on how the writing and teaching of Indian history affect national identity and public philosophy. The role of the historian as professional craftsman was lost to sight in the controversy over his role as ideologue of unity or disunity, as creator of sociopolitical reality, and as composer of literary forms that have political consequences.

Attention focused also—and critically so—on the incremental and *ad hoc* processes by which India had acquired a cultural policy.[3] The casual nature of Shankar's note to Chunder captures the amorphous, even protean, quality of cultural policy formation. It is more a loose aggregate of spontaneous decisions than a body of coherent doctrine expressing intent, and subject to policy choice and guidance. Although the procedures used to commission, examine, and license the textbooks in question were exemplary in comparison with the procedure used to challenge them, cultural policy formation was, and remains, *ad hoc*. Policies are essentially outputs of particular bureaus or outcomes of bargains among officials, rather than the results of deliberate choices based on coherent formulations that provide policy guidance, and are subject to public accountability.

The note's policy challenge also highlights the anomalous position of semi-autonomous government bodies in the scientific and scholarly arena. Charged with maintaining professional standards in the allocation of resources and honour, they are often swamped by political tidal waves. Neither governments nor scholarly communities have succeeded in creating procedures or conventions that assure autonomy. Although committed rhetorically to autonomy, both the Congress and Janata governments assumed that they could, and should, intervene in a tutelary and patrimonial manner on behalf of their very different worldviews and priorities.

---

[3]See Kapila Vatsyayan, *Some Aspects of Cultural Policy in India*, Paris: UNESCO, 1972.

The scholarly community of historians had few weapons with which to fend off political intervention. It proved impossible to disentangle the community's most plausible weapon—the defence of professional standards—from the merits of the issue. The secularists were convinced that Hindu-oriented historians were *ipso facto* unprofessional. The Hindu enthusiasts thought that professionalism was a cover for the wrong values and interests of the secularists. For reasons we elaborate below, the free-market solution, which under some circumstances might be an alternative to government patronage of learning, is not viable in the Indian context.

CULTURAL POLICY IN HISTORICAL AND POLITICAL PERSPECTIVE

The Janata government did not initiate attempts to influence the writing and teaching of history. Indian nationalists seeking a politically workable definition of Indian identity had struggled over the cultural orientation of the movement. Many of them, hesitant to attack British rule, adopted Muslim rulers as surrogate targets, with deeply divisive effects on the nationalist movement. Bipin Chandra, author of one of the textbooks involved in the controversy, argues that the vicissitudes of Indian nationalism fed communal history—that is, history that celebrates or denigrates particular religious, cultural, or ethnic communities. 'The teaching of Indian history has a great deal to do with the spread of communalism in the last 100 years. In fact, it would be no exaggeration to suggest that a communal historical approach has been, and is, the main ideology of communalism in India'.[4] This strongly stated view is supported by a variety of analyses and explanations: 'Communalism among the historians spread mainly because of its ability to serve as "vicarious" or "backdoor" nationalism. Communalism enabled them to feel nationalistic without opposing imperialism'.[5] For the most part, historians were prudent. They did not side with the colonial rulers, yet did not risk opposing them either. Backdoor nationalism, which took the form of regional or community history, 'could satisfy their nationalist urge and yet not be looked askance at by the authorities who encouraged any and all approaches which would create division in Indian society'.[6]

There are many examples of Chandra's proposition not only among nationalist historians, but also among the creators of nationalism. Tilak's famous speech praising the Hindu general Shivaji's 'treacherous' slaying of

---

[4]'Historians of Modern India and Communalism', in *Communalism and the Writing of Indian History*, by Romila Thapar, Bipan Chandra, and Harbans Mukhia, Delhi: People's Publishing House, 1969, p. 36.

[5]Ibid., p. 44.

[6]Ibid., p. 45.

the Bijapur (Muslim) general Afzal Khan,[7] and Bankim Chandra Chatterjee's (Hindu) ascetics fighting Muslim rule from the forest ashram, the Ananda Math, provide obvious examples of Chandra's backdoor nationalism.[8] However, some backdoor nationalism was sufficiently transparent enough for British authorities to be under no illusions about its meaning. Tilak's Afzal Khan speech figured in his treason trial.

Another element in the growth of communal history, according to Chandra, was the historical treatment of 'Hindus, Sikhs, and Muslims as distinct, separate socio-political entities'.[9] This treatment paralleled British official categories that reflected imperial ideology and policy.

'Islam' is made an active entity—almost given a personality. 'Islam' conquers, 'Islam' thinks, 'Islam' decides, 'Islam' benefits. ... The Maratha empire and states, Rajput states and chiefs, Jat chiefs, etc. are all lumped together as Hindu states, while the southern and northern states headed by Muslim rulers are described as Muslim states.[10]

Chandra's assertion is in accord with other scholarship on the subject. 'The very idiom of British rule after 1857,' writes Peter Hardy, 'encouraged the development of political consciousness by religious communities.'[11]

The tradition of communal history that Chandra describes is no monopoly of British or Hindu nationalist historians. Muslim orthodoxy in contemporary India has shown considerable enthusiasm for a Muslim communal history. One of India's most distinguished historians of Mughal history, Irfan Habib, whose analysis of the economic causes of the decline of the Mughal empire provides a model for social historians in the current generation, was reminded by the president of the Students' Islamic Union of India:

We want that every teacher of the [Aligarh Muslim University] should be loyal to the Islamic Faith and Community. He must not do anything that should be determined [sic] to the interests of Islamic culture, community, and this University. Not only the present statement of Irfan Habib, but his attitude in the past as well, was always inimical to Islam and the community.[12]

[7]See Stanley A. Wolpert, *A New History of India*, New York: Oxford University Press, 1977, p. 164, for a short account of the event. Wolpert refers to Shivaji's act as 'murder', but goes on to say that 'it marked a real birth of Maratha power'.

[8]Bankim Chandra Chatterjee, *The Abbey of Bliss: A Translation of Bankim Chandra Chatterjee's Anandamath* (Naresh Chandra Sen-Gupta, trans.), Calcutta: P.M. Neogi, 1906.

[9]Bipin Chandra, 'Historians', p. 47.

[10]Ibid., p. 47.

[11]Peter Hardy, *The Muslims of British India*, Cambridge (UK) and New York: Cambridge University Press, 1972, p. 116. See also p. 129, where Hardy speaks of the government 'endowing Muslims with a separate social as well as religious personality'.

[12]Cited in Romila Thapar, 'Academic Freedom and the AMU Crisis', *The Radical Humanist*, April, 1981. See also K.N. Raj, 'Irfan Habib and Basic Issues', *Mainstream*, XIX (52), 1981.

The attempts to emphasize communalism in the nationalist movement were countered by Gandhi and Nehru, each of whom in different ways sought to strengthen a comprehensive cultural policy. Gandhi pursued an inclusive strategy by seeking to incorporate religious symbolism relevant to Islam in his public rituals, Islamic linguistic forms in his definition of a national language, and Muslim political interests in his coalitions. Nehru's resolute rationalism and commitment to a 'scientific temper' in effect denied the relevance of religion to a national political identity. The secular cultural policy that he fashioned for the Indian National Congress became the dominant political paradigm after independence.

For a time, Nehru's *The Discovery of India* and *Letters from Prison* constituted a tacit statement of the Congress's cultural policy, in part because those who might have objected were reluctant to challenge a prime minister who commanded wide political support. But Indira Gandhi's accession to power in the mid-1960s marked the beginning of a more articulate and aggressive left secularism in institutional arrangements, ideological formulations, and scholarship. Congress governments founded, funded, and favoured the Jawaharlal Nehru University. Its nationally-recruited faculty and student body soon acquired a reputation for progressive perspectives. A progressive tone was imparted to many other national cultural institutions. Nurul Hasan, a leading Mughal historian of Marxist persuasion and former professor of history at Aligarh Muslim University, became education minister after Mrs Gandhi's impressive electoral victory in 1971. When, after 1977, Janata intervened in textbook certification and appointments to cultural bodies, it did so in the name of rectifying a decade of partisan cultural patronage by Congress governments to secularist and *soi-disant* left academia. The anonymous memorandum to Prime Minister Desai alleged that progressive secularists had colonized independent government-funded research organizations—such as the Indian Council of Social Science Research, the University Grants Commission, and the Indian Council of Historical Research.

The Janata view did not give sufficient recognition to important differences within the Congress. Lines of support and cleavage were by no means clear. Shifting ideological orientations and commitments to authoritarian and democratic regimes divided Congress adherents. The Congress's left or progressive ideological orientation had been evident since the 1969 split, when members of the Congress Forum for Socialist Action— especially Mohan Kumaramangalam, a former member of the Communist Party of India—became influential members of Mrs Gandhi's entourage.[13]

---

[13]For a telling account, see Francine Frankel, *India's Political Economy, 1947–1977: The Gradual Revolution*, Princeton, New Jersey: Princeton University Press, 1978, p. 407 ff.

The Congress-I began to shift in a more conservative and authoritarian direction after Kumaramangalam's death in May 1973. Yet left and right tendencies persisted side by side. Under the emergency (1975–7), when Sanjay Gandhi's influence on party and government became dominant, members of both factions moved towards a more conservative (private enterprise and anti-communist) economic and ideological position. However, Sanjay Gandhi took little interest in cultural policy, and many members of the secularist and/or left scholarly establishment, by adapting their views to the requirements of the new constellation of power, were able to retain their posts during the emergency. At the same time, the emergency divided progressive historians into two broad groups: those committed to constitutional democracy and the professional standards that helped to insulate scholarship from ideology and partisan issues; and those who thought the authoritarianism of the emergency was justified, and that scholarship benefited from ideological commitment and should serve publicly defined purposes.

When the Janata Party swept into power in 1977, the Desai-Jan Sangh sections of the party did not attend to these distinctions, but rather discerned a homogeneous left-secularist Congress ideological position among adherents of the Nehru dynasty. And they were somewhat justified. A distinct view of the relationship between scholarship and ideology, and its bearing on cultural policy, is indeed evident in a volume published on the eve of the emergency. Entitled *Towards a Cultural Policy*,[14] it contained papers and proceedings of a seminar held well before the emergency, in June 1972, at the Indian Institute of Advanced Study, Simla. The volume's contents, in the words of the institute's director and conference convenor, S.C. Dube, reflected the work of 'an interdisciplinary group of scholars, specialists working in diverse cultural fields, and practitioners of the arts'. Taking stock of the cultural situation in the country, the contributors analysed emerging trends and 'endeavored to evolve the broad outlines of a cultural policy for India'.[15] The quality and length of the papers varied greatly, as did their orientations to the relationship between scholarship and ideology, and its implications for cultural policy.

The possibilities of a left cultural policy were apparent in the 'policy guidance' provided by S.C. Dube, and chief guest and patron of the seminar, the education minister Nurul Hasan. Dube introduced his paper with the remark that,

[14]Satish Saberwal (ed.), *Towards a Cultural Policy*, Delhi: Vikas, 1975.
[15]Ibid., p. v.

at the suggestion of the Ministry of Education ... [the Institute] is holding a seminar in honor of Lenin. ... The seminar is not designed to be merely an act of homage to Lenin or a routine academic exercise. It is intended to provide a springboard for a realistic appraisal of the cultural situation in India that may lead to the emergence of an outline of a cultural policy.[16]

Dube went on to reject past approaches as mythic, myopic, arbitrary, and divisive. He asked, 'How can we redefine Indian-ness without glorification of segmental achievements of the past?'[17] The answer lies, first, in displacing self-appointed guardians of culture who are 'doomed to petrify', because 'they remain uninfluenced by the social and cultural milieu ... [and] abjure social responsibility'.[18] Obscuring the superstructure-substructure causal relationship, Dube argued that fundamental alterations in the structure of society are 'inevitable'. Even so, a cultural transformation is also imperative. 'It ... can be planned and guided. A cultural policy, thus, becomes necessary'.[19]

For Nurul Hasan, the conference was essentially a tribute to the memory of Lenin:

the man who worked for and led a successful revolution in which power was transferred from the hands of a small coterie of feudal lords and the nascent bourgeoisie. ... This small class of rulers ... produced great masterpieces of literature and art, but it was the culture of an oppressive class. ... Lenin ... emphasized the need to broad base culture [sic], the need to harmonize the great cultural achievements of this small class with the urges and aspirations of the masses, and the need to pursue a policy whereby all the various sections of the Russian empire which had been subject to the tyranny of Russification could come into their own and develop their culture.[20]

Applying his interpretation of Lenin's view of cultural policy to India, Hasan argued that Indians must adopt a different attitude towards the past. Much of it

is totally out of harmony with the urges of the masses. Indian society in the past, like societies in every other part of the world, was a class society sharply divided between the masses and those who appropriate the fruits of their labor and evolved theories and philosophies. ... The culture of the upper class was an injustice and supported an outlook which could only be sustained on the basis of obscurantism and revivalism.

[16]Ibid., p. 3.
[17]Ibid., p. 4.
[18]Ibid., p. 8.
[19]Ibid., p. 8.
[20]Ibid., p. 13.

Hasan then distinguished India's traditional culture from the culture of the upper class. Traditional culture was resilient; it could assimilate new ideas. Its eclecticism produced both irrationalism *and* a rejection of dogmatism, enabling the masses 'simultaneously [to] continue traditional modes of thought as well as adopt new modes of thought and value judgments. I am not pleading for the continuance of irrationalism [which by the eighteenth century had lost its progressive role] but I am pleading for this quality of Indian culture.'[21] What is needed today, according to Hasan, is not non-dogmatic irrationalism, but something akin to it: 'a composite culture which is characteristic of India'.[22]

It is possible to view these interpretations of history and their relation to cultural policy as expressing the dilemma faced by all responsible scholars: how to make their sense of craftsmanship and historical or social scientific 'truth' congruent with efforts to direct social change towards desirable goals. This is a dilemma of special poignancy for scholars to whom academic writing represents a form of praxis. From this point of view, Dube and Hasan were simply trying to clarify their own stance as intellectuals and scholars. However, their remarks were not merely personal clarifications by private scholars. Dube was in charge of India's leading centrally funded academic 'think-tank'; Hasan was minister of education. Under the emergency, they became even more influential. At the same time, it is difficult to identify any official programme with the policy guidance they provided. Even so, particularly under the emergency regime, when the Indian state patronized or created academic professional associations led by Congress-I party loyalists, those concerned with pleasing the powerful learned to scan attentively the views of such influential spokesmen. Like the prudent scholars, some Janata leaders perceived their views as the articulation of Congress cultural policy, against which they chose to do battle.

THE TEXTBOOK CONTROVERSY

Leadership of the new Janata government in 1977 fell to Morarji Desai, an 81-year-old self-proclaimed Gandhian. Desai's Hindu cultural revivalism, *noblesse oblige* high-caste attitudes, and economic conservatism provided the political and ideological conditions for an evolving *rapport* between him and like-minded members of the Jan Sangh faction. His Hindu revivalism first became apparent in policy terms early in the Janata period, when he sanctioned inquiries about the textbooks. Other policy initiatives that

[21]Ibid., p. 25.
[22]Ibid., p. 26.

appealed to an important section of the Jan Sangh appeared later. He was sympathetic to the freedom-of-religion bill which, by creating penalties for conversion, alarmed Christians; he supported a constitutional amendment that opened the way to banning cow slaughter throughout the country; and he was committed to nationwide prohibition.

The textbook controversy can be best understood in the context of the internal politics of the newly formed and fragile Janata Party.[23] Prime Minister Desai's efforts to undermine his principal rival for party leadership—Charan Singh, head of the agrarian Bharatiya Lok Dal (BLD) faction[24]—eventually complemented those of the Hindu-oriented Jan Sangh faction, which sought to make its influence in the party commensurate with its plurality of seats. Initially, the Jan Sangh established close working relations with the BLD factions at the state level. When it later challenged BLD leadership in four northern states, it jeopardized its national relationship with Charan Singh's faction, and moved closer to Desai.[25] It was this *rapprochement* that created a particularly receptive climate for the Janata government's Hindu cultural emphasis.

Before turning to a detailed analysis of the textbook controversy, which depicts Janata in a Hindu revivalist mode, it is important to recognize that Janata's foreign, economic, and state policies were very different in character. The Janata government proved to be more 'secular' and less ideologically anti-communist than many of its critics anticipated, given its RSS-Jan Sangh

---

[23]There is an extensive literature on the controversies of 1977–9. See, for example, L.K. Advani, *The People Betrayed*, New Delhi: Vision Books, 1978; A.B. Vajpayee, 'All Responsible for Janata Crisis', *Indian Express*, 2 August 1979; Janardan Thakur, *Indira Gandhi and Her Power Game*, New Delhi: Vikas, 1979; Nanaji Deshmukh, *R.R.S.: Victim of Slander*, New Delhi: Vision Books, 1979; Banu Sengupta, *Last Days of the Morarji Raj*, Calcutta: Ananda Publications, 1979.

[24]Lloyd I. Rudolph, and Susanne Hoeber Rudolph, 'Agrarianism in India and America', *Emerging Sociology*, II, 1980; Susanne Hoeber Rudolph, 'Agrarianism and Rural Development', and Lloyd I. Rudolph, 'Agrarianism in Comparative Perspective', papers presented at a seminar on 'Dynamics of Rural Development', held at Mussoorie, India, 23–25 May 1980, sponsored by the United States International Communication Agency, New Delhi, and published in *Proceedings* of the Seminar, New Delhi, 1980.

[25]The Janata Party had been formed by six groups: the Organization Congress led by Morarji Desai, the prime minister; the Jan Sangh, led by A.B. Vajpayee, the External Affairs Minister; the Bharatiya Lok Dal (BLD), led by Charan Singh, the home minister; the Socialist Party, led by George Fernandes, the minister of industries; the Congress for Democracy (CFD), led by Jajivan Ram, the defence minister; and dissident Congressmen, led by Mohan Dharia, the minister of commerce. *The Hindu* on June 24 [1977], gave the representation of these groups as follows: Jan Sangh 90; BLD 68; Organization Congress 55; Socialists 51; CFD 28; dissident Congressmen 6. Their numerical majority gave the two right wing groups—the Jan Sangh and the BLD—a dominant position, and the chief ministers who took office in Bihar, Haryana, Himachal Pradesh, Madhya Pradesh, Orissa, Rajasthan and Uttar Pradesh after the (state assembly) elections in June 1977 were all drawn from these two groups (*Keesing's Contemporary Archives*, 8 December 1978, p. 29343).

component and the prime minister's Hindu values. It improved India's relations not only with the United States (which was expected), but also with China (which was surprising) and Pakistan (which was considered unlikely). And it managed to maintain friendly relations with the Soviet Union. Its employment-oriented development strategy, featuring investment in agriculture and small-scale industry, proved to be an imaginative if incomplete effort to combine growth with redistribution. Many of these initiatives were carried forward by the post-1980 Congress-I government. Perhaps the Janata's most memorable contribution was in the realm of state policy—namely the restoration of constitutional democracy.

Among the most controversial cultural initiatives during Janata rule was a private member's bill introduced in parliament in December 1978 by O.P. Tyagi, a leading member of the Jan Sangh faction of the Janata Party. Euphemistically named the 'Freedom of Religion Bill', the proposed legislation made it a criminal offence to use 'force, fraud and inducement' to bring about religious conversions. Christians were alarmed because the bill seemed to challenge their constitutionally protected freedom to propagate their religion; they felt threatened because their philanthropic projects, such as hospitals and schools, could be regarded as 'inducements'. Although supposed to be a private member's bill, it was not only supported by much of the Jan Sangh faction and others, but it also had the tacit approval of the prime minister.[26]

[26]For a comprehensive treatment of the bill, including similar acts in Madhya Pradesh, Orissa, and Arunachal Pradesh, and court decisions that upheld the validity of the state acts, see Kananaikil, Jose, *Reaching Inward from the Periphery: The Experience of the Scheduled Castes in India*, Ph.D. dissertation, University of Chicago, 1981. An inter-denominational delegation of Christian leaders was given to understand by the prime minister on 7 April 1979 in Shillong that the Freedom of Religion Bill would go through substantially unchanged. When the delegation asked him to arrange for its withdrawal, he responded, 'It will not be done' (mimeo, no author, no date [*circa* spring 1979], attached to M.A.Z. Roiston, General Secretary, National Christian Council of India, 'A Report on the Situation of Christians in Arunachal', Nagpur, 8 January 1979). See also Mathai Zachariah (ed.), *Freedom of Religion in India*, Nagpur: National Christian Council of India, 1979, for a critical review of the private member's bill, prior state acts, and court decisions; and Richard W. Lariviere, 'The Indian Supreme Court and the Freedom of Religion', *Journal of Constitutional and Parliamentary Studies*, IX (2), 1975, for a review of earlier court decisions. The conversion to Islam of 2000 to 3000 harijans at Meenakshipuram, Kurayor, Ilamanur, Athiyoothu, and other villages of Tirunelveli and Ramanathpuram districts of Tamil Nadu between February and August 1981 raised a storm in the country, and led to a new anti-conversion bill—by this time supported by Mrs Gandhi's Congress-I government— that required converts to register their change of religion with the government. See George Mathews, 'Politicization of Religion; Conversion to Islam in Tamil Nadu', *Economic and Political Weekly*, XVII (25 and 26), 1982. An early version of this paper was read at the South Asia Political Economy Workshop, University of Chicago, January 1982.

The government introduced the Constitution (Fiftieth Amendment) Bill making cow protection a concurrent subject—that is, one on which both the union and state governments can legislate. While heretofore the states had exercised exclusive jurisdiction in this matter, the amendment was to enable the central government to ban all cow slaughter in all states. Such a legislation would have had particular impact on west Bengal and Kerala, the two states whose non-Janata governments were explicitly and unequivocally opposed to such a ban, in part because of their strong communist parties, and in part because of their large and influential Muslim and/or Christian populations. The proposed amendment aroused criticism and opposition in the Janata itself, and was ultimately abandoned.

Desai's efforts to impose prohibition on the country were more successful than his moves to stop conversions or end 'cow slaughter', although at the end of his twenty-eighth month term in office, he was far from achieving his goal of total prohibition. Public drinking in bars, clubs, and restaurants was banned in most states, and the number of dry days (no liquor sold in stores) per month substantially increased.

It was Desai's cultural policies, which appealed to the Jan Sangh faction but alarmed the Socialist faction, that triggered the conflict over secularism in the Janata Party. Secularism was not the only issue that motivated Charan Singh or Raj Narain—or even Madhu Limaye, the erstwhile Socialist Janata general secretary who led the attack on the RSS. But it was central to the power struggle against Desai and, in time, served to justify the successive splits that destroyed the party.[27]

The textbook controversy began at the end of May 1977, with the above-mentioned note on the four history books from V. Shankar to Education Minister P.C. Chunder.[28] (Shankar had been secretary to Vallabhai Patel, the Iron Sardar and deputy prime minister who, until his death in 1950, had challenged Prime Minister Jawaharlal Nehru's secular and socialist ideas and policies.) The books at issue were *Medieval India* (1967) by Romila Thapar; *Modern India* (1970) by Bipan Chandra; *Freedom Struggle* (1972) by Amales Tripathi, Barun De, and Bipan Chandra; and *Communalism and the Writing of Indian History* (1969) by Romila Thapar, Harbans Mukhia, and Bipan Chandra. In August 1977, at the height of the controversy, a fifth book was published—*Ancient India*, by R.S. Sharma. Thapar, Chandra, and Mukhia were professors at the Centre for Historical Studies, Jawaharlal Nehru

[27]See Janardan Thakur, *Indira Gandhi and Her Power Game*, Ch. V, particularly pp. 125 ff.; and Barun Sengupta, *Last Days of the Morarji Raj*, especially pp. 55–8.
[28]See fn 2.

222 THE REALM OF INSTITUTIONS

University; Sharma had been head of the Department of History, Delhi University, and was for some years director of the Indian Council for Historical Research (ICHR); Tripathi was head of the Department of History, Calcutta University; and De was director of the Institute for Social Sciences, Calcutta. They were influential and productive scholars from some of India's most important intellectual institutions and departments. Within the broad parameters of close attention to economic determinants, their views varied widely, most importantly with respect to the authoritarian emergency regime imposed by Mrs Gandhi in June 1975, but also with respect to methodology, especially the relative importance of ideal and material factors in historical explanation.

Three of the books (by Sharma, Thapar, and Chandra) were published by the National Council for Educational Research and Training (NCERT) for use in schools. The volume by Chandra, Tripathi, and De was published by the National Book Trust on the occasion of the twenty-fifth anniversary of Indian independence. The book by Thapar, Mukhia, and Chandra was published by the progressive People's Publishing House after its three essays were read (in an abbreviated form) at a seminar organized in October 1968 by All-India Radio on 'The Role of the Broadcaster in the Present Communal Situation'.

The most hotly-contested issue in the controversy was the interpretation of 'medieval' Indian history, a period when Muslim rule prevailed over much of India. The focus of the controversy was the textbook historians' attention to social and economic history, and their propensity to explain conflict among elites primarily in political rather than religious terms. It was chiefly this issue that the anonymous memorandum to the prime minister raised. For example, Thapar's *Medieval India*, written in language appropriate for middle-school students, was scolded for its lack of anti-Muslim and pro-Hindu enthusiasm. An examination of the book suggests that the main fault was not a skewing of generally-known facts, but an absence of the requisite fervour:

Memorandum: 'For example, Mahmud Ghazni's destroying of Hindu temples has been justified on the ground that he wanted to plunder them. His proud claim as breaker of idols has been almost ignored.'

Thapar, *Medieval India*: 'Mahmud attacked only the temple towns in Northern India. He had heard there was much gold and jewelry kept in the big temples in India, so he destroyed the temples and took away the gold and jewelry. ... He could claim, as he did, that he had obtained religious merit by destroying images' [p. 36].

Memorandum: 'In a very subtle manner Aurangzeb's religious intolerance which led to the revolts in many parts of the country has been defended. ... Among the causes of the downfall of the Mughal empire, Aurangzeb's contribution, particularly his policy of religious intolerance, had not been listed at all.'

Thapar, *Medieval India*: 'To make matters worse, Aurangzeb was influenced by an orthodox Muslim group and he decided that he would rule in accordance with the laws of Islam. This was a policy different from that of his ancestors who were tolerant and liberal rulers. Besides, it was quite a wrong policy for a country such as India which has always had a mixture of all kinds of people and religions and where no type of orthodoxy could have worked. Aurangzeb did not understand the problems of India as well as Akbar had done. He became unpopular when he introduced *Jaziya* and when he destroyed temples. What he did not realize is that the job of a king is to rule efficiently and that religion should not be allowed to interfere with the government' [pp. 152–3].

The memorandum also protested Bipin Chandra's critical treatment of the nationalist generation: 'The nationalists such as Tilak and Aurobindo Ghose have been held responsible for creating disunity between Hindus and Muslims.' The implication of this and other citations is that critical treatment of the communal views of some heroes of the nationalist movement is unacceptable in a government publication. The memorandum concludes by complaining about the communist infiltration of the Indian National Congress and cultural institutions under the control of Congress governments.

An element in the controversy that was never explicitly confronted was the issue of how to write history—the problem of method and historiography. The disputants disagreed not only about what questions to ask and what theories and concepts to use in answering them, but also about the intimately related questions of where to look for evidence and what counts as evidence.[29] These disputes reflected in part the methodological differences among generations of historians. The reliance on texts for categories and evidence, which characterized the older generation and its scholarship through the 1940s, had been gradually supplemented by innovative approaches grounded in archaeological remains and physical evidence, and in socioeconomic frameworks of explanation. It has also been supplemented by a critical sociology-of-knowledge perspective on the texts themselves. However, the

[29]For a discussion of the efforts by self-identified 'younger historians', some of whom were progressive, to establish new concepts, explanatory frameworks, and techniques for identifying new forms of evidence and re-interpreting conventional forms, see *Problems of Historical Writing in India*, Proceedings of the Seminar held at the India International Centre, New Delhi, 21–25 January 1973. In their introduction to this collection, S. Gopal and Romila Thapar identify the overall theme of the seminar as 'the emergence of new techniques and methods of interpretation', and state as its purpose 'a probe to see what problems most required attention, both at the level of historical reconstruction in research *and at the level of teaching history* as a discipline of the Social Sciences and the Humanities' (emphasis added).

approach of younger historians is resented by those for whom *Manusmriti* is a sacred text, and not a Brahminic rationalization of the dominance of the high (twice-born) castes within Hindu society.

Some of the disputed textbooks are not beyond criticism, although one of the problematic elements—the reductionist treatment of British imperialism in India—might not trouble the author of the memorandum. *Freedom Struggle*, by Chandra, *et al.*, offers a rather pronounced historical materialist interpretation. The motives behind British actions on the subcontinent are pictured as being exclusively economic in character. Motives of an ideological kind, which might expand the framework of an explanation—evangelicalism, utilitarianism—are neglected. There is no attention to the relationship between the diverse and often contradictory British policies in India and the shifting fortunes in Britain of parties and leaders. While British historians and policy-makers are rightly castigated for a false homogenization of 'Hindus' and 'Muslims', the authors of *Freedom Struggle* regard all Englishmen as the same. They fail to differentiate among policies and ideologies of British parties. The consequences of imperialism are deemed uniformly negative: that is, the impoverishment of India. British industrial development grew on the 'economic underdevelopment and cultural backwardness of India'.[30]

The Indian National Congress, in its early phases, is pictured as being uniformly in support of progressive and nationalist economic policies. The complexities and anomalies created when early Congressmen nervously resisted as too radical the peasant-oriented policy of Congress founder and friend, Allan Octavian Hume, or when Punjab Congress lawyers opposed the progressive and pro-peasant Punjab Land Alienation Act launched by British officials, do not figure in the account.[31]

Communalism, too, loses its complexity. Communalism was certainly in part a creation of British political ideology and strategy. The authors acknowledge that it was also a result of the religious and local symbolism used by regional nationalist leaders in Maharashtra, Bengal, and Punjab to broaden the base of popular mobilization. For the authors of *Freedom Struggle*, however, communalism remains mainly an imperialist creation. They argue that Sir Saiyed Ahmed Khan, the pre-eminent leader of the 'modernist' Islamic revival in the late nineteenth century, became apprehensive about Congress

[30]*Freedom Struggle*, New Delhi: National Book Trust, 1972, pp. 30–1.
[31]For a discussion of Hume's peasant strategy and its negative reception among Congressmen and English officials, see John R. McLane, *Indian Nationalism and the Early Congress*, Princeton, New Jersey: Princeton University Press, 1977, p. 114 ff. McLane elaborates on the formulation of Congress land policies in the latter part of the nineteenth century, including the Punjab Land Alienation Act. See Chs 6–8.

nationalism because 'the British also pulled strings behind the scenes'. They reject as 'contrary to facts and unscientific and irrational'[32] Sir Saiyed's views and those of other Muslim leaders that the diversity of Indian society and Muslim corporate interest and identity are incompatible with a common Indian nationalism. Presumably, in the absence of British manipulation, a scientific and rational attitude would have led Sir Saiyed to a Congress nationalist perspective.

The textbook writers follow Jawaharlal Nehru in their belief that the religious dimension of the Pakistan demand was a mystification[33] created by Muslim landlords, who 'were afraid that the increasingly radical agrarian program of the Congress would undermine their semi-feudal position'.[34] The authors' explanatory framework cannot easily account for the fact that 'modernist' Muslims were British loyalists, and orthodox Muslims pro-Congress nationalists. In fact, any political mobilization not based on class is suspect. Even Gandhi's campaigns on behalf of India's dispossessed communities did not qualify: 'A new trend away from mass movements was the revival of Gandhiji's old concern for gaining support from the Harijans, Scheduled Castes and Tribes.'[35] In brief, the interpretive consistency of *Freedom Struggle* is achieved at the expense of attention to causes and explanations more in accord with the complexity and indeterminacy of Indian history—a shortcoming, no doubt, but one that is hardly a reason for withdrawal.

The battle over the propriety of the prime minister's suggestion that the textbooks be withdrawn from circulation raged in the press, journals of opinion, and in the parliament throughout 1977, and in early 1978.[36] On

---

[32]*Freedom Struggle*, p. 103.

[33]*Discovery of India*, New York: Anchor Books, 1959, pp. 301–16.

[34]*Freedom Struggle*, p. 209.

[35]Ibid., p. 186.

[36]In addition to the extensive coverage in English and Hindi dailies, *Mainstream* ran articles by prominent historians on 10, 24, and 31 December 1977, and 7 and 14 January, 4 February, and 4 March 1978, as did *Seminar* (221 and 222, January and February 1978), with articles by S. Gopal ('The Fear of History') and Ashis Nandy ('Self Esteem, Autonomy and Authenticity'). *Economic and Political Weekly*'s extensive coverage of the textbook controversy began with a blunderbuss attack on 'left academics' as misguided and self-serving Marxists by Sumanta Banerjee, 'Devaluation of Marxism by Leftist Academics', XIII (14), 8 April 1978. A letter entitled 'Left Academics and the Writing of History', and signed by seventeen historians, mostly from the main target of Banerjee's attack, the Centre for Historical Studies, Jawaharlal Nehru University, rebutted aspects of his article in XIII (17), 29 April. Bipin Chandra, then head of the Centre and one of Banerjee's principal targets, answered more fulsomely in 'Devaluation: Of What and By Whom?' XIII (198), 6 May. Four more issues of *Economic and Political Weekly*, XIII (19, 23, 29, and 37), 13 May, 10 June, 22 July, and 16 September, further discussed the issues of Marxist interpretation and JNU governance raised by Banerjee. Contributors included Barun De, M. Jyothi Prakasam, Sumanta Banerjee, Alice Thorner, Vasanthi Raman, Aswini K. Ray, Vijay Singh, and Harbans Mukhia. *Past and Present* (Oxford)

29 July 1977, it was discussed in the Rajya Sabha (upper house) of parliament. The education minister, P.C. Chunder, allowed that some British historians distorted Indian history, but avoided direct comment on the impugned textbooks. V.P. Dutt, a professor at Delhi University and a progressive China scholar and Congress-I member, warned that medieval history had been used by communal forces to divide the country, and pleaded for a history that promoted integration. Nurul Hasan took a position similar to the one he had expressed in 1972 at the Simla seminar on cultural policy. In his opinion, medieval Indian society, like all medieval societies, was exploitative. The religious beliefs of the rulers and the ruled were irrelevant. At the same time, Hindus and Muslims had developed common cultural traditions while retaining their own religions. It was the job of the NCERT to commission textbooks that would provide school children with wholesome history.

The practical consequences of the prime minister's suggestion became clear when R.S. Sharma's book, *Ancient India*, published in 1977 at the height of the controversy, was withdrawn in July 1978 by the Central Board of Secondary Education from the syllabus of Class XI in the 1,100 board-affiliated schools. The board's chairman, R.P. Singhal, said at the time that there was no plan to withdraw Thapar's *Medieval India*, and that no decision had yet been taken on a third prescribed textbook, Chandra's *Modern India*. Although the books were not formally withdrawn, their distribution was sharply curtailed.[37] Minister of State for Education Renuka Devi Barkataki told the Lok Sabha on 12 August that the board had acted in consultation with the NCERT and the Ministry of Education. She said the book contained some 'controversial passages'. She also listed in her statement another thirty-one books, including fourteen history textbooks, which an expert committee of the NCERT had, on the basis of 'objective criteria', recommended for withdrawal from school use. R.S. Sharma's book does not seem to have been considered in the light of the NCERT criteria, as it was not among the thirty-one books screened by the committee.[38]

It would seem that the decision to de-license R.S. Sharma's book was taken independently and at the highest levels—a surmise strengthened by

---

carried a signed editorial in its November 1977 number. *The Hindu* carried commentary in its weekly supplement. See also Aligarh Historians' Group, 'The R.S.S. Camp in the ICHR: Its First Fruits', *Social Scientist*, 7 (August–July) 1978–9, p. 58 ff.

[37]Interview with a high-ranking education official under the Janata and Congress-I governments.

[38]For an account of the minister's statement and a list of the books recommended for withdrawal, see *Data India*, 21–27 August 1978, pp. 533–4. 'Of the 31 books recommended to the States for withdrawal, 27 were considered unsuitable because their content or tenor militated against national integration or because they reflected vestiges of imperialist thinking on India. Four books were considered to have material which was not up to date or not of a high standard.'

the fact that the government denied Sharma a passport in October 1977, preventing him from leading an eight-person ICHR delegation to attend a conference in the USSR on 'Ethnic Problems of the Early History of the Peoples of Central Asia in the Second Millennium B.C'.[39] (that is, the question of who the Aryans were). Sharma had already been relieved as director of ICHR.

The alternative establishment Janata had in mind was composed of historians broadly identified with the Bharatya Vidya Bhavan, a government-sponsored organization established in 1938 as a national institution to promote education, art, and culture. Its eleven-volume *The History and Culture of the Indian People* had been edited by the late R.C. Majumdar,[40] an eminent historian, formerly professor at Dacca and Banaras, and past president of the All-India History Congress. Majumdar's historical writings in the 1950s with Kali Kinkar Datta dealt with Mughal history in a manner reminiscent of the celebratory interpretations by Vincent Smith, doyen of the British Indian historians of the pre-World War I period. For Smith, Mughal rule constituted one of the glorious eras of Indian history. By the 1960s, Majumdar had adopted a more Hindu nationalist position.[41] Muslims had become foreigners in the land. Interpreting Gandhi's 1919 alliance with Indian Muslims concerned about the Allied treatment of the *khalif* of defeated Turkey, he writes:

If a hundred million of Muslims are more vitally interested in the fate of Turkey and other Muslim states outside India than they are in the fate of India, they can hardly be regarded as a unit of the Indian nation. By his own admission that the *khilafat* issue was a vital one for Indian Muslims, Gandhi himself admitted in a way that they formed a separate nation; they were in India but not of India.[42]

[39]For details and background of this event, see Vijay C.P. Chaudhury's polemical account, partisan to the textbook writers, *Secularism Versus Communalism: An Anatomy of the National Debate on Five Controversial History Books*, Patna: Navdhara Samiti, 1977, pp. 69–79.

[40]The eleven-volume *The History and Culture of the Indian People* was published in Bombay by the Bharatya Vidya Bhavan, various years. Majumdar died at age 92, in February 1980.

[41]R.C. Majumdar, H.D. Raychaudhuri, and Kali Kinkar Datta, *An Advanced History of India*, London: Macmillan, 1953. A comparison of the treatment of the *Khilafat* issue in *An Advanced History* (p. 984) with that in volume XI of *The History and Culture of the Indian People*, Bombay: Bharatiya Vidya Bhavan, 1969, p. 319, suggests the nature of Majumdar's shift. Vincent Smith's *Akbar the Great*, Delhi: S. Chand, 1966 (second edition, third Indian reprint), is an influential work characteristic of British historiography of the medieval period.

For a critique of such Akbar eulogies on the ground that they flow from a personalized view of history and that no medieval state could 'by its very nature, be secular', see Harbans Mukhia, 'Medieval Indian History and the Communal Approach', in *Communalism and the Writing of Indian History*, by Thapar, Mukhia, and Chandra, p. 23. 'The communal historian can also afford to shower praises on Akbar's liberalism, for having done that he would be free to condemn every other ruler with the charge of dogmatism' (p. 27).

[42]*Struggle for Freedom*, vol. XI of *History and Culture of the Indian*, p. 319.

Majumdar's approach, which would limit Indian identity to only those whose roots can be shown to be wholly indigenous, raises a host of complex problems. Among these are the problem of interpreting the continuous immigration of new peoples through the Khyber Pass, and the even more complex question of the origin of the peoples referred to as the Aryans. While the evidence is complex, it is difficult to imagine any credible historical reconstruction that would deny that Vedic civilization itself had elements that were 'foreign'. The search for 'the indigenous' may well be an infinite regress.[43]

Janata's efforts to reconstitute the historical establishment began with an abortive attempt by some members to promote the appointment of Kali Kinkar Datta as chairman of the ICHR. Author of *Modern Indian History* and *Advanced History of India*, Datta had served as vice-chancellor of both Magadh and Patna Universities. Intimations of his appointment were subjected to such severe professional criticism[44] that his name was withdrawn. In the meantime, the Janata government reconstituted the council with people considered more sympathetic towards the Janata's point of view. 'The powers of certain senior officials, known for their progressive outlook, were ... reduced to bring them in line with government's thinking. And some, it is alleged, bent over backward to please Janata leaders.'[45]

By March 1980, just after the Congress returned to power, the publication programme of the ICHR had been 'virtually in cold storage for the past two years'.[46] The impasse featured the Janata government's efforts to block translations into Indian languages of the works of disfavoured authors, including the textbook authors, and to transfer of the *Towards Freedom Project* (a history of India's freedom struggle in ten volumes) to the Bharatya Vidya Bhavan, whose interpretation of history had been questioned by the earlier council members on the grounds it was 'obscurantist and communal'. The pre-Janata council had refused to translate most of the books brought out by the Bhavan in the series *History and Culture of the Indian People*, edited by Majumdar.[47] The Janata government pressed the council to revise its translations and publications programme to bring it more in line with the Bharatya Vidya Bhavan's historical perspective. After

[43]See Romila Thapar's discussion of the question in 'Communalism and the Writing of Ancient Indian History', in *Communalism and the Writing of Indian History*, p. 11. For an important new study on the archaeological, linguistic, and textual evidence linking Harappan and Aryan peoples and cultures, see Malati Shendge, *The Civilized Demons: The Harappans in the Rgveda*, New Delhi: Abhinav Publications, 1977.

[44]See Chaudhury, *Secularism*, pp. 32–41, for a vituperative version of the criticism.

[45]Hasan Suroor, 'Historians in Cold Storage', *The Statesman*, 9 March 1980.

[46]Ibid.

[47]Ibid.

the Indian History Congress (India's oldest and largest professional body of historians) strongly endorsed the textbook writers,[48] the Janata government encouraged the creation of, and helped to fund, the Indian History and Culture Society. It attracted a variety of members, including some sympathetic to the RSS, and others unsympathetic to the textbook 'establishment'. A distinguished Muslim historian became its first president.

In 1978, A.R. Kulkarni, a respected historian not directly involved in the textbook controversy, was appointed chairman of the ICHR. In May 1981, at the end of Kulkarni's term and sixteen months after the Congress had returned to power, the late Niharranjan Ray, a respected cultural historian less involved in these cultural battles (but quite active in Bengal), became chairman. Ray's initial act was to suspend the research grants of ten historians appointed under Janata auspices, and order an inquiry into the manner in which they were funded.[49] Clearly, the problem of maintaining an autonomous realm for quasi-government agencies charged with supporting culture had not been solved yet.

IMPLICATIONS OF CULTURAL POLICY FOR POLITICS AND INDIAN IDENTITY

We conclude by returning to the origins of the textbook controversy, and some observations on its bearing on cultural policy. Prime Minister Desai was urged in a confidential memorandum to not only proscribe certain textbooks, but to also appoint a committee to investigate the infiltration by persons of 'communist' persuasion into academic positions, research grants, publication subsidies, and teaching positions. His suggestion to the education minister that the textbooks be withdrawn from circulation in the schools was accompanied by a more general campaign against so-called 'communist' historians and social scientists. They were said to be entrenched in the ICHR, JNU's Centre for Historical Studies, the Institute for Social Studies, and even the University Grants Commission (UGC), the Indian Council for Social Science Research (ICSSR), and the NCERT. From these bastions they propounded a wrong and dangerous view of Indian history and culture, and promoted the partisan and personal interests of those who thought as they did.

The response to the Janata cultural fundamentalist attack was to depict it as part of an effort to destroy some of India finest institutions and most

[48]See Romila Thapar, 'Sources of Encroachment on Academic Freedom', *Radical Humanist*, 43 (11), 1979.
[49]*The Statesman*, 19 and 23 April 1981.

promising careers. Both sides became deeply suspicious of their opponents' motives and goals. In time, the secularism issue surfaced within Janata itself, contributing to its demise.

Janata's cultural policy has to be understood not only in terms of the prime minister's endorsement of policies and cultural interpretations that challenged and sought to displace what he perceived to be the Congress's excessively secularist and progressive formulations, but also in terms of Janata's response to the historic opportunity its 1977 electoral victory created. Janata was driven by two contradictory impulses, the first statesmanly, the second partisan. Its statesmanly objectives included restoring the constitution and reconstituting the party system in a two-party mode. Its partisan objective was to exploit the powers of incumbency in order to consolidate and expand its party advantage. Its loosely consolidated factions seized the opportunity to allocate patronage and resources to their respective minions. It tried to displace what were perceived to be Mrs Gandhi's beneficiaries and acolytes in cultural and academic posts.

While Janata made solid advances towards its first objective of restoring the constitution, it proceeded to destroy itself in pursuit of the second. The intra- and inter-party struggle over power, spoils, and ideology destroyed Janata's fragile credibility and unity. In the process, it also aborted the short-lived period of the national two-party competition.

The secularist issue within the party took the form of an attack on 'dual membership'—that is, simultaneously belonging to Janata and the RSS. The attack became credible and effective in the wake of two distinct but mutually reinforcing developments: a factional re-alignment that involved the erstwhile Jan Sangh shifting its support from Charan Singh's BKD to Desai's Congress-O; and Desai's tilt towards a cultural orientation and policy initiatives that were more Hindu-communalist than Gandhian.

The textbook authors were in a poignant position. As opponents or critics of Mrs Gandhi's authoritarian regime, a number of them had been supporters of persons now associated with the Janata. At the same time, they were long-term beneficiaries of the Congress governments' policies and resources that supported their secularist social scientific and/or progressive history. In Janata's eyes, they seemed appropriate targets for a partisan reallocation of cultural and academic posts and resources. Thus, the communalist attack was not wholly ideological: it was also intended to provide access to resources, organizations, and career opportunities for those who had been in the political and academic wilderness for a generation or more.

The textbook controversy raised two complementary issues in the making of cultural policy, one instrumental, and the other constitutive: the role of partisan or personal interests in the allocation of scholarly resources and authority; and the political consequences that historical interpretations have for Indian identity and public philosophy. Neither is easily resolved.

Could personal and partisan struggles over resources, prestige, and scholarly standards have been avoided if the central government had abandoned the practice of selecting (that is, officially commissioning, prescribing, and/or producing) textbooks for use in the proportionately small but enormously influential centrally-controlled school sector? This was the position taken by Ashis Nandy, who damned both sides in the textbook controversy for countenancing state intervention and patronage. For Nandy, it was the rules of the game, not the writing and teaching of good or bad history, which were at fault in India's cultural policy: '[T]he votaries of academic freedom today [1978] are the ones who have systematically tolerated if not built the organizational means and the theoretical justification for state interference in intellectual affairs. ... [They] are fighting in Professor Majumdar an aspect of themselves they have never disowned.'[50] But what happens when textbooks are selected from private publishers by bureaucracies representing state education departments, principals, or boards of study? There is little evidence to suggest that they consistently prefer scholarly, engaging texts published by independent, established firms to shoddy or partisan ones. Economically and politically vulnerable firms spring like mushrooms from the soil of cosy patron-client relationships between local educational institutions and entrepreneurs. Given the well-documented limitations of India's myriad and often ephemeral private-sector publishing firms, the practice of commissioning and/or selecting texts by agencies of the central government, in consultation with professional historians, has a better chance of protecting scholarly standards than does risking the debilitating effects of an imperfect market.

If the central government is to encourage and protect scholarly standards, better means are required to insulate nominally autonomous bodies from the consequences of the partisan political struggle and efforts at personal aggrandizement. Organizations such as the ICHR, NCERT, and National Book Trust are meant to be autonomous bodies capable of acting on scholarly and professional criteria. They attempt to combine state financing and personnel selection with the putative benefits of autonomous, authentic, valid scholarship, and its presentation in school texts. Autonomy, however, is conditioned by the motives of those who offer appointments, and the expectations of those who accept them. The textbook controversy

---

[50]'Self Esteem, Autonomy and Authenticity', *Seminar*, 222 (February), 1978, p. 26.

and the related struggle over the leadership and policies of the ICHR make clear that the insulation and agreed norms required for autonomy have been, and will continue to be, difficult to realize in India.

Can different procedures or conventions lend non-partisan legitimacy and professional authority to autonomous bodies such as the ICHR? If decisions about the selection of personnel and the allocation of patronage had been more even-handed, as that between different schools of thought and research traditions, could the inevitable backlash that accompanies power and policy shifts have been made compatible with professional autonomy? Greater tolerance of interpretations and methodologies might have strengthened rather than divided the scholarly community of historians served by the ICHR. Perhaps the depth and variety of cleavages among historians—cleavages that are sharpened by the congruence of methodological and substantive positions (for example, left, secular, social history vs. right, communal, textualist history)—defy solution by the equitable procedures that recognize diversity. For S. Gopal of the Centre for Historical Studies at JNU, R.C. Majumdar in his later years was not only wrong, but also incompetent.[51] Bringing secularists and communalists under cover of a common definition of professionalism may be as difficult as getting a professional consensus on the origins of man from creationists and evolutionists in American school systems. Scholarly communities having a significant degree of consensus can more assuredly insist on the preservation of their autonomy, whereas deep cleavages invite political intervention by the government.

The textbook controversy renewed a century-old effort to articulate a national identity and public philosophy for India. Partition, followed by the Nehru consensus on the secular state, left many unanswered questions, including ones about India's minorities. Not least among them was how to interpret the role of Muslims in Indian history. The incorporation—or alienation—of seventy million people (11 per cent of the population) depends in considerable measure on historical interpretation. Interpretation, in turn, depends on historiography—the criteria scholars accept and use for historical research. Historiographical and interpretative differences go beyond positive and negative evaluations of Muslim conquest and rule, and their alien or assimilated relationship with Indian culture, to arrive at a question not unique to India: namely, whether the scholarly pursuit of historical knowledge can be compatible with the creation of a shared national identity and public philosophy.

[51]'The Fear of History', *Seminar*, 221 (January), 1978, p. 2.

Nehru's secularism was based on a commitment to a scientific humanism tinged with a progressive view of historical change. Gandhi's secularism was based on a commitment to the brotherhood of religious communities based on their respect for and pursuit of truth. The elites of the founding generation used, but did not replenish, the political and cultural capital that Nehru's and Gandhi's leadership created.

While Congress secularism has served Muslims well, it has not faced up ideologically to the causes and consequences of a persisting Muslim cultural identity for India's national identity and public philosophy. The textbook writers, for the most part, sympathized with Nehru's position. He had avoided or minimized the issue of a Muslim presence by interpreting Muslim historical and contemporary interests in political and class rather than religious terms; by claiming that there was a scientific humanist and progressive culture and a secular state public philosophy to which Muslims could and should be assimilated; and by applying a double standard to Muslim and Hindu communalism. Gandhi united his commitments to social pluralism and brotherhood through his understanding that, like a diamond, truth— including religious truth—was multi-faceted. Adherents to different faiths could respect each other as a brotherhood of truth-seekers. His formulation came closer than Nehru's to accommodating a distinct Muslim presence in the Indian nation and state. Gandhi's approach has been abandoned by the Congress, and betrayed by the Janata communalist group. When the Janata cultural fundamentalists challenged the Nehru cultural settlement by raising the textbook controversy, they made apparent that many Hindus— and some historians—did not adhere to that settlement or its public philosophy of a secular state, and equal citizenship for all religious minorities.

We are grateful for comments to members of the South Asia Political Economy Workshop at the University of Chicago, where a previous version of this paper was read. Ingrid Grinde and Sunita Parikh have conducted research under our guidance on similar problems for their MA papers in the Master of Arts Program in the Social Sciences, the University of Chicago. Their research has helped us with subsequent drafts.

10

Demand Groups and Pluralist Representation in India*

LLOYD I. RUDOLPH AND SUSANNE HOEBER RUDOLPH

Interest-group representation in India is marked by pluralist rather than corporatist forms and processes; its pluralism differs from that in other industrial democracies. Our conceptual vocabulary for the discussion of representation introduces three terms, *demand group*, *state-dominated pluralism*, and *involuted pluralism*, to designate aspects of the organization and representation of interests that distinguish pluralism in India. Unlike organized interests, the demand group relies on *ad hoc* rather than bureaucratic organization. It uses mass mobilization more than expert knowledge and technical bargaining, but combines issue and movement politics with the politics of organized interests. Other characteristics of the Indian variant of pluralism are its domination by the state, and its tendency towards excessive multiplication and fragmentation, a process we call involution. Finally, the pervasive and powerful state not only constrains and manipulates interest group activity, it is also itself a major interest, competing with and usually surpassing societal interests. On the one hand, the state sets policy agendas. It controls legal and economic incentives, and both fosters and manipulates involuted pluralism. On the other, in its various industrial, financial, and commercial manifestations, it commands more resources than the societal interests with which such manifestations of the state compete. State producer interests and policy bodies occupy much of the representational 'space' that is occupied in other industrial democracies by pluralist and corporatist structures and processes. They also speak and act on their own behalf as institutional interests in the context of governmental pluralism.

*Originally published as 'Demand Groups and Pluralist Representation in India', in *Journal of Commonwealth and Comparative Politics*, XXIV (3), November 1986, pp. 227–38.

Two parameters or initial conditions affect the organization of producer interests in India: (*i*) location in the organized or the unorganized economies; and (*ii*) the dominance, within the organized economy, of the public sector. That only 10 per cent of all workers are in the organized economy, and 90 per cent in the unorganized, affects the base on which the formal representation of interest thaws, and shapes the type of interest-group organization specific to India. The demand group, a particular variant of interest representation that we discuss below, is in part a consequence of the scale of India's unorganized economy. Within the organized economy, about two-thirds of the salaried and wage workers are employed by public-sector firms or the government, and of the 100 largest firms, public-sector firms control 76 per cent of the paid-up capital employed.[1] Such state domination of the organized economy is a pre-condition for its domination of pluralist representation. Formally organized interests are more common and more important for policy choice and implementation in the organized economy than they are in the unorganized, where *ad hoc* issue and movement politics using agitational and symbolic means play a larger role.

PLURALISM AND NEO-CORPORATISM: SOME CONCEPTUAL DISTINCTIONS

In treating representation in terms of pluralist and corporatist modes, we take interest rather than class as the basic motivating and organizing principle of political economy. Unlike most Marxist treatments, which take it as axiomatic and pre-determined that only the mode and relations of production define social formations, and that class so defined is the ultimate determinant of consciousness and action, we treat interest phenomenologically and contingently. Interests can be expressed through a variety of social formations—class, caste, tribe, or status group; religious, linguistic, or territorial community; profession or occupation defined in terms of skill, knowledge, and ethos, as well as in terms of property relations. The existence, goals, and ascendance of such social formations are as much a matter of context and choice as of objective determination.

The most common conceptualization of pluralist representation is interest-group pluralism.[2] American in its origin and development and closely

---

[1] For argument and evidence, see Chapter 1 of our *In Pursuit of Lakshmi: The Political Economy of the Indian State*, Chicago: University of Chicago Press, 1987.

[2] For a review of relevant theory, see J.D. Greenstone, 'Group Theories', in *The Handbook of Political Science*, by F. Greenstein and N. Polsby (eds), Reading, MA: Addison-Wesley, 1975, vol. 4, and Cyril E. Black and John P. Burke, 'Organizational Participation and Public Policy', *World Politics*, 35 (3), 1983.

related to liberalism, it became in the 1950s and 1960s a conceptual export that followed in the wake of the then rising curve of American world power and influence. It posits an equilibrium model of competing but ultimately harmonious organized interests. Anybody who feels the need to represent his or her interest can participate by joining with like-minded persons in a formal organization. Tocqueville held that America's associational life helped to combine liberty and democracy. Unless equal, but isolated and powerless, individuals were to combine in associations, democracies would be prone to tyranny, and citizens would be unable to limit and influence state action. Associations in democracies would constrain and direct popular sovereignty.

Like classical theories of market economics, interest-group pluralism relies on an equilibrium model for reconciling the pursuit of individual interest with the realization of the public good. An invisible hand is said to guide market transactions and interest-group bargains in ways that translate private interest into public. Just as buyers and sellers in markets get the goods they prefer for the prices they want to pay, so too do competing interest groups in policy arenas produce a policy outcome that is in the public interest. Persuasion, bargaining, and deliberation among interdependent but competing interests eventuate in harmonious equilibria that approximate what is best for all and for each.

In America, for some time the frontier, abundance, and a rapidly expanding economy obscured, if not eliminated, the zero-sum possibilities of interest-group competition. In time sympathetic as well as hostile critics showed in a variety of ways how the practice of interest-group pluralism led to consequences that were not anticipated by the model. Private power became the master of public power as vested interests appropriated public authority and resources by capturing state agencies. Just as inequalities of income, wealth, and power made for market imperfections, which contradicted the assumption that consumers and workers could engage in mutually beneficial exchanges with producers and employers, so did the absence or inequality of organizational and political resources enable vested interests to dominate policy choice and implementation. Many of those most in need of representation did not or could not benefit from interest groups. Members lost control or were alienated as interest-group bureaucrats became organizational masters. Those who managed interest organizations found it difficult to distinguish their personal goals and interests from those of the members they were intended to serve.

Contradictions became increasingly manifest between party government and executive leadership on the one hand, and the representational infrastructure through which interest-group pluralism operated on the other. Instead of the equilibrium and harmony that yielded the public interest, stalemate among interests and among separated and balanced institutions became common. The multiplication of, and competition between, interests often blocked legislative action.

Despite these and other criticisms, interest-group pluralism as theory and practice persists in America, India, and other industrial democracies because it is more than an explanation of societal-state relations. In part, it persists because associational life, like class, is a common feature of industrial democracies. It also persists because the right of citizen voters to associate independently is perceived as an essential aspect of liberty. If organized interests often represent the rich and the powerful more than the poor and the oppressed, if 'overmighty subjects' in industrial democracies sometimes dominate policy and the state, at other times associations limit state power in ways that protect their members' values and interests, the workers in Poland who in 1980 rallied behind Solidarity to challenge an oppressive regime, and the disadvantaged minority communities (Muslims, Harijans) who in 1977 helped to turn Indira Gandhi's authoritarian regime out of office, suggest that liberty to associate can serve both unvested and vested interests. As long as sovereignty-seeking states and the elites that staff them serve themselves, the right to association and to independent representation that interest-group pluralism makes possible will remain a collective good.

Pluralism and neo-corporatism can be viewed as contrasting models of state-society relations. They posit contrasting patterns for the organization and representation of interests, and for the formulation and choice of public policy. The pluralist model arose from a normative theory that values liberty for individuals, and for the voluntary associations they should be free to form. Voluntary associations are meant to pursue the interests of their members independent of state sovereignty or the compulsions of corporate and bureaucratic governance. Pluralist forms and processes of political participation and representation are held to determine public choices of policies and leaders in ways that both limit and direct state action. For these reasons, the pluralist organization and representation of interests has an elective affinity to politics, which emphasize voter sovereignty rather than politics that favour state sovereignty.

Neo-corporatism, as a model for the organization and representation of interests, echoes medieval and mercantilist forms for the compulsory and monopolistic representation of interests. Status orders (for example, estates, *Stände*), craft producers (for example, guilds), and state-licensed pre-industrial commercial and manufacturing companies structurally prefigure neo-corporatist forms and processes of representation. At the same time, neo-corporatism is a response to the concentration, bureaucratization, and interdependence of producer interests in industrial economies.

The neo-corporatist model posits vested, hierarchical, monopolistic, and compulsory apex bodies for producer interests organized in firms, unions, and professional associations.[3] Led by bureaucratic professionals, apex bodies negotiate with each other and with state agencies to gain benefits, avoid losses, and concert policy in well-established policy arenas. State civil servants and apex-body professional bureaucrats shape policy agendas and bargain over the formulation and choice of policy for whole industries, sectors, or the national economy. Whether by *de facto* appropriation or *de jure* command, apex bodies acquire not only collective, but also parastatal (public) authority, which enables them to govern and compel 'members'— the individuals involved in firms, unions, and professional associations— as well as the lesser intermediate organizations joined together in peak associations. The neo-corporatist organization and representation of interests has an elective affinity to politics that favour state over voter sovereignty, and public over private power in policy-making.

Viewed historically, pluralism in contemporary industrial democracies has been associated with older patterns of policy determination by legislatures, and neo-corporatism with the functional representation of organized producer and professional interests. As cabinet or presidential governments have come to limit the influence of voters and interests acting through legislative representatives, the influence of the permanent government and of functionally organized producer groups has increased. The growth of oligopoly and monopoly in industry, labour, and professional markets was paralleled by the growth of hierarchical representative bodies that tended to impose policy choices rather than reflect members' preferences, and to govern by compulsion rather than by consent. In these emergent historical conditions, the pluralist vision of open, voluntary, competitive, but ultimately harmonious, organized interests became harder to sustain. Concerting the functional interests of organized producers with professional counter-players

---

[3]See, for example, Stephen S. Cohen, *Modern Capitalist Planning: The French Model*, Cambridge, M.A.: Harvard University Press, 1979; L. Panitch, 'The Development of Corporatism in Liberal Democracies', *Comparative Political Studies*, 10 (1), 1977; Richard Wiley, 'Trade Unionism and Political Parties in the Federal Republic of Germany', *Industrial Labor Relations Review*, 2, 1974; Andrew Shonfield, *Modern Capitalism: The Changing Balance of Public and Private Power*, London and New York: Oxford University Press, 1969; Philippe C. Schmitter, 'Modes of Interest Intermediation and Models of Societal Change in Western Europe', and Gerhard Lehmbruch, 'Liberal Corporatism and Party Government', both in *Comparative Political Studies*, 10 (1), 1977, and the composite volume edited by Suzanne Berger, *Organizing Interests in Western Europe: Pluralism, Corporatism and the Transformation of Politics*, New York: Cambridge University Press, 1981. Gabriel A. Almond's review of this volume traces the connections between the more recent corporatist literature and the older pluralist writings, appropriately upbraiding the recent literature for its professional amnesia concerning the earlier, 'Corporatism, Pluralism and Professional Memory', *World Politics*, 35 (2), 1983.

in the permanent government was said to be a more appropriate means to reconcile private and public power, and private and public interests than pluralism's invisible hand guiding many competitive and conflicting interests to public-interest outcomes. As neo-corporatist representation, bargaining, and concertation in state-sanctioned policy arenas became more institutionalized, they tended to rival or displace not only legislative determination of policy, but also pluralist representation.

In contrast to the Anglo-American world which is the home of pluralism,[4] Western Europe, Japan, and Latin America have proved more hospitable to neo-corporatism. State-society relations in India are closer to the Anglo-American than the continental European world. India's associational life has not moved in the direction of a few monopolistic and compulsory apex bodies, capable of hierarchical domination of members' choices, but continues to sustain a large variety of competitive associations, especially in the fields of labour and industry. In 1975, the Gandhi government's authoritarian regime attempted to displace pluralist by neo-corporatist forms in the organization and representation of interests. This effort proved abortive when the electorate in 1977 repudiated authoritarian rule, and with it the initial attempts at state corporatism. What distinguishes Indian from Anglo-American pluralism is the emergence of the demand group as a representational form especially responsive to the unorganized sector; the extraordinary multiplication and fragmentation of pluralist associations which we call involution; and the role of the state sector, which crowds organized interests to the margin of the political and policy arenas, and fragments their potential countervailing power.

THE DEMAND GROUP AS PLURALIST ACTOR IN POLITICS AND POLICY

In examining Indian pluralism, we conceive of interest groups as encompassing two forms, organized interests and demand groups. We use the phrase 'demand groups' to signal that this unit of Indian pluralism exhibits different characteristics than do organized interests in other industrial democracies.

[4]'The interest group structure can be characterized as pluralist ... even increasingly so in its multiplicity, autonomy and fragmentation.' Philippe C. Schmitter and Donald Brand, 'Organizing Capitalists in the United States: The Advantages and Disadvantages of Exceptionalism', Paper presented at the meeting of the American Political Science Association, September 1979. Schmitter and Brand lay much of the causal burden for American pluralism on the anti-trust tradition (p. 69 ff). Grant McConnell, *Private Power and American Democracy*, New York: Knoff, 1966, represents the pluralist critique. See also T. Lowi, 'American Business, Public Policy, Case Studies and Political Theory', *World Politics*, 16, 1964, and *The End of Liberalism*, New York: Norton, 1969; and P. Bachrach, *The Theory of Democratic Elitism: A Critique*, Boston: Little Brown, 1967.

Formally organized interests exist in India and affect state-society relations and the policy process, but they have not been as important as demand groups, a more spontaneous and less formed type of collective action. Demand groups are a form that interest representation can take in competitive, open democracies when political mobilization of mass publics outstrips or overflows the formal institutions of the political process.[5] They are an expression of movement and issue politics. They do not so much replace organized interests as incorporate and transcend them. Unlike movement politics in other industrial democracies, which are usually an alternative to and competitive with organized interests, in India the combination in demand groups of movement politics and formally organized interest groups tends to be complementary rather than competitive. By raising new issues and mobilizing support for them, demand groups try to transform state and national policy agendas and gain bargaining advantages.

Formally organized interests work in institutionally defined policy arenas. They attempt to influence legislatures, bureaucratic agencies, and sometimes party policy. They develop elaborate organizational infrastructure, including a headquarters bureaucracy, means of internal communication for members, external communication to relevant publics, and research staffs. Their means of influence is technical and professional expertise and knowledge, and legal and legislative skills. The idea of an organized interest group implies a certain professionalization of the representative process. The force of its case rests on technical persuasiveness as much as, or more, than the pressure of numbers.

Demand groups, by contrast, do not work primarily in institutionally defined policy arenas. They are less likely to rely on expertise and lobbying skill than on symbolic and agitational politics. The tactics and style of demand groups have become a highly elaborated political art form that speaks to India's indigenous political culture, mobilizes support, influences public opinion, and gains bargaining advantages. Its *ad hoc* and spontaneous tactics include public dramas such as *padyatras* (political pilgrimages); *hartals* (shutdowns); *rasta rokhos* (road blockages); and *gheraos* (lock-ins). The grandfather of such public dramas was Gandhi's salt march to the sea in 1930. One of the more striking post-independence manifestations was agrarian leader Charan Singh's 'birthday party' in 1979, when 100,000 north Indian cultivators arrived at Delhi's Boat Club grounds by tractor and bullock cart to attend the extravaganza.

---

[5]Mobilizations that overflow formal political processes bear a family resemblance to what Huntington calls political decay. Our point is that such mobilizations are problematic, but not necessarily degenerative. See Samuel P. Huntington, *Political Order in Changing Societies*, New Haven: Yale University Press, 1968.

Interest groups work more *in camera*, demand groups out of doors. Demand groups tend to agitate first and bargain later. The force of their case rests on its dramatic visibility and demonstration of massive support, and sometimes on the disruption of public services. The transactions of organized interest groups take place between the knowledgeable professional and bureaucratic counter-players, while the transactions of demand groups take place between supporters mobilized in favour of an issue on the one hand, and governmental elites and public opinion on the other. While organized interests represent functionally specific producer interests—dockworkers, steel workers, tobacco growers—the demand group represents whole sectors—agriculture, students, workers. Demand groups attempt to mobilize on behalf of the collective good of a sector rather than to garner gains for functionally specific interests.

The demand group escapes some of the oligarchical aspects of formally organized interests, dominance by the organization's bureaucrats and professionals ('the iron law of oligarchy'), and a propensity to under-represent or ignore the less well-placed members and the disadvantaged among potential constituencies.[6] Demand groups arise when organized interests and political parties fail to represent or reach them. Since demand groups attempt to mobilize large numbers, they must appeal to and involve the poor and powerless even if they do not deliver equal benefits to them.

Groups characterized by the qualities we ascribe to the demand group have fared badly in that part of the development literature which emphasizes state capacity at the expense of participation.[7] These accounts portray an associational life that helps the state regulate and reduce demands. Thus, Almond contrasts 'sporadic, latent, diffuse, particular and affective' groups whose style is 'constant, manifest, specific, general and instrumental'.[8] The latter play a 'regulatory role ... in processing raw claims ... and directing them in an orderly way and in an agreeable form through the party system, legislature and bureaucracy'.[9] This formulation implies that there is no ground between 'responsible' interest groups that collaborate with the state, and anomic shapeless and implicitly dangerous behaviour.

[6]For an analysis which calls for interest groups that can serve as more efficient and broad-based channels for increased participation, see Stein Rokkan, 'Mass Suffrage, Secret Voting and Political Participation', in *Political Sociology*, by Lewis Coser (ed.), New York: Harper Torchbooks, 1966.

[7]See, for example, Huntington, *Political Order in Changing Societies*; Gabriel Almond, 'A Functional Approach in Comparative Politics', in *The Politics of the Developing Areas*, by Gabriel Almond and James Coleman (eds), Princeton, NJ: Princeton University Press, 1960; Gabriel Almond and G. Bingharu Powell, *Comparative Politics: A Developmental Approach*, Boston: Princeton University Press, 1966.

[8]Almond, 'A Functional Approach', pp. 33–8.

[9]Ibid., pp. 35–6.

Samuel Huntington portrays political decay as the outstripping of institutional processes by political mobilization. In his view, parties and interest groups contribute to development when they filter demands and insulate established political leadership from inchoate political demands. Almond, too, finds that organized interests, by reducing and regulating the expression of demands, protect the government against demand overloads. Both regard 'spontaneous' demand from below as a threat to vulnerable political institutions rather than as a form of political participation. As Robert Bianchi points out in his critique of this approach, 'Almond appears to regard ... interest articulation as the most expendable function'.[10]

In our analysis, demand groups articulate communities of interest that are unrecognized by institutional processes. They are more often a reaction to inflexible and unresponsive institutionalization than manifestations of 'excessive' mobilization. Effective demand groups usually signal that the institutional process—parties, organized interests, legislatures, and bureaucracies—are insufficiently accessible or responsive, unable or unwilling to hear the voices of unrecognized constituencies.

The natural habitat of the demand group is India's unorganized economy, which outnumbers the organized economy nine to one. While there is a far from absolute correlation between the presence of formal interest organizations and location in the organized sector of the economy, organized interests are more common and effective in it. At the same time, the scale of the unorganized economy (agriculture, small-scale industry, and commerce) affects the balance between organized interests and demand groups in Indian politics and policy. Demand groups share the less bureaucratized and less professional character of producers in the unorganized economy. The difference between organized interests and demand groups is also shaped by different levels of consciousness and articulation. As producers and as voters, potential supporters of demand groups have had little or no experience with organized representation and participatory politics. Organized interests assume that there is a 'group' with an interest that it knows and wishes to advance.[11] The problem is to represent a manifest interest. The demand group has yet to recognize itself; it is still 'becoming'. The problem of demand groups is to create the group consciousness of an interest, as well as to represent it.

---

[10]Robert Bianchi, *Interest Groups and Political Development in Turkey*, Princeton: Princeton University Press, 1984.

[11]For a view that assumes that interests already exist, as against the emphasis here on the demand group as a form that is becoming, see Berger, *Organizing Interests in Western Europe*. Berger's own formulation begs the question of representation of the unorganized and unmobilized. The demand group creates consciousness and organization as part of the process of representation and bargaining.

Demand groups are lineal descendants of the opinion out of doors and the 'self-appointed' and 'self-serving associations' that, according to Edmund Burke and George Washington, threatened the republican government and representative democracy. Today, as in the late eighteenth century, the 'opinion out of doors' that demand groups mobilize is perceived by authorities and vested interests as threatening governability. However, world time casts a different light on demand groups in contemporary India. Universal suffrage, associational life, organized opinion, and political parties have become, as they were not in the late eighteenth century, legitimate aspects of representative democracy. The opinion out of doors that helped to establish civil, political and, later, social rights were thought to be unfortunate and dangerous aberrations that could be eliminated once their goals were achieved. But this was not to be. Persistent discrepancies between the formal equality and actual inequality of political and economic power left ample scope and justification for the persistence of issue and movement politics. Demand groups persist, but create dilemmas. They perfect democracy and promote more equal bargaining by mobilizing the voters and lower constituencies slighted or ignored by organized interests. But they create problems of governability when they jeopardize public order and a government of laws.

INDIAN VARIANTS OF PLURALISM

The validity of interest-group pluralism as an explanatory social science concept has been vitiated by the anomalies and contradictions that have accompanied its application in industrial democracies. Nevertheless it remains, with class-based theories, one of the reigning paradigms for explaining society-state relations in governance and policy. Efforts to keep it viable as a social science theory have produced variants that recognize the paradigm, but make significant amendments or innovations to it.[12] Two variants we find helpful for explaining state-society relations and the policy process in India are state-dominated pluralism and involuted pluralism.

Under state-dominated pluralism, the political arena is populated by relatively autonomous interest groups, but they are overshadowed by an omnipresent state. Much of the organizational and representational 'space' occupied by pluralist actors and processes in the Anglo-American world,

[12]See, for example, David Greenstone's suggestion that the transformation of previously quiescent groups into significant political actors demanding major social change need not be accounted for by a stability-disruption-protest model, but can be accounted for by focusing on a class-like objective interest analysis, identifying large stable social groups as the units of analysis, and recognizing that such groups may come to an increased recognition of previously unrecognized objective interests. Greenstone, 'Group Theories', p. 290.

and by societal corporatism in Western Europe, is in India occupied by state agencies. This is not surprising in a state that opted, in the industrial policy resolutions of 1948 and 1956, for a mixed economy in which the public sector would dominate the 'commanding heights'; in the 1960s nationalized finance capitalism—banks and insurance; and had at its command a proliferating series of long-term state lending institutions. By occupying the commanding heights of industrial and finance capital, the state also came to occupy the commanding heights of the representational infrastructure. At the same time, the line between the public and private sectors has become increasingly obscure as state-controlled lending institutions and equity holders—the Life Insurance Corporation of India, Unit Trust, etc.— have acquired sufficient equity in private-sector firms to give them, potentially, the power to control management.

The pervasiveness of the state in India also affects the professional and occupational associations that occupy autonomous space in most other industrial democracies. If the 'free professions' constitute a significant part of the autonomous associations in which European middle-class society organizes itself, this is less true in India. The vast majority of doctors, scientists, engineers, teachers, and professors are employees of government organizations. Since the government is the principal employer of managers, technicians, and clerks, generally speaking the white-collar class, the interests of India's non-capitalist non-property owning middle classes are closely related to those of the state.

The state's prominence does not mean that there are no arenas of group autonomy. The political sociologist has a different story to tell from the political economist. Religious communities, caste associations, cultural, ethnic, and linguistic groups, a large range of non-producer social forces generally, lie beyond close regulation or manipulation by the state. If, in the economic arena, the state occupies much of the 'space' that in America and Europe is occupied by pluralist and corporatist forces, in the social arena it occupies less space. As a consequence, it faces powerful political and policy challenges from cultural, ethnic, and linguistic groups.

The state dominates pluralist representation through its direction of the policy process as well as through its control of public-sector industrial and finance capital and its employment of professionals. The state controls the policy agenda, for example, policy initiatives and choice; directs, through the use of incentives and sanctions, the organizational and market behaviour of organized interests, firms, and industries; and powerfully influences particular policy arenas by establishing favoured relationships with one among a plurality of organized interests in that arena.

The state controls the policy agenda to a remarkable degree. As Stanley Kochanek put it in his *Business and Politics in India*:

Policy initiatives usually come from government ... not from the larger society ... so most groups are forced to take a negative or defensive rather than a positive stance ... the pattern of public policy ... has concentrated vast powers in the hands of government officials. This power enables them to control and regulate the internal affairs and external conduct of business, trade unions, and other organizations ... far from being ... an outcome of interest group activity, as group theory would have it, public policy in India exerts a significant impact on group mobilization and on behaviour.[13]

State control of the policy agenda is most clearly expressed in the Planning Commission's perspective, Five-Year and annual plans. *Inter alia*, targets for most of the investment in the organized economy and for infrastructure (power, irrigation, transport, etc.) are set by Planning Commission allocations. State incentives and sanctions, what critics at home and abroad call the permit licence raj, are exercised through governmental licensing of production and production levels, control of foreign exchange, imports, and determination of agricultural prices and input costs. The state's monopoly of credit, together with its taxing powers provides it with extraordinarily powerful means to encourage or deter market and organizational behaviour.

The state's establishment of a special relationship with one of many organized interests in particular policy arenas is best illustrated by the arena of industrial relations, where the state, under Congress governments, has maintained a special relationship with INTUC (Indian National Trade Union Conference). Congress party governments have been in power at the Centre almost continuously since independence. INTUC, the Congress-affiliated trade union federation, has for the most part followed the party's, and thus the government's and the state's, policy line. INTUC does not have a licensed monopoly to represent organized labour, as would be the case under neo-corporatist arrangements. There are strains in its relationship with state agencies and the Congress-I party. They arise when INTUC tries to simultaneously maintain its competitive position in a pluralist universe, as well as its special relationship with Congress governments. But without government support and patronage, INTUC could not have remained India's largest trade union federation, and without INTUC collaboration Congress governments could not have been as successful as they have been in manipulating and controlling organized labour and industrial relations policy.

---

[13]S. Kochanek, *Business and Politics in India*, Berkeley: University of California Press, 1974, p. xii.

The second distinctive pluralist variant found in India is involuted pluralism. It has been one of the ways that the state has dominated interest-group pluralism. Involution refers to a continuing process and the resultant structural condition, the excessive multiplication of less effectual units. A leading example is the agricultural involution that Geertz observed.[14] Pluralist involution contrasts with the opposite of oligopolistic and monopolistic tendencies of interest-group pluralism, which can eventuate in neo-corporatism. We use involution as a metaphor for the decline or loss of vigour. Involution results when a viable, intensively elaborated pattern of development is extensively elaborated by continuous replication of units. Such replication not only weakens each successive unit, but also weakens all units collectively, and thus the activity as a whole. In this sense, more becomes less. It is a regressive debilitating process that results in decreasing effectiveness or entropy, the reverse of evolution.

We have shown elsewhere how the impact of the state on industrial capitalism includes a mild form of involution, as smaller private capitalist firms are encouraged to multiply by the structure of incentives and disincentives deployed by the state's economic management.[15] Similarly, the state has advanced a pronounced process of involution among the organized workforce so that an increasing number of trade unions compete for a limited constituency of easily organized workers.[16] In both instances, the effect of involution is to enable the state to manipulate an increasing number of weaker units. Involuted pluralism as a form of representational mediation strengthens state sovereignty as against voter sovereignty.

What is distinctive about pluralist representation in India is the presence of two novel actors, the demand group and the state as the largest producer interest, and two novel structural variants, state-dominated pluralism and involuted pluralism. These elements of the representational infrastructure have an independent effect on the prevailing balance between state and voter sovereignty. Demand groups favour the ascendancy of voter sovereignty while the state's role as producer, state-dominated pluralism, and involuted pluralism favour the ascendancy of state sovereignty.

[14]C. Geertz, *Agricultural Involution; The Process of Ecological Change in Indonesia*, Berkeley: University of California Press, 1970, pp. 81–2.

[15]See our *In Pursuit of Lakshmi*, Chapter 1.

[16]Ibid., Chapter 10.

11

The Iconization of Chandrababu
Sharing Sovereignty in India's Federal Market Economy*

LLOYD I. RUDOLPH AND SUSANNE HOEBER RUDOLPH

I n this chapter we try to explain how in the 1990s India moved from a command economy to a federal market economy. Under conditions of a federal market economy, the states command a larger share of economic sovereignty than they did under the conditions of a centrally planned economy. Whether they do well or badly economically depends more on what they do for themselves. States can act in ways that transform their initial economic situation; agency can modify structure.

We argue that a necessary condition of the shift from a command to a federal market economy has been the economic liberalization policy launched in 1991 by the Narasimha Rao Congress government. Its sufficient condition, we argue, is the displacement of public investment by private investment as the engine of economic growth. The states have become the principal arena for private investment. Their competition for private investment has generated races to the bottom and to the top. The states seem to be learning that is better for them to forgo short-term benefits and adopt the mutually advantageous benefits of cooperation over the longer term. At the same time that the states of the federal system are learning that is better for them to cooperate than to defect, the union government in New Delhi is transforming itself from the interventionist, tutelary state of a centrally planned economy and the permit-licence raj to the regulatory state of a federal market economy that tries to enforce fiscal discipline, and ensure transparency and accountability in market and federal processes.

*Originally published as 'Iconisation of Chandrababu: Sharing Sovereignty in India's Federal Market Economy', in *Economic and Political Weekly*, 5 May 2001, pp. 1541–52.

CHIEF MINISTERS AS ENTREPRENEURS

Benedict Anderson gave us nations as 'imagined communities', Satish Deshpande gave us 'imagined economies', and Tim Mitchell gave us the 'national economy ... as a representation'.[1] Economies, like nations, can be understood as constructions, products of symbols and rhetoric as well as of theorists' and practitioners' concepts and categories. This chapter starts with the contrast between the way India's economy was imagined in Jawaharlal Nehru's time, and the way it has come to be imagined in the post-liberalization era, a centralized planned economy in the 1960s, and a federal market economy[2] in the 1990s. Commonly understood as sites for 'truck, barter and exchange' and getting the prices right, economies are also sites for symbolic dramas. In the symbolic politics of imagined economies, actors appear on a public stage. They speak from scripts that go beyond the positivist world of the professional economist, beyond the interests and preferences of capital and labour, consumers and producers, buyers and sellers. The federal market economy is populated by persons, places, and relationships that constitute a coherent symbolic world.

[1]Benedict Anderson, *Imagined Communities: Reflections on the Origin and Spread of Nationalism*, London: Verso, 1983. 'Communities are to be distinguished, not by their falsity/ genuineness, but by the style in which they are imagined', p. 15.

The phrase 'imagined economies' is taken from Tim Mitchell's paper, 'At the Edge of the Economy', presented at the South Asia and Middle East (SAME) workshop, University of Chicago, 2 February 1995. The argument about the recent invention of the idea of the economy is made in Mitchell's 'Fixing the Economy', *Cultural Studies*, 12 (1), 1982, pp. 82–101.

Satish Deshpande, 'Imagined Economies; Styles of Nation-Building in Twentieth Century India', *Journal of Arts and Ideas*, 25–26 December 1993, pp. 5–35. 'If nations are indeed "imagined communities" as Benedict Anderson has so persuasively suggested, then I would argue that one of the dominant modes in which the Indian nation has been imagined is a community of producers, as an economy. ...' pp. 5–6.

[2]We distinguish Barry Weingast's deductive use of a model, 'market preserving federalism' (MPF), to assess and judge Indian federalism from our use of a Weberian style ideal type, a federal market economy, which enables us to organize our inductive analysis of ideas and practices in India. Sunita Parikh and Barry Weingast conclude that

the Indian case far better illustrates what occurs in the absence of market-preserving federalism ... India's federalism retains the hierarchy of federalism but eliminates the main mechanisms that sustain strong markets. States are not free to set their own economic policies. Nor can they capture the gains from policies that foster economic growth.

Sunita Parikh and Barry R. Weingast, 'Response' to Jonathan Rodden and Susan Rose-Ackerman, 'Does Federalism Preserve Markets?' and Ronald I. McKinnon and Daniel Rubinfield, 'Commentaries', *Virginia Law Review*, 83 (7), 1997, p. 1611.

As will become clear from our analysis below, we come to quite different conclusions.

See also Barry R. Weingast, 'The Economic Role of Political Institutions: Market-Preserving Federalism and Economic Growth', *Journal of Law, Economics and Organisation*, 11, 1995.

In the 1950s and 1960s, the heyday of India's Five-Year Plans, Prime Minister Jawaharlal Nehru cut a heroic figure as chairman of the Planning Commission that he put at the centre of India's industrial modernization. The Indian state would occupy the commanding heights of the economy. Nehru imagined big dams as temples for a powerful Indian nation. As the new millennium opens, the heroic age of centralized planning has become a fading memory. In the 1990s drama of economic liberalization, state chief ministers play leading roles in India's emergent federal market economy. They are seen on front pages, covers of news magazines, and television screens, making and breaking coalition governments, welcoming foreign statesmen and investors, dealing with natural disasters and domestic violence. By March 1995, a perceptive Raja Chelliah could observe that

The relative spheres of activities of the two levels of the government have been thrown into a flux. The scope for real decentralisation of economic power has been greatly increased and new vistas have opened up for creative and innovative activities by the subnational level governments.[3]

By the end of the 1990s, state chief ministers became the marquee players in India's federal market economy.

What has attracted media and policy attention in recent years is the competition among the states for international notice, and for domestic and foreign private investment. State chief ministers and their finance and industries secretaries have gone abroad, to the US, Western Europe, and Japan, in search of private investors, including non-resident Indians (NRIs). As the new millennium opened, India's state capitals attracted world leaders. Bill Gates and Bill Clinton came to Hyderabad; Yoshiro Mori and Li Peng to Bangalore. Clinton's visit capped Andhra chief minister Chandrababu Naidu's relentless efforts to be known as India's most successful chief minister. From Dallas to Davos, he promoted his ambitious plans to transform Andhra Pradesh from a middle into a top-ranking state.[4] As leader of one of a growing number of politically successful state parties, the Telugu Desam, his efforts to promote and use information technology caught the national imagination. Earlier, counter-intuitively, it had been Jyoti Basu, the long-serving Communist

[3]Raja Chelliah, *Towards Sustainable Growth: Essays in Fiscal and Financial Sector Reforms in India*, New Delhi: Oxford University Press, p. 19.

[4]In the annual ranking of states compiled by *Business Today*, which ranks twenty-six states according to the perceptions of CEOs about states as investment destinations, Andhra went up from twenty-second in 1995 to third in 1999. 'State of the States', *Business Standard*, 29 December 1999. Insofar as perceptions as much as 'objective conditions' shape investment behaviour, this is a consequential measure.

chief minister of Bengal, who had taken the lead in aggressively wooing job and revenue-generating capital.[5] By mid-2000 it was S.M. Krishna, Karnataka's Congress chief minister, who appeared to be showing India its economic future. As *Outlook* put it, 'Watch out, Naidu, S. M. Krishna is winning both panchayat polls and investors' (25 June 2000, pp. 16–18). In a world of federal competition in which some observers fear that a race to the bottom will make worse off all the states, Naidu and Krishna seemed to be pursuing a race to the top that could make better off both.

The defining event that shifted attention to the states as arenas of economic decision-making occurred in 1993 when the Government of Maharashtra (GoM), India's most industrialized state and home of India's pre-eminent global city, Mumbai, began negotiations with the Texas energy giant Enron to build a $3.5 billion, 2000 megawatt power plant. The negotiations revealed the down as well as the upside of autonomy. States can seize the opportunity provided by the Centre's diminished influence and resources to shape, for better or for worse, their own fates. On 8 December 1993 the GoM and the Maharashtra State Electricity Board (MSEB)[6] signed a Power Purchase Agreement (PPA) with Dabhol Power Company, Enron's India subsidiary, for the supply of about 2000 MW of power. Described as 'one of the largest contracts (civilian or military) in world history, and the single largest contract in (India's) history', it involved total energy investment of $3.5 billion over the life of the twenty-year contract and, as estimated in 1996 on the basis of then prevailing indexed fuel costs, $34 billion over the same period to be paid by the MSEB to Dabhol/Enron.

What is important so far as our story is concerned is the fact that the Government of India (GoI) played at best a supporting role. In September 1994, it provided a sovereign counter-guarantee, a decision it came to regret. The GoI's agents, for instance, a cabinet committee, the finance minister, and the Central Electricity Authority (CEA), opposed the project. So did the World Bank. The GoI was cajoled, bullied and, for all practical purposes, pushed aside by the GoM, whose actions some have called shady, foolhardy,

[5]See Aseema Sinha's case studies of Bengal, Gujarat, and Tamil Nadu in 'From State to Market—via the State Governments: Horizontal Competition after 1991 in India', paper presented at the Association of Asian Studies Annual Meeting, Boston, 11–14 March 1999.

[6]Our account of the Enron episode is largely based on the carefully researched, highly critical book by Abhay Mehta, *Power Play: A Study of the Enron Project*, New Delhi: Orient Longman, 1999.

Also useful is Sidharth Sinha, 'Private Participation in Power: Dabhol Power Company— A Case Study', and his 'Appropriate Return to Equity in Private Power Projects: Dabhol Power Project Company—A Case Study' in *Infrastucture Development and Financing: Towards a Public– Private Partnership*, by G. Raghuram, Rekha Jain, Sidharth Sinha, Prem Pangotra, Sebastian Morris (eds), New Delhi: Macmillan, 1999, pp. 122–60 and 161–9.

or illegal. More recent reflections indict the project and its failure to use competitive bidding instead of non-transparently negotiated 'memos of understanding', as leading to 'a perpetuation of old command-and-control habits' and an invitation to corruption rather than an instance of liberalization.[7] The actions were also potentially disastrous for the GoM and possibly for New Delhi, whose sovereign guarantee could make it financially liable if the GoM/MSEB finds itself unable to pay its bills for the high cost electric power it is committed to purchase over the twenty years of the contract.[8]

As we write in 2001, eight years later, the financial and political ups and downs of the Enron deal continue to rivet the country's attention on state-level economic decision-making. It suggests that sharing economic sovereignty and economic decentralization carry hazards as well as opportunities.

Our use of the term 'federal market economy' is meant to draw attention to the fact that the new imagined economy evokes not only the decentralization of the market, but also new patterns of shared sovereignty between the states and the Centre for economic and financial decision-making. This increased sharing shifts India's federal system well beyond the economic provisions of its formal constitution. Over the last decade, it has become clear that if economic liberalization is to prevail, it is the state governments and their chief ministers that can and must break the bottlenecks holding back economic growth. Can they and their governments negotiate a path that avoids surrender to populist pressures and yet effectively responds to the inequalities generated by market solutions?[9]

[7]Amulya Reddy, 'Lessons from Eaton', *The Hindu*, 6 January 2001.

[8]In early 2001, Enron did indeed invoke the government of India's sovereign guarantee when MSEB appeared unable to meet its payments for November and December 2000. According to state power minister Padmasinh Patil, this was no freebee for the GoM, as GoI 'will, in turn, recover it from funds allocated to the state government'. *Business Line*, 7 February 2001.

[9]We are not alone in attending to the federal dimension of economic reform and decision-making. Rob Jenkins breaks new conceptual and empirical ground in *Democratic Politics and Economic Reform in India*, Cambridge: Cambridge University Press, 1999. It goes beyond previous work on economic reform in India. His Chapter 5, 'Political institutions: Federalism, informal networks, and the management of dissent' offers strong evidence for the existence of an emergent federal market economy, pp. 119–71.

See also Aseema Sinha, 'From State to Market; India and the Theory of Market Preserving Federalism', paper presented at the APSA annual meeting, Washington, DC, 31 August–4 September 2000, and her MS 'Mapping Economic Reform: Federalism and the Politics of Economic Reform in India', University of Wisconsin Press.

We have benefited as well from John Echeverri-Gent's work on a 'decentred polity'. It theorizes and explains the economic decision-making and party system transformations of India's federal system, and relates them to the shift in the 1990s from an interventionist to a regulatory state. See his 'Politics in India's Decentred Polity', in *India Briefing: Quickening the Pace of Change*, Armonk, NY: M.E. Sharpe, 2001. Echeverri-Gent developed his conceptual distinction between an interventionist and a regulatory state in his work on SEBI's regulation

If state chief ministers have become marquee players in the drama of the federal market economy, business leaders, economic regulators, and a new breed of policy intellectuals can be found in conspicuous supportive roles. They overshadow the actors who, in Nehru's time, shared the limelight focused on the centrally planned economy, the able but now almost invisible deputy chairman of the Planning Commission in New Delhi's Yojana Bhavan, K.C. Pant; the more visible union finance minister, Yashwant Sinha; and other economic ministers and secretaries to government. As profit has come to be seen as a measure of productivity rather than a symbol of greed and of anti-social gain,[10] the media increasingly depicts India's businessmen (there are still few women) as persons to respect and emulate. Kumaramangalam Birla, Ratan Tata, Dhirubhai Ambani,[11] the young heirs of old business houses and the energetic builders of new; IT entrepreneurs such as Wipro's Azim Premji and Infosys' S. Narayana Murthy, are all persons with whom state chief ministers do business, the entrepreneurs and managers who are said to make things happen and make the economy grow. With India's move

---

of the Bombay Stock Exchange. He calls SEBI India's first independent regulatory agency in 'Governance Structures and Market-Making: Regulating India's Equity Markets in a Globalising World', paper presented at the University of California, Santa Cruz, November 1998.

The Observer Research Foundation's *Economic Reforms: The Role of the States and the Future of Centre-State Relations*, New Delhi: Observer Research Foundation, 1996, is written from the perspective of an earlier paradigm in the study of federalism and Centre-state relations in India, for example, Balbeer Arora's essay, 'India's Federalism and the Demands of Pluralism' in Nirmal Mukarji and Balbeer Arora (eds), *Federalism in India: Origins and Development*, New Delhi: Vikas Publishing House, 1992. Lawrence Saez examines many of the federal issues in 'Federalism Without a Centre: The Impact of Political Reform and Economic Liberalisation on India's Federal System', Ph.D. dissertation, University of Chicago: Political Science Department, 1999.

The government of Rajasthan, provides an example of the entrepreneurial breaking of bottlenecks that can characterize the use of, in Rob Jenkins' phrase, 'stealth' in the sharing of sovereignty or decentring of the polity. Blocked by the provisions of the obsolete Telegraph Act, 1885, and the Wireless Telegraphy Act, 1933, from attracting investment to upgrade telecommunications in Rajasthan, including new developments in information technology, the government contracted for project designs for laying a fibre optic cable or 'spine' throughout Rajasthan, and sought investors to implement it. The cable would not violate the two acts, which barred private companies from transmitting voice messages on telephone ground lines. The acts did not bar transmitting data or digital information (communication, Arvind Mayaram, Secretary to Government for Industries, December 1999).

[10]For a discussion of profit and the profit motive in pre-liberalization India, see Lloyd I. Rudolph and Susanne Hoeber Rudolph, *In Pursuit of Lakshmi*, Chicago: University of Chicago Press, 1987, pp. 26–7. See also Jeffrey D. Sachs, Ashutosh Varshney, and Nirupam Bajpai (eds), *India in the Era of Economic Reforms*, New Delhi: Oxford University Press, 1999, pp. 21–2.

[11]See Hamish McDonald's serious biographical and analytical economic history, *The Polyester Prince: The Rise of Dhirubhai Ambani*, Sydney: Allen and Unwin, 1998. Through summer 2000, Ambani succeeded in preventing the sale of the book.

from a centrally planned, state-dominated economy to a decentralized federal market economy, the economic views, philosophies of life, and ways of living of India's successful businessmen have come to attract some of the respect and admiration that were earlier enjoyed by the sentinels guarding the economy's commanding heights.

Also overshadowing the images of an increasingly obsolescent Nehruvian interventionist state are the administrators and policy intellectuals of India's emergent 'regulatory state'[12]—persons such as Reserve Bank of India (RBI) Chairman Bimla Jalan, Securities and Exchange Board of India (SEBI) Chairman D.R. Mehra, former National Council of Economic Research (NCAER) Director General, Rakesh Mohan (now economic adviser to the government), and Confederation of Indian Industries (CII) Director General, Tarun Das.

THE FEDERAL MARKET ECONOMY: CAUSES AND REASONS

Economic liberalization, the dismantling of the 'permit-licence raj', and an increasing reliance on markets proved to be enabling factors for the emergence of the federal market economy. The dismantling of controls provided a window of opportunity for enterprising state governments. However, economic liberalization tells only part of the story concerning the emergence of a federal market economy. It was a necessary, but not a sufficient condition. Equally important was the marked decline in public investment and, as a consequence, of the Centre's financial leverage. Capital expenditure of both the Centre and the states as a ratio of the total government expenditure declined from 31.2 per cent in 1980–1 to 14.62 per cent in 1995–6.[13] The central government no longer had the resources to finance large capital investments on its own. Further borrowing was constrained by large external and internal deficits,[14] and by rising interest

[12]Lloyd I. Rudolph and Susanne Hoeber Rudolph, 'Redoing the Constitutional Design: From an Interventionist to a Regulatory State', in *The Success of India's Democracy*, by Atul Kohli (ed.), Cambridge: Cambridge University Press, 2001.

[13]D.K. Srivastava, 'Emerging Fiscal and Economic Issues', *Seminar*, 459, November 1997, p. 501.

[14]The fact that to be eligible to join the European Union monetary community (the Euro), states had to bring down their fiscal deficits to 4 per cent of GDP provides a comparison with the Indian situation. It has been hard pressed since liberalization began in 1991 to keep the domestic deficit below 6 per cent of GDP. Man Mohan Singh as finance minister in the Narasimha Rao government (1991–6) brought the deficit down from 8.3 in 1990–1 to 5.7 in 1992–3. Subsequently it fluctuated, 7.4 per cent in 1993–4, 6.1 per cent in 1994–5 and 5 per cent in 1998–9. The Government of India, Ministry of Finance, Economic Division, *Economic Survey, 1996–97*, Ministry of Finance, New Delhi, 1997, Table 2.2, 'Components

rates that increase the costs of carrying new debt and rolling over old debts.[15] In 1998–9, interest payments as a ratio of the Centre's revenue receipts were 52 per cent.[16] The Centre's deficit and the interest payments it entailed made it increasingly difficult for it to help the states with investment funds or bailouts. The Centre's gross assistance to states' capital formation declined from 27 per cent of the Centre's revenue expenditure in 1990–1 to 12 per cent in 1998–9.[17] This sharp decline proved an incentive to some states prepared to take advantage of the economic liberalization climate to pursue private investment. However, economic forces were not alone in moving India from a centralized planned economy to a federal market economy. Political forces were equally important.

The movement from a command economy to a federal market economy is as much to do with changes in the party system as it is to transformations in economic ideology and practice. Independent causal chains may have resulted in economic liberalization and the transformation of the party system during the 1990s, but once in place, the two phenomena began to interact in ways that proved mutually reinforcing. The dominant Nehru-Gandhi party system that enabled Congress party governments to engage in centralized planned investment gave way from 1989 onwards to a regionalized multiparty system and coalition governments, in which state parties play a decisive role.

Since the ninth national election in 1989 returned a hung parliament, coalition governments have given ample scope to state parties. Atal Behari Vajpayee's 1999 majority included 120 of 300 MPs from single-state parties.[18] His National Democratic Alliance (NDA) government can be understood as a federalized coalition. Economic and political decentralization were working in tandem.

---

of Gross Fiscal Deficit of the Central Government', p. 19; the same for 1999–2000, Table 2.1, 'Trends in Parameters of Deficit of Central Government', p. 27.

India's external debt stood at $33.8 billion when Rajiv Gandhi took over as prime minister in 1984–5; it rose to $60.6 billion by the end of his term in 1988–9; had risen to $85.5 billion in 1991–2; rose to $101.1 billion in 1994–95 but declined to $93.7 billion in 1995–6; and had risen only slightly to $97.7 billion in 1998–9. World Bank, India, *Sustaining Rapid Economic Growth*; World Bank, Washington, DC, 1997, Table A3.1 (a), p. 78; and *Economic Survey, 1999–2000*, Table 6.12, 'India's External Debt Outstanding', p. 110.

[15]*Economic Survey, 1996–97*, p. 26

[16]Table 2.2, 'Receipts and Expenditures of Central Government', *Economic Survey, 1999–2000*, p. 8.

[17]Table 7.1, 'Gross Capital Formation from Budgetary Resources of the Central Government', *Economic Survey, 1999–2000*, Appendix, p. s38.

[18]Kewal Varma counted the BJP, Congress, CPI, and CPM as national, *Business Standard*, 29 October 1999.

As shown in Figures 11.1 and 11.2,[19] between the tenth national election in 1991 when economic liberalization began and the thirteenth in 1999, the votes and seats of national parties declined 10 per cent each, from 77 and 78 per cent to 67 and 68 per cent respectively. The votes and seats of state parties,

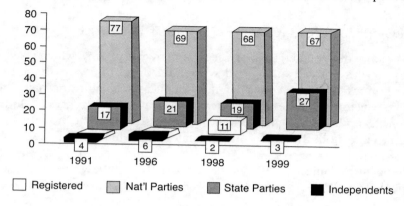

Figure 11.1: Rise of State Parties' Percentage of Votes

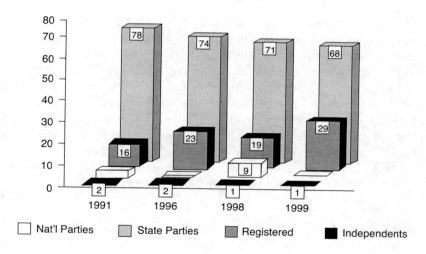

Figure 11.2: Rise of State Parties' Percentage of Seats

[19]The data found in the table on votes and the table on seats in four national elections, 1991, 1996, 1998, and 1999, have been compiled from Election Commission of India, *Elections in India: Major Events and New Initiatives 1996–2000*, New Delhi: Election Commission of

by contrast, have risen 10 and 13 per cent, from 17 and 16 per cent to 27 and 29 per cent respectively. Regional parties now play a pivotal role not only in a multiparty system and in the formation and conduct of coalition governments, but also in the dynamics of the federal market system.

FROM PUBLIC TO PRIVATE INVESTMENT IN STATES

Our story of the emergence of a federal market economy, which provides states with a greatly increased scope and opportunity to shape their economic fate, begins with a paradox, the success of failure, or snatching a partial victory from the jaws of defeat. As we have already suggested, India's deficits, both at the Centre and in the states, seemed to be mounting and intractable. Both the Centre and the states had bankrupted themselves by borrowing money to pay for things they could not afford. It was this desperate condition, the foreign exchange crisis of 1991, which precipitated the reforms. Sachs, *et al.* put it this way:

The foreign exchange crisis of July, 1991 not only gave the IMF and World Bank an opportunity to insist on policy change, but also reform-oriented bureaucrats inside the government to pursue their long cherished agenda. A possibility of financial collapse led to a new resolve at the governmental level.[20]

At the Centre, the downward slide to deficit financing began with borrowing to pay for Rajiv Gandhi's extraordinary mid-1980s military modernization programme. For two years running, India spent more per annum on weapons purchases (over $4 billion each year) than any other country.[21] In the Rajiv Gandhi era, the GoI abandoned the fiscal conservatism that it had inherited from the raj and had continued to practice for almost four decades. Like other developing countries in the 1980s, its debt mounted as a result, *inter alia*, of annual budget deficits, and of having succumbed to the

---

India, 2000; Lok Sabha Poll; An AIR Analysis, News Service Division, All India Radio, Government of India, New Delhi, 1991; Election Commission of India, Statistical Report on General Elections, 1996, to the Eleventh Lok Sabha, Volume I (National and State Abstracts), New Delhi: Election Commission of India, 1996; Ibid. for 1998 and for 1999; URL for the Election Commission of India: http://www.eci.gov.in, where data for the 1996, 1998, and 1999 elections are available online.

The data on votes and seats are presented according to Election Commission definitions for national party, state party, registered party, and independents.

[20]Jeffrey D. Sachs, Ashutosh Varshney, and Nirupam Bajpai (eds), *India in the Era of Economic Reforms*, New Delhi: Oxford University Press, 1999.

[21]For details see Lloyd I. Rudolph, 'The Faltering Novitiate: Rajiv Gandhi at Home and Abroad', in *India Briefing 1989*, by Marshall M. Bouton and Philip K. Oldenburg (eds), Boulder, Colorado: Westview Press /New York: The Asia Society, 1989.

temptations offered by commercial banks. In the states, deficits were the consequences of the populist exploitation of soft budget constraints such as subsidies,[22] administrative pricing, and labour redundancy. The single largest source of state deficits has been state electricity boards (SEBs). State governments have so far proved unwilling to levy or unable to collect adequate user charges for piped water, irrigation, and electricity. Some states have provided free electricity to cultivators, while others charge nominal prices. A lot of electricity is unmetred or stolen; the late power minister, Mohan Kumaramangalam, thought the amount might be as high as 40 per cent.

The reluctance of states to collect user charges is the fruit of a long-term secular political trend, the political hegemony in the 73 per cent of the population still classified as rural[23] of those we have elsewhere called 'bullock capitalists', small to medium-sized self-employed independent agricultural producers.[24] They overlap with other backward classes (OBC), and less privileged castes such as the Yadavs. Together, bullock capitalists and OBCs constitute the largest and among the best organized voting constituency in most states. Their emergence into political power roughly coincides with the decline of financial discipline in the 1980s.[25] As bullock capitalist/OBC cultivators consumed more and more electricity to irrigate second, third, and even fourth crops, they used their votes to resist efforts to collect user charges. No amount of proof showing that cheap or free electricity disproportionately benefited the better-off farmers could alter the perception that increased user charges formed an anti-poor policy. In 1996–7, the commercial losses of SEBs were estimated to be over Rs 9000 crore.[26]

[22]According to Rakesh Mohan, subsidies accounted for 14.7 per cent of GDP in 1998–9. Of this amount, only 4 to 6 per cent were 'justified', that is, helped the poor for whom subsidies are intended. India has moved away from pricing public goods, Rakesh Mohan told the 16–18 December 1999, Confederation of Indian Industries-sponsored conference on infrastructure development. When public utilities such as electricity were private, they covered their costs and made money, or went bankrupt. He noted that 50 per cent of rural households have no electricity connections, with the consequence that the subsidized price benefits the relatively better-off who have connections, not the poorest. Because power does not pay for itself, and hence generates no money for investment, expansion has to come from money borrowed at 12–14 per cent.

Paying for expansion this way becomes one of the major components of subsidies. Notes on Rakesh Mohan's remarks, 16 December 1999.

[23]Table 9.1, 'Population of India—1991', *Economic Survey 1999–2000*, s-114.

[24]Lloyd I. Rudolph and Susanne Hoeber Rudolph, *In Pursuit of Lakshmi*, Chicago: University of Chicago Press, 1987, p. 50.

[25]Interview, K.C. Pant, Deputy Chairman, Planning Commission, February 2000.

[26]Confederation of Indian Industry, *An Overview of the Challenges for Infrastructure Development in India; Background Paper for Infranet '99*. Prepared by Pricewaterhouse Coopers, CII, New Delhi, 1999, p. 21. For data on electricity charges as of 1998 by state and category, that is, domestic, commercial, etc., see Central Electricity Authority, *Average Electric Rates and*

By 2001–2, the power subsidy burden was expected to be a staggering Rs 41,238 crore (almost $10 billion), with Rs 29,461 crore (over $6 billion) attributable to agriculture.[27] Who will bell the bullock capitalist/OBC cat?

Ahluwalia uses more discreet language to characterize India's deficit crisis:

Over the years, both the centre and the states have seen a burgeoning of non-Plan expenditure in the face of inadequate buoyancy of revenues. They have responded by resorting to larger and larger volumes of borrowing. The process has led to a steady build up of debt, which in turn has generated a rising interest burden.[28]

Ahluwalia's Table 10, 'Interest Payment as Percentage of Total Revenue' (in India's fourteen largest states), shows that the ratio of interest payments to tax revenues increased from 7.7 per cent in 1980–1 to 13.1 in 1990–1, and to 17.6 per cent in 1996–7. The 10 per cent increase over seventeen years radically reduced the capacity of states to finance development expenditures from current revenues, and made them more dependent on borrowing. Interest payments as a percentage of the total revenue in two of India's poorest states, Uttar Pradesh and Orissa, as measured in per capita income, have increased by 17 per cent in seventeen years. Surprisingly, in Bihar, the poorest state, the percentage increase is much less, but for an unattractive reason. Bihar has borrowed proportionately less because it substantially reduced its level of Plan or development expenditure. Better-off states with low percentages of interest payment to total revenues in 1996–7 are Haryana (11.83 per cent), Tamil Nadu (12.33 per cent), Karnataka (12.55 per cent), Maharashtra (12.70 per cent), and Madhya Pradesh (13.74 per cent).

Duties in India, New Delhi: Government of India, Central Electricity Authority, April 1998. The CEA's structure and functions are described in the *Central Electric Authority and Indian Power Sector*, CEA, New Delhi, October 1996.

[27]*Economic Survey, 2000–2001*, Table 9.4, p. 176. For the overall picture vis-à-vis power, see pp. 174–7.

The Economic Times, 23 February 2001, reporting on the recently released *Economic Survey. 2000–2001*, commented with regard to the Rs 41,238 crore, 'That's enough money to add 8,000 MW of new capacity to the national grid. Which, by the way, is almost half of National Thermal Power Corporation's (NTPC's) total capacity built over the last 50 years.'

'The hidden subsidy for agriculture and domestic sectors,' *The Economic Times* continued, '... which was at a modest Rs 7,449 crore in 1991–92 (accounting for 1.1 per cent of GDP) has been increasing at an alarming rate. It currently accounts for 36 per cent of gross fiscal deficit of state governments.'

The subsidy bill of the power sector includes losses incurred by the state electricity boards from transmission and distribution. Such losses included theft and non- and poor metering. T and D losses for 2001–2 are estimated by the *Economic Survey, 2000–2001* at Rs 25,000 crore.

[28]Montek Singh Ahluwalia, *The Economic Performance of the States in the Past Reforms Period*, New Delhi: NCAER, 2000, pp. 33–4. See also Reserve Bank of India, *State Finances: A Study of Budgets, 1999–2000*, Mumbai: Reserve Bank of India, January 2000. Some of Ahluwalia's tables draw on this document, as do we for some of our arguments.

The large current deficits in the states are recent, and not entirely of their own making. They are victims of the union government in New Delhi. The Government of India, in the form of I.K. Gujral's United Front government, made the profligate decision in 1997 to further increase the Fifth Pay Commission's budget- and inflation-busting recommendation of a threefold increase in central government employees' basic pay. Under severe pressure, state governments soon followed suit.[29]

So runs the story of defeat. What is the story about snatching a partial victory from the jaws of defeat? As public expenditure in India's federal states has declined, private investment in many states has come to the rescue. Surprisingly, even though the Centre's and the states' mounting deficits have led to a decline in the scale of public or planned investment for growth, there is 'no statistically significant relationship between state plan expenditure as percentage of SDP (state domestic product) and growth performance across states in either ...' the 1980s or 1990s.[30] The lack of correlation between state planned expenditure and the growth performance should not surprise us, Ahluwalia argues, because it is total investment that affects growth, and almost three-fourths of the gross fixed investment at the national level comes from the private sector, private corporate investment accounting for 38 per cent, and private household investment accounting for 33 per cent.[31]

This brings us to the heart of our argument on India's emergent federal market economy: the decline of central public investment and growth of private investment gives the federal states, the immediate sites of private

[29]For more details on the Fifth Pay Commission, see Nirupam Bajpai and Jeffrey Sachs' essay, 'Fiscal Policy in India's Economic Reforms', in *Era of Economic Reforms*, by Sachs, Varshney and Bajpai (eds), pp. 96–7. Also see Nirupam Bajpai, and Jeffrey Sachs, 'The State of State Government Finances', *The Hindu*, 6 December 1999.

[30]See Ahluwalia, *Economic Performance*, section on 'Investment and Growth in Individual States', pp. 20–5, including his discussion of Table 8, 'Plan Expenditures as a Percentage of SDP (state domestic product)'. In the fourteen largest states that Ahluwalia analyses, the ratio of state plan expenditure to SDP declined from an average of 5.7 per cent in the 1980s to 4.5 per cent in the 1990s.

The decline of 1.2 percentage points in state plan expenditures almost certainly hides an even larger decline in investment for new capacity, because of the increase in the revenue component of the Plan ... There is considerable variation across states in the ratio of state plan expenditure to SDP ... (but) there is no statistically significant relationship between state plan expenditure as a percentage of SDP and growth performance across states ... in the 1980s or the 1990s', p. 21.

[31]'Public sector investment at the national level is only about 28 per cent of total investment and this includes both the centre and the states.' Three-fourths of the national-level gross fixed investment comes from the private sector, 38 per cent from private corporate investment, and 33 per cent from private household investment. At 28 per cent of the total investment, public investment by the Centre and the states accounts for about 6.8 per cent of the GDP, of which state plans account for only one-third. Ahluwalia, *Economic Performance*, p. 22.

investment, a greatly expanded role in economic liberalization, and in promoting investment and growth. They do so in highly variable ways that are as contingent on agency—that is, policy initiatives, leadership, good governance—as on structure, for example, the previous economic position. Ahluwalia enumerates the elements affecting growth: it would be

simplistic ... to focus on investment as the critical determinant of growth ... efficiency of resource use (i.e., its productivity as measured by ICOR[32]—incremental capital-output ratio—the number of investment dollars needed to produce one more dollar of real GDP, a ratio that depends in part on technological innovation) is at least as important as the level of investment. Efficiency in turn depends upon many other factors such as the level of human resource development, the quality of infrastructure, (and) the economic policy environment. ...[33]

We would argue that two factors that make for efficiency of resource use, the level of human resource development and the quality of infrastructure, are dependent on investment. While human resource development—a low public priority in India—remains primarily, if not exclusively, the domain of public investment,[34] attracting private investment in infrastructure has become an arena of intense competition among states.

Success in attracting private investment in infrastructure depends on the boldness, imagination, and tactical and strategic skills of civil servants

[32]Paul Krugman elucidates the role of ICOR with illustrations from 'Asian' economies and from the former Soviet Union.

The debate over Asian productivity still rages (in 1999) ... Asia achieved remarkable rates of economic growth without correspondingly remarkable increases in productivity. Its growth was the product of resource mobilisation rather than efficiency ... As in the case of the Soviet Union ... given the lack of rapid productivity growth, Asia was bound to run into diminishing return. By 1997 Malaysia was investing more than 40 per cent of GDP, twice its share in 1970; Singapore was investing half its income. These rates of investment sure could not be pushed much higher; and merely maintaining them would not be enough to sustain growth ... Given rising ICORs, growth could be sustained only via an ever-increasing investment rate, and that just wasn't going to happen (pp. 33–4).

[33]These factors can reinforce or contradict each other; they cannot be read in mutual isolation. For example, Ahluwalia points out that Kerala ranks high in 'human resource development' where literacy is taken as the best available proxy measurement, but low in 'economic policy environment'. This can help to explain why Kerala, which ranked as the most literate state in 1981, 1991, and 1997, remained in the middle ranks over those years in 'Annual Rates of Growth of Per Capita Grass State Domestic Product', Tables 2 and 5. He also points out that although the levels of literacy in the 'slow growing states' of Bihar, UP, and Orissa are distinctly lower than the average for all states (see his Table 9, Total-Literacy Rate, *Economic Performance*, p. 50), there is no statistically significant correlation between the growth of SDP and the level of literacy.

[34]We say primarily, but not exclusively, because both education and health, hitherto arenas for public investment, are under increasing pressure to recoup larger proportions of their running and capital expenses from hitherto nominal 'user charges'.

and politicians at the state level, not least the state chief ministers.[35] The economic policy environment and quality of governance[36] are distinctly in the political domain, too. Rob Jenkins persuasively shows that, under conditions of a democratic politics that opens the way for vested interests to stymie economic liberalization, politicians have to be able to 'succeed by stealth', conceding form to gain substance, going around rather than confronting obstacles, invoking continuity to bring about change.[37]

CHANGING RANK: ACCELERATING AND DECELERATING GROWTH

Over the past two decades, the 1980s and 1990s, variable growth among India's states has produced marked disparities. Some have argued that the effect of liberalization on the federal system has been to make better-off states richer, and worse-off states poorer. This is not an adequate summary of the problem. The propensity of some states to grow did not coincide with their per capita income ranking, or their ranking on a poverty index. Thus, of India's fourteen largest states, the first and third highest with respect to per capita income, Punjab and Haryana, and the second and third lowest with respect to per capita income, UP and Bihar, experienced declining growth rates between the pre-liberalization 1980s and the post-liberalization 1990s. The rest of the fourteen largest states increased their growth rates, some markedly more than others. This suggests that, as the states have been forced to rely upon themselves financially and politically, they have had, perforce, to take responsibility for their economic fate.

Examining the ranking of states over time as measured by per capita domestic product indicates movement in the middle ranges, but stability

[35]For a recent overview of investment opportunities in infrastructure, see Cabinet Secretariat, Government of India, and National Council of Economic Research with assistance from Arthur Andersen, *India's Infrastructure: Investment Opportunities*, New Delhi: GoI and NCAER, 1997. The publication deals with investment opportunities in power, oil and natural gas, coal, mining, roads, urban infrastructure, telecommunications, civil aviation, and ports.

[36]On the importance of good governance for attracting private investment, see The World Bank, *The State in a Changing Word; the World Development Report, 1997*, published for the World Bank by the Oxford University Press, New York, New Delhi, etc. According to the Bank, private investors are more likely to invest when they perceive 'predictability of rulemaking, political stability, security with respect to crimes against persons and property, reliable judicial enforcement and freedom from corruption'. Figure 2.4, p. 37, shows three scatter grams that indicate a close relationship between 'credibility' (reliable state institutions as specified above) and economic performance, pp. 34–8.

[37]See Rob Jenkins, *Democratic Politics*, where he observes that 'One of the skills which reforming governments must possess is the capacity to cloak change, which tends to cause anxiety among those privileged by the status quo, in the appearance of continuity', p. 176. In our reckoning, leadership includes not only chief ministers and their cabinet colleagues, but also entrepreneurial civil servants.

Table 11.1: State Rankings by Per Capita Domestic Product

State	1980–1	1990–1	1997–8	+Higher/–Lower Rank
Andhra Pradesh	9	8	9	0
Bihar	14	14	14	0
Gujarat	4	4	4	0
Haryana	3	2	3	0
Karnataka	6	7	7	−1
Kerala	7	9	6	+1
Madhya Pradesh	10	11	11	−1
Maharashtra	2	3	2	0
Orissa	11	13	13	−2
Punjab	1	1	1	0
Rajasthan	13	10	10	+2
Tamil Nadu	8	5	5	+3
Uttar Pradesh	12	12	12	0
West Bengal	5	6	8	−3

at the top and bottom (Table 11.1, 'State Rankings by Per Capita Domestic Product, 1980–1, 1990–1, 1997–8').

West Bengal dropped by three positions and Orissa by two. Rajasthan and Tamil Nadu climbed by three, and several others moved up or down by one position, but Punjab, Maharashtra, and Haryana remained in the top three, and Bihar, UP, and Orissa made up the bottom three.

Growth in SDP depends to a considerable extent on investment. We can learn a lot about relative success and failure by studying how investment in individual states has been doing over the past two decades, one pre-liberalization, and the other post-liberalization. As Ahluwalia puts it,

the economic performance of the individual states ... has received less attention than it deserves in the public debate on economic policy—there is very little analysis of how individual states have performed over time and the role of state government policy (and, we would add, leadership) in determining state level performance. ...[38]

[38]'The Plan document ... is not disaggregated into targets for the growth of State Domestic Product in individual states nor does it report the growth performance of different states in the past, nor analyse the reasons for differences in performance across states. The Annual Economic Survey brought out by the finance ministry is also silent on these issues' (Ahluwalia 2000, p. 1).

Unfortunately, there is no reliable information about what it is that can be taken to be the principal cause of variation, the total level of investment, or gross fixed capital formation in individual states. Precisely specifying the causes of investment variation awaits better state-level data.

The degree of dispersion in growth rates across states increased significantly in the post-liberalization decade. In the 1980s, the range of variation in the growth rate of SDP was from a low of 3.6 per cent per year in Kerala, to a high of 6.6 per cent in Rajasthan, a state at the time near the bottom in per capita SDP. The spread between low and high was less than a factor of two. Post-liberalization, in the 1990s, the variation was much larger, from a low of 2.7 per cent per year for Bihar, to a high of 9.6 per cent per year for Gujarat, a factor exceeding 3.5.

When differences in the rates of growth of population are taken into account and we judge the states in terms of growth rate per capita, the disparities in performance across states become even more marked.[39] In the 1980s, the variation in growth rates per capita ranged from 2.1 per cent in Madhya Pradesh to a high for Rajasthan of 4 per cent, a ratio of 1:2. Post-liberalization in the 1990s, the difference between the highest and the lowest per capita growth rates increased to a ratio of 1:7, with Bihar and UP barely growing at 1.1 per cent and 1.2 per cent respectively, and Gujarat and Maharashtra surging ahead at 7.6 per cent and 6.1 per cent.

Nationally, although growth per capita accelerated in the 1990s, it decelerated in the three poorest states, Bihar, UP, and Orissa. Growth in per capita SDP also decelerated in the two richest states per capita, Haryana and Punjab, but their deceleration, unlike that of the three poorest states, was from a relatively high level of growth in the 1980s.

High growth performance was geographically and politically dispersed, a finding that seems to undermine theories about backward and dynamic regions, or unsuitable and facilitative party ideologies. The six states whose SDP grew more than 6 per cent in the 1990s included Gujarat (9.6 per cent, west, BJP), Maharashtra (8 per cent, west, Congress, then Shiv Sena–BJP), West Bengal (6.9 per cent, east, CPI[M]), Tamil Nadu (6.22 per cent, south, AIADMK, then DMK), Madhya Pradesh (6.17, north, Congress), Rajasthan (6.54, west, BJP, then Congress).

The 'BIMARU' states, Bihar, Madhya Pradesh, Rajasthan, and UP, which Ashish Bose grouped under this acronymic pun because they allegedly shared 'sick' demographic characteristics such as high fertility rates and low

[39]See Ahluwalia's Table 2, 'Annual Rates of Growth Per Capita Gross Domestic Product, ibid., p. 44.

female literacy, have been stereotyped as the backward India that is dragging down an economically progressive India. They are not, however, homogenous as far as economic performance is concerned. Bihar and UP performed poorly in the 1980s, and performed even worse in the 1990s. But Rajasthan and Madhya Pradesh have done fairly well. Indeed, in the 1980s Rajasthan was India's fastest growing state (6.6 per cent) and in the 1990s, it was among the half dozen states that grew at over 6 per cent (634 per cent). MP's growth in the 1980s at 4.56 per cent was below the national average of 5.24 per cent, but in the 1990s, it joined the top performers by accelerating to 6.17 per cent.

The surging growth of several poor states such as Rajasthan and Madhya Pradesh and the lagging growth of some rich states such as Punjab and Haryana suggest that poverty is not a trap and wealth no guarantee. States can act in ways that transform their initial economic situation.

RACE TO THE TOP VS RACE TO THE BOTTOM

It is both a virtue and a vice of federal systems that they generate interstate competition. Such competition can take the virtuous form of a race to the top, or the vicious form of a race to the bottom. The race to the top takes the form of attracting private investment by providing a skilled and committed labour force and a good work culture, good infrastructure, especially power, transport and communication, and good governance.

The race to the bottom is driven by competition to provide a variety of concessions that, allegedly, will attract private investment, but that force the state to forego needed revenues. R. Venkatesan and Sonalika Varma note in their NCAER study (1998) of policy competition among the states that offering incentives to attract direct investment 'is akin to a "prisoner's dilemma" in that it is collectively rational not to give incentives to attract direct investment, while at the same time it is individually rational to provide incentives'.[40] According to their study, such concessions can be categorized as financial in situations where a state government provides funds for investment; fiscal, where the government reduces the tax burden for the incoming industry; and others, such as power tariff concessions, assistance with project analysis, and design.[41]

---

[40]Venkatesan and Varma, 1998, p. 59. The authors go on to say that investment decisions are 'a function of a wide range of factors ... (such as) political stability, infrastructure availability, extent of labour unrest, presence of good backward and forward linkages, incentives provided (sic!), attitude of the bureaucracy towards the investors, etc.'

[41]Financial incentives are 'defined as those where the government is directly involved in the financing of the projects and comprise: provisions of funds for financing investment

Before turning to the consequences of using incentives to attract direct investment, let us explore the question: do the incentives that trigger the race to the bottom matter? Do they do the trick? One answer is provided by the results of a survey of managers 'based largely in north India', but including the southern state of Tamil Nadu. The results show 'the top ranking factors influencing the decision to invest are related to infrastructure (namely transport, energy, telecommunications and water)'. According to the survey, 'neither financial nor fiscal incentives are important, but good quality infrastructure that investors rank as the most important factor in investment decisions (is)'.[42] Venkatesan and Varma add to this generalization that 'surveys and statistical analysis on the relative importance of incentives over other determinants reveal that incentives play a limited role in the FDI locational decision'. There is

a relatively weak but somewhat positive relationship between incentives and investment. ... (But) it would wrong to assume that incentives offered by states are irrelevant as a source of attracting FDI. When fundamental determinants across states are similar, incentives help the foreign investors towards making a particular locational decision.[43]

Rob Jenkins (2000) argues that concessions to attract direct investment, and, more broadly, tax competition among states, 'further de-link states' economic fates from one another—contributing to the pattern of provincial Darwinism that has reduced the effectiveness of resistance among state-level elites'. In a footnote to this sentence, he qualifies this race to the bottom view of interstate competition by observing that

there have been some moves to counter this trend. ... At a CII summit in January 1995 West Bengal chief minister Jyoti Basu strongly emphasised the need to end

---

operations; government involvement in fixed capital investment for new industrial units; financing and other assistance in setting up technologically pioneering and prestigious units; expansion and diversification of existing units'. Fiscal incentives—'mainly aim at reducing the tax burden and (or providing subsidies) to an investor. These include: provisions for various sales tax exemptions; deferment of tax schemes; octroi exemptions (an indirect tax); reductions and exemptions of other taxes such as property taxes; other incentives such as export based incentives.' Other incentives—'many other incentives are also provided to help in the setting up of projects. These include: help in formulating project analysis; allowances for subsidising services like generating sets; feasibility reports; incentives for modernisation schemes, special incentives and all other incentives that cannot be classified under a common head but basically which increase the economic viability of a foreign unit by non-financial means' (Venkatesan and Varma 1998, p. 45).

[42]R. Venkatesan and Sonalika Varma, *Study on Policy, Competition Among States in India for Attracting Direct Investment*, New Delhi: NCAER, 1998, p. 49.

[43]Ibid., pp. 50–1.

the interstate taxation war and incentive war to woo investors because it would ultimately be of zero gain to the states and result in loss in revenue.[44]

By early 2001, Jyoti Basu's view, that the states should avoid a beggar your neighbour interstate competition, was gaining ground.[45] The finance ministers and secretaries of the states had joined together to get the Centre to promote a uniform system of sales taxes among the states, and to 'do away with tax incentives wars'. By January 2000, implementation had progressed in most states. By February 2001, state finance ministers had agreed that on 1 April 2002, the states would adopt a uniform CENVAT (central value added tax) as the country's principal excise tax.[46] If incentives and state sales tax

[44]The Rob Jenkins (2000) gloss and quote are from his *Democratic Politics*, pp. 132–3. The Jyoti Basu quote is from *Asian Age*, 6 January 1995, as cited by Jenkins, fn 34, p. 133.

Chief ministers and finance ministers met in conference on 16 November 1999, and decided on unified floor rates for sales tax. *Economic Survey, 1999–2000* reported an 'implementation of uniform floor rates of sales tax by states and union territories from January 1, 2000', Box 2.5, p. 38.

An interview with Mahesh Purohit, professor at the National Institute of Public Finance and member-secretary of the empowered committee of state finance ministers to monitor sales tax reform, stated in an interview in *Business Line*, 13 February 2001, that he was confident about VAT being introduced by 1 April 2002. Its introduction would be accompanied by the reduction of a, by then, uniform Central Sales Tax (CST) from 4 to 3 per cent by 1 April, and then to 1 per cent by 1 April 2003. Purohit said that the CST at 4 per cent as of 2000–1 yielded about Rs 9,000 crore. 'We are considering,' Purohit said, 'three rates of value added tax—a low tax rate for some necessary items, a high rate for luxury items and a general rate for all other products. What this general rate would be—which will the floor rate—is the crucial question, and we are working on it now.'

Purohit said that two additional interstate committees were assisting the empowered committee of state finance minister to monitor sales tax reforms, the committee of finance secretaries and a committee of state commissioners of tax. *Business Line*, 13 February 2001.

[45]Interview with P.V. Rajaraman, secretary, finance, government of Tamil Nadu, 4 February 2000, Fort St. George. Rajaraman told us that Tamil Nadu and Maharashtra, over the course of five years, made competitive offers with respect to freehold land and infrastructure. Continuing this way for five years caused serious revenue loss. The race to the bottom was halted by cooperative efforts by the states to institute a common sales tax. The finance ministers were said to be influenced by a speech made by Raja Chelliah on the need for tax reform.

[46]The 'first decisive steps' towards replacing the existing sales tax regime with a system of value added tax, a VAT or, in this case, a CENVAT, were taken on 16 November 1999 when the finance ministers of the various states met in the capital, New Delhi. Mahesh Purohit said on 12 February 2001 that, having pushed the zero date back on year from 1 April 2001 to 1 April 2002, he was 'fully confident that by that date VAT would be introduced by in all the major states'. *Business Line*, 13 February 2001.

Earlier, a *Business Standard* headline of 11 January 2000 had announced a 'January 15 deadline for uniform sales tax'. The story read in part—

Penal action is being contemplated against states not implementing the decision to adhere to uniform sales tax floor rates and to phase out sales-tax related incentive schemes by January 15. This was decided at the meeting of the standing committee of state finance ministers which asked the 13 states which had not implemented the decision to do so

competition create a situation akin to that of a prisoner's dilemma, it is also true of such situations that iteration, communication, and learning can lead to cooperation rather than defection. This seems to be what is happening in an attempt to moderate, if not eliminate, the race to the bottom.

THE REGULATORY STATE AS CONSTRAINT ON AUTONOMY

We have argued that a federal market economy is fast replacing a Nehruvian centralized command economy in the country's economic imagination and practice. The Centre's hazardous financial condition,[47] and the decline of central planning[48] and public investment that accompanied it, have forced the states to become more self-reliant. However, there is a paradox. Even as the Centre becomes less able to intervene through its control of public investment, permits, and licences, it assumes a new role as a regulator concerned with market imperfections and state fiscal discipline. As the Centre's role as an interventionist state has faded, its role as regulatory state has grown. The Centre has attempted to impose hard budget constraints on the states. So too have market-oriented international and domestic credit-

---

by the stipulated date. During their meeting in November, states and union territories agreed to implement uniform sales tax floor rates and to do away with tax incentives war from January 1. West Bengal finance minister, Asim Das Gupta, the convener of the meeting, ... told reporters that Maharashtra, West Bengal, Gujarat, Andhra Pradesh, Kerala, Assam and Tripura had already implemented the decision. He said Delhi and Uttar Pradesh, which bad partly implemented the decision, had agreed to do so in toto. With respect to the union territories, ... Yashwant Sinha (the union finance minister) assured the meeting that necessary steps would be taken so that same compliance is reached by them.

For an overview of tax reform challenges and proposals, see Chelliah's 'An Agenda for Comprehensive Tax Reform', in *Towards Sustainable Growth; Essays in Fiscal and Financial Reform in India*, by Raja J. Chelliah (ed.), New Delhi: Oxford University Press, 1996, pp. 138–59.

Meanwhile, just under the wire, the Tamil Nadu government announced on 27 October 1999 that Ford India, which had recently established a $450 manufacturing plant in the state, had been granted a concessional 1 per cent *ad valorem* sales tax rate for vehicles and parts manufactured in the state, and sold interstate to registered dealers or governments. This concession would be valid for fourteen years, from 1 November 1999 (*The Hindu*, 28 October 1999).

[47]In early 2000, the Centre's fiscal deficit was hovering at 5.6 per cent despite persistent efforts to bring it down to the 4 per cent that has become something of a world standard. Interest payments on the deficit had risen to an alarming 50 per cent of central revenue (*The Hindu*, 14 March 2000).

[48]The Planning Commission, 'finding itself somewhat marginalised in the decision-making mechanism of the central government', prepared a confidential internal note in April 2000, urging that it be given a much larger coordinating role in the federal system. 'In the domestic sector the commission feels that it should be allowed to play the role of an arbitrator whenever there is "lack of harmonization" of policy between various tiers of government and also between regions in the country'. It seems clear that the Commission was seeking to define a new regulatory role for itself in the federal market economy (*The Hindu*, 11 April 2000).

rating agencies. Such agencies evaluate 'economies' by assigning grades such as A, B, and C, which affect interest rates and thus the cost of capital.[49] Financially strapped states cannot borrow at viable rates to build the infrastructure that promises growth—and, sometimes, to meet current expenditures—unless they can demonstrate that they command the income streams to pay back the loans. As bonds become a greater component of public finance, credit-rating agencies loom ever larger as the market's guardian of hard budget constraints.[50]

India's states are also being exposed to the discipline of international lenders such as the World Bank and the Asian Development Bank. Andhra Pradesh chief minister, Chandrababu Naidu, led the way by negotiating the first state-level World Bank development loan. By mid-2000 five more states had followed Andhra's lead. States who want development loans are being obliged to observe a third form of conditionality in addition to that of the Centre and the credit-raters, namely the discipline that demonstrates to the WB, the ADB, and other international lenders that they are credit worthy.

Why is there a need to impose and monitor hard budget constraints? To a greater or lesser degree, India's states are deeply in debt. For years their politicians have competed by offering voters give-away populist measures. Especially prominent among them are subsidies for agricultural inputs, for example subsidies for irrigation, fertilizers and, most importantly, electricity. Agricultural subsidies are directed to the single largest block of voters, the enormous constituency of agricultural producers.[51] Students pay a purely

[49]In February 2001, CRISIL downgraded a Maharashtra state government-supported bond issue, explaining it had done so because of the GoM's non-payment of monthly dues to Dabhol Power Corporation, the Enron affiliate (*The Economic Times*, 6 February 2001).

[50]Thomas L. Friedman has popularized the relationship between credit-rating agencies and the hard budget constraints of market competition in *The Lexus and the Olive Tree*, New York: Random House, 2000, with his terms, the 'golden straitjacket' and the 'electronic herd' of 'faceless stock, bond and currency traders sitting behind computer screens all over the globe ... and big multinational corporations ... This herd ... is beginning to replace governments as the primary source of capital for both companies and countries to grow,' p. 109.

For hard (and soft) budget constraints, see Janos Kornai, *Vision and Reality, Market and State; Contradictions and Dilemmas Revisited*, New York: Routledge, 1990.

[51]The importance of subsidies for agricultural inputs has to be imagined in the context of the 65 per cent of the workforce located in the agriculture sector, and the almost 70 per cent of the population that live in what are classified as rural or town areas.

In October 1997, while out of power, Bal Thackeray, leader of the Shiv Sena, a Maharashtrian regional party, promised farmers free electricity. In 1999, when the Shiv Sena formed the state government in coalition with the BJP, the BJP leader Gopinath Munde announced that this promise was not viable. By that time, the earlier promise had seriously affected the payment of electricity charges (*The Economic Times*, 13 January 1999). Punjab, too, supplied free electricity to farmers (*Outlook*, 28 December 1998).

Until recently, agricultural/rural electricity consumers had been subsidized by industrial

nominal amount for a college, professional, or postgraduate education. Public utilities do not come close to even recouping their costs, let alone generating income for maintenance or investment in improved technology or expansion. State public corporations do not generate profits, and default regularly on the loans for covering their losses.[52]

At the end of December 1999, Nirupam Bajpai and Jeffrey Sachs were noting with alarm the state of the states' finances:

the revenue expenditure under non-developmental heads is expected to rise (in 1997–98) by about 20 per cent over an increase of 14.8 per cent in 1996–97; interest payments and administrative services would account for over 60 per cent of the total increase in revenue expenditure in 1997–98 ... the revenue deficits of the state governments have been rising since 1987–88. Large and persistent revenue deficits have implied a diversion of high-cost borrowings for consumption purposes, leading to a declining share of investment expenditures ... the investment outlays of the states as a ratio of the GDP declined from 2.8 per cent in 1990–91 to ... 2.2 per cent in 1997–98. An expenditure pattern of this type has had ... wide ranging implications such as for the adequacy and quality of infrastructure (*The Hindu*, 6 December 1999).

The states have been in the habit of covering shortfalls occasioned by their failure to recover the cost of services through overdrafts on the Centre, a practice referred to by government financial bodies as 'gap-filling'. One can imagine the softness of soft budget constraints in India when one considers that until the Tenth Finance Commission, 'successive finance commissions established a tradition of unconditional debt forgiveness ... These developments built expectations that the states need not be overly concerned with mobilising resources since ever-expanding and politically more expedient financing would be forthcoming.'[53] By the late 1980s, and certainly by the time the Narasimha Rao government launched economic

---

consumers whose rates were four to five times higher than those paid by agriculturalists. As the agricultural sector's consumption of electricity in particular states mounted (in Rajasthan, over the past ten years, it had jumped from 10 to 40 per cent of an expanding total supply, so that in 1999–2000 it equalled the industry's proportion), the system of cross-subsidization from industry to agriculture broke down, opening the way in 2000 to raise user charges from the agricultural economy.

[52]Loan defaults by state corporations, especially electricity and roadways corporations, are heavily implicated in the very high level of non-performing assets of public-sector banks. Frequently, such loans are backed by state government guarantees. State industrial, commercial, and service corporations have been 'notorious for defaulting on their debt and their (respective state) governments had earlier shown no interest to honour their obligations' ('Double Whammy; As State Corporations' Finances Worsen, States are Dragged Down', *Business Standard*, 21 October 1999).

[53]World Bank, India, *Sustaining Rapid Economic Growth*; World Bank, Washington, DC, 1997, p. 21.

liberalization in 1991, the Centre lost its capacity to routinely bail out state governments. Faced with mounting deficits that drove up the interest rates, it found it increasingly difficult to borrow for investment in economic growth, much less to finance state government deficits. Faced with the consequences of its own imprudence, the Centre has turned into an advocate for and enforcer of fiscal discipline on the states. To that end, and to cope with the state deficits' debilitating effect on the Centre's fiscal deficit, Prime Minister A.B. Vajpayee, Finance Minister Yashwant Sinha, Power Minister Suresh Prabhu, and Planning Commission Deputy Chairman K.C. Pant called on state chief ministers assembled in New Delhi to agree to a time bound one-time settlement of the states' Rs 26,000 crore power arrears. The finance minister suggested that 'we could think of issuing bonds and hold them till such time that the SEBs are in a position to pay', and the prime minister called on the states 'to revise agriculture tariff to raise it to at least 50 per cent of the average cost in three years'.[54]

The Centre is not without the means to enforce fiscal discipline on the states. Under the constitution, states must solicit and receive central government permission for all foreign borrowing and, *de facto*, for domestic borrowing as well.[55] The Centre exercises significant influence over lending institutions.[56]

[54]See front page story in *The Economic Times*, 4 March 2001, 'One-Time Settlement for SEBs Mooted; Centre to Power Reforms'.

[55]Article 293 (1) restricts state borrowing to domestic lenders: 'the executive power of a state extends to borrowing within the territory of India upon the security of the consolidated Fund of the state. ...' Equally decisive for the Centre's enforcement for fiscal discipline is Article 293 (3). It requires states that owe money to the Centre to obtain the Centre's consent to borrow: 'A state may not without the consent of the government of India raise any loan if there is still outstanding any part of a loan which has been made to the state by the government of India.' Since all states owe money to the GoI, the condition applies to all of them. Borrowing by state corporations often avoids this permission.

World Bank loans to state governments involve intensive negotiations between individual states and the Bank, but because they are foreign loans, they have to be processed and cleared by the central government. WB loans reach particular states as 70 per cent loan, 30 per cent grant. In fact the Centre, in return for additions to its foreign exchange balance, lowers the interest rate states pay, and absorbs the risk of variable foreign exchange rates.

[56]The Power Finance Corporation (PFC), for example, has used its leverage to nudge states to set up state electricity regulatory boards, devices to move the setting of electricity rates out of the hands of politicians and into a cost recouping process. In 1999, the PFC was offering a 5 per cent subsidy on loans taken where states set up such boards. Since then, central loans are threatened to be withheld where states do not take such steps (*The Economic Times*, 5 January 1999).

In October 1999, when the financial standing of many public-sector banks was in jeopardy as a result of heavy exposure to the non-performing assets of state-level corporations, observers thought the 'Reserve Bank of India (RBI) might come out with a list of criteria regarding such issues. This could include a limiting amount for such corporation as well as compulsory rating for them' ('State Corps May be Told to Adhere to Specific Norms', *Business Standard*, 27 October 1999).

It can also use the substantial energy supplies it controls through its ownership of the large thermal and hydel projects operated by the National Thermal Power Corporation (NTPC) and the National Hydel Power Corporation (NHPC) to enforce fiscal discipline on state electricity boards. Like California's reliance on states in the US northwest, many Indian states rely on the Centre for the viability of their power supply. The NTPC, the NHPC, and Coal India can and sometimes do use their control of power to deny supplies to defaulting states.[57] Despite the demise of the 'permit-licence raj', the Centre still reviews large foreign and domestic investment proposals.

Whether the constitutionally mandated finance commissions, appointed every five years to recommend the allocation of certain centrally collected taxes between the Centre and the states and among the states,[58] are agents of profligacy or discipline is subject to heated political debate. Southern and western state politicians and civil servants think they see a protector of fiscally irresponsible and incompetent northern states.[59] Traditionally, as heirs of the redistributive philosophy of the founding generation, the finance commission was seen as the rectifier of unacceptable disparities among the federal states.[60] The Eighth, Ninth, and Tenth Commission recommendations down to the year 2000 tilted central tax devolution markedly towards equalizing the financial condition of the states, rather than encouraging effort and effectiveness. After states began to routinely operate in deficit in the

[57]'Recently, the central public enterprises have been instructed by the central government to discontinue supplies to states in arrears. Thus Coal India has implemented a "cash and carry" policy for supplies to the State Electricity Boards (SEBs) in arrears, and the National Thermal Power Corporation has, at times, cut power supplies' (World Bank 1997, p. 21).

[58]See Constitutional Articles 280 and 281, which deal with the finance commission. Commissions make recommendations to the government, and the government places its version of the FC's recommendations before the parliament for its approval. FC recommendations are generally accepted with minor modifications. See 'Don't Shoot the Commission' (*Economic and Political Weekly*, 23 September 2000, pp. 3451–2, for exceptions).

Finance Commissions awards during the Nehru-Gandhi era were sometimes encroached upon by the Planning Commission, which in its heyday and even now makes developmental grants that cannot always be distinguished from grants-in-aid of revenue.

Made up of a chairman and four members appointed by the president of India from knowledgeable and distinguished persons, commissions are asked to 'determine what proportion of the receipts from designated taxes collected by the union government must be passed on to the states and how much in addition must be provided as grants-in-aid to states in need of such assistance after taking account of the amounts likely to accrue to them by way of tax devolution' (*Economic and Political Weekly* 2000, pp. 3451–2).

[59]Interviews with chief secretaries, finance secretaries, industry secretaries in Maharashtra, Andhra Pradesh, and Tamil Nadu in February 2000.

[60]'Under the aegis of national planning, it has been the declared policy to ensure balanced development of all regions ...', Chelliah, *Sustainable Growth*, p. 25. Like other observers, Chelliah notes that intention to the contrary not withstanding, 'interstate disparities have ... increased'.

1980s, finance commissions equally routinely, but without incentives or consequence, preached deficit reduction.[61] The Tenth Finance Commission, recommending for the period 1995–2000, rewarded indices of backwardness (large population, low per capita income) to the extent of 85 per cent while rewarding effort and initiative, such as infrastructure building and tax mobilization, by a meagre 15 per cent.[62] The Eleventh Finance Commission Report (2000), which reduced the percentage high income that states would receive in the total tax devolved by the Centre to the states from 13.14 to 9.75 per cent, also reduced the share of the middle-level states. In the wake of that report, Naidu, the Andhra CM and supremo of the TDP, a key component of the governing NDA coalition, declared war on the commission. He led a revolt of eight high and middle states publicly in August 2000. They challenged the traditional role of the finance commission as federal equalizer, and condemned it for encouraging fiscal and reproductive profligacy.[63] The call led to a marginal adaptation by the commission in a supplementary report. Whether finance commissions are competent under the constitution, as the Eleventh Commission claims to be, to make its grants conditional on fiscal discipline is being debated.[64]

The Centre can also pass a defining legislation from a constitutionally enumerated list of current subjects on which both the Centre and the states may legislate.[65] One of those subjects is electricity. The Electricity Act 2000, a Centre-initiated piece of legislation, places the central electricity authority and the newly established central and state electricity regulatory

[61]Madhav Godbole, 'Finance Commissions in a Cul-de-sac', *Economic and Political Weekly*, XXXVI (1), 2001, pp. 29–30.

[62]M.M. Sury, *Fiscal Federalism in India*, Delhi: Indian Tax Institute, 1998, pp. 81, 181.

[63]The criticisms and calls for redress of the Eleventh Finance Commission awards were initiated by Andhra Pradesh's chief minister, Chandrababu Naidu. He implied that the commission was using a formula that rewarded feckless high population growth, low economic growth states such as Bihar and Uttar Pradesh, and penalized successful low population growth, high economic growth states such as Andhra Pradesh and the seven other states who had joined Chandrababu's campaign. The campaign did not succeed in changing the overall framework of the Eleventh Finance Commission's award, but did succeed in having additional funds of Rs 53 billion allocated to the low population growth, high economic growth states.

The Economic and Political Weekly, in its issue of 23 September 2000, editorialized in alarm that 'never until the Eleventh Finance Commission has the report of any commission been subject to the kind of attacks and charges that have followed the publication oaf the report of this commission ...'. At the same time, it admitted that 'the task of allocating funds ... is undoubtedly a formidable one, especially when the goals to be achieved happen to embody fundamental conflicts between equity and efficiency', pp. 3451–2.

[64]Commissioner Amaresh Bagchi dissented from the Eleventh Finance Commission's conditionalities on this ground.

[65]Constitution of India, List III, Concurrent, item 38.

authorities in a dominant position with respect to state electricity planning and management.[66]

In recent years, the Centre has increasingly asked states to accept conditionalities in return for permissions and resources. Prime Minister Vajpayee, in May 2000, told the country's chief ministers assembled for a rare meeting of the interstate council, that 'the union government has taken some difficult decisions to contain subsidies at the centre. The states would be well advised to do the same.' There was no alternative, he added, to the 'new viable sustainable paradigm of a financial regime'.[67] No power supplements would be available to states unless they impose user fees on electricity, and show that the fees provide a reliable income stream for payments to the Centre for the energy supplied. He also told the chief ministers, in a constitutionally controversial move, that there would be no release of funds allocated by the finance commission until a state provides credible evidence demonstrating that it will mobilize the resources needed to meet the requirements of its own budget. And there would be no loans from the Centre without establishing an escrow account based on revenue income or user fees that guarantee the repayment of the loan. While in all of these assertions the bite has routinely fallen short of the bark, and intent fallen victim to postponement, they do reflect the new regulatory role of the Centre.

It would be wrong to suggest that the states regard the new fiscal discipline entirely as a burden. It is also a way in which to establish and defend the state governments' autonomy from local political pressures. 'It is not your friendly state governments who are making these oppressive demands. Our hands are tied by central interference and control.' Something analogous happened at the national level at the outset of liberalization in 1991. Prime Minister Narasimha Rao and his finance minister, Manmohan Singh, were able to shelter their fledgling hard budget constrained liberalization measures against political attack by pleading that without such measures, international lenders would not help India avoid default. Similarly, state chief ministers can now blame the imposition of user charges for services on the Centre, even while benefiting from the financial and

[66]See memorandum by Pramod Deo, principal secretary, energy, government of Maharashtra, 'The Electricity Bill 2000—A Critical Appraisal', no date, ca May 2000, which provides a history of the legislation and suggests the ways in which states can shape their own energy regime if their legislation precedes the passage of the central act.

[67]'Share the Burden of Hard Decisions: PM', (*The Hindu*, 21 May 2000). Not that the chief ministers acquiesced supinely. 'There is no reason,' said Maharashtra Chief Minister Vilas Rao Deshmukh, 'why the centre should take decisions which affect millions of families across the country on its own without taking popular governments in the states into confidence.'

political independence they make possible. It remains to be seen whether politicians can supply firm power for most of the working day and, if so, whether, when they levy and collect user charges for it, they will be re-elected.

But the Centre as regulator and fiscal disciplinarian is not the only constraint with which states have to deal as the price of their new-found autonomy. They also have to deal with the hard budget constraints required by faceless, apolitical, credit-rating agencies. With fewer and fewer public investment funds available for infrastructure investment in power plants, bridges, roads, ports, and telecommunications, states have increasingly turned to private borrowing, usually in the form of bonds. Their capacity to borrow at a reasonable cost in terms of the interest rate to be paid depends on their ranking by credit-rating information systems of India (CRISIL) or CARE, the two major domestic credit-rating agencies. CRISIL downgraded Maharashtra's credit rating in October 1999 just as the state was about to issue bonds to fund four irrigation projects. CRISIL pointed to the deterioration in the fiscal situation of India's richest state after it matched the Centre's pay raises for government employees.[68] Foreign private investors, like domestic ones, make their investment and interest rate decisions in the light of credit ratings, but foreign investors pay attention to international raters such as Standard and Poor's.[69] Working for and achieving favourable credit ratings have increasingly become a powerful incentive for states to practise fiscal discipline, and implement hard-budget constraints. The market, like the Centre, has begun to regulate state economic thinking and conduct.

What are the implications for a federal market economy of coalition governments based on one national party such as the BJP and several politically decisive state parties? Is a BJP-led central government prepared to tighten the fiscal screws on a BJP-controlled state government? Would it be tempted to use central government discretion and resources to help woo

---

[68]When CRISIL downgraded the bonds of four state corporations charged with Konkan irrigation, Krishna valley development, Tapi irrigation, and Vidarbha irrigation, it blamed the 'persistent rise in (Maharashtra's) ... revenue and fiscal deficit to higher levels' on the 'revision in pay scales or state employees following recommendations of the Fifth Pay Commission'. 'Fiscal recovery in the long run,' CRISIL wrote, 'would be contingent on the state government's willingness to speedily implement significant revenue augmentation and fiscal reform measures' (*Business Standard*, 7 October 1990). CARE, another major domestic credit-rating agency, had come in with a more favourable rating earlier that year for bond issue to support a Godavari project (*The Economic Times*, 8 January 1999).

[69]Indian papers regularly carried the credit ratings of international and domestic credit-rating agencies such as Standard and Poor's and CRISIL. See, for example, the report by Standard and Poor's in March 2000, affirming its triple-'B'/'A'-3 local currency sovereign credit rating, and its double-'B'/single-'B' foreign currency sovereign credit ratings for the Republic of India (*Hindustan Times*, 22 March 2000).

voters in a state assembly election where its candidates are fighting from behind? Would it want to tighten fiscal discipline on a laggardly UP, where its government was already in deep trouble politically? Would a coalition government be prepared to resist the demands made by key state parties in its coalition? Will one result of state parties playing a more important role in national politics be to compromise the Centre's role as market regulator and guardian of fiscal discipline?[70] Such a tendency will be countered by the depth and seriousness of the Centre's and the states' fiscal deficits, and by pressure from coalition partners and departmental bureaucrats to preserve some appearance of even-handedness. To address deficits, India's states will have to be able to collect user fees for services provided and to attract private investment, both foreign and domestic, to upgrade and expand not only their physical infrastructure, but also their education and health services.

CONCLUSION

The emergence in the 1990s of a federal market economy that replaced a Nehruvian permit-licence raj and centrally planned economy followed the launching of economic liberalization in 1991. The market economy it fostered was a necessary but not sufficient condition for the formation of a federal market economy. The sufficient condition was the transformation of India's party and government system from a one-party dominant majority party system to a regionalized multiparty coalition government system. The economic and political causal chains proceeded more or less independently until 1989–1991, when they intersected. The result of that intersection was a mutually reinforcing relationship that helps to account for the formation of a federal market economy. The states in India's federal system command more economic and political sovereignty than they did under a Nehruvian planned economy; their voices matter more in economic and political decisions. States are challenged to be more self-reliant; increasingly, they have to navigate as tubs on their own bottoms. However, they are also faced with new restraints on their enhanced autonomy. As the Centre's interventionist and tutelary role has faded, its role as regulatory state has expanded. The states have found that the price of more freedom is more responsibility for growth and fiscal discipline.

[70]Kewal Varela argued in October 1999 that as 120 of the 300 members of the governing coalition in parliament were from single state parties (he counted the BJP, Congress, CPI, and CPI [M] as national), the state voice at the Centre had grown. He also argued that increased regional influence at the Centre means that the fiscal deficit will not be contained. 'Globalisation versus localisation', *Business Standard*, 29 October 1999.

12

Redoing the Constitutional Design
From an Interventionist to a Regulatory State*

Lloyd I. Rudolph and Susanne Hoeber Rudolph

O n 27 January 2000, President K.R. Narayanan, in an address in the central hall of parliament to mark the golden jubilee of the republic and the constitution, asked whether 'it is the constitution that has failed us or we who have failed the constitution'.[1] The president was responding critically to the appointment of a commission 'to comprehensively review the Constitution of India in the light of the experience of the past 50 years and to make suitable recommendations'.[2] Unlike the presidential speech at the

---

*Originally published as 'Redoing the constitutional design: from an interventionist to a regulatory state', in Atul Kohli (ed.), *The Success of India's Democracy*, Cambridge: Cambridge University Press, 2001, pp. 127–62.

[1]The full text of the President's golden jubilee speech is given in *Seminar,* 487, March 2000, pp. 88–90, and in *Mainstream,* 38 (8), 12 February 2000, pp. 9–11. Accounts of the debate surrounding the speech are given, *inter alia,* in *The Asian Age,* 28 January 2000 and *Business Line,* 1 February 2000. See Mitra and Ahmed (2000) for an overview.

[2]This is the language of the BJP's 1998 manifesto. Although the BJP, like the other twenty-one parties of the National Democratic Alliance (NDA), dropped its manifesto in favour of a common minimum programme on which all parties of the coalition contested the thirteenth national election in 1999, the language of the minimum programme and the post-election government announcement closely followed the language of the BJP's 1998 manifesto. This manifesto is given in Aggarwal and Chowdhry 1998, pp. 43–4.

The NDA government asked former chief justice and former chair of the National Human Rights Commission, M.N. Venkatachaliah, to chair an eleven-member commission. His acceptance was conditioned on an understanding that he would have a say in choosing the commission's members, and that there would be no change in the constitution's 'basic features', a term made famous by the landmark *Keshavananda* (1973) case. Justice Venkatachaliah's conditions seemed to exclude the 'presidential form of government' favoured by BJP ministers of the NDA government who sought 'stability'. The president obliquely addressed those seeking 'stability' in his golden jubilee address by placing accountability above stability, 'which could slip into an authoritarian exercise of power'. *Mainstream,* 12 February 2000, p. 10.

opening of parliament, President Narayanan's golden jubilee address was not written for him by the government of the day. It represented an autonomous presidential perspective. Widely reported and much discussed in print and in the electronic media, the speech deepened and accelerated a national debate on the constitution that the NDA government's action had provoked. The speech also signalled that presidents have been able to be more independent of prime ministers and cabinets since 1989, when coalition governments displaced majority party governments.[3] Such basic changes in the party system and in electoral outcomes show that a constitution is a living thing, a process, and not just a blueprint; a work in progress, not a monument.

Because a constitution is a living thing, we read the word 'constitution' to mean more than its formal aspect, more than a text frequently amended by parliament and interpreted by the Supreme Court.[4] We also mean the conventional constitution, consisting of widely recognized and commonly accepted rules, practices, and institutions, and the symbolic constitution, consisting of collective representations, signifiers, and metaphors that help to define 'India' and Indianness. Regardless of whether constitutions are formal, conventional, or symbolic, their meaning is continually contested, and their legitimacy is subject to renewal.[5]

Attending exclusively to the formal constitution would mean missing

---

On 23 February 2000, when President Narayanan opened the budget session of parliament, he read from a text written for him by the government. Nevertheless, his words seemed to show traces of his own input. 'While keeping the basic structure and salient features of the Constitution inviolate,' he told parliament, 'it has become necessary to examine the experience of the past 50 years to better achieve the ideals enshrined in the Constitution.' He assured his listeners that the recommendations of the review commission 'will be presented before Parliament'. *Hindustan Times*, 24 February 2000.

[3]After eight national elections, 1952 through 1984, which yielded eight majority governments, five subsequent national elections, 1989 through 1999, produced four coalition governments and one minority government.

[4]Like the United States, India has a written constitution whose provisions are subject to amendment and judicial review. In India the doctrine and practice of judicial review was challenged by the claim that a sovereign parliament had unlimited powers of amendment. In particular, Prime Minister Indira Gandhi in 1976 tried, by having the parliament adopt the forty-second amendment, to override the Supreme Court's decision in *Keshavananda Bharati* (1973) that parliament's power to amend the constitution be limited by the constitution's basic structure or 'essential features', for example, holding free and fair elections. The forty-second amendment made parliament's claim to unlimited sovereignty explicit. Minerva Mills (1980) invalidated the two clauses of the forty-second amendment meant to reverse *Keshavananda*. For a detailed account, see Lloyd I. Rudolph and Susanne Hoeber Rudolph 1987, *In Pursuit of Lakshmi: The Political Economy of the Indian State*, Chicago: University of Chicago Press, Ch. 3; and D.D. Basu, 1999, *Shorter Constitution of India*, Agra, Nagpur, New Delhi: Wadhwa & Company, Law Publishers, pp. 1138–49.

[5]A longer revised version of this chapter appeared as a chapter in our forthcoming study, 'Living with Difference: Economic, Political and Cultural Dimensions of Sharing Sovereignty in India's Federal System'.

out on the fundamental changes in constitutional ideas and practices that distinguished the Indian state of the 1990s from that of the 1950s. Neither the party system nor the Planning Commission, central forces in creating the constitutional order, are mentioned in the formal constitution. Attention to the conventional constitution directs us to analyse change in the party and federal systems, and the changing balance of power between branches and units of government. It highlights, as no close analysis of formal constitutional provisions can, the erosion of the centralized Nehruvian state and economy that prevailed for four decades after independence in 1947. Analysis of the conventional constitution reveals that in the 1990s a multiparty system, including strong regional parties, displaced a dominant party system; market ideas and practices displaced central planning and a 'permit-license raj'; and the federal system took on a new lease of life with the federal states gaining ground at the expense of the Centre. With the launching of economic reform in 1991, a centralized, tutelary, interventionist state, whose political and administrative elites were committed to the notion that they knew best and could do best, was challenged by an increasingly decentralized regulatory state and market economy whose politicians and entrepreneurs turned to voters, consumers, and investors for ideas and actions.

The formal constitution, too, was not static. The balance of power between central institutions that was provided for in the formal constitution was reshaped by the practice of actors responding to historical challenges. The balance shifted in favour of the Supreme Court, the Election Commission, and the president at the expense of parliament, the prime minister, and the cabinet. Here, we address changes in only one aspect of the formal constitutional design, the contribution of enhanced roles for the Supreme Court, the president, and the Election Commission to the emergence of a regulatory state.[6]

RENEGOTIATING THE BALANCE OF POWER: THE JUDICIARY, THE PRESIDENCY AND THE ELECTION COMMISSION

We have noted that since the onset of economic reform in 1991, the Indian economy has moved away from central planning by an interventionist state and moved towards market competition fostered by a regulatory state. Something similar happened in the conduct of politics: a dominant party

---

[6]We have borrowed the term 'regulatory state' in the sense used in this chapter from Matthew C.J. Rudolph, who is working on a comparative study, 'Making Markets: Financial Organization, Economic Transitions, and the Emergence of the Regulatory State in India and China', Ph.D. proposal, Department of Government, Cornell University, 1998.

system and majority governments have given way to a multiparty system and coalition governments. In institutional terms, the displacement of an interventionist by a regulatory state has meant a diminished executive and legislature and enhanced regulatory institutions—less scope for cabinet and parliament, more scope for the Supreme Court, the election commission, and the president.

The role of regulatory institutions is more procedural than substantive, more rule-making and enforcing than law-making and policy-making. Regulatory institutions are needed not only to create, sustain, and perfect markets, but also to ensure procedural fairness in the election and operation of a multiparty system, and in the formation and conduct of coalition governments in a federal framework. The difficulties and failures of transitions to market economies and to democracy in a variety of settings have revealed their dependence on the rule of law and a viable state.[7] The emergence in some Eastern European states, and particularly Russia, of what Max Weber would have called political capitalism,[8] the accumulation of wealth through power rather than entrepreneurship, has been accompanied by fraud, crime, and violence. The result suggests that transitions to a market economy and democracy require more than privatization and liberty.

Such considerations also apply to India even though the economic and political transitions it has experienced have been less traumatic than those in Eastern Europe and Russia. Three constitutionally mandated institutions, the Supreme and high courts, the president, and the Election Commission, became more visible and effective in the 1990s as the reputations and authority of political executives (union and state cabinets) and legislatures (parliament and state assemblies) lost ground. During the Nehru/Gandhi years of Congress dominance, political executives and legislatures benefited from association with the (declining) political capital of the nationalist era's struggle against colonial rule and for independence; the one-party-dominant party system; and the authority and resources of a command economy. As these three predisposing conditions lost their potency, political

---

[7]Stephen Holmes, 1977, 'What Russia Teaches us Now: How Weak States Threaten Freedom', *The American Prospect*, no. 33, pp. 30–40.

[8]For a systematic development of the idea of and practice of political capitalism in Eastern Europe and Russia with special attention paid to Bulgaria, see Ganev, 1999.

Thomas L. Friedman (1998) argued that the ultimate test of US policy in China is 'how well the US uses its influence to promote a more rule-of-law system in China—one that first constrains the Chinese state and then gradually lays an institutional foundation that can carry Chinese society forward after the inevitable collapse of the Communist Party or its evolution into an electoral body'. Chaudhry (1997) shows how the quality and strength of institutions have determined economic viability and market success and failure in Yemen and Saudi Arabia.

executives and legislatures receded, opening space and creating opportunities for courts, presidents, and election commissioners to act in ways that emphasized their constitutional roles as the regulatory mechanisms of democratic politics.[9]

The fading of structural conditions that supported the pre-eminence of executives and legislatures by itself does not account for their fall from grace. Prime and chief ministers, legislators, and the civil servants who served them discredited themselves in the eyes of India's educated middle classes[10] who, as producers, consumers, and citizens, cared about the reliability and security that a government of laws promised to deliver. A burgeoning constituency, the middle classes responded in the mid-1980s to Rajiv Gandhi's promises to provide a clean government and a high-tech, reformed, environmentally friendly economy that would take India into the twenty-first century. After Rajiv disappointed them, the symbolic politics and practical measures spawned by the Supreme Court, the president, and the Election Commission spoke to their attitudes, moods, and interests. The Bofors scandal that drove Rajiv Gandhi from office in 1989 symbolized the pervasiveness of corruption. From *bakshish* for the little guy to bribes for his boss to 'commissions' for the governing elite, office was seen to serve as a source of income. Permit-licence raj had become 'rent raj'. Intimidation, violence, and black money were being used to win elections. In the early 1990s an unprecedented number of ministers at state and national levels were indicted for taking bribes.[11] The complexity and fragility of the coalition

[9]For an authoritative overview of the complex 395-article constitution that came into force on 26 January 1950, see D.D. Basu, 1994, *Introduction to the Constitution of India*, New Delhi: Prentice Hall of India.

[10]We use 'educated middle classes' as a portmanteau phrase to refer to the old, raj era as well as new professional and Green Revolution-era middle classes insofar as their education, which usually includes some English, enables them to share an information (media) and consumer (market) culture. We are aware that these differences are further cross-cut by the cultural variations that mark India's federal states. A Mumbai-wallah is not the same as a Calcutta-, New Delhi-, or Chennai-wallah, although many share enough in the way of attitudes, moods, and interest to speak on occasion of national middle classes—readers of the national weekly magazines and buyers of nationally advertised brands.

[11]The most spectacular cases of the 1990s were associated with illegal transactions which the seized diary of businessman S.K. Jain was said to have documented. According to accounts leaked to the press, nine serving or former ministers were implicated by illegal payments and use of foreign exchange. Subsequently, all charges were dropped. In 1993, then Prime Minister Narasimha Rao was accused of having had Rs 10 million paid to four Jharkhand Mukti Morcha MPs to secure their support in a confidence vote designed to bring down his government. Large sums of cash were found in Telecommunications Minister Sukh Ram's house at the height of decision-making about which firms were to be awarded contracts for providing regional service contracts. The then chief minister of Bihar, Laloo Prasad Yadav, was forced to resign and was temporarily imprisoned over a $280,000,000 cattle fodder scam.

governments formed after 1989 on the basis of hung parliaments (and hung state assemblies), their rapid turnover, and their dependence on regional parties created complexities and ambiguities that further enhanced the role of the regulatory branches of government.

As executives and legislature were perceived as being increasingly ineffectual, unstable, and corrupt, the Supreme and high courts, the presidency, and the Election Commission became the objects of a middle-class public's hopes and aspirations, only partially fulfilled, that someone would defend a government of laws and enforce probity and procedural regularity.

JUDICIAL ACTIVISM

India's judiciary, a Supreme Court created by Article 124 and state high courts created by Article 214, are important components of India's written constitution. In the era of unstable, short-lived coalition governments in the 1990s,[12] the Supreme Court's judicial activism helped to repair and correct the Indian state. The court played a critical role in approximating a framework of lawfulness and predictability that has had some success in protecting citizens' rights, limiting malfeasance, and safeguarding environmental and other public goods.

The court's judicial activism marks a novel turn in India's constitutional history. In the first four decades of the court's existence, it was pitted against the Nehru and Gandhi governments' efforts to expand parliamentary sovereignty at the expense of judicial review.[13] The contest arose because the

---

The degradation of the early to mid-1990s came against the background of the Bofors case, the allegation that Prime Minister Rajiv Gandhi and/or those closely associated with him had accepted substantial 'commissions' when the GOI placed an order for $1.4 billion worth of artillery pieces with Bofors, a Swedish armaments firm. The charges against Rajiv Gandhi as of 2000 remained unsettled. They haunt his memory and hover like a dark cloud over the Congress party presidency of his widow and political heir, Sonia Gandhi.

[12]Between 1989 and 1999 eight governments held power: V.P. Singh's Janata Dal minority coalition government 1989–91; S. Chandrasekhar's six-month minority government, 1990–1; Atal Behari Vajpayee's minority BJP government, thirteen days in June 1991; P.V. Narasimha Rao's mostly minority Congress government, 1991–6; Deve Gowda's minority United Front government succeeded by Inder Kumar Gujral's minority UF government, 1996–8; Atal Behari Vajpayee's two BJP-led coalition governments, 1998–9 and 1999–2004.

[13]India's written constitution and contested practice of judicial review does not mean that those who framed India's constitution were committed, as the US framers were, to protecting liberty by constructing a system of separation of powers and checks and balances. It is important to remember that even the US constitution did not explicitly provide for judicial review of legislative acts, that is, laws passed by the two Houses of Congress, the House of Representatives, and the Senate, and presented to and signed by the president. It was Chief Justice John Marshall who, in *Marbury vs Madison* (1803), established 'the principle of judicial review and the Supreme Court's sovereign right to interpret the meaning of the Constitution' by striking down the Judiciary

framers of India's constitution created a hybrid that joined the parliamentary sovereignty of the British model[14] with the judicial review of the US model.

The first clashes between parliamentary sovereignty and judicial review occurred when the court in *Golak Nath vs State of Punjab* (1967) invoked the constitution's protection of fundamental rights,[15] particularly the right to property, to challenge the Nehru government's land reform legislation. The decision restricted parliament's competency to amend fundamental rights.[16] A more momentous round of confrontations surrounded the emergency regime (1975–7) imposed by Indira Gandhi.[17] Using the Congress party's parliamentary majority to pass the forty-second amendment (1976), she tried to eliminate the court's use of judicial review to limit parliament's power under Article 368 to amend the constitution. She did not succeed. An earlier landmark case, *Keshavananda vs State of Kerala* (1973), persisted, and was again upheld in the *Minerva Mills* case in 1980.[18] In *Keshavananda*

Act of 1789 (Ellis 1998, p. 267). The next time the court declared a legislative act unconstitutional was fifty-four years later in 1857, when, in the Dred Scott case, it held the 1820 'Missouri Compromise' law barring slavery in northern territories unconstitutional.

The relative ease with which the contemporary US Supreme Court declares legislative acts unconstitutional should not obscure Marshall's innovation or judicial review's very tentative beginnings. For a more detailed analysis in a comparative framework, see Rudolph and Rudolph 1987, pp. 103–26.

[14]The term 'parliamentary sovereignty' refers to the pre-eminence of a hyphenated entity, cabinet-in-parliament. The executive, the prime minister, and his or her council of ministers or cabinet, is elected by the legislature and is dependent on its continuing support. Put another way, the prime minister and his ministerial cabinet colleagues are members of parliament and have the confidence of the lower house. They do not confront the legislature as a contrary force. The Indian Supreme Court invoked a conventional English characterization when it referred to the relationship as 'a hyphen which joins, a buckle which fastens', in *Ram Jawaya vs State of Punjab*, 1955, 2 SCR 225.

[15]Basu 1994, p. 433, Table VI.

[16]*Golak Nath vs State of Punjab*, A 1967 SC 1643. It reversed *Shankari Prasad vs Union of India* 1951 AIR (SC) 458, which held that no part of the constitution was unamendable, and *Sajjan Singh vs State of Rajasthan* 1964 AIR (SC) 845. The Indira Gandhi government's response to *Golak Nath* was the twenty-fourth amendment which modified Article 368, the amendment clause, so as to make the fundamental rights provided for by part III of the constitution susceptible to parliamentary amendment.

[17]For a discussion of Supreme Court opinions in relation to the court's internal struggles and to varying political environments, including the emergency regime, see Baxi 1980. See also Rudolph and Rudolph 1987, pp. 118–20.

[18]The cases are *Keshavananda vs State of Kerala*, A 1973 SC 1461 (FB) and *Minerva Mills vs Union of India*, A 1980 SC 1789. In the *Minerva Mills* case, the court invoked *Keshavananda* to declare invalid, because they attacked the basic structure of the constitution, the two clauses of the forty-second amendment meant to reverse *Keshavananda*. The first prohibited court review of laws that contravened fundamental rights if parliament declared that they gave effect to directive principles of state policy; the second proscribed judicial review of constitutional amendments. See Rudolph and Rudolph 1987, p. 117. For a thoughtful consideration of the issues in the *Minerva Mills* case, see Noorani 1981, pp. 293–300.

the justices agreed that, using Article 368, governments could amend fundamental rights, but held that there were certain *basic features* of the constitution that could not be altered.

If, therefore, a Constitution Amendment Act seeks to alter the basic structure or framework of the Constitution, the Court would be entitled to annul it on the ground of *ultra vires*, because the word 'amend,' in Art. 368, means only changes other than altering the very structure of the Constitution, which would be tantamount to making a new Constitution.[19]

The practice of judicial review survived the buffeting of the 1970s, though the court emerged chastened. It showed skill in recapturing its role in the 1980s when, by beginning to entertain public interest legislations (PIL)—similar to class action suits in the US—it laid the basis for the judicial activism of the 1990s. As the court's PIL version of judicial activism suited Indira Gandhi's (1980–4) and Rajiv Gandhi's (1985–9) populist agendas, the two Congress prime ministers did not perceive PIL as a threat to their governments' claim to parliamentary sovereignty. The court's decisions and actions in the pre-economic reform phase of judicial activism sought to enforce citizens' fundamental rights[20] and, more broadly, to protect the human rights of the poor and the powerless. The court sought to safeguard human rights against state abuses, for example, police brutality and torture, custodial rape, and inhuman treatment in jails and 'protective' homes.[21] In the late 1980s and early 1990s, the court extended its judicial activism to protecting the viability of public goods, for example, clean air and water, and uncontaminated blood supplies.

In the mid-1990s the court's judicial activism turned in yet another direction. Coinciding with the rise of precariously balanced coalition governments and a marked increase in ministerial-level corruption, the Supreme Court moved to restore the independence of the Central Bureau of Investigation (CBI), the union government's principal investigative agency. As far back as January 1988, after Prime Minister Rajiv Gandhi had been implicated in the payment of illegal commissions by the Swedish armament

---

[19]Basu 1994, p. 151.

[20]Ibid., p. 433, Table VI.

[21]The judges, led by Chief Justice Bhagwati, were initially responding to a case (*Upendra vs State of U.P.* [1981] 3 Scale 1137 SC) in which two law professors complained that the fundamental rights of the inmates of a protective home were being violated by the government (Basu 1999, p. 270).

After the initial encouragement given to PIL by Chief Justice Bhagwati in the early 1980s, there was a lull of some years. PIL resumed in 1993 with the twenty-month term of Justice M.N. Venkatachaliah, who 'set the tone for a new activism'. He was soon followed by Justice, later Chief Justice, J.S. Verma and Justice Kuldip Singh (Gupta 1996).

firm, Bofors, for a gun deal with the GOI, the CBI was made subject to 'the single directive', that is, 'prior consultation with the Secretary of the Ministry/ Department concerned before ... [the CBI] takes up any enquiry, including ordering search. ... Without this concurrence, no enquiry shall be initiated by the [CBI].'[22]

'Prior consultation' and 'government concurrence' meant that prime ministers, who also controlled CBI appointments, promotions, and transfers, dominated CBI initiatives and actions. The extent of control was highlighted with the discovery of the 'Jain diaries', a record of payments to politicians by an influence-peddling commission agent, S.K. Jain.[23] As news of the Jain diary's contents spread, seemingly implicating not only cabinet ministers and leading politicians but also the then sitting prime minister, Narasimha Rao, the CBI's inability to act without government concurrence seemed to some including, eventually, Supreme Court justices, unconscionable. There was a 'common belief', a leading news magazine reported, 'that it is the near complete abdication of responsibility by the Government as well as Parliament which has created the conditions for the current bout of judicial activism'.[24]

A Supreme Court division bench headed by then Justice, later Chief Justice, J.S. Verma, 'felt it was necessary to free the CBI from the Prime Minister's charge to eliminate any impression of bias'. The court asked the CBI to not furnish information to Prime Minister Rao regarding the details of the investigation. This meant that for all practical purposes, the CBI would report only to the Supreme Court with respect to the investigations and charge sheeting (indictments) that arose from the information found in the Jain diaries.[25] After issuing directives removing the CBI from direct executive supervision, the court asked it to follow up on evidence found in the diaries. They implicated many leading politicians with respect to illegal foreign exchange violations, bribes, and kickbacks. With court prodding and supervision, twenty-six politicians were indicted, including seven of Prime Minister Narasimha Rao's cabinet colleagues.[26]

---

[22]For more details see Rani 1998, pp. 24–6, and Jha and Kang 1996.

The January 1988 order was issued by the then minister of state of the personnel department, P. Chidambaram. The personnel department ministerial portfolio is usually held by the prime minister, often, as in this case, with a minister of state to assist him.

[23]See note 10 for details.

[24]Jha and Kang 1996, p. 13.

[25]Ghimire 1996.

[26]Vineet Narain and Kamini Jaiswal, both civil rights lawyers, 'persuaded the Supreme Court to get the CBI to hasten its investigations in the multi-crore havala transactions case' (Jha and Kang 1996). Several of those indicted were not prosecuted, for example, Madhavrao Scindia and Sharad Yadav. 'Law Makers or Breakers? 39 MPs have Criminal Cases Pending Against Them', Outlook, 14 August 1996, pp. 6 and 9.

While most of those implicated by the Jain diaries were found to be not guilty,[27] the court, supported overwhelmingly by middle-class public opinion, persisted in its role as upholder of norms and agent of good government.[28] On 18 December 1997, after the Rao Congress government had been rejected by the electorate, the Supreme Court in a landmark judgment made its arrangements of March 1996 permanent. It did so by removing the 'single directive' (government concurrence) that governed CBI investigations, and by giving the CBI director a minimum two-year term in office.[29] These actions left the CBI somewhat freer to investigate ministerial cases on its own cognizance, and to follow up on *prima facie* cases it had left unattended because it lacked 'government concurrence'.

Not surprisingly, the court's judicial activism with respect to the CBI and on other matters precipitated counter-moves to limit the court initiatives.

Further investigation and court reviews of procedure and evidence led to the dropping of charges, including those against the Jain brothers. *Deccan Chronicle*, 10 February 2000. Already as of December 1997, according to a CBI spokesman, '20-odd charge-sheeted politicians were sitting pretty in their bungalows. All but two charge sheets have been thrown out in the preliminary stages for lack of prima facie evidence. ... The Supreme Court pressurized us [the CBI] into charge-sheeting these politicians' (Rani 1998, p. 25).

[27]By 1999, observers worried whether, with the retirement of Justice Kuldip Singh and others of the activist generation, the court would retreat from its role as anti-corruption watchdog. See *India Today's* comments on the reversal of the Rs 50 lakh exemplary damage assessed against former petroleum minister Satish Sharma for mishandling his discretionary powers to award petrol pumps (16 August 1999).

[28]An opinion poll conducted in February 1996 found that 89 per cent of urban respondents felt that the judiciary was doing 'a commendable job', and 94 per cent that 'the judiciary should continue to cleanse the system'. 'Judiciary is doing a great job; An Outlook-MODE opinion poll finds overwhelming support for judicial activism', *Outlook*, 6 March 1996, p. 18. The sample was made of up 551 respondents from Delhi, Bombay, Calcutta, Madras, and Bangalore. Another urban poll in October 1996 found that 75 per cent of the sample thought politicians were corrupt and 73 per cent thought the court was proceeding fairly against them. The results of the poll are reported in *Outlook*, 23 October 1996. A total of 1,234 interviews were conducted on 9–10 October by MODE in five cities—Delhi, Bombay, Madras, Calcutta, and Bangalore. For details of the results see pp. 8 and 9.

According to CPI-M spokesperson H.K.S. Surjeet, 'Politicians of all hues—including those who were part of the government in the last five years—unanimously subscribe to the view that the judiciary stepped in to compensate for a weak, listless executive ... "a vacuum created by an executive that has stopped functioning." The judiciary, he says, has "stepped in largely on behalf of the people and is seen to be doing so in popular perception."'

Ramakrishna Hegde, former chief minister of Karnataka, spoke of the '"unhealthy camaraderie between legislators and civil servants" [that] has led to the latter abdicating their responsibility to discharge their duties without fear or favor.' Sushma Swaraj, BJP spokesperson, believed that 'judicial activism has come into play because of the failure of the executive'. At the same time, she, like politicians across the party spectrum, thought that judicial activism was 'a dangerous trend in itself'. *Outlook*, 23 October 1996, pp. 6 and 7.

[29]Rani 1998, p. 24; *India Today*, 29 December 1997, pp. 30–1.

The careers and political survival of leading politicians were at stake. One counter-move was an initiative to remove the constitutional prohibition (Article 121) against parliamentary discussions of the conduct of Supreme Court or high court judges. Another was a conclave called by the then speaker of the Lok Sabha, Purno Sangma, to address the question of judicial activism. It concluded that 'the judiciary was exhibiting a dangerous tendency to encroach on legislative and administrative foundations beyond its ambit [and] that the judges were populists playing to the gallery in the recent spate of widely-publicized corruption trials'.[30]

The court's activism arose not only as a response to state processes, but also from the interplay between state and civil society. The 1980s saw an extraordinary burgeoning of non-governmental voluntary organizations and social movements dedicated to a wide variety of goals and causes, from opposing environmental degradation and big dams (Narmada, Tehri) to exposures of child and bonded labour, Dalit (ex-untouchable) empowerment, and historical and cultural preservation. In the early 1990s there may have been between 50,000 and 100,000 NGOs at work in India.[31] Together with an array of individual litigators, for example, Goldman Environmental Prize winner M.C. Mehta and H.D. Shourie of Common Cause, NGOs used PIL to advance their agendas. In the 1980s and more so in the 1990s, a growing synergy linked Supreme and high court justices, a resurgent civil society, and reform-minded members of the middle classes.

Public interest litigation could begin and flourish in India because its Supreme Court exercises original jurisdiction not only with respect to disputes between different units of the federation (Article 131), but also with respect to the enforcement of fundamental rights (Article 32). The evolution of the court's original jurisdiction under Article 32 led to the so-called 'epistolary jurisdiction'[32]—recognizing postcards from victims of state impropriety and lawlessness as writ petitions, including postcards from jail inmates. In the early 1980s Chief Justice P.N. Bhagwati and Justice Krishna Iyer took the

---

[30]*Outlook*, 23 October 1996, p. 6.

[31]See Mary Katzenstein, Uday Mehta, and Usha Thakkar, 1997, 'The Rebirth of Shiv Sena: The Symbiosis of Discursive and Organizational Power', *Journal of Asian Studies*, 56(2), May, pp. 371–91; Kothari 1993, 'Social Movements and the Redefinition of Democracy', in Philip Oldenburg (ed.), *India Briefing, 1993*, Boulder Co.: Westview Press; and Gail Omvedt 1993, *Reinventing Revolution: New Social Movements and the Socialist Tradition in India*, Armonk, NY: M.E. Sharpe.

[32]The term seems to have been coined by Upendra Baxi.

The legal meaning of Article 32 was expanded through aggressive litigation by social activist lawyers acting on behalf of social movements and NGOs to override the principle that only the person who has suffered injury by reason of violation of his or her legal rights or interest is entitled to seek judicial redress.

lead in promoting this novel jurisdiction. The court further modified Article 32 by allowing PIL litigators to bring class action suits on behalf of the poor, oppressed, and victimized because, in the court's view, they are often not in a position to represent their own interest.[33]

Supreme and high court activity on behalf of environmental and other public goods has been as striking as that on behalf of victims of state lawlessness. Attracting most media coverage were actions to save the Taj Mahal from the effects of pollutants. By 1992, the Supreme Court had ordered the closure of 212 industries near the Taj Mahal that were in chronic violation of environmental regulations. It took similar action with respect to 190 polluters on the banks of the Ganges river.[34] In 1996 and 1997 it extended its enforcement rulings to industrial violators in the heavily polluted Delhi. Even more than its PIL actions, its environmental enforcement efforts generated resistance from powerful interests, and suffered from civic inertia. In 1999, the Delhi government was requesting two years' grace for non-complying polluting industries. In February 2000, however, the Supreme Court ordered the closure of outlets emitting pollutants into the Yamuna river, and threatened to jail for contempt state government officials who obeyed Delhi environment minister A.K. Walia's and industry minister Dr Narendra Nath's orders to keep them open.[35] It remains to be seen whether constituencies for human rights and environmental protection will continue to support the court's judicial activism.

[33]The court enlarged the concept of 'persons aggrieved' to include public-spirited individuals or associations, 'provided only he ... is not actuated by political motive or other oblique motive' (Basu 1999, p. 289).

Basu suggests that these decisions have carved a legal space beyond conventional adversarial law, 'involving collaboration and cooperation between the Government and its officers, the Bar and the Bench, for the purpose of making human rights meaningful for the weaker sections of the community' (ibid., p. 291).

The enlargement of the concept, together with the invoking of original jurisdiction, has led to a horrendous overload of the courts, with a backlog, in 1995, of 28 million cases in the Supreme Court and the eighteen high courts; 37,000 of these were accounted for by the Supreme Court, and 765,426 by the Allahabad high court in India's largest state, Uttar Pradesh.

For a running discussion of the overload problem by legal professionals sympathetic to public interest legislation, see the annual publication of the Indian Law Institute, *Annual Survey of Indian Law*. See especially the discussion by Parmanand Singh, 'Public Interest Litigation', in the *Annual Survey of Indian Law*, 1988, vol. xxiv. For a wider, sympathetic discussion of what he calls social action litigation, see Baxi 1985.

[34]Indian Law Institute, *Annual Survey of Indian Law*, 1992, vol. XXVIII, p. 251. The actions were in enforcement of the Environmental Protection Act of 1986. In 1999 the Supreme Court directed Uttar Pradesh to set up a monitoring committee including the PM petitioner who brought the relevant case to supervise steps to improve Agra drinking water supply and sewage facilities. *The Hindu*, 24 November 1999.

[35]*Hindustan Times*, 27 February 2000.

In the context of the hung parliaments and coalition governments of the early 1990s, the court acted formally to change the balance of power between the judiciary and the executive. Supreme Court judgments in 1991 and 1993 shifted the authority to appoint and transfer Supreme Court and high court judges from the president of India acting on the advice of his council of ministers (the prime minister and his cabinet) to the president acting on the advice of the chief justice of the Supreme Court.[36] Until the early 1990s, Article 124, which establishes and constitutes the Supreme Court, was understood to mean that while the president would consult with (take the advice of) the chief justice and such judges of the Supreme Court and the state high courts as he deemed necessary, he would ultimately act on the advice of his council of ministers (the government of the day) in appointing the chief justice and other justices of the Supreme and High courts.[37] Until 1993, there was 'a consensus of opinion that "consultation" does not mean concurrence';[38] the president and his council of ministers could have serious conversations with the chief justice or other justices, but in the end the council of ministers' advice was to prevail.

All this changed in 1993. The governing case, *S.P. Gupta vs Union of India* (1982),[39] was modified by a decision of 6 October 1993, which gave legally binding powers to the chief justice's advice to the president. The judgment, *Union Government vs Advocates on Record* (1993), gave primacy to the chief justice's views as against those of the political executives, Centre and state,

---

[36]The background to this shift in authority lies in Indira Gandhi's highly political use of the appointment powers. In advising the president about court appointments, she overrode the seniority convention that was thought to govern the appointment of the chief justice. She also intimidated judges with the threat and practice of transfers. The seniority rule, which was and is part of the conventional constitution, was designed to protect the autonomy of the court. Transfer rules had a similar aim.

An early Law Commission report recommended that judges not be appointed to the high courts of their home states in order to insulate them from parochial and familial influences. However, this protective device has also been used by the executive as a convenient weapon of harassment. Judges who had served for years in a particular state and who had children in school have been abruptly uprooted and sent to distant states with different cultural traditions and languages on the grounds that they were too close to the public they served. Indira Gandhi's abuse of the appointment and transfer power put the question of the appointment and transfer of judges at the Centre of the struggle over the constitutional balance of power. For a more detailed discussion of the appointment and transfer struggles, see Rudolph and Rudolph 1987, pp. 112–16.

[37]Basu 1999, p. 382.

[38]Ibid., p. 381.

[39]*Gupta vs Union of India*, A.1982 SC 249, laid down that the president, acting with the council of ministers' advice, has primacy among those consulted. In *Subhash vs Union of India*, 1991, I SCJ 521, a three-judge bench asked for a nine-judge bench to modify *Gupta* and declare that the chief justice should have primacy in the appointment of high court judges. See Basu 1999, p. 551.

in the appointment and transfer of high court and apex court judges.[40] In practice, the chief justice acted within a small collegium consisting of the second most senior member of the apex court and, in the case of state high court appointments, the Supreme Court justice from the relevant state. There were differences between the justices about whether the chief justice could override his brother justices.[41]

The new assertiveness of the court drew a predictable response from the now disenfranchised executive. The 1996 United Front government headed by Prime Minister Deve Gowda charged the law ministry with drawing up legislation to reverse the court's expansion of its powers.[42] Its task was made easier when it was alleged that the highly reputed then Chief Justice J.S. Verma might have committed (a minor) malfeasance. Minor malfeasance was also found in the record of M.M. Punchhi, the justice slated to succeed Verma as chief justice.[43]

The fall of the United Front government temporarily ended efforts to return the last word in the choice of judges to the political executive. However, the legal profession and the judges' unease with vesting all power in the chief justice led to yet another step. In November 1998 a nine-judge bench mandated a collegium of five, the chief justice and his four most senior colleagues, to make appointments, and implied but did not explicitly provide that the chief justice could not override its recommendations.[44] In

[40]See *Data India, A Weekly Digest of India News* 1993, p. 776. The Bar Council of India, an interest group of lawyers, called for a uniform transfer policy, and specifically recommended that the first assignment for judges not be in their home state to check the possibility of their favouring legal practice by their relatives. Ibid., 1993, p. 858.

A three-judge bench of the Supreme Court (the twenty-five justices can meet in partial benches) offered the following reassuring statement to lawyers and the public: 'The Chief Justice of India, as the pater familias of the judiciary, can be safely relied upon in his wisdom to ensure that transfer of a judge is so effected as to cause him minimum inconvenience.' Ibid., p. 116.

[41]*India Today*, 6 October 1997. Chief Justice M.M. Punchhi was said to have favoured the override position.

[42]*India Post*, Chicago, 27 December 1996.

[43]A group of anti-establishment lawyers, several active in public interest litigation, feared that the prospective future chief justice, M.M. Punchhi, had doubts about *Union Government vs Advocates on Record* (1993), giving the chief justice the last word on appointments and transfers. Justice Punchhi had joined Justice A.M. Ahmadi in a dissent from the judgment in *Union Government*.

The anti-establishment lawyers also feared that as chief justice, Punchhi would put self-imposed restrictions on the flood of PIL cases. *India Today*, 6 October 1997. The lawyers tried but failed to prevent Punchhi's appointment. In the event, Justice Punchhi succeeded Justice Verma as chief justice.

[44]'We have little doubt,' the decision said, 'that if even two of the judges forming the collegium express strong views, for good reasons, that are adverse to the appointment of a particular person, the chief justice of India would not press for such appointment.' *India Today*, 9 November 1998.

January 2000 NDA Prime Minister Atal Behari Vajpayee advanced the idea of a National Judicial Commission to monitor the ethical conduct of the judiciary, and to take responsibility for the appointment, removal, and transfer of judges.[45] Somehow such a commission, its proponents argued, would be exempt from the ordinary temptations of power that afflict the judicial and presidential nominating process. 'It should not be left in the hands of either government or chief justice assisted by four judges,' ventured ex-chief justice P.N. Bhagwati, 'because they are all human beings.'[46]

The high judiciary promptly took steps to ward off the challenge such a commission would pose. The annual conference of chief justices (of both state and the Centre) passed a fifteen-point code of conduct, and promised to devise 'in-house procedures' to implement self-regulation.[47] The promise was, however, met with scepticism. Ex-chief justice J.S. Verma, for example, argued that 'neither the impeachment procedure nor internal judicial machinery is workable'.[48] The constitutional design in this, as in other respects, remains a project in the making.

THE PRESIDENT STEPS FORWARD

The presidency, like the judiciary, became more visible and influential in the era of hung parliaments and coalition governments that began in 1989. Nehru's claim in the Constituent Assembly on behalf of parliamentary sovereignty that 'No Supreme Court and no judiciary can stand in judgment over the sovereign will of Parliament representing the will of the entire community' began to ring hollow when governments, lacking the two-thirds majority in both houses that is required to pass a constitutional amendment, could no longer try to override Supreme Court judgments.

Although Article 53 vests the 'executive power of the Union ... in the President', as constitutional head of state he is expected to act as an agent of the political executive (the council of ministers or cabinet), not as a principal. But the office has a residual identity separate from cabinet, parliament, and the civilian and military services—an identity beyond government and opposition, beyond partisanship, as representative of the interests of the nation. The rise of coalition governments and the spread of corruption—in the political executive, legislatures, and civil services—have provided a space for presidents, as well as for the courts and the Election Commission, to act as guardians of fairness and constitutional balance.

[45]*The Times of India*, 21 January 2000.
[46]*The Hindu*, 20 February 2000.
[47]*The Times of India*, 7 December 1999.
[48]*The Statesman*, 4 November 1999.

The Constituent Assembly assumed that Indian presidents would conduct themselves like modern British monarchs: as head of state, he or she would act on the advice of the council of ministers, that is, the prime minister and cabinet, observing the conventions of collective responsibility. Rajendra Prasad, president of the Constituent Assembly and, after 1950, India's first president, articulated the standard in this way: 'It is hoped that the convention under which in England the King always acted on the advice of his ministers would be established in this country also and the President would become a constitutional President in all matters'.[49]

This understanding was not, however, made part of the constitution, but left to convention. In 1951, after becoming president of India, Rajendra Prasad saw the matter rather differently. Advised by his council of ministers to assent to a Hindu Code Bill to which he was adamantly opposed, he wrote to Prime Minister Jawaharlal Nehru stating that he wished to act solely on his own judgment when giving assent to bills, sending messages to parliament, and returning bills to parliament for reconsideration.[50] Prasad put forward his position even more succinctly in a speech to the Indian Law Institute in 1960: 'There is no provision in the Constitution which in so many words lays down that the President shall be bound to act in accordance with the advice of his Council of Ministers'.[51]

The president's dual identity—as voice of the government of the day and guardian of constitutional propriety—formulated by President Rajendra Prasad in the early days of the republic, reappeared dramatically in President K.R. Narayanan's golden jubilee address of 27 January 2000, and in the speech he gave when opening parliament on 23 February. Both speeches dealt with the NDA government's efforts to revise the constitution in the light of fifty years' experience. In the first, speaking on his own as president, he argued that parliamentary government and accountability were more in keeping with the basic structure of the constitution than with the 'presidential' system and stability favoured by the government. By the time he spoke on 23 February, what the government had him say reflected the intense national debate launched by his golden jubilee address of 27 January. The government was no longer asking that revisions include radical departures from the parliamentary form, a directly elected political executive, or a fixed-term parliament.[52]

[49]Basu 1994, p. 184.

[50]The act would have erased Hindu personal law. Prasad's tactics led to the bill being withdrawn twice, toned down, rewritten, and divided into three separate bills. For details see Austin 1996, p. 140 and Levy 1973.

[51]Basu 1994, p. 184.

[52]In his golden jubilee address on 27 January 2000, President Narayanan had quoted Dr B.R. Ambedkar, law minister in the Nehru government that dominated the Constituent Assembly-cum-parliament of 1947–50: 'Dr Ambedkar explained that the Drafting Committee

Under the emergency regime which she imposed on 25 June 1975, Indira Gandhi tried, in the forty-second amendment (1976), to put parliamentary sovereignty in an unassailable position by removing any ambiguity with respect to presidential discretion.[53] One clause of the amendment provided that 'There shall be a Council of Ministers with the Prime Minister at the head to aid and advise the President who shall, in the exercise of his functions, act in accordance with such advice'.[54]

Even if such a clause had existed in June 1975 when Indira Gandhi, as prime minister, had the then president Fakhruddin Ali Ahmed declare a national emergency (Article 352),[55] it would be hard to call her actions constitutional. Her midnight letter 'advising' President Ahmed to sign the emergency proclamation had not been discussed by the council of ministers, and nor did its members sign the request. When President Ahmed objected, stating that the council of ministers had not agreed collectively or signed her letter to him, she replied that she would have her cabinet colleagues sign 'first thing tomorrow morning'. The president succumbed;[56] his late-night signature enabled the prime minister to utilize the element of surprise in the midnight arrest of opposition leaders and the closure and/or censorship of newspapers.

After Mrs Gandhi was turned out of office in 1977, Morarji Desai's Janata government passed another omnibus Amendment Act, the forty-fourth, in 1978. It gave the president some discretion in responding to the advice of his council of ministers. It took the form of a suspensory veto, that is, the president was allowed to return bills for reconsideration. If he was again advised to sign by the council of ministers, he would then have to do so.[57]

[of the Constitution], in choosing the parliamentary system for India, preferred more responsibility to more stability, a system under which the Government will be on the anvil every day.' *Mainstream*, 12 February 2000, p. 10. See also *Hindustan Times, The Hindu*, and *The Statesman*, 24 February 2000.

[53]Rudolph and Rudolph 1987, pp. 107–19.

[54]Basu, 1994, p. 185.

[55]For an account of the three national emergencies declared under Article 352, including the third by Prime Minister Indira Gandhi on 25 June 1975, and the forty-second amendment, *inter alia*, substituting the phrase 'armed rebellion' for 'internal disturbance' used by Mrs Gandhi, see Basu 1994, Ch. 28.

[56]She wrote to the president: 'I would have liked to have taken this to Cabinet but unfortunately this is not possible tonight. I am, therefore, condoning or permitting a departure from the Government of India (Transaction of Business Rules, 1961), as amended up-to-date by virtue of my powers under Rule 12 thereof. I shall mention the matter to the Cabinet first thing tomorrow morning.' Government of India 1978b, p. 25.

Such exercise of the prime minister's power was banned after the end of Indira Gandhi's emergency by Article 352 (3), which requires the union ministers of cabinet rank, headed by the prime minister, to recommend the proclamation of an emergency before the fact and in writing.

[57]Basu, 1994, p. 185.

The request for reconsideration is a more powerful device than might appear at first sight, as it provided the president with a lever to call into question and direct public attention to a problematic piece of legislation or act of the executive. President R. Venkataraman used this provision of the forty-fourth amendment in 1987 to express his displeasure about a postal bill that would have authorized the government to open the mail of suspect persons. The bill was withdrawn.[58] President Shanker Dayal Sharma did not assent to two ordinances sent to him on the eve of the 1996 parliamentary elections by the Narasimha Rao government. Both could be read as efforts to influence the outcome of the impending election. One extended reservations for seats in legislatures, places in educational institutions, and jobs in the government to Dalit (Scheduled Caste) Christians, the other moved up the date of the eleventh parliamentary elections.[59] President Narayanan returned for reconsideration a resolution of the cabinet invoking presidential rule (Article 356) against a majority government in Uttar Pradesh.

The transformation of the party system and the rise of coalition governments have profoundly affected the president's role in the constitutional design. In the era of Congress party majorities, presidents had few responsibilities in the making of governments. The constitutional design was clear: ask the leader of the majority party to form a government. But when the era of minority and coalition governments began in 1989 with the defeat of the Rajiv Gandhi-led Congress party by the V.P. Singh-led Janata Dal/National Front, the constitutional design needed to be reworked in both practice and precedent. The regulatory role of the presidency expanded as uncertainty and discretion began to characterize the process of selecting a government.

President Ramaswami Venkataraman in 1989 and 1991, President Shankar Dayal Sharma in 1996, and President Kocheril Raman Narayanan in 1998 and (possibly) 1999 were all faced with hung parliaments. No party commanded a majority; several claimed they could form viable coalition governments. Under such circumstances, should a president use his discretion in deciding which of several party leaders to invite to form a government? The leader he invites gains a tremendous advantage over his rivals because he can use offers of ministerial posts and material incentives to win over lesser parties and pliable or wavering members.[60] The track record of state

---

[58]R. Venkataraman 1975, *My Presidential Years*, New Delhi: HarperCollins, p. 36.

[59]*Outlook*, 3 April 1996.

[60]We read the failure of BJP leader Atal Behari Vajpayee to gain the confidence of the Lok Sabha in June 1996 and of NDA leader Nitish Kumar to gain the confidence of the Bihar Vidhan Sabha in March 2000 as exceptions to this generalization due to special circumstances. In June 1996, the BJP was still regarded as a pariah by the non-Congress opposition parties. The Bihar NDA was badly divided by rivalries between coalition parties and their leaders.

governors suggests that the use of discretion can be influenced more by partisan and personal preferences than by concern for making a viable, stable government. The constitution offers no specific direction for what the president (or governors) should do when a single party or pre-poll alliance fails to gain a majority of seats. Until President R. Venkataraman's tenure as president, precedent too provided little guidance.[61]

When President Venkataraman inaugurated the era of coalition governments, he shaped the constitutional design for making governments by creating constructive precedents and making the process transparent. Like Presidents Sharma and Narayanan after him, he had a long association with the Congress party and its governments. Before being sworn in as president on. 25 July 1987, midway through Rajiv Gandhi's prime ministership, Venkataraman had served as vice president to President Zail Singh. During his two terms as president he dealt with the formation of the V.P. Singh, S. Chandrasekhar, and P.V. Narasimha Rao governments.

Venkataraman regarded himself as a '"copybook' president [who] would act strictly according to the rules'.[62] His most basic rule was to first ask the largest party to form the government and, within two or three weeks, to test its majority on the floor of parliament.[63] If the party with the most seats declined or failed to gain the confidence of the House, he would ask the next largest party to try.

On 1 December 1989, after the ninth parliamentary election had produced India's first hung parliament, President Venkataraman began to turn this rule into a convention. He told a National Front delegation headed by V.P. Singh that 'as the largest single party [Congress-I] had not staked a claim to form the government, I invite you [V.P. Singh] as the leader of the second largest party to form the government and take a vote of confidence of the House within 30 days'.[64] When the V.P. Singh government fell in

---

Governor V.C. Pande's hurried decision to call Nitish Kumar was widely regarded as a poor precedent. The Congress and other opposition parties denounced his decision as unconstitutional, and called for his removal. See 'Pande's Haste Baffles Opposition', *The Hindu*, 4 March 2000; 'Bihar Governor Acted in Haste: Karunanidhi', *Hindustan Times*, 14 March 2000.

[61]See Jha 1996 for a useful overview of presidential conduct in the making of governments.

[62]Venkataraman 1975, *My Presidential Years*, p. 405.

[63]This rule eliminated as far as possible the hazardous path of a personal headcount which, at the state level, had often produced bizarre scenes of coercion and instant horsetrading in the governor's office. All three presidents followed the rule of asking the leader of the largest party (or, if he failed, the next largest party) to establish that they commanded the confidence of the House, not in the president's residence, the Rashtrapati Bhavan, but 'publicly' on the floor of the parliament. These days publicly can mean before a national TV audience tuned in to broadcasts of confidence debates and voting.

[64]Venkataraman 1975, *My Presidential Years*, p. 275, and *Outlook*, 15 May 1996, p. 7.

November 1990, President Venkataraman asked the Congress-I party leader of the opposition, Rajiv Gandhi, 'whether he was able and willing to form a viable government. The Congress [I] did not stake a claim for forming the government but offered unconditional support to Shri Chandra Shekhar.'[65] In June 1991, when the Congress-I emerged as the single largest, but not the majority, party in the tenth parliamentary election and P.V. Narasimha Rao was elected its parliamentary leader, President Venkataraman sent him a letter which read: 'As the leader of the Congress [I], the largest party in the Lok Sabha, I appoint you as the Prime Minister of India and invite you to form the council of ministers. I advise you to establish your majority in the Lok Sabha within four weeks.'[66]

After the eleventh parliamentary election in May 1996, President Sharma followed Venkataraman's precedents. Sharma, who served from 1992 to 1998, came to the president's office with a reputation for impartiality. In

Madhu Dandavate, who was chairman of the meeting that elected V.P. Singh leader, handed over a letter to President Venkataraman saying that 'the BJP with 85 members and the Left Front with 52 members had pledged their support to the National Front government' (Venkataraman 1975, p. 275).

[65]'Thereafter, the President sounded the Bharatiya Janata Party and the Left Front whether they would be able and willing to form a viable government. On both parties expressing their inability to undertake the responsibility, the President enquired from Shri Chandra Shekhar if he was in a position to form a viable government. Shri Chandra Shekhar responded to the offer and produced evidence of support to his group from the Congress [I], AIADMK, Bahujan Samaj Party, Muslim League [and other lesser parties and independent members]'. The president declared himself satisfied *prima facie* that Chandra Shekhar had the strength to form a viable government.

Also influencing his judgment about the formation of a minority Chandra Shekhar government was President Venkataraman's 'considered opinion' that it was 'not in the national interest to plunge the country into general election at this time', a time when the Mandal reservations for other backward castes and building a Ram temple at Ayodhya were convulsing the country. Venkataraman 1975, p. 373.

See Jha 1996, p. 5, for another gloss on the formation of the Chandra Shekhar government. 'Aware of the "ugly incident in our parliamentary history" when Indira Gandhi first extended support to Charan Singh in 1979 and then withdrew it within a week, Venkataraman probed the nature of the support and the minimum period it would last.' Only when Rajiv Gandhi assured him that his support to Chandra Shekhar was 'neither temporary nor conditional' did he agree to allow him to form a government. 'I asked Rajiv Gandhi if this support would continue at least one year. He replied, "Why one year? It may extend to the life of Parliament"' (ibid., p. 7).

[66]Ibid., p. 464. Rao's government won its vote of confidence with the help of the AIADMK, the Jayalalitha-led Tamil Nadu party with which the Congress was allied in the 1996 election.

Rao's Congress government almost lost a vote of confidence in 1993. It was saved by the votes of a small party seeking statehood, the Jharkand Mukti Morcha (JMM), to which Rao seems to have committed himself in exchange for their votes in the confidence motion. He is also accused of making a large sum of money available to the JMM MPs. As of this writing this matter was *sub judice*.

1984, as governor of Andhra Pradesh, he had reversed Indira Gandhi's controversial use of Article 356 (of which more below) to oust the chief minister of Andhra, N.T. Rama Rao, when it became clear that NTR still commanded a majority in the assembly. 'His innings as governor alone was enough to endear him to the non-Congress parties and convince them of his sense of fair play.' Later, after serving as governor of Punjab and Maharashtra, Sharma showed courage and independence as Rajya Sabha chairman.[67] To the discomfort of the Narasimha Rao government, Sharma used the authority of the presidency to tell state governors at a seminar he organized that they should observe constitutional standards before calling for president's rule under Article 356. Sharma, himself a legal scholar and teacher, no doubt welcomed President Venkataraman's precedents, but also charted his own constitutional path.

His big moment came in May 1996 after the eleventh parliamentary election. Confronted with a hung parliament in which the Hindu nationalist BJP had won the most seats, with the United Front in second place and the Congress in the third, he first asked the BJP parliamentary party leader, Atal Behari Vajpayee, to form a government and gave him two weeks to gain the confidence of the House. When, after thirteen days, Vajpayee failed to convince any other party to cross the aisle to his side, the President turned to the second-largest grouping, the United Front, a fourteen-party coalition. With Congress's outside support it won a vote of confidence. The UF government lasted for nineteen months, until December 1997.

In March 1998, after the twelfth parliamentary election, President Narayanan followed the Venkataraman and Sharma precedents when he asked the BJP, again the largest party in a hung parliament, to form a government and gain the confidence of the House. Having worked hard since its failure in June 1996 to persuade voters and potential coalition partners that it was capable of being centrist and moderate, the BJP succeeded this time where it had failed in 1996.

However, in the era of coalition governments the Venkataraman rule, that the president should first ask the largest party to try to form a government, is not the sure guide it appears to be. The 1999 parliamentary election could have resulted in an outcome likely to cast the rule into doubt by raising the question as to whether the proper candidate for government was the 'largest party' or the largest pre-poll alliance. The National Democratic Alliance led by the BJP consisted of twenty-two parties. Each party had agreed to give up its manifesto, adopt a common programme, and campaign in support of it. Each party also agreed to recognize Atal Behari Vajpayee as the leader of

---

[67]For further details of Sharma's career see Jha 1996, pp. 5–10.

the NDA, and as the NDA's candidate for prime minister. Prior to the result being known, the country debated whether the president, in calling on the single largest party to try and form a government, should turn to the BJP or the Congress, the two principal conventional parties, or the NDA, an alliance made party-like by its pre-poll agreement on a common minimum programme and leader. Congress spokespersons had also tried to pre-empt possible claims by the NDA to 'single largest party' status by arguing that if, hypothetically, Congress won 180 seats, BJP 175, and the NDA a narrow majority with 275 seats, the president was bound by precedent to call the Congress first as the 'single largest party' to try to form a government.[68] The election results rendered moot, for the moment, the question whether the president should count a pre-poll coalition such as the NDA as 'the single largest party'. Congress did badly, winning only 112 seats, 32 less than in the previous parliament. The BJP won about the same number of seats as it held in the previous parliament, 182. The NDA, however, with 296 seats, won a comfortable majority of twenty-five, largely because the BJP's regional party allies did better than anticipated.

The formulation by presidents of non-discretionary conventions, such as first calling the single largest party, tends to affect the conduct of governors who at the state level play an analogous role to the president at the union government level. Like presidents, governors have dual identities, first as a spokesperson and symbol for governments of the day, the second as a non-partisan public person speaking and acting on behalf of the common good. The second identity is meant to come to the fore when, like the president at the national level, governors choose a party leader who is to try and form a government and (unlike the president) recommend to the president the removal of a government and the imposing of 'president's rule' under Article 356 of the constitution.[69]

In the run-up to the twelfth national election in 1998, President Narayanan tried to get state governors to follow presidential precedents in forming governments, and to use impartial and transparent procedures. At stake was a five-month effort by the National Front government at the Centre to topple the government of India's largest state, Uttar Pradesh. Not only

[68]Jairam Ramesh speaking for the Congress Party, Door Darshan, election programme, 7 October 1999.

[69]Article 356 lists provisions in case of failure of the constitutional machinery. The principal provision says that 'if the President, on receipt of report from the Governor of a State is satisfied that a situation has arisen in which the government of the State cannot be carried on in accordance with the provisions of this Constitution [e.g., the government has lost its majority and no alternative government can be formed, the government cannot maintain law and order], the President may by Proclamation assume to himself all or any of the functions of the Government of the State.' See also below for a discussion of the Article.

did the president reverse an 'unconstitutional' use of Article 356 in October/ November 1997, but also at the end of February 1998, on the eve of the twelfth parliamentary election campaign, he, along with the Allahabad high court and the Supreme Court, prevented UP governor Romesh Bhandari from arbitrarily dismissing Kalyan Singh's BJP government and replacing it with Jagdambika Pal's Congress/Samajwadi government. President Narayanan reprimanded Governor Bhandari for dismissing the Kalyan Singh government 'in a partisan manner' designed to help the ruling United Front and Congress in the upcoming election. Bhandari had not allowed a trial of strength in the assembly, and had hastily sworn in Jagdambika Pal as chief minister.[70] A 'landmark' Supreme Court verdict reinstalled Kalyan Singh and gave him an opportunity to prove his majority. The procedure that the court mandated for the notoriously unruly and often violent UP assembly was 'unprecedented in constitutional history': a vote of confidence had to be held on the floor of the assembly through signed ballots, which was also exposed to public gaze by TV coverage.[71]

The steps that the court prescribed underlined that fairness, transparency, and civility were matters of both low and high politics. Knowing the UP legislators too well, the Speaker had got the ballot box chained. The hall was made free of microphones to avoid their misuse as missiles, as witnessed in 1997 and 1995. Entry was restricted to members, personnel on duty, and

[70]'"Why must I resign?" UP Governor Romesh Bhandari justifies his actions', *Sunday*, 8– 14 March 1998, p. 30.

[71]See *The Hindu*, 27 February 1998, and *India Abroad*, 27 February 1998. On 25 February 1998, the wire services were writing 'Mr Bhandari's [the UP governor's] position became untenable when he chose to ignore the advice of the President [Narayanan] and went ahead with the dismissal of the Kalyan Singh Government instead of giving it an opportunity to test its strength in the State Assembly.'

I.K. Gujral, whose UF government was about to lose badly in the twelfth national election, ducked a decision that would have displeased his defence minister, former UP chief minister Mulayam Singh Yadav, and Congress president Sitaram Kesri, upon whose support the Gujral's government depended. Gujral's dubiously constitutional view was that 'the Center didn't come into the picture because ... right or wrong, the Governor acted at his level, in the exercise of his discretion'. Gujral's justification flew in the face of the president's 'advice' to Bhandari and the Supreme Court decision the president's advice reflected, *S.R. Bommai vs Union of India*, which made the use of Article 356 subject to judicial review. India Server News Briefs for 25 February 1998, brief@Indiaserver.com, and Muralidharan 1998c, pp. 4–7.

Atal Behari Vajpayee's BJP coalition government won its vote of confidence on 29 March. Bhandari's friends at court had been removed by the results of the twelfth national election which were known by mid-March. In the certainty that Vajpayee would do what Gujral feared to do, Bhandari submitted his resignation on 16 March 1998, thereby justifying President Narayanan's view of the impropriety, not to say unconstitutionality, of his conduct. Pradhan 1998b, p. 15.

the media. Mobile phones, pagers, briefcases, and even file covers (which, experience shows, could be used as missiles) were not allowed. Perhaps what prevented the rival groups from getting in on the act were the sword of Damocles that hung over them in the form of the Supreme Court interim order directing that a floor test between Kalyan Singh and Jagdambika Pal be held, a warning that 'Violence in any form would be taken serious note of', and the full gaze of the video cameras.[72]

President Narayanan stayed aloof from the controversy surrounding Bihar governor V.C. Pande's decision in early March 2000 following a state assembly election to ask NDA leader Nitish Kumar, rather than Rashtriya Janta Dal (RJD) leader Rabri Devi, to form the government. A retired IAS officer appointed by the NDA government at the Centre, Pande hastily turned to NDA leader Kumar even though Kumar's shaky pre-poll coalition had fewer seats than Devi's RJD, and despite the fact that Congress leaders in Delhi had told him that Congress's Bihar MLAs would support an RJD-led government.[73] After two days, well before his allotted time, Nitish Kumar gave up and resigned. The fact that a Rabri Devi RJD coalition government quickly won a vote of confidence intensified the clamour against the governor's precipitous and apparently partisan action.

Under Article 356, governors can recommend the suspension of state governments and the imposition of 'president's rule', a critical feature of the constitutional design that the Constitutional Review Commission appointed in February 2000 is certain to examine. Article 356, which allows the president to assume the government of a state in case 'the government of a State can not be carried on in accordance with the provisions of [the] Constitution', is vulnerable to partisan use by the party or parties in charge of the central government. Pliant state governors, themselves appointed, transferred, and dismissed by union governments of the day, can report to the council of ministers the failure of the constitutional machinery in particular states. The council of ministers then advises the president to suspend or

[72]Pradhan 1998a, pp. 28–31, and India Server News Brief, 27 February 1998, brief@indiaserver. com.

[73]The RJD with 123 seats claimed to be the single largest party. With the votes of its pre-poll ally, the CPI-M, it also claimed to be the largest alliance. Before Governor Pande invited Nitish Kumar, the NDA leader, to form a government, Pande had been informed by phone from New Delhi that the Congress Party would support an RJD government and that a letter to that effect was on its way. With Congress seats, an RJD-led government could credibly claim 161 of the 163 seats needed for a majority, while the most the Kumar-led NDA could muster were 151 members.

The press widely supported the view that the governor's hasty action carried overtones of partisanship. See, for example, the *Hindustan Times* and *The Hindu* for 4 March 2000.

dismiss the government, and to carry on its administration in his name for six months to two years.[74] In comparison with the 1960s and 1970s, the Article has been somewhat more protected since the onset of coalition governments in 1989 from abuse by state governors and union governments.

Article 356 was intended as a measure of last resort in times of severe governmental crisis.[75] Starting in 1957, when Indira Gandhi as Congress party president arranged for the dismissal of a CPI-M (Communist) government in Kerala, Congress governments began using Article 356 routinely to remove troublesome opposition state governments. It was used 100 times between 1950 and 1994, mostly by Congress governments.[76] Perhaps its most constitutionally problematic use was in 1977 by the Janata Party government, which took power after Indira Gandhi's emergency regime. Claiming that the Congress 'opposition' governments of nine northern states that had been independently elected in separate state elections had lost their mandate as a result of the Janata Party's parliamentary election victory, the Janata government used Article 356 to impose president's rule on all nine. When a Congress government was returned to power in 1980, its prime minister, Indira Gandhi, used the Janata government precedent to justify the dismissal of nine independently elected Janata state governments.

Reports on reforming the federal system were commissioned in the 1980s by Karnataka, Tamil Nadu, and West Bengal, all states ruled by opposition parties and eager to loosen the hold of the Centre. As a co-optive measure, Indira Gandhi appointed a central body, the Sarkaria Commission. Sarkaria, not surprisingly, found that Article 356 had been misused, and recommended its replacement. One of the reasons the BJP as an opposition

[74]Article 352 allows a presidential proclamation of emergency if there is an imminent danger of war, external aggression, or armed rebellion. It was the vehicle of Indira Gandhi's national emergency in 1975. The term 'armed rebellion' was substituted by the forty-fourth amendment for the weaker 'internal disturbance' to raise the criteria by which an emergency might be declared. Indira Gandhi had used the weaker phrase to justify her action. An emergency declaration under Article 352 does not result in the suspension of the state government, but does allow the national parliament to exercise concurrent powers with state assemblies.

The much more commonly used Article 356 allows a proclamation stating that the state legislature and executive authority of a state can be suspended because of a failure of the constitutional machinery. In this case the president may delegate the functions of government to his appointees, generally serving civil servants, but sometimes retired ones— thus 'president's rule'.

[75]Dr B.R. Ambedkar, a principal architect of the constitution, told the Constituent Assembly that 'the proper thing we ought to expect is that such articles [as 356] will never be called into operation, that they remain a dead letter'. CAD, vol. IX, p. 177, cited in Basu 1994, p. 311.

[76]Congress governments held power between 1952 and 1977, from 1980 to 1989, and from 1991 to 1994. For further details see Basu 1994, p. 335, table XXI, and pp. 459–61, which details the use of Article 356 by state and date. See also Dua 1979, 1985, and Rudolph and Rudolph 1987, pp. 101–2.

party had dropped its commitment to a centralized, unitary state and opted for a decentralized, federal state was its response to Congress's abuse of Article 356.[77]

As long as union governments commanded secure majorities (1952–89), it was difficult for presidents to resist partisan use of Article 356. The rise of coalition governments has changed the rules of engagement. During the era of hung parliaments, from the ninth national election in 1989 through the twelfth in 1998, when no single party commanded a parliamentary majority, central governments were a little more sparing in their use of Article 356. These days a party at the Centre that manages to use Article 356 for partisan advantage against a rival party in a federal state risks finding itself on the receiving end. Even so, the temptation of a short-term gain often weighs strongly.

It has been noted above that in October 1997 Prime Minister Gujral's National Front government concurred in UP with Governor Bhandari's attempt to supersede Kalyan Singh's BJP government. President Narayanan invoked his prerogative to return the Gujral government's directive for reconsideration, thereby blocking what was widely seen as a partisan act.[78] The BJP, which headed a coalition government at the Centre in 1998, was itself tempted to make partisan use of Article 356. To do so would have contradicted its declared policy position in the manifesto it had adopted for the 1998 election,[79] and would have risked repudiation by the president.

---

[77]See, for example, Government of Karnataka (1983), Government of Tamil Nadu (1971), and Government of West Bengal (1978). For a summary of some of the regional demands for decentralization in the early 1980s, see Saez 1999, Ch. II. See also Government of India 1988.

[78]After the UP Bahujan Samaj Party Chief Minister Mayawati had withdrawn her party from a BSP–BJP coalition government, a BJP government led by Kalyan Singh had won a confidence vote on the assembly floor. President Narayanan had been so informed by home ministry observers. Mulayam Singh Yadav, defence minister in the UF government, UP Samajwadi Party leader, and former UP chief minister, led the faction in the UF cabinet supporting president's rule for UP. In effect, he wanted to use his role at the Centre to his advantage in UP politics. Other regional party leaders in or associated with the UF government, such as West Bengal's CPI-M chief minister Jyoti Basu, Tamil Nadu's DMK chief minister M. Karunanidhi, and Andhra Pradesh's Telugu Desam chief minister Chandrababu Naidu, were opposed in principle and for practical political reasons to the use of Article 356 in UP.

The Congress party was supporting the UF government from the outside. Without its votes the UF government would fall. Sitaram Kesri, the octogenarian Congress president, pressed Prime Minister I.K. Gujral to use Article 356 against Kalyan Singh's BJP government in the expectation that under president's rule, with Romesh Bhandari in charge as governor, Congress would be able to restore its fortunes in India's largest state.

For more details on the machinations surrounding this important constitutional event see *Sunday's* (2–8 November 1997) cover story, 'Enemy or Friend? I.K. Gujral's refusal to toe Mulayam Singh Yadav's line in UP has a ripple effect on ruling relationships', pp. 14–25.

[79]Aggarwal and Chowdhry 1998, p. 143: 'The Party is committed to take necessary steps to prevent misuse of article 356 of the Constitution.'

In the event, the BJP resisted the demand of its troublesome key coalition partner, the Tamil Nadu regional AIADMK headed by the scheming Jayaram Jayalalitha, to topple the government of Jayalalitha's arch rival, Tamil Nadu's DMK chief minister M. Karunanidhi. It paid a heavy price when Jayalalitha withdrew AIADMK support and the BJP-led coalition fell.[80] Earlier, on 12 February 1999, the BJP-led government had initiated the use of Article 356 to remove an RJD Rabri Devi government in Bihar after it failed to prevent two major massacres of Dalits by an upper-caste private army. It was widely believed that the Rabri Devi government could not maintain law and order. At the same time, it continued to command a legislative majority. The Centre's move in this case appeared to have the approval of the president as well as the support of national public opinion. However, this effort to use Article 356 proved abortive when Congress reneged on its commitment to support the move in parliament.[81]

Another arena for a presidential regulatory role was created in the 1990s by the rapid turnover in governments. When a government falls and an

[80]Jayalalitha had been chief minister of Tamil Nadu between 1991 and 1996. She and her party were routed from office in the 1996 state assembly elections, in part because voters perceived her and her government as corrupt and vicious. Two years later she allied her AIADMK party with the upper-caste BJP in the twelfth parliamentary election of 1998, an event that must have made Periyar (great leader) E.V. Ramaswamy Naicker, the religion- and upper-caste hating leader and founder of the anti-Brahmin Dravidian movement, turn in his grave.

The BJP, with only 179 parliamentary seats, needed help from almost 100 MPs to form a government, and had to keep their support to stay in power. Jayalalitha levied pressure for almost a year, threatening periodically to withdraw.

When two earlier Karunanidhi DMK governments fell victim to the Congress abuse of Article 356, the BJP as an opposition party at the Centre and as an occasional state governing party was outspoken in its condemnation. For details of the BJP coalition's efforts to stay in power in the face of coalition partners' threats, see Dasgupta 1998, pp. 12–17.

[81]Not that there were no ambiguities about the disinterested nature of BJP conduct. On the one hand, the RJD government headed by Rabri Devi, wife of RJD leader Laloo Prasad Yadav, had an unenviable record for massive corruption and populist inefficiency. On the other hand, there was strong partisan pressure within the BJP by its coalition partners, Samata party leaders Nitish Kumar and George Fernandes, opposed to the Rabri Devi RJD government in Bihar, to oust that government at all costs. The governor, S.S. Bhandari, a long-time RSS *sanchalak*, was generally regarded as a crucial partisan connection for the Centre. In October 1998 the Centre attempted to oust the Bihar government without the backing of Dalit massacres, but was invited by the president to reconsider. In the event, the February ousting failed because the Congress party made it clear that it would not support the ousting in the Rajya Sabha, the upper house, where the BJP-led alliance lacked a majority. It presumably denied support because it feared that if the partisan Governor Bhandari was in charge of president's rule in the state, he would favour the BJP and Samata parties and disfavour Congress and its potential ally, the RJD. *India Today*, 22 February, 1 March, and 8 March, 1999.

In November 1999, when there was another massacre, this time by left terrorists, of Muslims belonging to a competing left faction, Congress called for the dismissal of the government. By that time its alliance with the RJD had soured. *The Times of India*, 20 November 1999.

election is called, as happened in 1998 and 1999, the president has the authority to designate a caretaker government. The caretaker government will hold office until an election can produce a new parliament and a new government. What actions is it proper for such a government to take, given its limited authority and time in office? In 1999, the BJP government fell on 26 April and a new post-election government was not installed until October. During this six-month period the Vajpayee caretaker government conducted and concluded a limited war in the Kargil sector of Kashmir, carried on intensive negotiations with respect to the Comprehensive Test Ban Treaty, and tried to move ahead with economic liberalization.

A caretaker government is no longer responsible to the legislature; it has lost its confidence. If it is responsible to anything or anyone, it is to the president who has authorized its existence. The president has no constitutionally explicit means for holding a caretaker government responsible. Much depends on what kind of political issue he is willing to challenge a caretaker government on. During the six months of the Vajpayee caretaker government in 1999, the opposition petitioned the president to require the government to debate the conduct of the Kargil war in the Rajya Sabha. The opposition also petitioned President Narayanan to halt the government's bailout of the telecommunications industry, a major and costly policy initiative.[82] The president placed both demands before the caretaker government. It responded by modifying rather than acceding to the Kargil demand, stating that it would discuss the onset and conduct of the Kargil war at an all-party meeting rather than allow a full-fledged parliamentary debate on the war. It turned down the telecom demand.[83]

In the era of a multiparty system and coalition government, presidents have played a more active role. They have made use of their constitutional powers to influence the formation and dismissal of governments at the state and union levels. Presidents have elaborated rules for the government-making process, and made the procedures transparent. At the union level, presidents have adhered to the rules set out by President Venkataraman. At the state level, the use of Article 356 now seems closer to the position Dr B.R. Ambedkar intended for it, '*a matter of last resort*'. It has been restored to a matter of last resort in part because state governments and regional parties have gained authority in the operation of the federal system; in part because state governors and the union governments and presidents that appoint them have recognized the political prudence and constitutional desirability of a governor who is both independent and impartial; and,

[82]'Chronology of Events', *Mainstream*, 37 (30), 1999 pp. 33–4.
[83]'Chronology', *Mainstream*, 37 (29), 1999, p. 33; 32, 1999, p. 31.

most importantly, because presidents have found constitutional grounds and appropriate occasions to act independently of the union executive in the public interest.

ELECTION COMMISSION ACTIVISM

Starting in 1991 with the tenure of T.N. Seshan as chief election commissioner (CEC), the Election Commission (EC) joined the Supreme Court in improving the legal conditions that make representative government and democratic participation possible. This is not to say that the EC had not been a bulwark for free and fair elections in India before 1991.[84] But in the 1990s, with the electoral process threatened by criminalization, violence, bribery, and gun-toting candidates portrayed in daring television exposés, the EC gained national prominence as a prime force in restoring and maintaining free and fair elections in India. Polls suggested that the public trusted it more than any other political institution.[85] Like the court and the presidency, the EC was supported by urban middle classes who welcomed its ability to expose and limit the lawlessness and corruption of politicians, state officials, and the police. Together with the court and the presidency, the EC has contributed to the making of a regulatory state in India.

The EC is a constitutional body. Article 324 vests the 'superintendence, direction and control of elections ... in an Election Commission'. The EC consists of a chief election commissioner and 'such number of other Election Commissioners, if any, as the President may from time to time fix. ... When any other Election Commissioner is so appointed the Chief Election Commissioner shall act as the Chairman of the Election Commission.' The commission's independence is assured by clause 5 of Article 324, which provides that 'the Chief Election Commissioner shall not be removed from his office except in like manner and on like grounds as a Judge of the Supreme Court', that is, by each house of parliament, by a special majority, and on the grounds of proved misbehaviour or incapacity. Other election commissioners may not be removed by the president except on the recommendation of the chief election commissioner.[86] The only path available to the executive to influence the Election Commission is to pack

[84]Rudolph and Rudolph 1987, pp. 89–91.

[85]In a nationwide poll conducted by the Centre for the Study of Developing Societies for the Indian Council of Social Science Research and *India Today* just after the eleventh national election in June and July 1996, 62 per cent of 15,030 respondents rated the Election Commission as trustworthy, the highest score, followed by 59 per cent for the Supreme Court. *India Today*, 31 August 1996. For an extended discussion of this survey result, see de Souza 1998, pp. 51–2 and Note 1.

[86]For provisions and practice beyond the language of Article 324, see Basu 1994, pp. 365–6.

it, a strategy made possible by a constitutional clause that allows multiple members of the commission to be appointed. The flamboyant, arrogant T.N. Seshan, CEC from 1991 to 1996, became for a time a hero of middle-class reform.[87] He fought successfully to keep the commission a one-man show until he was reined in by the Narasimha Rao government's appointment of two additional commissioners.[88] The 1996, 1998, and 1999 national elections provided no evidence that adding two commissioners had weakened the Election Commission's considerable capabilities.

The commission's task is enormous. It deals with an electorate of 600 million,[89] 57 per cent of whom vote.[90] Contrary to Western electoral behaviour,

[87]'More than any politician, sportsperson or film star, it is the Election Commission which has managed to stay consistently in the limelight during the last five years, thanks largely to the consummate knack of its colourful chief, T.N. Seshan, in dramatising issues and non-issues': Mahalingam 1996, p. 14.

[88]Differences over whether there should be additional election commissioners began just a week before the commencement of the ninth national election when the Rajiv Gandhi Congress government, on 16 October 1989, appointed two more commissioners. The move 'created a suspicion that it was an attempt to compromise the independence of the Commission'. The incoming National Front returned the commission to a one-person body as of 2 January 1990.

Taking advantage of a provision in Article 324 that allowed the appointment of additional election commissioners to act with the chief election commissioner, the Narasimha Rao government in September 1993 attempted to rein Seshan in by appointing two commissioners, M.S. Gill and G.V.G. Krishnamurthy. Seshan, charging that the appointments were motivated by the Congress party's desire to prevent his reform of a corrupt electoral system, challenged the appointments before the Supreme Court, asking the court to block the appointments on constitutional and procedural grounds.

A constitution bench headed by then Chief Justice A.M. Ahmadi and including the next chief justice, J.S. Verma and Justice N.P. Singh upheld the constitutionality of the appointments and ruled out all *mala fide* intentions of the ruling party.

The court also remarked on Seshan's 'insustainable' decisions, 'abrasive public utterances, appearances on commercial television and in newspaper ads'. The court opined that 'Serious doubts may arise regarding his decisions if it is suspected that he has political ambitions' (in 1997 Seshan stood unsuccessfully for president of India against K.R. Narayanan), and accused him of being 'totally oblivious to a sense of decorum and discretion that his high office requires, even if his cause is laudable' (Fernandes 1995, pp. 28–35).

Shortly after the thirteenth parliamentary elections the BJP-led coalition was thought to be favouring a five-person commission in order to get its own appointees in place. Such intent was denied. *The Hindu*, 24 November 1999.

[89]The 600-million strong Indian electorate elects about 5,000 representatives to the national parliament and the state assemblies. Elections have been held at regular intervals since 1952. There have been twelve national or parliamentary elections since 1952. A national election requires 900,000 polling stations scattered from Cape Cormorin at the tip of India to the Himalayas in the north. The electoral process requires 4.5 million persons to administer. They are seconded from state and local government services, and temporarily placed under the authority of the Election Commission. By the end of 1999, each of India's 600 million voters was supposed to have a photographic identity card.

[90]Unlike the US, where registration is the citizen's responsibility, in India it is that of the state. The 57 per cent average turnout across twelve national elections is that much more impressive because it is a proportion of the total eligible electorate. See Gill 1998, pp. 24–7.

participation is higher in state and local elections than in national elections, and higher among the poorly educated and lower castes and classes than the better educated and higher castes and classes. 'The poor, the underclass, the uneducated, the former untouchables, tend to vote not less but more than the others.'[91] M.S. Gill, CEC from January 1997,[92] recognizing the imperfections of the electoral process, nevertheless claimed, not implausibly, 'that these inadequacies do not affect the overall outcome of elections, either at the state or the national levels. ... Those who govern do so because the voters chose them.'[93] The proof lies, he argued, in the defeat of incumbent parties, chief ministers, and prime ministers. In 1996, for example, Narasimha Rao's Congress government was badly defeated. It was Congress's third loss at the national level in the last six elections. Between 1993 and 1997, in the elections for all of India's twenty-five state assemblies the incumbent party lost in nineteen.[94]

The EC's most visible success has been in getting India's parties and candidates in the eleventh (1996), twelfth (1998), and thirteenth (1999) national elections to comply with its code of conduct.[95] The code is divided into seven sections: general conduct; meetings; processions; polling day; polling booths; observers; and party in power. Rules of conduct are specified under each heading. One rule that dramatically changed the feel and spirit of Indian elections and benefited the urban landscape was the ban on pasting posters and notices on walls and buildings, and that on vehicles with loudspeakers. Under 'party in power', the code bars ministers and other authorities from making promises of financial grants for the construction of roads, provision of drinking water facilities, or the laying of foundation

[91]Ibid., p. 25. There are those that argue that one of the determinants of higher levels of voting among lower castes including, in particular, Dalits, lower classes, and marginal persons, is the improvement of protection and associated decline of intimidation and the security environment surrounding voting. Intimidation was, and to an extent still is, practised by upper over lower castes, but it seems to have declined substantially as a result of EC measures, including those taken by T.N. Seshan to bring central security to bear on the voting process.

[92]Seshan's term as CEC ended in December 1996. He was succeeded as CEC by Commissioner Manohar Singh Gill. J.M. Lyngoh was appointed as election commissioner at this time. G.V.G. Krishnamurthy stayed on as the third commissioner.

[93]Gill 1998, p. 25.

[94]Ibid., p. 26.

[95]The code, under a court ruling, becomes operative with EC notification of the dates for the campaign and the polling dates, usually three spread over about ten days. (This enables the EC to use a finite number of personnel and facilities in several polling places.) The code is not statutory, although its provisions are recognized and enforced by the courts. It originated in 1983 as a voluntary agreement, an 'all-party consensus', among all recognized political parties, and was renewed by the political parties before the 1996 (eleventh) election in November–December 1995 (Venkatesan 1996, pp. 29–31).

stones for projects of any kind from the time elections are announced. Ministers may not combine official visits with electioneering and/or use official machinery (for example, helicopters) or personnel during the official campaign period. Parties are prohibited from campaigning from places of worship or making appeals based on caste or communal (religious) feeling.[96] Not all the rules are complied with all the time, but they are taken seriously, in part because it suits incumbent candidates and their opponents to use them to monitor each other.

In 1999 there were some complaints that the EC's enthusiasm for fairness had overreached itself. The Madras high court and the Andhra high court termed the EC's ban, new in 1999, on the dissemination in the media of opinion polls, exit polls, or electoral ads, 'arbitrary', 'discriminatory', and 'unreasonable'. The commission claimed it was protecting voters from inappropriate influences on their voting decisions. When the commission appealed to the Supreme Court for support, the court refused and lifted the EC's ban on media use of voting survey results prior to the closure of the polls.[97]

Enforcement of rules, for instance for polling day and polling places— against 'booth capturing', 'ballot snatching', intimidation, and violence— was partly in the hands of local officials deputed to serve the EC, partly in

[96]Here are a few of many examples of the application of these rules. After the 1996 election was announced, Prime Minister Narasimha Rao was forced to abandon a 20 March foundation-stone laying ceremony for a Rs 7,000 crore oil refinery at Azadpur in Rae Bareli, Uttar Pradesh. State governments had to postpone until after the election the tendering process for liquor and tendu leaf concessions.

Section 123 of the Representation of the People Act, 1951, makes promoting 'feelings of enmity or hatred between different classes of [citizens] ... on grounds of race, caste, community [read religion] or language' a corrupt electoral practice warranting disqualification of a victorious candidate from elected office. Section 125 enables the prosecution of 'any individual' who uses appeals to the criteria mentioned in Section 123. The Indian Penal Code (Section 153A) provides for the proscription of political organizations that advocate the views proscribed in Section 123.

After the 1989 national election, the Bombay high court disqualified Manohar Joshi (later Maharashtra chief minister) and other BJP and Shiv Sena candidates under Sections 123 and 125, which gave legal backing to EC code of conduct rules for campaigning on a 'Hindutva' platform. In 1995 the Supreme Court overturned the Bombay high court's judgment, holding that it was not proved that the candidates had appealed to religion by speaking of Hindutva, and that in any case candidates did not necessarily consent to the conduct of their election agents who appealed to religion. Sukumar Muralidharan writes that 'the decision appalled all those who had watched the growing salience of religion, caste and communal appeals in electioneering with a sense of alarm' (Muralidharan 1998b). In 1999, however, the president accepted a recommendation of the Election Commission to strip Shiv Sena leader Bal Thackeray of his voting rights for violating the Representation of the People Act during the 1987 by-election by invoking religion to promote a candidate. 'Chronology', *Mainstream*, 37 (33), 1999.

[97]'Chronology', *Mainstream*, 37 (39), 1999.

the hands of central security forces (a legacy of the Seshan years), and partly in the hands of 1,500 EC observer teams equipped with video cameras. Their footage not only provided evidence of wrongdoing to the EC, but could also expose criminal conduct to national audiences.

During the six months in 1999 in which India was ruled by a caretaker government, the president and the Election Commission worked in parallel to keep the rules fair for the opposition. The opposition parties wanted strict prohibition of government acts of patronage that could function as pre-election incentives to voters. Both the president and the EC supported the opposition's resistance to a major bailout of telecom operators disadvantaged by an earlier bidding process.[98] The commission barred the government's monopoly broadcast facility from allocating 150 new FM stations to private parties in forty cities, and prevented the government from issuing an ordinance that would have given the government-controlled television system the exclusive rights for five years to direct home television.[99] On the other hand, the commission did not forbid a 10 per cent hike in support prices for ten agricultural commodities—higher than the Agricultural Prices Commission had recommended—or a 5 per cent hike in the inflation allowance for central government employees.[100]

The EC's task continues to be an uphill one. In the face of what CEC Gill called a 'democratic upsurge', a rising tide of democratization that brings with it 'social unrest and political instability', the commission, he believed, must 'assert its constitutionally guaranteed independence more fiercely than ever' if India is to continue to hold free and fair elections. In 1999 the upsurge was as usual particularly visible in relatively lawless Bihar, where the commission found itself the target of accusations stating that it had not adequately controlled partisanship among its army of local officials and observers. The commissioners were particularly disturbed by a lame duck minister's charge, quickly proved false, that the EC had colluded in the printing of extra ballot papers for use in ballot stuffing in key Bihar constituencies.[101]

The EC faces two immediate challenges: criminalization of politics and making the parties internally democratic. In increasing numbers, 'criminal

[98]'Chronology', *Mainstream*, 37 (29), 1999. The government resisted on the ground that the decision about telecom preceded the issuance of the code of conduct.
[99]'Chronology', *Mainstream*, 37 (30), 1999, and (32), 1999.
[100]'Chronology', *Mainstream*, 37 (39), 1999.
[101]The charges were brought by Defence Minister George Fernandes, not famed for conspicuous moderation, who charged that he had the information from the Bihar state intelligence bureau chief. The EC was supported by the secretary to the central government home ministry in its assertion that the IB had no such information, and that printing extra papers was a routine back-up precaution. The EC asserted that the papers were intentionally printed out of state, in Calcutta, to assure their security. 'Chronology', *Mainstream*, 37 (41), 1999.

elements' have taken advantage of 'loopholes' in the law to be nominated and elected to parliament and state assemblies. No parties are exempt from the charge of criminalization. The EC has tried to close one loophole by prohibiting criminals convicted in a lower court from contesting elections during the long period when their appeals are being heard by higher courts. Parties that conduct their internal business in 'an entirely undemocratic manner' have been directed to conduct organizational elections 'in accord with their own constitutions', a directive with which, the EC claimed, it 'got all parties to comply', a claim which may have been premature.[102]

The latest frontier for fair electoral practices is the struggle to insulate a new tier of state-level election commissions, put in place to conduct elections to local bodies, from the political interference of state governments. Enthusiastic about their own autonomy from central government control, most state governments are less enthusiastic about the new third tier of the federal system, mandated in 1992 by the seventy-third and seventy-fourth amendments of the constitution. It further decentralizes political power to local bodies. State governments have been scrambling to control those institutions, such as state-level election commissions, that ensure the autonomy and viability of these grassroots foundations of power.[103]

Tough longer-run problems remain, which will not be unfamiliar to US and other Western publics. One is what to do about campaign finance, particularly the role of 'illegal' money,[104] both the black money generated

---

[102]Gill 1998, p. 26. A maladroit effort by Commissioner G.V.G. Krishnamurthy in December 1997 on the eve of the twelfth national election to enforce the internal democracy standard on the Shiv Sena failed. M.S. Gill, with help from President K.R. Narayanan, was able to smooth over the situation.

In 1993 Seshan had 'put all parties on notice ... "that they should constitute their various governing bodies/committees and elect their office bearers at different levels in accordance with their own party constitutions within a reasonable time"' on pain of de-recognition by the EC, that is, loss of legitimacy with which to contest elections and non-recognition as a national or state party (Muralidharan 1998a).

[103]The governments of Karnataka and Andhra Pradesh both promulgated ordinances affecting the parameters and timing of local elections. Andhra sought to appoint special officers for *panchayati raj* bodies. The Andhra election commissioner, K. Madhava Rao, moved the Andhra high court against the Andhra government ordinance. The Karnataka government sought to postpone local government elections by issuing an ordinance redefining *panchayat* boundaries. The Karnataka election commissioner complied with the Karnataka government's ordinance, but a public interest petition moved the high court to block the ordinance. The court declared that the legislative power of the state government in this matter was extinguished by the constitution. When the Karnataka government appealed the Karnataka high court decision to the Supreme Court, it stayed the high court order. The issue was pending at this writing. *The Hindu*, 19 February 2000. For the constitutional basis see Basu 1999, pp. 761–77.

[104]According to Sukumar Muralidharan, Seshan in his later years (1994–6) resurrected long-neglected ceilings on election expenses and enforced them despite their obvious inadequacy. He also tells us that 'a loophole in the [electoral] law that allowed parties to meet

in India's vast underground economy that finds its way to parties and candidates, and the often related money that parties and candidates spend above the limits set by EC rules. Another is how much and in what way the state should fund elections. Since the Indian state owns the most widely viewed and heard television and radio stations, the EC is 'considering the establishment of a fair mechanism for allotting time to political parties and candidates during election campaigns. Given free, this time will ... amount to indirect state funding for campaigns.'[105]

A review of the role of the constitutionally mandated Election Commission over the past decade suggests that the strengthening of its regulatory role has coincided with the period during which confidence in cabinet and parliament, the instruments of a developmental, interventionist state, has eroded. The EC has played its role as envisioned in the formal constitution by strengthening free and fair elections, the necessary conditions for representative democracy. In the 1990s, under the mixed blessing of T.N. Seshan's leadership, and in the late 1990s under the strong but fair hands of M.S. Gill, the EC improved the conditions under which elections were held in India. The high levels of public trust in the EC suggest that the Indian electoral processes diverge strikingly from the tainted ones common in other developing and some developed nations.[106]

CONCLUSION

We read 'constitution' to include symbolic, conventional, and formal dimensions. Our examination here of some aspects of the formal constitution in the 1990s reveals major modifications in India's constitutional design. Our story of an interventionist state giving way to a regulatory one shows how process, agency, and event modified and redirected the effects of structural determination and path dependency. The initial triumph of a developmental,

---

a candidate's expenses with little restraint was plugged by a parallel intervention from the Supreme Court ... that no party was exempt from the requirements of submitting income tax returns'. The Congress-I was the main target of this ruling, 'but it managed to meet the deadline imposed by the court'. This dual system of vigilance—between the EC and the Income Tax authorities—makes it conceivable that the abuse of money power in elections could be curbed' (Muralidharan 1998b).

[105]Gill 1998, p. 26. Gill's claims have to be qualified by the impact of satellite TV. For example, 'there are satellite television channels in all the four southern languages ... The question ... is what impact these channels will have on the electorate [in the 1996 national election] ... there are ... indications that these channels influence the masses far more than the print media' (Panneeselvan 1996).

[106]See fn 84 for the 1996 survey results by the Centre for the Study of Developing Societies showing the EC with the highest trust rating at 62 per cent, ahead of the Supreme Court.

interventionist state was foreshadowed at a symbolic level by Nehru's rejection in 1945 of Gandhi's imagined village as the lodestar of economic development and state formation. After independence and partition, with Gandhi, Sardar Patel, and Subhas Chandra Bose dead, Jawaharlal Nehru and his supporters in the party and the civil service were free to construct a state suitable for a dominant party system and a planned economy. After 1989, both the planned economy and the centralized state have gradually given way to a regulatory state more suited to coalition governments in a multiparty system, to economic decentralization, and to more independent and competitive federal states. Judicial activism and an independent president and Election Commission have filled the space partially vacated by a less ambitious, less capable, and more constrained parliamentary executive. Our analysis of India's emergent constitutional design reveals how a relatively centralized, interventionist, and tutelary state is being replaced by a relatively decentralized regulatory state willing to rely on, but not surrender to, a market economy and self-reliant (and sometimes self-destructive) civil society.

13

New Dimensions of Indian Democracy*

SUSANNE HOEBER RUDOLPH AND LLOYD I. RUDOLPH

Conventional wisdom has it that India is the world's largest democracy, but few have recognized that it is so against the odds. The Indian experience runs against the widely held view that rich societies are much more likely to be democratic than poor ones, and that societies with large minority populations are prone to ethnic cleansing and civil war. Democracy in India, a poor and notoriously diverse country, has succeeded for more than half the twentieth century, and seems likely to succeed in the twenty-first, too. India's democracy has proved substantial as well as durable. Electoral participation has been higher than in the United States, elections have been free and fair, governments have alternated at the Centre and in the states, and free speech and association are constitutionally protected and widely practised. However, democracy is subject to challenge and change. This essay examines why and how democracy in India during the 1990s responded to a variety of challenges. These may be summarized under seven headings:

1. *A more prominent role for federal states in India's political system.* The states are making themselves heard and felt politically and economically more than they ever have in the half-century since India gained its independence from Britain.

2. *The transformation of the party system.* The era of dominance by the Indian National Congress has ended. Congress remains a major party, but it must now operate within a multiparty system that includes not only the nationally influential BJP, but a host of significant regional and state-based parties as well.

---

*Originally published as 'New Dimensions of Indian Democracy', in *Journal of Democracy*, 13 (1), January 2002, pp. 52–66.

3. *Coalition government.* Stable central governments based on parliamentary majorities have given way to coalition governments that must depend on constellations of regional parties. In this regard, India has become like Italy or Israel, both places where small parties can make or break governments and thereby affect the whole nation.

4. *A federal market economy.* Economic liberalization has been marked by a decline in public investment and a rise in private investment, the displacement of the federal Planning Commission by the market, and the emergence of the states as critical actors in economic reform and growth. The result has contributed to a transformation of India's federal system.

5. *The central government as regulator.* Despite what the above points might suggest, India's central government is not fading away. The Centre is holding on, but its role has changed. The Centre had previously acted as an intervenor; now it acts as a regulator. In the economic realm, it monitors the initiatives of the several states. It tries (albeit mostly without success) to enforce fiscal discipline. In the political realm, the Centre acts—through regulatory institutions such as the Supreme Court, the presidency, and the Election Commission—to ensure fairness and accountability. Since the emergence of the first coalition government in 1989, this role as 'policeman' or honest broker has grown, while the interventionist institutions, the cabinet, and parliament, have waned in significance.

6. *A social revolution.* In most states, and to a significant extent at the Centre as well, there has been a net flow of power from the upper to the lower castes. Indian politics has experienced a sociopolitical revolution that, in varna terms, has meant a move from a brahmin (priests, intellectuals) toward a shudra (toilers) raj.

7. *Centrism has held against extremism.* The imperatives of centrist politics have checked the momentum of Hindu fundamentalism. India's diverse and pluralist society, the rise of coalition politics, and the need to gain the support of the median voter have transformed the Hindu-nationalist BJP from an extremist to a centrist party.

THE RISE OF THE STATES

In recent years, the twenty-eight states of India's federal system have played a more prominent role in India's public life. Not least has been their contribution to helping India live peacefully with difference. In a world where armed strife has increasingly taken the form of civil war and ethnic cleansing—of the ninety-six recorded conflicts between 1989 and 1996, only five were between sovereign states—India's federal system has helped to keep cultural and ethnic differences within relatively peaceful bounds.

In thinking about something with which to compare India's federalism, the multilingual European Union seems more appropriate than does the United States. Much like the English and the Italians, the Hindi speakers of the state of Bihar in the shadow of the Himalayas and the Tamil speakers of Tamil Nadu at the subcontinent's southern tip speak quite distinct languages. They share little history and few points of contact. Their traditional rulers, legends, and folk cultures are distinct from one another. Their socioeconomic profiles are as different as those of Sweden and Portugal. Bihar is poor and mostly illiterate. Tamil Nadu is prosperous and advanced. No contrast between any two of the fifty US states comes anywhere close. Forty years ago, there seemed good reason to fear that Selig Harrison was right to warn that India's 'fissiparous tendencies', particularly its linguistic differences, would soon lead to Balkanization or dictatorship. Today such worries seem unpersuasive. The federal system has helped India to live peacefully with its marked difference.

How anomalous is a multinational federal state? India reminds us that the nation-state as we know it is a relative historical newcomer, with roots in the post-Revolutionary, post-Napoleonic Europe of the nineteenth century. The nation-state reached its apogee after the two world wars. Before 1914, the numbers of people and extent of territory ruled by nation-states were dwarfed by those which lay under the sway of multinational entities such as the Habsburg, Ottoman, and Romanov empires, or the maritime dominions of Britain and other European colonial powers. After 1945, the working out of Woodrow Wilson's doctrine of self-determination had seemingly conferred sovereignty on enough aspiring 'nations' to bring the era of the multinational state to a decisive end. The nation-state, said many scholars, stood revealed as the natural end towards which the history of state formation had been tending.

This claim was soon belied, however, by the formation of the European Community and its successor, the European Union. On 1 May 2001, the *New York Times* reported the proposal by German chancellor Gerhard Schroeder's Social Democratic Party of 'a far-reaching plan ... to turn the European Union into a more centralized federal system'. The EU was becoming more like the sovereignty-sharing Holy Roman Empire than the warring nation-states of World War I. Had the Holy Roman Empire become the dominant polity in the twelfth century, the process of state formation in Europe would have conformed more closely to the world norm. The path that marks the rise of India's federal, multinational state since 1947 also tracks the emergence of an alternative to the increasingly outmoded nation-state.

By promoting peace among their constituent parts, both the EU and the vast federal republic that is India are saving the world from a great deal of trouble and strife. If it has done nothing else, the EU, the creation of a Europe bloodied, exhausted, and chastened by two gigantic and terrible wars, has radically reduced the prospect of conflict among its member states. Something similar is true of India. Each of its twenty-eight federal states could well be a nation-state unto itself. The largest, Uttar Pradesh, has more people than Germany and France combined, and is nearly as populous as Russia. If Uttar Pradesh and its neighbours were sovereign nation-states, there would be that many more countries living in the Hobbesian world of anarchy and self-help. Instead of ending in domestic arbitration, the dispute between Tamil Nadu and Karnataka over the Krishna River water rights could have led to war. The internal conflicts within Punjab and Assam, like the civil wars that roiled Congo-Kinshasa during the 1990s, could have been made worse by outside forces seeking strategic gain. As it is, the international community has quite enough to occupy it as a result of the long-standing dispute between India and Pakistan over the fate of Kashmir, India's northernmost and only Muslim-majority state.

The story of India's state formation since independence has included a story of rising influence on the part of the federal states. At independence in 1947, India inherited the British-brokered constitution of 1935. It embodied two possibilities, a centralized authoritarian 'vice-regal' state and a decentralized, or federal, parliamentary state. Mohammad Ali Jinnah, the 'great leader' of Pakistan, chose the former option, in effect acting as the successor to Lord Louis Mountbatten, the British raj's last viceroy and governor-general of India. Jawaharlal Nehru, despite his personal penchant for centralized rationalization, selected the latter course and became the prime minister of a parliamentary government in a federal system.

Each choice was a fateful one. Pakistan has known parliamentary democracy for barely half of its five decades as an independent country. The rest of the time, it has been run by generals and authoritarian bureaucrats. Its civilian political landscape has been profoundly troubled, and its unsteady constitutional mixture of unitary and federal features contributed to the violent secession of East Pakistan (present-day Bangladesh), and a related war with India in 1971. India reinforced the federal character of its constitution in 1956 by implementing a sweeping 'states reorganization' that redrew state boundaries on the basis of language. Mohandas K. Gandhi had set the stage for this as early as 1920, when he reformed the Indian National Congress by creating twenty Provincial Congress Committees (PCCs) based on regional languages. Arguably, Gandhi's far-seeing decision to provide a form of political expression for ethnocultural identities such as Hindustani, Tamil, and Bengali opened the way for greater popular participation under conditions of democratic pluralism.

Gandhi's linguistic reforms, like his strong support of Muslim causes, flowed from his inclusive understanding of what Indian nationalism should mean. Inclusive nationalism is reflected in the opening years of the twenty-first century by Indians' capacity to live with dual and overlapping national identities, regional and trans-regional. As one Tamil writer has put it, 'Tamil is my mother, India is my father', a gendered metaphor that captures how the linguistic-cultural 'home space' fosters a 'subjective' sense of care and affection, while the national 'civic space' promotes a due respect for the 'objective' virtues of security, discipline, and the rule of law.

THE PARTY SYSTEM TRANSFORMED

The dominant-party system of the Nehru-Gandhi era that led to the formation of Congress majority governments was replaced after the ninth parliamentary election in 1989 by a regionalized multiparty system and coalition governments. The 1989 elections resulted in India's first hung parliament. V.P. Singh's Janata Party, which held the largest bloc of seats in the 545-member Lok Sabha, became the nucleus of India's first coalition government. Each of the four national elections since that watershed has led to a coalition government, in which parties based in single states have been key. Today, for instance, the coalition government that came out of the 1999 elections is led by Prime Minister Atal Behari Vajpayee of the BJP, but includes in its 300-seat majority fully 120 members from single-state parties.

According to the EC's classification of parties (national, state, registered, and independents) and its declared election results, the four national ballotings held from 1991 to 1999 saw national-level parties' vote share drop from 77 to 67 per cent, while the proportion of seats they controlled slid from 78 to 68 per cent. By contrast, parties based in single states went from 17 per cent of the votes and 16 per cent of the seats to 27 and 29 per cent, respectively.

The shift from dominant-party to multiparty politics and the rise of state parties at the expense of national parties have undone the centralizing thrust of the 1950 constitution. One telling sign of this is the reduced use of Article 356, the 'president's rule' clause that was used—some would say misused—by majority-party governments at the Centre to remove irksome state governments. With state-based parties now holding the balance of power in New Delhi, freewheeling invocations of Article 356 are a thing of the past.

COALITION GOVERNMENTS

The third major feature of contemporary Indian democracy, the rise of coalition governments, is implicit in what we have said about the transformation of the party system from a dominant to a multiparty system. Strong central governments based on sturdy one-party majorities in the Lok Sabha have given way to precarious coalitions that must cater to state parties in order to survive. Since the era of coalition government began in 1989, coalitions have differed in their ideological make-up and caste composition, but all have depended on sub-national parties, particularly those from the southern states of Tamil Nadu and Andhra Pradesh. Following Indian politics since 1989 has become rather like following Italian or Israeli politics, where smaller parties can and do hold national governments hostage in order to advance narrow partisan agendas.

In the thirty-two years from 1947 to 1989, India had a total of five prime ministers. There have already been six in the twelve years since coalition government began. But perhaps the suggestion of instability carried by these numbers is deceptive. The Narasimha Rao government lasted five years (1991–6), longer than a US presidential term. Until a corruption scandal threatened to trip it up in March 2001, the second government under A.B. Vajpayee seemed likely to complete its five-year term. And at the time of this writing in November 2001, it is still carrying on. Even the combined burden of scandal, Vajpayee's poor health, and dissension in the ranks could not overcome the absence of any viable alternative to him as a national leader.

Now that coalition governments are the order of the day, how are we to judge them? If we think of India as analogous to a potential EU federal government, composed of fifteen former nation-states, each with its own identity and interests, we might appreciate the fact that coalition governments can give federal units weight and voice. Coalitions can soften extremism. The BJP, for instance, began as a predominantly north Indian party dedicated to Hindutva (Hindu nationalism), but has had to shelve that agenda in order to accommodate key coalition partners, especially secular state parties from south India that care little for anti-Muslim 'communalism'.

However, this happy outcome is not the only possible result of coalition politics. The unedifying tale of Jayalalitha Jayaram, the corrupt and vindictive chief minister of the ruling AIADMK party in Tamil Nadu, seems to provide a lesson in how coalitions can be hijacked. For years, she shamelessly used the threat of bringing down the Rao and Vajpayee governments to shield herself from the legal consequences of the abuses that she committed while in the post of chief minister of Tamil Nadu between 1991 and 1996. Re-elected to that post in May 2001 and sworn in by a faint-hearted governor after she brushed aside the EC's ruling that her criminal convictions disqualified her from office, she was turned out only after the Indian Supreme Court upheld the Commission in a landmark September 2001 ruling.

While the final disposition of the Jayalalitha case may have reduced the danger of state parties blackmailing coalition governments, there are other exigencies that can undermine or threaten coalition governments. One is the bloated, ineffective cabinets that are the by-products of efforts to cobble together ruling coalitions by handing out ministerial appointments. Another is legislative gridlock, as coalition partners and their constituencies jockey for advantage and block ministerial initiatives. The Vajpayee government's difficulties in keeping economic liberalization moving owe something to this effect. The cabinet is committed to privatizing more public-sector undertakings, to enacting an exit policy for labour, and to promoting new initiatives in energy, telecommunications, and transport-infrastructure policy, but political conflicts among ministers have stymied its efforts.

It is clear that coalition government based on a region-favouring multiparty system is a mixed blessing. It has made it possible to avoid ethnic cleansing, civil war, and extremist politics by facilitating the country's capacity to live with difference and support centrist politics. At the same time, however, coalition government has weakened the country's ability to pursue economic liberalization or achieve vigorous economic growth.

A FEDERAL MARKET ECONOMY

When you opened your daily copy of the *Times of India* back in the 1950s or 1960s, you could read all about the big dams, steel mills, and other mega-projects that master planner P.C. Mahalanobis and his colleagues were launching at the national Planning Commission. The celebrities of the command economy and the 'permit-licence raj' were the bureaucrats, administrators, economists, and other experts who were helping Prime Minister Nehru build a modern industrial economy of which the government held the commanding heights. Today, a decade after the turn towards economic liberalization, newspapers and magazines feature stories about state chief ministers such as Chandrababu Naidu of Andhra, S.M. Krishna of Karnataka, and surprisingly, Jyoti Basu, who until recently headed the Communist government of the state of Bengal. These stories describe how the chief ministers of various Indian states are travelling the world to meet with business leaders, woo investors, and persuade the likes of Bill Clinton or Bill Gates to endorse the idea of investing in the future of Kerala, Karnataka, or Tamil Nadu.

Economic liberalization, the dismantling of the permit-licence raj, and an increasing reliance on markets have fostered the emergence of the 'federal market economy'. But economic liberalization is only part of the story. Equally important has been the marked decline in centrally directed public investment, which has reduced the central government's financial leverage and opened up new fields of initiative for enterprising state governments.

In the 1990s, India's deficit-ridden central government found that it could no longer afford planned investment. The Centre's gross assistance to states' capital formation declined from 27 per cent of its revenue expenditure in 1990–1 to 12 per cent in 1998–9. The more alert state governments have moved in to fill the gap by securing private investment and multilateral assistance. The decline of central public investment and the growth of private investment have given the federal states a greatly expanded role in economic liberalization, and in promoting investment and economic growth.

Our use of the term 'federal market economy' is meant to draw attention not only to the decentralization of the market and the shift to a region- and state-based multiparty system, but also to new patterns of shared sovereignty between the states and the Centre for economic and financial decision making. This increased sharing shifts India's federal system well beyond the economic provisions of its formal constitution. Over the past decade, it has become even clearer that if economic liberalization is to prevail, state governments and their chief ministers must break through the barriers that are holding back economic growth.

THE CENTRAL GOVERNMENT AS REGULATOR

Despite the fading of Nehru's vision of a strongly centralized, development-guiding state, the Centre is holding. But it is holding in a different way. Regulation is replacing direct intervention as the Centre's preferred mode of affecting both the polity and the economy. Since 1991, economic liberalization has meant the abandonment of the permit-licence raj and central planning. But federal regulatory agencies remain active in monitoring markets for goods, services, and capital to ensure that they perform competitively and effectively. Politically, the shift from one-party dominance to fragile coalition governments has changed the balance among institutions at the Centre. The cabinet and parliament, the traditional initiators of intervention, have ceded pride of place to regulatory institutions such as the presidency, the Supreme Court, and the EC—enforcers of rules that safeguard the democratic legitimacy of the political system.

The role of regulatory institutions is more procedural than substantive, more about enforcing rules than making law and policies. Regulatory institutions are needed not only to create, sustain, and perfect markets, but also to ensure procedural fairness in elections, in the operation of a multiparty system, and in the formation of coalition governments. The travails that many countries around the world are now experiencing as they strive to establish democracy and markets show how vital the rule of law and a viable state are to both. Russia and some other post-Soviet and East European states suffer from what Max Weber called 'political capitalism', meaning the accumulation of wealth through political power (often wielded deceitfully and coercively) rather than economic enterprise and open competition. Transitions to a market economy and to democracy require more than privatization and liberty. They require fair regulatory mechanisms.

Although India's case is far less dramatic, a similar logic applies. In the economic arena, the role of the Centre as regulator has been to monitor the states in the name of fiscal discipline. For a few years after 1991, the Centre backed state-level economic initiatives with sovereign guarantees, but is now reluctant to do so. Under Article 293 of the constitution, the Centre must approve all foreign loans contracted by the states, and has de facto veto power over all domestic borrowing as well. In the spirit of 'Do as I say, not as I do', the Centre tries to make the states accept fiscal discipline by imposing conditions that look suspiciously like those which the International Monetary Fund demands of faltering national economies—and enforces them with a similarly wide latitude of discretion.

The political front has seen a parallel decline of interventionist institutions and an enhancement of regulatory ones. The Supreme Court, the presidency, and the EC became more visible and effective in the 1990s as the reputations and authority of ministers, cabinets, and legislatures suffered. During the Congress party's heyday, executives and legislatures had benefited from association with the Congress-dominated party system, the (declining) political capital left over from the independence struggle, and the authority and resources made available to politicians by the existence of a command economy.

Today, all this has changed. The complexity and fragility of the coalition governments, their rapid turnover, and their dependence on region- and state-based parties have sapped the executive capacity of governments. As ministerial executives and legislatures have receded, they have made room for judges, presidents, and election commissioners to act in ways that highlight their constitutional roles as regulators who make democratic politics possible by ensuring that the game is not rigged.

Structural conditions alone do not tell the whole story of this shift. National prime ministers, state chief ministers, legislators, and civil servants have discredited themselves in the eyes of India's growing, well-educated, and increasingly influential middle classes. As taxpayers, investors, producers, consumers, and citizens, middle-class Indians care a great deal about the reliability and security that cannot be had apart from good governance and the rule of law. In the mid-1980s, they responded to Rajiv Gandhi's promises to provide clean government and a high-tech, environmentally friendly economy that could carry India into the twenty-first century. Rajiv disappointed them, leaving office under a cloud in 1989 after a scandal involving an arms deal with the Swedish Bofors company. The early 1990s saw an unprecedented number of state and national ministers indicted for taking bribes, and the BJP's carefully cultivated reputation for probity will not recover quickly from the Tehelka scandal of March 2001, which was blown wide open by hidden-camera videotapes showing top figures in that party taking bribes.

Amid this atmosphere of public disillusionment and hunger for integrity, the symbolic and practical words and deeds of the Supreme Court, the president, and the EC have taken on a new significance. These institutions, despite weaknesses of their own, are now the repositories of middle-class hopes and aspirations for steady, transparent, and honest government.

The Supreme Court's judicial activism marks a particularly novel turn for a body that spent the first four decades after independence mostly defending the rights of property owners against land redistribution. The court's decision in the 1980s to begin taking a stand vis-à-vis rights abuses against the poor and powerless and to hear cases based on public-interest legislation—the Indian equivalent of the US class-action lawsuit—paved the way for the judicial activism of the 1990s. With executive power slipping and wobbly coalition governments the order of the day, the court's activism emphasizes lawfulness and predictability, often in the face of state abuses. Despite overloaded dockets and an often-glacial pace of adjudication, the court has had some success in protecting citizens' rights, limiting police brutality and inhuman treatment in jails, and safeguarding environmental and other public goods.

In the mid-1990s, coinciding with a marked increase in ministerial-level corruption, the Supreme Court moved to assert the independence of the Central Bureau of Investigation (CBI), the union government's principal investigative agency. That such a proceeding should have achieved even partial success highlights the relative shift in the balance between the executive and regulatory functions of the central government. The CBI had been barred from investigating a department or its minister without prior consultation with and the concurrence of the secretary-to-government of the ministry concerned. 'Prior consultation' and 'government concurrence' meant that prime ministers, who also controlled CBI appointments, promotions, and transfers, dominated CBI initiatives and actions. In a landmark judgment, the court removed the requirement of government concurrence that governed CBI investigations, and gave the CBI director a minimum two-year term of office. These actions left the CBI somewhat freer to investigate ministerial cases on its own cognizance.

India does not lack environmental legislation, but neither does it lack powerful interests ready to block the enforcement of such laws. In the late 1980s and early 1990s, the Supreme Court—prompted in some cases by assertive NGOs—began to redress the balance by acting to protect such public goods as clean air and water, and safe blood supplies. At stake in some of these cases were two of India's greatest assets, the Taj Mahal and the Ganges river. To protect the sixteenth-century mausoleum from further damage by air pollution, the court had by 1992 closed 212 nearby businesses for chronic violations of environmental regulations. Almost 200 polluters along the banks of the Ganges found themselves similarly shuttered by court order. In 1996 and 1997, the court began beefing up the enforcement of clean air and water laws in the heavily polluted Delhi area. By early 2000, the court had ordered polluting buses and cars off the roads and shut down enterprises that were emitting pollutants into the Yamuna river. When the environmental minister and industry minister of the National Capital Territory defied the court by trying to keep the outlets open, the court countered by threatening to jail non-complying local officials for contempt.

The transformation of the party system and the rise of coalition government have also opened the way for the president to play a regulatory role. In the era of Congress party majorities, presidents had little to do beyond the pro forma duty of asking Congress's leader to form a government. Since 1989, however, the exercise of presidential discretion has become crucial in determining the make-up of governments. Presidents in turn have leveraged this new-found influence into a bigger regulatory role for their office.

Although Article 53 vests the 'executive power of the Union' in the president, the president, like modern British monarchs, is expected to act at the behest of the cabinet rather than as a principal. As a constitutional head of state indirectly elected through a weighted voting system in which all federal and state-level elected legislators participate, the president retains a separate and potentially highly prestigious identity as steward of the nation's interests. He stands apart from and above mere partisan or bureaucratic politics. In the 1990s, presidents Shankar Dayal Sharma and K.R. Narayanan acted in ways that stressed the autonomy of their office. This was most striking when each resisted political pressure to invoke Article 356, the 'president's rule' clause, as part of a plan to unseat a state government for partisan advantage. President Narayanan also delivered a remarkable address on the fiftieth anniversary of independence (27 January 2000), in which he questioned the BJP-led government's efforts to change the constitution by replacing an executive responsible to parliament with a directly elected president, and protecting parliament against dissolution by fixing its term.

Unlike in other national contexts where presidential powers have been used to undermine or destroy democratic institutions, in India recent presidents have exercised their powers on behalf of democratic transparency and accountability.

Starting in 1991 with the tenure of T.N. Seshan as its chief, the EC joined the Supreme Court and the president in strengthening constitutional government and democratic participation. The Commission is a constitutionally mandated central body whose fixed terms make it independent of the political executive. While the Commission had been a bulwark of free and fair elections in India before 1991, its task became more difficult in the 1990s as India's sprawling electoral process came under well-publicized threats from terrorists and criminal gangs bent on using force to impede or distort the expression of the people's will. The EC gained national fame as a restorer and defender of free and fair voting. Polls indicate that the public trusts it more than any other political institution. When the Supreme Court backed the Commission by removing Jayalalitha from office in September 2001, it enhanced the Commission's role as the guardian par excellence of the democratic process in India. Like the court and the presidency, the Commission draws enthusiastic support from the educated, urban middle classes, who are eager for solutions to the problem of official corruption and lawlessness. It is not too much to say that the Commission, the court, and the presidency are the three vital pillars of the new regulatory state in India.

A SOCIAL REVOLUTION

Since 1947, Indian society has experienced a social revolution with massive political consequences. Political power in the states, and to a significant extent at the Centre, has moved from the hands of the so-called twice-born upper castes into the hands of lower-caste groups, known in Indian parlance as the 'other backward castes' (OBCs) and the Dalits (former 'untouchables').

In early post-independence elections, social prestige translated readily into political power. Upper-caste patrons—coming from a social stratum that contained about a fifth of the populace—could tell their lower-caste dependents how to vote, and elections produced state and national cabinets dominated by officials from upper-caste backgrounds. In the fifty-four years since independence, the OBCs and Dalits—together about two-thirds of the population—have displaced the upper castes in the seats of power in many state cabinets. At the turn of the twenty-first century, lower-caste chief ministers are no longer rare, and at least one national cabinet—the one that headed the National and Left Front governments of Deve Gowda and I.K. Gujral in the mid-1990s—had almost no upper-caste members. The logic of 'one person, one vote' in free and fair elections has put power in the hands of the more numerous lower castes.

Analysts of developing countries often stress the importance of economic growth for political stability and legitimacy. What they notice less often is the contribution that social mobility can make to political stability and legitimacy. Status as well as income matter for both. In India, the 'status growth' enjoyed by members of the once-reviled lower castes has been rapid, and this seems to have palliated much discontent with the relatively slow pace of economic growth.

THE CENTRE HOLDS

In the early 1990s, the BJP and its Hindu nationalism appeared to be on the march. Today, centrist structural constraints, coalition politics, and the ideological moderation imposed by the need to attract the median voter have forced the BJP to gradually abandon communalist extremism in favour of a position much nearer the middle of the spectrum.

In 1992, such an outcome seemed unlikely. Two years earlier, BJP leader L.K. Advani had completed an all-India *yatra* or pilgrimage featuring an image of a martial but caged Lord Ram, the site of whose birthplace at Ayodhya in Uttar Pradesh was said to have been usurped by a sixteenth-century Muslim mosque known as the Babri Masjid. Everywhere it went Advani's yatra had drawn large crowds, seemingly galvanizing Hindu militants and swelling the BJP's electorate: BJP support jumped from a mere 9 per cent of the vote and two seats in the 1984 general election to 11 per cent and eighty-six seats five years later, and then to 20 per cent and 117 seats—more than a fifth of the Lok Sabha—in 1991. On 6 December 1992, young Hindu extremists acting in the presence of BJP leaders and before the eyes of a global television audience stormed the Babri Masjid and tore it down stone by stone. Hindu-versus-Muslim communal violence exploded across northern and western India. Observers split over the likely impact of this episode, with some claiming that this assault on a prominent Muslim place of worship would fuel the rise of Hindu nationalist politics, and others maintaining that it would discredit them. The future was more complex than either group expected.

In retrospect, it appears that the destruction of the Babri Masjid, instead of being the harbinger of a new BJP surge, was the crest of a wave. The violence of the assault and its wanton indifference to life and property shocked many of the moderate Hindus who had been providing the BJP with the bulk of its support. In the 1993 state assembly elections, the BJP lost heavily in four states, especially in its core state of Uttar Pradesh—India's largest state and the heart of the populous 'Hindi Belt' across the north-central part of the subcontinent.

Yet the BJP did not collapse, and even gained ground. In the 1996 general election it took 20 per cent of the vote and 161 seats, though it could not form a government because no other party would join it. In 1998, the BJP garnered 25 per cent of the vote and 182 seats—its best showing ever. (In the 1999 balloting, the party held on to its seat share, but saw its voter support drop slightly to 24 per cent.) Having absorbed the lesson of 1996, the party turned decisively towards moderation two years later. Led by the avuncular and moderate A.B. Vajpayee, it managed to put together a governing coalition, known as the National Democratic Alliance (NDA), by working mostly with regional parties. Conspicuously absent from the NDA's pre-election programme were such divisive Hindu-nationalist agenda items as calls for stripping Kashmir of its special constitutional status, demands that a Hindu temple be raised on the site of the Babri Masjid, and promises to override Muslim personal law via a uniform civil code.

In recent years the BJP's upper-class leadership has realized that electoral success depends on lower-caste support and on living with difference. This explains the party's about-turn on the Mandal Report, a government white paper that recommends set-asides for OBCs in school admissions and civil-service employment. The BJP, it would seem, is now seeking to exploit the very social revolution it once bitterly criticized. Whatever manoeuvring the leadership may be doing, however, it would be going too far to suggest that the Centre of gravity of the entire BJP now lies stably in the middle of the Indian political spectrum, or that Indian voters now believe it does. Important organizations affiliated with the party, such as the Hindu-extremist Vishva Hindu Parishad (the VHP—Universal Hindu Organization), are showing signs of serious alienation from what they see as the BJP's excessive centrism. The Swadeshi Jagran Manch (Homemade-Products Promotion Council) continues to challenge economic liberalization. Vajpayee is still shutting the extremists out of the central advisory positions they crave, but his health is failing. The Tehelka tapes have taken a terrible toll on the BJP's good name. State assembly elections as well as by-elections for the Lok Sabha have lately gone badly for both the BJP and its coalition partners. The successful efforts by the BJP family of 'saffron' organizations to infiltrate India's cultural organizations and activities and to rewrite the history texts used in schools in order to paint Muslims as invaders and foreigners have produced a backlash. Hindu extremists have turned from seemingly politically counter-productive and more dangerous Muslim targets to the softer targets of India's far smaller Sikh and Christian minorities.

AFTER VAJPAYEE?

What can we say about the prospects for democracy in India? We take as given the prior consolidations of democracy—for example, the realization of free and fair elections; alternating governments; freedoms of speech, press, and association; and the more or less successful transition from an interventionist to a regulatory state.

Our story of new dimensions suggests that democracy in India has proved resilient and adaptable. Absent an exogenous shock, centrist politics and coalition governments seem capable of providing stable, if not always effective, government. With the BJP vote share peaking at 24 per cent, upper-caste Hindu extremist politics seems to have slowed. To remain viable as a contender for national office, the BJP will have to continue to reach out to lower castes and minorities and be able to form coalitions with secularist state parties. Judging by its wins and performance at the state level, the Congress seems to be regaining its capacity to practice centrist, inclusivist politics.

The problem for the future is that A.B. Vajpayee has become physically weak and psychologically weary, and there is no comparable alternative to him. Congress leader Sonia Gandhi's dynastic legitimacy does not compensate adequately for her political inexperience and foreign provenance, but to date, no one can challenge her.

Business as usual may not be good enough; the country needs to gain, not lose, momentum. A viable regulatory state may have displaced a failing interventionist one, but if India is to prove its mettle, the country's political and economic life needs to be revitalized.

Index